FREE MOVEMENT OF PATIENTS IN THE EU

FREE MOVEMENT OF PATIENTS IN THE EU

A Patient's Perspective

Gabriella Berki

intersentia
Cambridge – Antwerp – Portland

Intersentia Ltd
Sheraton House | Castle Park
Cambridge | CB3 0AX | United Kingdom
Tel.: +44 1223 370 170 | Fax: +44 1223 370 169
Email: mail@intersentia.co.uk
www.intersentia.com | www.intersentia.co.uk

Distribution for the UK and Ireland:
NBN International
Airport Business Centre, 10 Thornbury Road
Plymouth, PL6 7PP
United Kingdom
Tel.: +44 1752 202 301 | Fax: +44 1752 202 331
Email: orders@nbninternational.com

Distribution for Europe and all other countries:
Intersentia Publishing nv
Groenstraat 31
2640 Mortsel
Belgium
Tel.: +32 3 680 15 50 | Fax: +32 3 658 71 21
Email: mail@intersentia.be

Distribution for the USA and Canada:
International Specialized Book Services
920 NE 58th Ave. Suite 300
Portland, OR 97213
USA
Tel.: +1 800 944 6190 (toll free) | Fax: +1 503 280 8832
Email: info@isbs.com

ISBN 978-1-78068-575-5
D/2018/7849/4
NUR 820

British Library Cataloguing in Publication Data. A catalogue record for this book is available from the British Library.

Édesanyának és Édesapának

To Mum and Dad

FOREWORD

The free movement of patients and the right to cross-border medical care is a topical issue that since the development of the case law of the Court of Justice of the EU at the end of the 1990s has gained considerable interest. Not only is it a right which affects European citizens, it also concerns a domain where there is a conflict of competence between the national Member States and the European Union. Notwithstanding that healthcare is still, as confirmed in the European Treaties, a domain of national competence, the European Union has had a growing indirect influence through its case law on free movement of services and goods. While for decades the European Coordination Regulations on the social security of migrant workers has been considered the natural and only instrument dealing with cross-border healthcare, the case law of the Court has opened a new path directly based on the Treaty provisions. As a result, and striving for more legal certainty, a Patient Mobility Directive was enacted. This has led to a situation where today the rights to cross-border medical care can be found in three European instruments: the Coordination Regulations, the Patient Mobility Directive and the Treaty provisions. Needless to say this creates a complex legal situation.

In this book, which is the result of a joint PhD awarded by Ghent University in Belgium and the University of Szeged in Hungary, Gabriella Berki describes the different provisions of cross-border healthcare in a detailed way, emphasising the still existing gaps, the discrepancies (persons covered, rights obtained, tariffs of reimbursement, etc), the not always very successful interrelation between these texts, as well as the legal complexity, often leaving the patient in an unclear position.

The topic has already gained a great deal of attention in literature and Ms Berki is not the first author to describe these problems. However, in her book she approaches these problems in an innovative way. The original, fresh perspective from which the topic is dealt with is to her credit. She focuses on the rights concerned from a patient's perspective and scrutinises all provisions by asking one question: can we say that these provisions allow the patient to look for the best medical treatment regardless where in the European Union this may be (if possible at a favourable price)? Are these provisions protecting the interests of the patients or rather the national healthcare systems and the social security institutions? When elaborating this approach, she also develops an extensive list of policy proposals. The issue of cross-border medical care is still evolving. Not least through the case law of the Court and the introduction of the European citizenship, European citizens and patients have gained a new status of rights within the European Union that allows them to rely more and more directly on primary EU provisions. It may therefore not be excluded that some of the provisions of secondary EU legislation will be questioned from a patient's perspective. The author rightly points out that the optimistic view on cross-border healthcare, resulting from the first cases of the Court, has perhaps not always been completely translated into this secondary legislation, leading to a deterioration of the patient's situation. However, on the other hand, not least in these times of economic crisis, there is a fear that people will abuse their right to free movement to profit from more beneficial systems and thus abuse cross-border medical care, leading to medical tourism. Furthermore, other legal, political and financial barriers may complicate the optimisation of the patient's situation. The most important barrier is presumably the actual division of competence in healthcare between the national Member States and the European Union. It is doubtful whether these political situations will take place and it will be extremely difficult to circumvent such political barriers. For that reason, this book is also interesting beyond the academic world.

The author has made her voice heard in this topical issue of cross-border medical care and thus contributed to its further debates.

Professor Dr Yves Jorens
Ghent University

PREFACE

For, after all, the foundation of our whole nature, and, therefore, of our happiness, is our physique, and the most essential factor in happiness is health, and, next in importance after health, the ability to maintain ourselves in independence and freedom from care. There can be no competition or compensation between these essential factors on the one side, and honour, pomp, rank and reputation on the other, however much value we may set upon the latter. No one would hesitate to sacrifice the latter for the former, if it were necessary. We should add very much to our happiness by a timely recognition of the simple truth that every man's chief and real existence is in his own skin, and not in other people's opinions; and, consequently, that the actual conditions of our personal life, health, temperament, capacity, income, wife, children, friends, home, are a hundred times more important for our happiness than what other people are pleased to think of us: otherwise we shall be miserable.

(Schopenhauer)[1]

Being a patient is possibly never easy. In the vast majority of cases, it is – at best – an inconvenient situation to be in. This unease might well be intensified if someone is seeing a doctor abroad in an unfamiliar setting. What are the obstacles a border-crossing patient faces and how can these barriers be overcome? These are the questions which particularly fascinated me during the years of my research. My ambition was to detect and to bring a better understanding of those legal issues which are potentially problematic when

1 A. Schopenhauer, *Wisdom of Life*, Cosimo Classics, New York 2007, p. 54.
The original quote in German reads as follows: 'Denn überhaupt ist die Basis unseres Wesens und folglich auch unseres Glückes unsere animalische Natur. Daher ist für unsere Wohlfahrt Gesundheit das Wesentlichste, nächst dieser aber die Mittel zu unserer Erhaltung, also ein sorgenfreies Auskommen. Ehre, Glanz, Rang, Ruhm, soviel Wert auch mancher darauf legen mag, können mit jenen wesentlichen Gütern nicht kompetieren, noch sie ersetzen: vielmehr würden sie erforderlichenfalls unbedenklich für jene hingegeben werden. Dieserwegen wird es zu unserm Glücke beitragen, wenn wir beizeiten die simple Einsicht erlangen, daß jeder zunächst und wirklich in seiner eigenen Haut lebt, nicht aber in der Meinung anderer, und daß demnach unser realer und persönlicher Zustand, wie er durch Gesundheit, Temperament, Fähigkeiten, Einkommen, Weib, Kind, Freunde, Wohnort usw. bestimmt wird, für unser Glück hundertmal wichtiger ist, als was es andern beliebt aus uns zu machen. Der entgegengesetzte Wahn macht unglücklich.' A. Schopenhauer, *Aphorismen zur Lebensweisheit (Separatausgabe aus 'Parerga und Paralipomena')*, F. A. Brockhaus, Leipzig 1886.

obtaining healthcare abroad and to examine whether these can be solved with the legal tools currently available on the European level. The main question behind this research was how the current landscape of European cross-border patient mobility legislation can be improved in a way that better serves patients' interests while respecting the responsibilities of the Member States in this field.

Principally, this book aims to analyse the European legal framework governing cross-border patient movements from a strictly patient-centred approach. I confess that as a social lawyer, my main interest is the social status of the individual. Thus, when I chose the rather well-researched topic of cross-border patient mobility, I set my focus on an aspect which seemed lacking: I approached the subject from the perspective of the patients. By doing this, I was led by Schopenhauer's thought who said that 'für unsere Wohlfahrt Gesundheit ist das Wesentlichste.'[2]

Admittedly this book is one-sided to a certain extent, implying a demand-side approach and setting aside the providers' market-based and the Member States financial interests. Since I observe each occurring problem through this filter, some observations or suggestions may be seen as provocative and hold potential for debate. As I see it, evoking an exchange of views and different opinions is one of the missions of academic writing, thus while I hereby act as an advocate of patients, I seek to bring on board arguments from the other sides involved in cross-border healthcare situations as well – especially in the last part of the book.

The legal framework under scrutiny in the book is far from simple. It is far from perfect too. It is complex on multiple levels: it both applies different rules to diverse scenarios and different legal tools to the same situation. When I think of the possibilities a patient might have when in need of healthcare, I imagine a maze with a mouse in it looking for the cheese. The mouse knows exactly what it wants, it just does not know how to get there. There are various paths to follow, but the dilemma is: which one leads to trouble and which one leads to fulfilment?

In order to reach my goal, I examined the legislation in its totality, paying special attention to the interrelations of the different legal tools, rather than studying the various legal paths separately. Furthermore, as a starting point of my research, I formulated an axiom with the aim to articulate patients' needs properly: *Patients wish to benefit from the most effective, highest quality healthcare provided as quickly as possible for the most favourable price.*[3] The order of the different elements in this sentence does not necessarily indicate an order of preference. Whether it is the quality, the timeliness or the price which holds the highest importance for a patient, varies from person to person.

---

2 It can be translated as 'the most essential factor in happiness is health.' SCHOPENHAUER, above n. 1.

3 The expression '*the most favourable price*' must be understood as the amount of money which is to be paid by the patient him/herself.

However, when obtaining healthcare, each of these factors is relevant. From the intriguing issues identified throughout this research, the present book details three key areas of patient mobility, namely legal complexity, financial affordability and information obstacles.[4]

This book is based on my doctoral dissertation which was defended in the summer of 2015 at the Ghent University in Belgium. Since then, my interest in the coordination of healthcare schemes and cross-border patient mobility has not diminished and I have continued to work in this domain. Recently, I participated in a reporting exercise whose aim was to revisit certain issues of access to healthcare in another Member State and to provide the European Commission with an in-depth analysis of different legal scenarios of cross-border healthcare.[5] This exercise, besides the experience of numerous conferences and expert discussions inspired me to update and extend my manuscript and to write this book, which was completed on 30 April 2017. I hope it can serve as a compass in the maze.

---

4 Since issues related to quality and patient safety require specialised expertise in healthcare protocols and are not directly related to social security matters (not included into the Social Security Coordination Regulations either), and as they raise questions related to e.g. cross-border medical liability and cross-border remedy for medical malpractice, which are deserving as a subject of another book, they are beyond the scope of the present research. However, quality is an important concern for patients and a leading factor in the quest to obtain healthcare abroad, so the in-depth observation of legal problems related to that field holds great potential for future research.

On the issues related to quality and patient safety, see among others European Commission, *Special Eurobarometer 327: Patient safety and quality of healthcare*, 2010; H. Legido-Quigley, I.A. Glinos, K. Walshe, B. van Beek, C. Cucic and M. McKee, 'Quality and safety' in M. Wismar, W. Palm, J. Figueras, K. Ernst, E. van Ginneken, *Cross-border Health Care in the European Union – Mapping and analysing practices and policies*, European Observatory on Health Systems and Policies, Brussels 2011 and V. Paskalia, 'Cross-border Healthcare in the EU: And What if Something Goes Wrong?' *European Journal of Health Law* 2016, http://booksandjournals.brillonline.com/content/journals/10.1163/15718093-12341435 (accessed 22.04.2017).

5 G. Strban (ed.), G. Berki, D. Carrascosa and F. Van Overmeiren, *Access to healthcare in cross-border situations*, FreSsco Network, Ghent 2017.

ACKNOWLEDGEMENTS

I believe that most achievements do not belong to one single person. I certainly consider mine as team work. Each and every one of my team has carried out his/her job wonderfully: some did the cheering and supporting part, some did the pushing and criticising part and some were simply listening on the other side of the table when that was needed.

This book is the icing on the cake, the baking of which took me several years and I cannot possibly be grateful enough for having had all these amazing people around me. Without even attempting to enumerate everyone I owe my thanks, I would like to express my gratitude to my PhD-supervisors, Prof. Yves Jorens and Prof. József Hajdú and to the members of my doctoral defence committee, Prof. Saskia Klosse, Rob Cornelissen, Prof. Grega Strban and Filip Van Overmeiren, all of whom contributed to the betterment of my work. Similarly, special thanks go to my friends and colleagues both at the Ghent University and the University of Szeged.

The process which has led me to writing this book was one of the greatest personal and professional experiences of my life. It was not only an exciting task but a real adventure which challenged my skills. I feel lucky because of the unique opportunity this work has given me: I was inspired by the outstanding work experience I gained abroad, by the people I met and the joy I found in researching. What is more, it not only brought new relationships into my life but also put the old ones into new perspectives. My friends and family never ceased to stand by me during this – sometimes thorny – procedure and I love them for this as well. Thanks to all of you!

Szeged, 30 April 2017
Gabriella

CONTENTS

TABLE OF CASES

COURT OF JUSTICE OF THE EUROPEAN UNION

EFTA COURT

TABLE OF TREATIES, INSTRUMENTS AND LEGISLATION

TREATIES AND ANALOGOUS INSTRUMENTS

EU LEGISLATION AND POLICY DOCUMENTS

NATIONAL LEGISLATION AND POLICY DOCUMENTS

LIST OF TABLES AND FIGURES

TABLES

FIGURES

LIST OF ABBREVIATIONS

AC	Administrative Commission
AG	Advocate General
BR	Basic Regulation, Regulation (EC) No 883/2004 of the European Parliament and of the Council of 29 April 2004 on the coordination of social security systems
CFREU	Charter of Fundamental Rights of the European Union
CJEU	Court of Justice of the European Union
COE	Council of Europe
DG	Directorate General
DG EMPL	Directorate General Employment, Social Affairs and Inclusion
DG SANTE	Directorate General Health and Food Safety
ECJ	European Court of Justice
ECLI	European Case Law Identifier
EEA	European Economic Area
EEC	European Economic Community
EESSI	Electronic Exchange of Social Security Information
EFTA	European Free Trade Association
EHIC	European Health Insurance Card
EP	European Parliament
EPF	European Patients' Forum
EU	European Union
ICT	Information and Communication Technology
ILO	International Labour Organization
IR	Implementing Regulation, Regulation (EC) No 987/2009 of the European Parliament and of the Council of 16 September 2009 laying down the procedure for implementing Regulation (EC) No 883/2004 on the coordination of social security systems
MPT	Maximum Processing Time
MS	Member State
MWT	Maximum Waiting Time
NEAK	Nemzeti Egészségbiztosítási Alapkezelő (Hungarian Healthcare Fund)
NCP	National Contact Point
NHS	National Health Service
OECD	Organisation for Economic Co-operation and Development
OJ	Official Journal

OMC	Open Method of Coordination
PA	Prior Authorisation
PD	Portable Document
PMD	Patient Mobility Directive, Directive 2011/24/EU of the European Parliament and of the Council of 9 March 2011 on the application of patients' rights in cross-border healthcare
PRC	Provisional Replacement Certificate
SED	Structured Electronic Document
SSGI	Social Services of General Interest
TCN	Third Country National
TEC	Treaty Establishing the European Community
TEEC	Treaty of Rome establishing the European Economic Community
TEU	Treaty on the European Union
TFEU	Treaty on the Functioning of the European Union
UK	United Kingdom
UN	United Nations
UNESCO	United Nations Educational, Scientific and Cultural Organization
WHO	World Health Organization

CHAPTER 1
SETTING THE SCENE

Community law provides patients with rights to cross-border care under Community law, but we need a clear, practical framework to reconcile greater individual choice with the sustainability of health systems overall. I hope that [...] we can realise the potential for European cooperation on healthcare to bring benefits to all.[6]

1. EXPLORING THE RESEARCH PROBLEM

I was sitting in the plenary session of the European Parliament (EP) in Strasbourg on 19 January 2011 when it approved by a large majority its legislative resolution on the Council position at first reading with a view to the adoption of a directive on the application of patients' rights in cross-border healthcare.[7] The success was celebrated and the new piece of legislation was welcomed as a game-changer in the domain of cross-border patient mobility. Whether it really is, that is a question I intend to answer in this book.

Data are hard to argue with. It is true that cross-border patient mobility is often stigmatised as marginal[8] in terms of the aggregate volume of patients and

---

6 Citation from the speech of the European Health and Consumer Protection Commissioner, Markos Kyprianou on 26 September 2006. European Commission, *Patient mobility: Commission to launch public consultation on EU framework for health services*, IP-06-1267, 2006.

7 P7_TA(2011)0007, European Parliament, *European Parliament legislative resolution of 19 January 2011 on the Council position at first reading with a view to the adoption of a directive of the European Parliament and of the Council on the application of patients' rights in cross-border healthcare.*

8 See, among others, G. France, 'Cross-border flows of Italian patients within the European Union – An international trade approach' *European Journal of Public Health* 1997, vol 7 suppl 3, p. 18; I.A. Glinos and R. Baeten, *A Literature Review of Cross-Border Patient Mobility in the European Union*, European Observatory on Health Systems and Policies, Europe for Patients Project, Brussels 2006, p. 12; I.A. Glinos, R. Baeten and N. Boffin, 'Cross-border contracted care in Belgian hospitals' in M. Rosenmöller, M. McKee and R. Baeten (eds.), *Patient Mobility in the European Union – Learning from experience*, European Observatory on Health Systems and Policies, Europe for Patients Project, Brussels 2006, p. 97; M. Rosenmöller, M. McKee, R. Baeten, I.A. Glinos, 'Patient mobility: the context and issues' in Rosenmöller et al., in this note, p. 2.; M. Wismar, W. Palm, E. van Ginneken, R. Busse, K. Ernst and J. Figueras, 'The Health Service Initiative: supporting the construction of a framework for cross border health care' in Wismar et al., above n. 4, p. 1;

healthcare costs related.[9] In most cases, obtaining medical treatment in a Member State other than the Member State of residence is considered as an *ultima ratio* by patients. Several studies have shown that European patients prefer to be treated as close as possible to their place of residence.[10] Nevertheless, cross-border patient movements are considered 'non-marginal for certain pathologies and/or geographical areas in particular countries'.[11] They are highly significant especially in border regions,[12] for smaller Member States, for rare diseases, and in areas that attract a large number of tourists.[13] Furthermore, the overall willingness to travel for healthcare seems to have increased in recent years.

F. Pennings, 'The Cross-border Health Care Directive: More Free Movement for Citizens and More Coherent EU Law?' *European Journal of Social Security* 2011, vol 13 issue 4, p. 437 and J.-P. Lhernould, 'Access to Healthcare by Cross-Border Patients' in S. Hennion and O. Kaufmann (eds.), *Unionsbürgerschaft und Patientenfreizügigkeit*, Springer, Berlin, Heidelberg 2014, p. 176.

9 In 2008, the European Commission estimated that 'around 1% of public healthcare budgets are spent on cross-border healthcare, equating to around €10 billion for the Community as a whole'. European Commission, *Communication from the Commission: A Community framework on the application of patients' rights in cross-border healthcare*. COM (2008) 415 final, 02.07.2008, p. 8.
Recent statistical data show that 'the budgetary impact of cross-border healthcare on total healthcare spending in kind is rather marginal as it amounts to only 0.3% of total healthcare spending in kind. Nonetheless, in absolute terms annual cross-border healthcare spending amounts to more than €3 billion.' F. De Wispelaere and J. Pacolet, *Coordination of social security systems at a glance: 2016 Statistical Report*, Network Statistics FMSSFE, Leuven 2016, p. 23.

10 W. Palm, J. Nickless, H. Lewalle and A. Coheur, *Implications of recent jurisprudence on the co-ordination of health care protection systems*, Association Internationale de la Mutualite, Brussels 2000, p. 7; Glinos and Baeten, above n. 8, p. 6.; I.A. Glinos, R. Baeten, M. Helble and H. Maarse, 'A typology of cross-border patient mobility' *Health and Place* 2010, vol 16 issue 6, p. 1147; H. Legido-Quigley, I.A. Glinos, R. Baeten, M. McKee, R. Busse, 'Analysing arrangements for cross-border mobility of patients in the European Union: A proposal for a framework' *Health Policy* 2012, vol 108 issue 1, p. 27. See also COM (2008) 415, above n. 9, p. 8 and Recital 39 of the Preamble of Directive 2011/24/EU of the European Parliament and of the Council of 9 March 2011 on the application of patients' rights in cross-border healthcare. OJ L 88 of 4 April 2011 (hereinafter also referred to as Patient Mobility Directive or PMD).

11 France, above n. 8, p. 18. See also Palm et al., above n. 10, p. 7.

12 Various research projects have been carried out in order to explore the cross-border use of healthcare in the frontier zones. For example in northern France and Belgium: M. Calnan, W. Palm, F. Sohy, and D.N.A. Quaghebeur, 'Cross-border use of health care – A survey of frontier workers' knowledge, attitudes and use' *European Journal of Public Health* 1997, vol 7 suppl 3, pp. 26–32; among the Nordic countries: K-G. Hem, B. Kalseth and A. Wilson, *Patient mobility in the Nordic Countries. Volume and obstacles*, http://www.nordicinnovation.org/Global/_Publications/Reports/2011/2011_patientMobility_report.pdf, 2011 (accessed 21.04.2017) pp. 36–50; among Belgian, French, German and Luxembourger frontier workers: J. Pacolet, F. De Wispelaere and A. De Coninck, *The social security rights of frontier workers – A survey on their knowledge, use and satisfaction, focusing on sickness benefits*, SSCALA Project, Leuven 2012; and more recently, among the BENELUX States: K. Jutten and P. Janssens (eds.), *Patients without borders: Cross-border patient flows in the BENELUX*, General Secretariat of the Benelux Union, 2016.

13 COM (2008) 415, above n. 9, p. 8.

At the same time, many patients still lack efficient and reliable information on their cross-border health rights,[14] which prevents them from using these rights which they are entitled to under Union law. Although the prioritisation of the Member State of residence is not surprising, in certain cases, receiving healthcare abroad proves to be not only desirable and feasible, but also inevitable. Therefore, providing European patients with a coherent, clear and logical legal framework, which enables them to claim their right to cross-border patient mobility when in need, is of great importance.

For a long time, two different, simultaneously existing legal schemes were applicable to cross-border medical treatments in the European Union. On the one hand, the so-called *regulation-based approach* governed by the rules of the European social security Coordination Regulations;[15] on the other hand, the *case law-based approach*, which is based on the relevant articles of the Treaty on the Functioning of the European Union (TFEU)[16] concerning the free movement of goods and services, and the connected cases[17] of the Court of Justice of the

---

14 A survey carried out in 2014 by the European Commission presented that an overall 43 per cent of European citizens were not aware of their entitlement to receive medical treatment in another EU country and to be reimbursed for that treatment by their national health authority or healthcare insurer. The level of ignorance was even higher in several Member States, for instance 47 per cent in Spain, 55 per cent in Italy and 67 per cent in Bulgaria. European Commission, *Special Eurobarometer 425: Patients' rights in cross-border healthcare in the European Union*, 2015, p. 31.

15 Regulation (EC) No 883/2004 of the European Parliament and of the Council of 29 April 2004 on the coordination of social security systems. OJ L 166 of 30 April 2004 (hereinafter also referred to as Basic Regulation or BR) and Regulation (EC) No 987/2009 of the European Parliament and of the Council of 16 September 2009 laying down the procedure for implementing Regulation (EC) No 883/2004 on the coordination of social security systems. OJ L 284 of 30 October 2009 (hereinafter also referred to as Implementing Regulation or IR).

16 The Treaty on the Functioning of the European Union, OJ C 83 of 30 March 2010. In this book, articles of the Treaty are referred to as numbered after the TFEU entered into force on 1 December 2009. However, when referring to case law, the old numbering (as numbered in the Treaty establishing the European Community or TEC) might be used.

17 The milestone cases are the following: C-120/95 *Nicolas Decker v Caisse de maladie des employés privés* [ECLI:EU:C:1998:167]; C-158/96 *Raymond Kohll v Union des caisses de maladie* [ECLI:EU:C:1998:171]; C-368/98 *Abdon Vanbraekel and Others v Alliance nationale des mutualités chrétiennes* [ECLI:EU:C:2001:400]; C-157/99 *B.S.M. Geraets-Smits v Stichting Ziekenfonds VGZ and H.T.M. Peerbooms v Stichting CZ Groep Zorgverzekeringen* [ECLI:EU:C:2001:404]; C-326/00 *Idryma Koinonikon Asfaliseon (IKA) v Vasileios Ioannidis* [ECLI:EU:C:2003:101]; C-385/99 *V.G. Müller-Fauré v Onderlinge Waarborgmaatschappij OZ Zorgverzekeringen UA and E.E.M. van Riet v Onderlinge Waarborgmaatschappij ZAO Zorgverzekeringen* [ECLI:EU:C:2003:270]; C-56/01 *Patricia Inizan v Caisse primaire d'assurance maladie des Hauts-de-Seine* [ECLI:EU:C:2003:578]; C-8/02 *Ludwig Leichtle v Bundesanstalt für Arbeit* [ECLI:EU:C:2004:161]; C-145/03 *Heirs of Annette Keller v Instituto Nacional de la Seguridad Social (INSS)* [ECLI:EU:C:2005:211]; C-372/04 *The Queen, on the application of Yvonne Watts v Bedford Primary Care Trust and Secretary of State for Health* [ECLI:EU:C:2006:325]; C-466/04 *Manuel Acereda Herrera v Servicio Cántabro de Salud* [ECLI:EU:C:2006:405]; C-444/05 *Aikaterini Stamatelaki v NPDD Organismos Asfaliseos Eleftheron Epangelmation (OAEE)* [ECLI:EU:C:2007:231]. See http://ec.europa.eu/social/main.jsp?catId=572&langId=en (accessed 09.02.2017).

European Union (CJEU).[18] There have been some remarkable differences between these two, parallel systems. As a result, the discrepancies of the concurrent legal tools have caused certain legal problems since the 1990s (e.g. the scope of application of the Treaty rules, different levels and mechanisms of reimbursement of medical costs occurred abroad, the question of post factum authorisation), and have raised serious doubts among patients (e.g. whether a prior permission from the competent authority is required in relation to the treatment abroad, which reimbursement regime is applicable in a certain situation, or which conditions must be met to use either of the different routes of cross-border patient mobility).

Consequently, it was indeed considered a remarkable success when the European Parliament voted in favour of a new Directive in January 2011, and after the second reading was approved by the Council on 28 February, a new piece of the legal framework on European patient mobility was born.[19] The Directive became known as the Patient Mobility Directive (or as other sources refer to it, Cross-border Healthcare Directive or Patients' Rights Directive).[20] The agreement of the EP and the Council put an end to a lengthy and complicated legislative procedure, which began in 2006, when healthcare services were excluded from the material scope of the so-called Services Directive[21] due to their special characteristics,[22] and the legislators decided in favour of adopting a separate legal instrument on healthcare service provision.[23]

---

18 Since the Treaty of Lisbon entered into force on 1 December 2009, the name of the Court changed to *Court of Justice of the European Union* (Articles 251–281 TFEU). In the relevant literature, the abbreviation ECJ (formerly used for European Court of Justice) and CJEU are both used. For the sake of simplicity, in this book the abbreviation CJEU is used.

19 The steps of the legislative procedure can be found on the EP's website: http://www.europarl.europa.eu/oeil/popups/ficheprocedure.do?lang=en&reference=2008/0142(COD) (accessed 09.02.2017).

20 Directive 2011/24/EU of the European Parliament and of the Council of 9 March 2011 on the application of patients' rights in cross-border healthcare. OJ L 88 of 4 April 2011.

21 Directive 2006/123/EC of the European Parliament and of the Council of 12 December 2006 on services in the internal market. OJ L 376 of 27 December 2006.

22 Baeten argues that the specific features of the healthcare sector such as third party payer involvement, moral hazard, information asymmetry, the principles of social solidarity and universal coverage distinguish medical services from the typical commercial services and make the application of the Services Directive to healthcare highly problematic. R. Baeten, *The proposal for a Directive on Services in the Internal Market applied to Healthcare Services.* http://www.ose.be/files/publication/rbaeten/baeten_2004_PaperHearingEP111104.pdf, 2004 (accessed 09.02.2017), p. 2. See also C.T. Carlstrom, 'The Government's Role in the Health Care Industry: Past, Present, and Future' *Economic Commentary*, 1 June 1994; and S. Shmanske, 'Information Asymmetries in Health Services. The Market Can Cope' *The Independent Review* 1996, vol 1 no 2, p. 191. Shmanske adds adverse selection to the list of special properties of health services.
Furthermore, see European Commission, *High level process of reflection on patient mobility and healthcare developments in the European Union*, 2003, p. 9. After the removal of health services from the Service Directive's scope, the European Council adopted the *Council Conclusions on Common values and principles in European Union Health Systems* (OJ C 146 of 22 June 2006).

23 R. Baeten, 'Health and social services in the internal market' in C. Degryse and P. Pochet (eds.), *Social Developments in the European Union 2006*, European Observatory

The Patient Mobility Directive not only intends to incorporate the findings of the CJEU on the provision of healthcare services[24] and to clarify its relationship with the existing framework of social security coordination. It also wants to facilitate cooperation among the Member States in the field of healthcare.[25] Moreover, its declared intention is to end the legal uncertainties relating to Union legislation on patient mobility.[26] Although satisfying this ambition is more than desirable from the patients' point of view, it is debatable whether the Directive can reach its target and fully tackle the problems mentioned above in order to develop the healthcare systems in the European Union in a patient-friendly way.

2. CONCEPTUAL BASICS

In order to analyse the legislation on cross-border patient movements within the European Union, the concept of *patient mobility* needs to be clarified at the outset. Therefore, in this chapter, the complex nature of European cross-border patient mobility is examined in general, including a typology of patient movements, border-crossing patients and their motivations to obtain healthcare abroad. Following this, the definition(s) of patient mobility used in this book are elaborated.

Let us first picture some possible scenarios. A Hungarian national breaks her leg while on holiday in Greece and receives necessary medical help in a Greek hospital. A Luxembourg national takes his daughter to Germany to receive treatment from a German orthodontist.[27] A Belgian national travels to France to undergo orthopaedic surgery which could be provided in better medical conditions abroad than in her home country.[28] Dutch nationals obtain

---

on Health Systems and Policies, Brussels 2007, p. 2 and W. Palm, M. Wismar, E. van Ginneken, R. Busse, K. Ernst and J. Figueras, 'Towards a renewed Community framework for safe, high-quality and efficient cross-border health care within the European Union' in Wismar et al., above n. 4, p. 30.
It is worth reading the EP's report on the benefits which a separate legal tool on cross-border healthcare services was expected to bring in this field. European Parliament, *Report on the impact and consequences of the exclusion of health services from the Directive on services in the internal market*, 10.05.2007, A6-0173/2007. The report was transformed into an EP resolution: P6_TA (2007) 0201.

24 In the Council Conclusions the European Council expressed its firm opinion that 'developments in this area should result from political consensus and not solely from case law'. Therefore, it was of high priority for the European Commission to develop a Community framework for safe, high quality and efficient health services including the relevant case law of the Court. Council Conclusions, above n. 22.

25 Article 1(1) PMD.

26 Ibid.

27 C-158/96 *Kohll*, 2.

28 C-368/98 *Vanbraekel*, 11, 16.

specific, experimental treatments in foreign hospitals because those treatments are not offered to them in the Netherlands.[29] A Greek resident who suffers from chronic heart disease is admitted to a German hospital while visiting his son in Germany.[30] A German national who is resident in Spain goes to Germany for family reasons and is diagnosed with a malignant tumour that needs to be operated on by a specialist in Switzerland.[31] A UK citizen suffering from severe arthritis of the hips travels to France to undergo hip replacement surgery there, reducing the predicted waiting time significantly.[32] A Bulgarian citizen, who was diagnosed with a malignant tumour of the eye, seeks advanced therapy in Germany instead of the much more radical Bulgarian treatment which would have involved the removal of the eyeball.[33] A Croatian national visits his friends in Sweden but he leaves his prescription medication at home and so seeks help at a local general practitioner.

These examples, most of them taken from the cases of the CJEU, nicely illustrate that the variation of patient movements are endless and that situations like the ones mentioned above can happen to any of us. Ever since people have travelled and have possibly needed healthcare, patient mobility has existed.[34]

From a practical point of view, the core concept of patient mobility can be described as a combination of two elements, namely the capability of moving and the necessity to obtain healthcare. Although patient mobility is a multifaceted phenomenon which encompasses various situations,[35] all these cases have the following two elements in common: the person concerned moves and he/she receives medical treatment outside the area where he/she resides. Therefore, in my understanding, it can be said that the broadest definition of patient mobility involves a person who moves into an area outside the area where he/she resides,

---

29 C-157/99 *Geraets-Smits and Peerbooms*, 25–26, 31–32, 38.

30 C-326/00 *Ioannidis*, 14.

31 C-145/03 *Keller*, 12–17.

32 C-372/04 *Watts*, 24–31.

33 C-173/09 *Elchinov*, 12–15.

34 A paper focusing on cross-border patient mobility highlights that this kind of mobility dates back to ancient times when borders were created. As an example, it refers to pilgrims in the Middle Ages who could rely on a network of monasteries providing free care in case of need. L. Bertinato, R. Busse, N. Fahy, H. Legido-Quigley, M. McKee, W. Palm, I. Passarani, F. Ronfini, *Cross-Border Health Care in Europe*, European Observatory on Health Systems and Policies, Brussels 2005, p. 1.

35 In another paper, eight possible scenarios of cross-border patient mobility were identified with the aim of proposing a typology of patient mobility with global relevance. The analysis was based on two dimensions of patient mobility, namely the types of patient motivations and the types of funding. The combinations of four types of motivations and two types of funding presented in the paper resulted in eight different situations. Glinos et al., above n. 10, pp. 1145–1155.
Mainil developed an even more sophisticated typology resulting in twelve types of transnational patient mobility. T. Mainil, *Transnational health care and medical tourism: Understanding 21st-century patient mobility – Towards a rationale of transnational health region development*, NRIT Media, Nieuwegein 2012.

and receives medical treatment in the latter area.[36] This broad concept can be further specified by posing questions to detect each relevant aspect of the above-mentioned basic elements.

2.1. THE MOBILITY ELEMENT: DIRECTIONS AND DETERMINANTS

If someone changes his/her place of stay, in the majority of cases there is a specific direction, a geographical area involved in the movement and a reason behind it. Therefore, in this section a distinction is made according to the direction of the mobility, the geographical area involved in the patient's movement and the determinants[37] of mobility are examined.

Mobility can take place within the same country (*domestic* or *intra-country mobility*) or between countries (*inter-country* or *international mobility*). When moving between different countries, borders[38] are crossed, so the latter type is also called *cross-border mobility*. This term is widely used in the European Union in relation to patient mobility. The countries concerned may either share a common border or be geographically further apart.[39] If the mobility

---

36 Glinos and Baeten (above n. 8, p. 18) define patient mobility as a 'general term to describe any kind of movement which involves patients moving beyond their catchment area or area of residence to access healthcare'. Similarly, in an article by Glinos et al. (above n. 10, p. 1146) cross-border patient mobility is described as 'involving a patient, who travels to another country for the purpose of receiving planned care'. The difference between these definitions and the concept outlined above lies in the fact that, in my view, the broad concept of patient mobility should not be limited to *patients* moving with the purpose of seeking *planned treatment* but should be extended to *persons* moving and receiving *occasional healthcare* abroad. The concept of the broad and narrow definition of patient mobility is to be detailed below.

37 Determinants should be understood as those factors which are decisive when a person considers obtaining medical treatment abroad.

38 According to the definition of the International Organisation for Migration a border is '(a) line separating land territory or maritime zones of two States or subparts of States. It can also refer to a region that is found at the margin of settled and developed territory'. International Organisation for Migration, *Glossary on migration*, http://publications.iom.int/bookstore/free/Glossary%202nd%20ed%20web.pdf, 2011 (accessed 31.07.2012), p. 14. Hereinafter the term *border* is to be understood as an international border separating two states.
Some authors note that different types of borders can be distinguished. Most remarkably, a distinction can be made between *fluid* and *rigid* borders, where the former is physically and geographically easy to cross and does not impose a serious administrative burden on the person concerned, whereas the latter creates a real barrier, which hinders persons from crossing it. Glinos and Baeten, above n. 8, p. 7.

39 Interestingly, Kangas distinguishes between *international* and *cross-border* mobility, reserving the latter exclusively for travel to adjoining countries, while indicating that international mobility involves a journey to a destination beyond neighbouring countries. B. Kangas, 'Traveling for Medical Care in a Global World' *Medical Anthropology: Cross-Cultural Studies in Health and Illness, Special Issue: Medical Travel* 2010, vol 29 issue 4, pp. 344–362.

occurs between two regions within the same country, we speak of *inter-regional mobility* (which is a specific type of intra-country mobility), although if the region extends beyond an international border, the term *regional cross-border mobility*[40] is used (which is a specific type of inter-country mobility). These types are categorised in Table 1 below.

Table 1. Types of mobility according to the geographical area involved

Direction of movement / Area involved	Moving between two places which are in the same region	Moving between two places which are in the same county	Moving between two places which are in different regions	Moving between two places which are in different countries
One region	*domestic*, (intra-) regional mobility	*domestic*, (intra-) regional mobility	–	regional *cross-border* mobility
One country	*domestic*, (intra-) regional mobility	*domestic*, (intra-) regional mobility	*domestic*, inter-regional mobility	–
Different regions	–	*domestic*, inter-regional mobility	*domestic*, inter-regional mobility	inter-country or *cross-border* mobility
Different countries	regional *cross-border* mobility	–	inter-country or *cross-border* mobility	inter-country or *cross-border* mobility

Source: The author's own summary.

Table 1 illustrates the possible directions of patient movements and the geographic area involved in a matrix. This book is limited to analysis of the *cross-border aspects of patient mobility* (in Table 1, they are marked in grey), thus excluding domestic, intra-country mobility situations from its scope. Hereinafter solely cross-border patient mobility within the European Union[41] is dealt with, even if its cross-border nature is not mentioned each time.

Although surveys show that the European citizens' cross-border mobility rate is still rather low,[42] in 2015 one-third of the respondents of an EU survey were

---

40 Glinos and Baeten, above n. 8, p.18.

41 In cross-border situations, at least two countries are involved. The original country is – in principle – the one where the person concerned is covered by the public health insurance scheme (*competent Member State* or *Member State of affiliation*), and the other one is where the medical treatment is provided (*Member State of treatment*).

42 'On average, only slightly more than two percent of EU citizens currently live in another EU Member State.' European Commission, *Eurobarometer: Geographical and labour market mobility*, 2010, p. 5. According to the Annual Labour Mobility Report, '(i)n 2014, around 11.3 million EU-28 and EFTA citizens of working age were living in an EU Member State

clearly open to travelling abroad to seek medical treatment, whereas another 16 per cent made it dependent on the country or the type of healthcare. All in all, on average about half of EU citizens would consider obtaining healthcare abroad as a viable option.[43]

In searching for the answer to why people tend to travel across borders to obtain medical treatment and what can motivate them, special attention has to be given to four basic factors[44] in my view, namely *familiarity* and *proximity, availability, price* or *affordability*, and *quality*.

First, *familiarity* and *proximity* are key drivers of mobility which are especially present in the border areas. People obviously feel more comfortable with a system they know and are more often willing to travel for healthcare when they are associated with the language,[45] the culture[46] and the healthcare

other than their country of citizenship, an increase of around 1.4% compared to 2013'. E. Fries-Tersch and V. Mabilia, *2015 Annual Report on Labour Mobility*, Network Statistics FMSSFE, Brussels 2015, p. 21.

43 *Special Eurobarometer 425*, above n. 14, p. 6. It is remarkable, however, that at the same time the proportion of EU citizens that actually received treatment in another Member State ranges from only 1 per cent in Bulgaria and 2 per cent in the UK, Estonia, Greece, Germany to 12 per cent in Italy and 16 per cent in Luxembourg with an EU-average of 5 per cent. *Special Eurobarometer 425*, p. 4.

44 Glinos and Baeten specify five key drivers, considering the factor of bioethical legislation a separate driver, whereas I include this type of treatment in the group of non-available treatments. Glinos and Baeten, above n. 8, p. 6. However, in a more recent article by Glinos et al. the very same four factors of motivation were identified as mentioned above. Glinos et al., above n. 10, p. 1147. On incentives and barriers see also Calnan et al., above n. 12, pp. 30–32.

Crooks and her colleagues, while dealing with medical tourism on an international scale, apply a different approach and identify three types of motivating factors, such as (1) procedure-based (e.g. illegal or non-available treatments, experimental procedures in the patient's country); (2) travel-based (e.g. increasing ease and affordability of international travel, frequency of flights to the key destinations); and (3) cost-based factors. V.A. Crooks, P. Kingsbury, J. Snyder and R. Johnston, 'What is known about the patient's experience of medical tourism? A scoping review' *BMC Health Services Research* 2010, vol 10, p. 271.

The data of a survey by the Techniker Krankenkasse showed that the key reason for the respondents in their decision for EU cross-border treatment was their former good experience. As other main drivers, the possibility to combine treatment with holiday, better healthcare and the unavailability of treatment were identified. C. Wagner and F. Verheyen, 'Aspects of Planned EU Cross-border Care' in Hennion and Kaufmann, above n. 8, pp. 105–106.

45 The Techniker Krankenkasse-survey concludes that a significant part of the responding patients opted for undergoing treatment in German-speaking countries (in Austria and Switzerland), so almost 80 per cent of the patients communicated in their native language during their treatment. Wagner and Verheyen, above n. 44, p.108.

46 In Crooks et al, religious accessibility is also added as an influencing factor, since 'patients may seek out facilities that observe the same religious protocols they do'. Crooks et al., above n. 44, p. 271. However, religious beliefs may result in a counter-effect when religious considerations are mirrored in the bioethical legislation of the given country. For instance, it can be clearly seen that strict laws on abortion or euthanasia may drive people abroad to obtain the requested services there.

system of the country they are heading to. It is not exceptional that people who migrated to another country return to their country of origin to obtain healthcare.[47] In border areas it is often seen that the closest healthcare provider happens to be settled on the other side of the border.[48] However, it should be noted that proximity has become relative in the last decades. Thanks to, among others, low budget airlines, ever bigger distances can be covered quite easily and even the farther points of Europe have become readily accessible.[49]

Secondly, the *availability* of the required treatments plays an essential role. Patients are highly motivated by inadequate availability, which can occur in two different ways. On the one hand, when the capacity is insufficient, the treatment concerned does exist and is covered by the national healthcare system in the Member State of affiliation, but cannot be provided within a justifiable time limit. This can be considered *relative unavailability*.[50] One-third of EU citizens say that they are willing to travel abroad in order to reduce waiting times and receive treatment more quickly than at home.[51] Rieder calls this 'the vector of time'.[52]

On the other hand, certain treatments may either not exist or not be covered by the national healthcare system. These are the cases of *absolute unavailability*. The reason behind this unavailability can be purely economic if financing the treatment or setting up the necessary infrastructure were too expensive and unreasonable.[53] This is the case for highly specialised treatments, which would result in inefficient investments if the population of the country is quite small.[54] However, the lack of providing certain treatments can be based on the

---

47 J. Connell, 'Contemporary medical tourism: Conceptualisation, culture and commodification' *Tourism Management* 2013, vol 34, p. 3.

48 For example, Dutch patients from the Dutch region Zeeuws-Vlaanderen often choose to receive medical treatment in hospitals in the northern part of Belgium, where they share a common language and are familiar with the culture and healthcare infrastructure. Glinos et al., above n. 10, p 99.

49 Among others, Glinos and Baeten, above n. 8, p. 9 and C. Perdue and S. Noble, 'Foreign travel for advanced cancer patients: a guide for healthcare professionals' *Postgraduate Medical Journal* 2007, vol 83 issue 981, p. 437.

50 In Glinos et al, this dimension is considered (un)*availability in terms of quantity of services* as opposed to (un)*availability in terms of types of care*, which more or less connotes the same as what I describe as *absolute unavailability*. Glinos et al, above n. 10, p. 1147.

51 *Special Eurobarometer 425*, above n. 14, p. 7. At the same time, evidence shows that – despite extensive waiting times – many patients prefer to be treated in their usual environment over travelling for (quicker) healthcare. P. Burge, N. Devlin, J. Appleby, C. Rohr and J. Grant, 'Do patients always prefer quicker treatment?: a discrete choice analysis of patients' stated preferences in the London Patient Choice Project' *Applied Health Economics and Health Policy* 2004, vol 3 issue 4, p. 192.

52 C.M. Rieder, 'Cross-border Movement of Patients in the EU: A Re-Appraisal' *European Journal of Health Law* 2016, http://booksandjournals.brillonline.com/content/journals/10.1163/15718093-12341419 (accessed 23.04.2017), p. 2.

53 Glinos and Baeten, above n. 8, p. 6.

54 For example, Maltese patients go to the United Kingdom for high-cost treatments because '(t)he investment cost is too high, the patients are too few and full-time professional staff

national bioethical legislation as well. There are numerous medical interventions which are judged diversely in the different Member States within the European Union.[55] Thus – in order to circumvent their own national laws[56] – patients travel abroad for instance for abortion,[57] reproductive care,[58] stem cell therapy[59] or even euthanasia.[60] European citizens seem most willing to travel abroad if

employed to perform this type of service will quickly become deskilled'. N. Azzopardi Muscat, K. Grech, J.M. Cachia, D. Xuereb, 'Sharing capacities – Malta and the United Kingdom' in Rosenmöller et al., above n. 8, p. 122.
Between Malta and the UK, this cooperation is based on a bilateral agreement. 'The services offered under the Malta-United Kingdom bilateral agreement are considered to be an extension to the healthcare services offered by the Maltese healthcare system, and when considering requests for treatment abroad, priority is given to healthcare services offered under this agreement.' Strban et al, above n. 5, p. 66. Reportedly, in 2015 '482 Maltese patients received planned treatment under the Malta-UK bilateral agreement.' F. De Wispelaere and J. Pacolet, *Planned cross-border healthcare*, Network Statistics FMSSFE, Leuven 2016, p. 22.

55 N. Lunt and P. Carrera, 'Medical tourism: Assessing the evidence on treatment abroad' *Mauritas* 2010, vol 66, p. 30.

56 W. Henn, 'Genetic screening with the DNA chip: a new Pandora's box?' *Journal of Medical Ethics* 1999, vol 25, p. 202; M. Brazier, 'Regulating the reproduction business?' *Medical Law Journal* 1999, vol 7, p. 191.
G. Pennings argues, however, in relation to reproductive tourism (the cross-border movement of patients to obtain specific types of medical assistance in reproduction that they cannot receive at home) that ethically controversial treatments should not be seen as circumvention of restrictive national laws, but rather as 'a safety valve that avoids moral conflict, and as such, contributes to a peaceful coexistence of different ethical and religious views in Europe'. G. Pennings, 'Legal harmonization and reproductive tourism in Europe' *Human Reproduction* 2004, vol 19 no 12, p. 2694. See also G. Pennings, 'Reproductive tourism as moral pluralism in motion' *Journal of Medical Ethics* 2002, vol 28, pp. 337–341 and M. Frischhut, 'Legal and Ethical Issues of Cross-Border Reproductive Care from an EU Perspective' in M.K. Smith and L. Puczkó (eds.), *The Routledge Handbook of Health Tourism*, Taylor & Francis, London, New York 2017.

57 Many cases have shown that adopting strict anti-abortion laws in the Member States does not result in women not undergoing these kinds of treatments. They are just forced to do it 'underground or abroad'. G. Price, 'Polish women increasingly head abroad for abortions' *Warsaw Business Journal*, 27 August 2010. See also A.M. E.W. Sterling, 'European Union and Abortion Tourism: Liberalizing Ireland's Abortion Law' *Boston College International and Comparative Law Review* 1997, vol 20 issue 2, pp. 385–406.

58 L. Nielsen, 'Procreative Tourism, Genetic Testing and The Law' in N. Lowe and G. Douglas (eds.), *Families Across Frontiers*, Kluwer Academic Publisher, The Hague 1996, pp. 831–848; Pennings, above n. 56; A. McKelvey, A.L. David, F. Shefield and E.R. Jauniauxc, 'The impact of cross-border reproductive care or "fertility tourism" on NHS maternity services' *BJOG: An International Journal of Obstetrics & Gynaecology* 2009, vol 116 issue 11, pp. 1520–1523; P. Thorn and S. Dill, 'The role of patients' organizations in cross-border reproductive care' *Fertility and Sterility* 2010, vol 94 no 1, p. 23 and Connell, above n. 47, p. 9.

59 K.A. Ryan, A.N. Sanders, D.D. Wang and A.D. Levine, 'Tracking the rise of stem cell tourism' *Regenerative Medicine* 2010, vol 5 issue 1, pp. 27–33; P.P. Song, 'Biotech pilgrims and the transnational quest for stem cell cures' *Medical Anthropology* 2010, vol 29 issue 4, pp. 384–402.

60 D.S. Miller and C. Gonzalez, 'When Death is the Destination: The Business of Death Tourism – Despite Legal and Social Implications' *International Journal of Culture, Tourism and Hospitality Research* 2013, vol 7 issue 3.

they cannot obtain the desired medical care in their home country.[61] However, it is worth mentioning that if the treatment is not illegal in the given country but simply not covered by the public healthcare system, the majority of this demand is usually absorbed by the private healthcare sector of the given country.

A third crucial factor is the *price* of the treatment. There are enormous differences between the medical costs in the various Member States, which are especially remarkable with regard to co-payments, the formal service fees which have to be paid by patients out of pocket.[62] Since receiving the same treatment abroad can result in considerable savings for patients[63] even with the additional costs considered, a significant percentage of the EU population chooses to seek cheaper healthcare abroad.[64] A clear trend can be seen of patient flow from the old Member States with higher prices towards the new Member States with lower prices[65] but good quality healthcare.[66]

Fourthly, the *quality* of the healthcare service is also one of the main driving forces prompting people to go abroad. In this regard they are also expressing their dissatisfaction with the national system in the country they live in.[67] Fifty three per cent of EU citizens indicated their readiness to travel for better quality.[68] In Rieder's analysis this appears as 'the vector of treatment'.[69]

---

61 *Special Eurobarometer 425*, above n. 14, p. 7.

62 C.C. Ros, P.P. Groenewegen, D.M.J. Delnoij, 'All rights reserved, or can we just copy? Cost sharing arrangements and characteristics of health care systems' *Health Policy* 2000, vol 52 no 1, p. 2. See also R. Robinson, 'User charges for healthcare' in E. Mossialos, A. Dixon, J. Figueras and J. Kutzin (eds.), *Funding health care: options for Europe*, Open University Press, Buckingham, Philadelphia 2002, p. 162.

63 Glinos and Baeten, above, n. 8, p. 6.

64 *Special Eurobarometer 425*, above n. 14, p. 7.

65 van den Bossche and Ploscar aptly call the phenomenon of travelling from developed to less developed countries due to costs and waiting lists 'reverse globalization'. A.-M. van den Bossche and P. Ploscar, 'Rights of Dental Patients in the EU – A Legal Assessment' *Journal of Forensic Odonto-Stomatology* 2012, vol 30 suppl 1, p. 6. See also Connell, above n. 47, p. 1.

66 A typical example is dental tourism, when patients coming from the United Kingdom, Ireland or Austria travel to Hungary or Poland for cheaper but high-quality dental care. L. Turner, 'Cross-border dental care: "dental tourism" and patient mobility' *British Dental Journal* 2008, vol 204 no 10, p. 553. See also Glinos and Baeten, above n. 8, p. 6.; Zs. Tolnai., B. Billik and P. Fuchs, 'Magyarország és a fogászati turizmus' (Hungary and the dental tourism) *Egészségügyi Gazdasági Szemle (Journal of Health Economics)* 2009, issue 4, pp. 34–40; A. Osterle, P. Balazs, J.J. Delgado, 'Travelling for teeth: characteristics and perspectives of dental care tourism in Hungary' *British Dental Journal* 2009, vol 206 no 8, pp.425–428; van den Bossche and Ploscar, above n. 65 and J. Winkelmann, M.M. Hofmarcher, E. Kovacs and G. Szocska, 'Cross-border dental care between Austria and Hungary' *Eurohealth* 2013, vol 19 no 4.

67 As Runnels and Carrera points out the fact '(t)hat patients seek access to care abroad says something about how health is construed and how domestic healthcare is regarded and, as such, reflects to a certain extent on the performance and responsiveness of domestic health care systems'. V. Runnels and P.M. Carrera, 'Why do patients engage in medical tourism?' *Mauritas* 2012, vol 73, p. 303.

68 *Special Eurobarometer 425*, above n. 14, p. 7.

69 Rieder, above n. 52, p. 2.

However, it should be mentioned that in numerous Member States, mainly in Central East Europe, it is a widespread habit to seek better quality treatment in the public sector by informally providing an extra 'under-the-table' payment – also called gratitude money – for the healthcare professionals.[70] Another solution can simply be to 'buy' better treatment on the private healthcare market. So patients in these countries tend to consider first to pay some extra within the public healthcare system or turn to a private provider, before deliberating the possibility of obtaining healthcare abroad.

It should be added that other determinants of patient mobility influencing patients' choice can also be identified, such as or receiving treatment from a renowned specialist.[71] Aside from these motivating factors, it should also be noted that many European patients prefer not to seek treatment abroad.[72] Reasons for this consist of arguments such as: they are satisfied with the medical treatments in their country; they find it more convenient to be treated near their home,[73] where it is much easier to keep in contact with family and friends; they are afraid of language difficulties which can be especially problematic in medical situations; they lack information about their rights and the medical treatment available abroad; or they simply cannot afford to be treated in other Member States, where they possibly have to pay upfront.[74]

2.2. THE HEALTHCARE ELEMENT: CONTENT AND ACTORS

Besides the realisation of cross-border movement, the other core element of patient mobility is to obtain healthcare in a country other than the country of residence. Therefore, it is necessary to summarise what is understood by the expression *healthcare* in this book. In this section, the types of healthcare and the categories of European mobile patients are briefly touched upon.

Healthcare, in a broad sense, is a complex system designed to cope with the social risk of sickness and injury.[75] While dealing with social issues

70 S. Allin, K. Davaki and E. Mossialos, 'Paying for "free" health care: the conundrum of informal payments in post-communist Europe' *Global Corruption Report* 2005, p. 63 and M. Lewis, 'Informal health payments in central and eastern Europe and the former Soviet Union: issues, trends and policy implications' in Mossialos et al., above n. 62, p. 184. The details and consequences of this phenomenon are nevertheless beyond the scope of this research.

71 *Special Eurobarometer 425*, above n. 14, p. 7.

72 See n. 8 above.

73 See n. 10 above.

74 *Special Eurobarometer 425*, above n. 14, p. 9.

75 Long-term care benefits – however connected – are not subject of this book. Still more so since they are excluded from the material scope of the Patient Mobility Directive. See Article 1(3)(a) PMD. Nevertheless, cross-border long-term care does exist, and that phenomenon is also of a great value for further research. K. Connolly, 'Germany "exporting" old and sick to foreign care homes' *The Guardian*, 26.12.2012.

as a consequence of sickness and injury, the social system needs to tackle two separate, but nevertheless interrelated, problems at the same time: on the one hand, the healthcare system aims to compensate the person who cannot carry out his/her working activity due to medical reasons for the loss of income, and on the other hand, it attempts to handle the health problem itself.[76]

The first aim indicated above can be achieved by offering the person sickness benefits in cash (*in pecuniam*).[77] These benefits can be considered as financial support to maintain the standard of living during the incapacity to work and are usually provided by means of a simple money transfer. Typically, this transfer evokes a *bipolar relationship* between the insured person and the health insurance fund, which makes the cross-border provision of the benefits rather smooth.

In this book, the term healthcare is to be understood in its more narrow meaning, also called medical care. According to the ILO (International Labour Organization), 'contingencies covered shall include any morbid condition, whatever its cause, and pregnancy and confinement and their consequences'.[78] Whereas the ILO's definition of medical care focuses on the social risks covered and the particular benefits included,[79] in the European Union, where the term sickness benefits in kind (*in naturam*) or healthcare services are more widely used, emphasis is put on the various methods of healthcare delivery. According to the Coordination Regulations these benefits intend 'to supply, make available, pay directly or reimburse the cost of medical care and products and services ancillary to that care'.[80] Similarly, the CJEU described them as benefits which are 'designed to cover care received by the person concerned, inter alia, by the direct payment or reimbursement of medical expenses incurred by that person's state.'[81]

From a functional point of view, healthcare can be defined as a collective phrase for all the '(g)oods and services provided to promote health, or prevent,

---

76 Similarly, in P. Watson, *Social Security Law of the European Communities*, Mansell Publishing, London 1980, p. 1.

77 See Part III of the International Labour Organization's (ILO) Convention concerning Minimum Standards of Social Security (ILO 102).

78 Article 8 of ILO 102.

79 In Article 10 of ILO 102 states that medical care: 'shall include at least (a) in case of a morbid condition (i) general practitioner care, including domiciliary visiting; (ii) specialist care at hospitals for in-patients and out-patients, and such specialist care as may be available outside hospitals; (iii) the essential pharmaceutical supplies as prescribed by medical or other qualified practitioners; and (iv) hospitalisation where necessary; and (b) in case of pregnancy and confinement and their consequences (i) pre-natal, confinement and post-natal care either by medical practitioners or by qualified midwives; and (ii) hospitalisation where necessary'.

80 Article 1(va)(i) BR. The Regulation's definition shows precisely the different types of healthcare funding.

81 C-160/96 *Molenaar* [ECLI:EU:C:1998:84], 32 and 34 (in the context of a statutory scheme of social insurance against the risk of reliance on care); C-372/04 *Watts*, 137 and C-466/04 *Acereda Herrera*, 29.

alleviate or eliminate ill-health'[82] or '(t)he total human and material resources that a nation or community deploys to preserve, protect, and restore health and to minimize suffering caused by disease and injury'.[83] It can be agreed upon that the function of healthcare is twofold: preventive[84] on the one hand and curative on the other.[85] It is an especially wide term including *self-care* (personal health maintenance, care provided by the person in need of healthcare himself/herself), *informal care* (care provided through an informal framework of family members, friends, etc) and *institutionalised care* (organised by a private or public body, care provided through a formal institutional framework). This book deals with the third form of healthcare.

During the research, examination was made solely of the sickness benefits in kind that are organised by the Member States within the European Union and are provided in the framework of a national healthcare system[86] according to the relevant legal regulations of the given Member State. In the course of the provision of these benefits a 'new' actor becomes involved: *the healthcare provider*, an individual or an institution that provides healthcare services. The result is – in contrast with the bipolarity of cash benefit provision – a *tripolar relationship*, in which the provider is the actor whom the insured person receives the benefit from and the healthcare fund plays the role of the 'third party payer' who ensures – at least partly – the funding for the health expenses.[87]

As mentioned above, in cross-border situations, within the European Union the provision of sickness cash benefits is properly coordinated by

82 A.J. Culyer, *The Dictionary of Health Economics*, Edward Elgar Publishing, Cheltenham, UK, Northampton, MA, USA 2005, p. 149.

83 J.M. Last, *A Dictionary of Public Health*, Oxford University Press, Oxford 2007, p. 156.

84 The Directive's definition, which says that 'healthcare means health services provided by health professionals to patients to assess, maintain or restore their state of health, including the prescription, dispensation and provision of medicinal products and devices' seems to miss the preventive side of healthcare. See Article 3(a) PMD.

85 Rehabilitation can be seen as a third pillar of healthcare.

86 Flear calls them *public health care systems*, which implies on the one hand that these schemes are – at least partly – publicly financed and on the other hand they are 'established, guaranteed and often funded and/or provided by the welfare states of the EU Member States'. M. Flear, 'Case C-385/99 V.G. Müller-Fauré v. Onderlinge Waarborgmaatschappij O.Z. Zorgverzekeringen U.A. and E.E.M. van Riet v. Onderlinge Waarborgmaatschappij Z.A.O. Zorgverzekeringen, Judgment of the Court of 13 May 2003' *Common Market Law Review* 2004, vol 41 issue 1, p. 209.

87 Employing a third party payer is an example of the implementation of a solidarity mechanism in the European public health insurance systems in order 'to share the costs for medical care between the sick and the well and to adjust for different levels of ability to pay'. European Parliament – Directorate General for Research, 'Health Care Systems in the EU: A Comparative Study', 1998, p. 10. On the different types of healthcare funding see OECD, EUROSTAT and WHO, 'A Proposal for the Main Categories of the Classification of Financing Schemes' http://www.oecd.org/dataoecd/17/32/41016651.pdf, 2008 (accessed 01.04.2012).

Regulation (EC) No 883/2004[88] and its Implementing Regulation.[89] However, the provision of sickness benefits in kind is greatly problematic and gives rise to numerous legal questions if the person concerned stays or resides abroad. Thus, these issues merit further detailed examination later in this book.

The *actors* involved in healthcare service provision are the insurer or healthcare fund, the healthcare provider and the insured person. In other words, they are the payer of the service, the provider of the service and the potential recipient of the service, also called the patient.[90] Since the topic is observed from the patients' point of view, meaning that the main focus is on their social rights concerning the cross-border healthcare provision, it seems necessary to take a closer look at this group. The Patient Mobility Directive defines a patient as 'any natural person who seeks to receive or receives healthcare in a Member State'.[91]

By analogy, a border-crossing patient[92] is any natural person who seeks to receive or receives healthcare in a Member State other than the State of affiliation. At this point, it must be noted that this book's scope is restricted to persons covered by a compulsory healthcare system; neither uninsured persons,[93] nor people subject only to voluntary healthcare systems are dealt with.

Nevertheless, according to one of the most widespread categorisations, five main categories of European border-crossing patients can be distinguished,[94] namely *temporary visitors*, *long-term residents*, *people living in the border areas*, '*posted patients*' and the '*real*' *mobile patients*, persons choosing to travel abroad in order to obtain healthcare.

The first group are *temporary visitors* who become in need of healthcare while staying abroad temporarily. These people travel for tourism, business, study or any other purpose. The point is that while they are visiting a country other than the country where they are covered by health insurance, they need

88 Article 21(1) BR: 'An insured person and members of his/her family residing or staying in a Member State other than the competent Member State shall be entitled to cash benefits provided by the competent institution in accordance with the legislation it applies.'

89 Articles 27–28 IR.

90 It is important to note that in case of *derived rights*, the patient is not the insured person him/herself, but regularly a family member. See Article 1(i) BR on the definition of family members.

91 Article 3(h) PMD.

92 They are also called 'transnational EU-patients'. K. Kesteloot, S. Pocceschi and E. van der Schueren, 'The reimbursement of the expenses for medical treatment received by "transnational" patients in EU-countries' *Health Policy* 1995, vol 33 issue 1, p. 43.

93 See on this issue J.-P. Lhernould (ed.), B. Schulte (ed.), J.-C. Fillon, J. Hajdú, H. Verschueren, *Healthcare provided during a temporary stay in another Member State to persons who do not fulfil conditions for statutory health insurance coverage*, trESS Network, Ghent 2010.

94 Bertinato et al., above n. 34, pp. 2–5; Rosenmöller et al., above n. 8, p. 6 and Lunt and Carrera, above n. 55, p. 28.

to use the health system in the country of stay. The European Health Insurance Card (EHIC)[95] was designed specifically for this group of people in order to avoid the need to return to the home country before the intended date of return.

The second category are the *long-term residents* who – in most of the cases – decide to retire to another Member State and wish to use the healthcare system of that country.[96] Examples are Scandinavian pensioners who spend the winters in the Mediterranean,[97] English pensioners living in Spain and currently anxious how Brexit will affect their access to healthcare[98] or Irish workers who return home after spending their working life in England.[99] In my opinion, we will face a similar phenomenon when the workers from the recently acceded East European countries, who sought employment in the old Member States, reach retirement age.[100]

In these two categories, the *mobility element* precedes the *healthcare element*, whereas in the other three groups first the need for healthcare occurs and then the patients cross the border(s) to obtain treatment.

The third category is *people living in the border areas*. Those who share close linguistic and cultural links with the people living on the other side of the border might be more willing to cross the border for treatment than to receive healthcare service in their own country, in an environment which they are less familiar or comfortable with. In border areas, special arrangements are often made between providers in order to share the capacities and ensure appropriate service for all even if the closest provider happens to be settled on the other side of the border.[101]

The patients belonging to the fourth category are encouraged to go abroad or even sent abroad by the insurer to receive the required treatment. They are

---

95 On the rules related to the usage of EHIC, detailed analysis can be found in, especially section 2.

96 On the migration patterns of the elderly, see A.M. Warnes and A. Williams, 'Older Migrants in Europe: A New Focus for Migration Studies' *Journal of Ethnic and Migration Studies* 2007, vol 32 issue 8, pp. 1257–1281. See also S. Kumpunen and L. Trigg, 'Intra-European retirement migrants' access to state-funded long-term care and health entitlements' *Eurohealth* 2013, vol 19 no 4.

97 S. Roberts, B. Schulte (eds.), C.G. de Cortazar, T. Medaiskis and H. Verschueren, *Healthcare for Pensioners*, trESS Network, Ghent 2009, p. 5. Here the authors distinguish two main groups of retirement migrants, namely those who move to another Member State on a permanent basis and fully integrate into the society of this Member State and those who 'retain their centre of interest in the country where they lived and worked and consider themselves to be resident in that country while they share their time between the two or more Member States'. p. 5.

98 L. O'Carroll, 'Hundreds of thousands of retired Britons in EU "may be forced to return"' *The Guardian*, 18.01.2017.

99 Bertinato et al., above n. 34, p. 4.

100 Warnes and Williams call them 'return migrants'. Warnes and Williams, above n. 96, p. 1262.

101 Bertinato et al., above n. 34, p. 4. See also n. 12 and 48 above and De Wispelaere and Pacolet, above n. 54, pp. 21–22.

also called '*posted patients*' or '*outsourced patients*'.[102] The reason behind this is usually the uneconomic situation regarding the infrastructure for certain, often highly-specialised treatments.[103] This problem can be easily solved by treatment abroad, which is 'actively managed by public authorities, seeking to ensure continuity of care, coverage of extra expenses and appropriate selection of providers abroad'.[104]

Lastly, the fifth group are patients *choosing to travel abroad* in the hope of receiving quicker, better or cheaper treatment there.[105] These are often self-managed arrangements, which are either not or, at most, partly funded by the insurer. The treatments obtained often fall outside of the circle that is covered by the public health insurance, such as cosmetic surgery or dental treatment.[106] This type of mobility is generally called *medical tourism*.[107]

Nevertheless, this typology reflects mainly on the practical circumstances of the various groups of patients and not on their legal status. Nevertheless, patients dealt with in the course of this research share some characteristics, namely they do reside in one Member State, but receive healthcare in another one; they receive medical treatment which is (or is supposed to be) in the benefit package of at least one of these countries; and the medical costs are (or are supposed to be) partly or fully covered by their health insurance.

2.3. THE DEFINITION OF CROSS-BORDER PATIENT MOBILITY

In the previous sections, the conceptual elements of patient mobility were discussed, although the term *patient mobility* is not mentioned literally in Union legislation: it is not a legal expression. It is a concept which was created by the literature and which not only includes the legal aspects of the phenomenon, but all issues related to mobile patients. The so-called Patient Mobility Directive itself

---

102 Lunt and Carrera, above n. 55, p. 28.

103 See n. 54 above.

104 Rosenmöller et al., above n. 8, p. 7.
Under the UK-Malta bilateral agreement, '(i)n addition to the medical treatment, approved patients are means-tested to assess whether they qualify for free air tickets. The Maltese health authorities also have accommodation agreements with various service providers who offer accommodation services to patients receiving treatment. Payment to these institutions is made directly by the Maltese health authorities. Patients receiving treatment in the United Kingdom are also provided with transport from and to airports and for hospital appointments'. Strban et al, above n. 5, p. 66.

105 On the motivating factors, see section 2.1. above.

106 Bertinato et al., above n. 34, p. 5.

107 On the different terms used in relation to patient mobility, see section 2.3. below.

uses the phrase *cross-border healthcare.*[108] Thus, before moving to the analysis of the legislation, it is indispensable to clarify the various terms and concepts.

Although *patient mobility* is a wide and complex phenomenon in itself,[109] it is regarded as a subset of the broader notion of *cross-border healthcare*. In the course of the high level process of reflection on patient mobility and healthcare developments in the European Union,[110] cross-border care was described as a general term which covers both cooperation in the border regions and more generally, care received in another Member State, without any implication of proximity.[111] In comparison, the Patient Mobility Directive defines cross-border healthcare as 'healthcare provided or prescribed in a Member State other than the Member State of affiliation'.[112] This broad approach is abstract enough to be able to absorb all the actors and types of cross-border healthcare provision and clearly shows that this concept is not restricted to patient mobility only.

Each healthcare provision which – in one or more elements – reaches beyond the national border and thus implicates at least one international element[113] is considered cross-border healthcare:[114] cross-border healthcare includes the cross-border mobility of all goods, services and persons related to healthcare. Four main fields can be distinguished, namely patient mobility,

---

108 Interestingly, the Committee on the Internal Market and Consumer Protection of the European Parliament suggested making a distinction between *cross-border health services* (which are situated on either side of a border common to two Member States in order to maintain and offer patients a high standard of access and care) on the one hand; and, on the other hand, *international health services* within the European Union (which must offer healthcare for the treatment of rare or orphan diseases and/or diseases which require rare and very expensive technologies or provide access to care which their Member State or State of residence cannot at present offer them). European Parliament – Committee on the Internal Market and Consumer Protection, *Report on the impact and consequences of the exclusion of health services from the Directive on services in the internal market*, 10 May 2007, A6-0173/2007, p. 26.
In my opinion, this terminology would have been confusing and the definitions too restrictive, thus it is right that the drafters of the PMD did not follow this approach, but applied a more general one. See n. 112 below.

109 See n. 35 above.

110 The high level process of reflection on patient mobility and healthcare developments in the European Union was convened by the European Commission following the conclusions of the Health Council on 26 June 2002. The Council and the representatives of the Member States meeting in the Council recognised that there would be value in the Commission pursuing a high level process of reflection, in close cooperation with the Council and all the Member States, particularly with health ministers and other key stakeholders.

111 Council Conclusions, above n. 22, see similarly in n. 24, p. 4.

112 Article 3(e) PMD.

113 In case of European cross-border healthcare, the international element must be a European one.

114 This definition resembles the concept of Peeters, who says that cross-border healthcare 'covers all situations, different from the one the patient is treated in his own Member State (the one he is socially insured in) by a local healthcare provider (established in that Member State)'. M. Peeters, 'Free Movement of Patients: Directive 2011/24 on the Application of Patients' Rights in Cross-Border Healthcare' *European Journal of Health Law* 2012, vol 19, p. 29.

the mobility of healthcare professionals, the mobility of health services themselves and institutional cross-border collaboration on healthcare.[115]

Health professionals[116] cross borders in search of higher wages, better working conditions, training and career opportunities, and new professional or personal experiences.[117] Provider mobility comprises all forms of mobility 'whether they are establishing themselves in another Member State or simply providing services on an occasional or temporary basis'.[118]

In certain cases, cross-border healthcare can be realised without either the patient or the provider moving: healthcare services can be provided from a distance. This means that the services 'move' across borders themselves by using modern information and communication technology (ICT) – typically telemedicine[119] – to transfer or exchange diagnostics, expert advice, tests or images.[120] In these cases the real mobility element is missing and is replaced by ICT.

Finally, cross-border healthcare also includes cross-border collaboration between healthcare providers – mainly between hospitals[121] – or between

---

115 Wismar et al., above n. 8, p. 2.

116 3 (f) PMD: '"health professional" means a doctor of medicine, a nurse responsible for general care, a dental practitioner, a midwife or a pharmacist within the meaning of Directive 2005/36/EC, or another professional exercising activities in the healthcare sector which are restricted to a regulated profession as defined in Article 3(1)(a) of Directive 2005/36/EC, or a person considered to be a health professional according to the legislation of the Member State of treatment'.

117 C. Jinks, B.N. Ong and C. Paton, 'Mobile medics? The mobility of doctors in the European Economic Area' *Health Policy* 2000, vol 54 issue 1, p. 57; B. Marchal and G. Kegels, 'Health workforce imbalances in times of globalization: brain drain or professional mobility?' *The International Journal of Health Planning and Management* 2003, vol 18 issue S1, p. 95; M. Wismar, I.A. Glinos, C.B. Maier, G. Dussault, W. Palm, J. Bremner and J. Figueras, 'Health professional mobility and health systems: evidence from 17 European countries' *Euro Observer* 2011, vol 13 no 2, p. 1.

118 M. Peeters, M. McKee and S. Merkur, 'EU law and health professionals' in E. Mossialos, G. Permanand, R. Baeten and T.K. Hervey (eds.), *Health Systems Governance in Europe – The Role of European Union Law and Policy*, Cambridge University Press, New York 2010, p. 592. On the recognition of health professionals' qualification see the European Parliament and Council Directive 2005/36/EC.

119 Telemedicine is the provision of healthcare services, through use of ICT, in situations where the health professional and the patient (or two health professionals) are not in the same location. It involves secure transmission of medical data and information, through text, sound, images or other forms needed for the prevention, diagnosis, treatment and follow-up of patients. European Commission, *Communication from the Commission to the European Parliament, the Council, the European Economic and Social Committee and the Committee of the Regions on telemedicine for the benefit of patients, healthcare systems and society*, COM (2008) 689 final, 04.11.2008, p. 3.

120 Wismar et al., above n. 8, p. 14.

121 One of the most successful cross-border arrangements functions between the Universitätsklinikum Aachen in Germany and the university hospital of Maastricht. 'The two institutes have agreed on a contract for top clinical patient care as well as research and training in the fields of cardiovascular diseases, oncology and transplant medicine.'

providers and insurance institutions to support patient flow or to ensure proper and adequate care for patients.[122]

Although theoretically these forms can be clearly distinguished, in real life situations, they often appear together in the context of cross-border healthcare provision and are inseparable.[123]

The opinions in legal literature on what can be considered as patient mobility differ slightly. Two main approaches can be observed: whereas Palm and Glinos say that '(f)ree movement of patients – or patient mobility, as it is commonly referred to – implies people accessing health care services outside their home state'[124] and thus patient mobility includes any type of patient movement involving consumption of healthcare services abroad, in another article, Glinos and her colleagues define cross-border patient mobility as 'the movement of a patient travelling to another country to seek planned healthcare',[125] narrowing the notion of patient mobility to scheduled care and excluding unplanned healthcare abroad from its scope.[126]

It is important to note that there are many widely used terms with similar meanings concerning persons receiving healthcare abroad. A clear distinction has to be made between them. One of the most commonly used expressions is *medical tourism*. I share the opinion that 'the industry-driven term[127] "medical tourism" insinuates leisurely travelling and does not capture the seriousness

http://www.english.azm.nl/info/azMorganisatie/6011 (accessed 17.08.2011). On the topic of cross-border hospital collaboration, see I.A. Glinos and M. Wismar, *Hospitals and Borders – Seven case studies on cross-border collaboration and health system interactions*, European Observatory on Health Systems and Policies, Brussels 2013.

122 In the framework of the HealthACCESS Project, six categories of cross-border collaboration were classified. R. Busse, M. Wörz, T. Foubister, E. Mossialos and P. Berman, *Mapping Health Services Access: National and Cross-Border Issues – Final Report*, HealthACCESS Project, 2006, p. 22.

123 For instance, one can easily picture a situation in which a doctor from Member State (MS) A needs to ask for the medical records of the patient affiliated with MS B, who travelled to receive healthcare in MS A, from his/her general practitioner in MS B. Or another situation, when a patient temporarily staying in MS C, whereas insured in MS D, when in need during his/her stay, prefers to visit a doctor in MS C, who originates from MS D, but came to establish a practice in MS C.

124 W. Palm and I.A. Glinos, 'Enabling patient mobility in the EU: between free movement and coordination' in Mossialos et al., above n. 118, p. 509.

125 Glinos et al., above n. 10, p. 1145. See n. 36 above.

126 Strban shares this view by stating that 'the notion of patient mobility can hardly be used for unplanned treatment, since a person is not moving as a patient, but only becomes one in another Member State'. G. Strban, 'Patient mobility in the European Union: between social security coordination and free movement of services' *ERA Forum* 2013, vol 14 number 3, p. 398.

127 In this context, *medical tourists* are looked at as consumers on the healthcare market. Lunt and Carrera, above n. 55, p. 28 and Connell, above n. 47, p. 2.

of most patient mobility'.[128] The term *tourism* is often affixed to diverse forms of patient movements, such as 'abortion tourism',[129] 'reproductive tourism',[130] 'stem cell tourism',[131] 'transplant tourism'[132] or even 'euthanasia tourism',[133] in which cases the intention behind the patient movement is far from the traditional notion of tourism. On the contrary, these are usually very delicate situations that involve persons who are desperately seeking the medical treatment which their state of health requires.[134] However, medical tourism also includes situations in which health services[135] and ancillary tourist services are closely linked together. *Health tourism* is a broader category. It encompasses not only medical tourism, which always relates to a medical intervention, but any travel with direct or indirect health purposes, such as recreation, sport activities or wellness services.[136] In Kincses et al., within the notion of health tourism, medical tourism and *recreation or wellness tourism* is distinguished. Within the latter, wellness and sport activities can be differentiated from *medical wellness*, which comprises 'measures guided by medical science, for sustained improvement of quality of life, and of the subjective sense of well-being, by means

---

128 Glinos et al., above n. 10, p. 1146.
Mainil observes that there is 'a shift between EU perceptions of patient mobility and Asian/US perceptions of the medical tourist'. In his opinion, whereas the former focuses on individual patients and thus the demand-side of healthcare, the latter follows a rather supply-side logic and puts the emphasis on the medical tourism industry. Mainil suggests that the term 'transnational healthcare' 'fits both types of discourse and practice'. Mainil, above n. 35, pp. 48–49.

129 See n. 57 above.

130 See n. 58 above.

131 See n. 59 above.

132 Henn, above n. 56, p. 202.; D. Budiani-Saberi and F.L. Delmonico, 'Organ Trafficking and Transplant Tourism: A Commentary on the Global Realities' *American Journal of Transplantation* 2008, vol 8, pp. 925–929.

133 See n. 60 above.

134 A. Whittaker, 'Pleasure and pain: Medical travel in Asia' *Global Public Health* 2008, vol 3 issue 3, p. 272; Song, above n. 59, p. 386.; Connell, above n. 47, p. 3.

135 These healthcare services most often are dental or cosmetic surgery services. For instance, in a research paper's definition of medical tourism, expressed emphasis is put on these treatments: 'travelling to a destination in another country to receive medical, dental and surgical care because the destination enables better access to care, provides higher quality care or offers the same treatment at a more affordable price'. Grail Research, *The Rise of Medical Tourism*, http://www.grailresearch.com/pdf/ContenPodsPdf/Rise_of_Medical_Tourism_Summary.pdf, 2009 (accessed 19.08.2011), p. 2.

136 Gy Kincses, I. Borbás, P. Mihalicza, E. Varga, and E. Udvardy, 'A gyógyturizmus tendenciái a világban' (Tendencies of health tourism around the world), *Egészségügyi Gazdasági Szemle* (*Journal of Health Economics*) 2009, issue 5, p. 34. See also J. Connell, 'Medical tourism: Sea, sun, sand ... and surgery?' *Tourism Management* 2006, vol 27, p. 1098 and P.M. Carrera and J.F.P. Bridges, 'Globalization and healthcare: understanding health and medical tourism' *Expert Review of Pharmacoeconomics & Outcomes Research* 2006, vol 6 no 4, pp. 447–454.
Connell says that health tourism is 'primarily concerned with low-key, therapeutic and non-invasive "procedures" – while allowing the inclusion of dentistry and check-ups, since that might lead to medical intervention'. Connell, above n. 136, p. 2.

of prevention and health promotion for which the individuals themselves assume responsibility, and motivation for a health-conscious lifestyle'.[137]

While browsing through the various definitions, an important issue must be kept in mind: although a great variety of patient movements can be detected in the European Union, basically two different types of cross-border patient mobility can be defined to which different legal rules apply.[138] As mentioned above, patient mobility contains two elements: border-crossing movement and the need for healthcare. However, it is decisive which component occurs first.[139]

On the one hand, insured persons might need healthcare while staying or residing abroad. They first cross the border, then become in need of healthcare. The reason for the border-crossing is legally irrelevant in this case; the point is that the mobility precedes the need for healthcare. So at the moment of going abroad the persons cannot be considered patients in a narrow sense because they do not seek to receive healthcare. On the other hand, people may choose to look for medical treatment abroad. Strictly interpreted, they are the real mobile patients who, when the need of healthcare arises, decide to travel to another Member State to obtain medical treatment.[140]

In theory, this distinction is rather clear-cut. However, it must be kept in mind that in real life the circumstances can be highly complicated, sometimes making it impossible to investigate which element of patient mobility appeared first. Still more so since the distinction is based on the *intention* of the person concerned: whether he/she travelled abroad for any other reason than receiving healthcare and became in need of medical intervention during the stay in the other country, or whether the purpose of his/her journey was exactly to obtain medical treatment outside his/her country of residence. This leads to the question how the intention of the patient can be ascertained.[141]

To sum up, according to the broad approach, cross-border patient mobility within the European Union can be defined as a situation in which the insured person receives healthcare in a Member State other than the Member State of affiliation. In other words, the Member State of treatment differs from the Member State of residence. Similarly, the CJEU considers it cross-border patient

137 This definition was created by the 1st Medical Wellness Congress 2007 in Berlin. http://i-m-w-a.com/definition.html (accessed 16.02.2017).

138 The Coordination Regulations have traditionally made a strict distinction between planned and unplanned care, which has remained until today. However, a change of approach can be seen, since the Patient Mobility Directive does not make such distinction and is applicable to both types. One might wonder whether the approach of the Regulations is still valid in today's circumstances and serves the interest of the patients. This issue is further dealt with in, below.

139 Palm and Glinos, above. n. 124, p. 529.

140 This double approach can be seen in the PMD's patient definition as well, as it distinguishes between persons who *seek to receive* healthcare in another Member State and persons who actually *receive* medical treatment outside the Member State of affiliation. Article 3(h) PMD.

141 This question is dealt with in detail in, below.

mobility, when a healthcare provider provides healthcare without moving from the Member State in which he/she is established for recipients established in other Member States.[142]

In the narrow approach, patient mobility means that the insured person *travels abroad to seek* healthcare in a Member State other than the Member State of affiliation (Table 2 below).

Table 2. The concept of patient mobility

<table>
<tr><th colspan="6">Cross-border healthcare</th></tr>
<tr><td colspan="3">Patient mobility</td><td rowspan="4">Professional mobility</td><td rowspan="4">Service mobility</td><td rowspan="4">Cross-border collaboration</td></tr>
<tr><td colspan="3">Broad approach to patient mobility</td></tr>
<tr><td rowspan="2">people needing healthcare while residing in a Member State other than the Member State of affiliation</td><td rowspan="2">people needing healthcare while staying in a Member State other than the Member State of affiliation</td><td>Narrow approach to patient mobility</td></tr>
<tr><td>people travelling to a Member State other than the Member State of affiliation to seek healthcare</td></tr>
</table>

Source: The author's own summary.

In this book, the phenomenon of patient mobility is analysed primarily from a legal point of view, without limiting the scope to planned treatments.

3. THE RIGHT TO ACCESS TO HEALTHCARE ACROSS BORDERS

In the first half of this chapter, the existence of the right to access to healthcare in another Member State was the focal point of the observations. The main question posed was whether people have the right under Union law to receive medical treatment beyond the borders of the country they are affiliated to.

Since it was shown in the above sections that the phenomenon of cross-border patient mobility includes two components,[143] it can be said that from a legal point of view, the right to cross-border patient mobility is a result of the fusion of two rights: *the right to move freely across borders* and *the right to health(care)*. In this section, first, the origins of these rights are outlined briefly. Then, the *right to cross-border patient mobility* itself is examined by analysing the legislative basics

142 C-211/08 *Commission v Spain* [ECLI:EU:C:2010:340], 48.
The CJEU defined cross-border service provision uniformly in relation to other services: see C-384/93 *Alpine Investments* [ECLI:EU:C:1995:126], 21 (financial services); C-243/01 *Gambelli and Others* [ECLI:EU:C:2003:597], 53 (betting services).

143 See sections 2.1. and 2.2. above.

of its different aspects in the European Union, such as healthcare, social security and public health, and the protection of migrants' social rights. Subsequently, the evolution of this right and its legislative background is dealt with.

3.1. THE RIGHT TO MOVE FREELY ACROSS BORDERS

Ever since the dawn of human evolution, humans have migrated:[144] it became a genuine characteristic of human history and also a part of mankind's survival strategy. However, the causes and methods of migration have changed enormously throughout the centuries[145] and certain limitations of such movements came into existence. Nowadays countries have the authority – as a part of their sovereignty – to regulate who can cross their borders either to enter the state or to leave it, and under which conditions. These arrangements are justified by safety issues on the one hand and by controlling and monitoring the flow across the national borders on the other.[146] The regulatory power of the states is nevertheless restricted by various legal instruments on both the international and regional level which aim to ensure the individual's right to move freely across borders.

On the international level, the human right treaties of the United Nations (UN) specify this right. Article 13(2) of the Universal Declaration of Human Rights[147] and Article 12 of the International Covenant on Civil and Political Rights stipulate that 'everyone shall be free to leave any country, including his own'[148] and this right:

> […] shall not be subject to any restrictions except those which are provided by law, are necessary to protect national security, public order […], public health or morals or the rights and freedoms of others, and are consistent with the other rights recognized in the […] Covenant.[149]

The *right to leave*[150] guaranteed by the aforementioned treaties was complemented by the *right to enter* in the International Convention on the

---

144 J.N. Wilford, 'Skull Supports Theory of Human Migration' *The New York Times*, 12.01.2007.

145 See, among others, D.S. Massey, J. Arango, G. Hugo, A. Kouaouci, A. Pellegrino and J.E. Taylor, 'Theories of International Migration: A Review and Appraisal' *Population and Development Review* 1993, vol 19 no 3, pp. 431–466 and R. Jennissen, *Macro-economic determinants of international migration in Europe*, Dutch University Press, Amsterdam 2004.

146 D. Jacobson, *Rights across borders: Immigration and the decline of citizenship*, Johns Hopkins University Press, Baltimore 1996, p. 21.

147 Article 13(2) of the Universal Declaration of Human Rights: 'Everyone has the right to leave any country, including his own, and to return to his country.'

148 Article 12(2) of the International Covenant on Civil and Political Rights.

149 Article 12(3) of the International Covenant on Civil and Political Rights.

150 On this issue in more details, see S.S. Juss, 'Free Movement and the World Order' *International Journal of Refugee Law* 2004, vol 16 issue 3, pp. 289–335; C. Harvey and

Protection of the Rights of All Migrant Workers and Members of Their Families, adopted by the UN in 1990.[151]

In the European region the European Union's legislation on free movement is the most remarkable. European integration is based on the so-called four fundamental freedoms covering the free movement of persons, services, goods and capital.[152] Originally, when the predecessor of the European Union, the European Economic Community (EEC), was established in 1957, its Founding Fathers[153] aimed to open the borders of the Member States – with the intention to support the functioning of the common market – only for workers and their family members.[154] Thus, the promotion of the freedom of movement of workers and the removal of all possible obstacles which may hinder the flow of labour force were major concerns of the European Union from its very creation.[155] Throughout the decades, this purely economic approach became out of date as the Community re-evaluated its aims and extended its field of activities. Nowadays, the Treaty on the Functioning of the European Union ensures 'the right to move and reside freely within the territory of the Member States'[156] for each European citizen[157] 'without any discrimination on grounds of nationality'.[158]

It can be concluded from this that *EU citizens do hold the right under Union law to cross borders freely* within the European Union and travel to another Member State, and that the mobility element of patient mobility is thus ensured on a theoretical level.

R.P. Barnidge, *The right to leave one's own country under international law*, http://www.qub.ac.uk/schools/SchoolofLaw/Research/HumanRightsCentre/Publications/ResearchReports/researchfilestore/Filetoupload,56100,en.pdf, 2005 (accessed 16.07.2013).

151 Article 8(2) of the International Convention on the Protection of the Rights of All Migrant Workers and Members of Their Families: 'Migrant workers and members of their families shall have the right at any time to enter and remain in their State of origin.'

152 On the four freedoms, see C. Barnard, *The substantive law of the EU: the four freedoms*, Oxford University Press, Oxford, New York 2010.

153 On the political leaders who mainly inspired the creation of the European Community, see https://europa.eu/european-union/about-eu/history/founding-fathers_en (accessed 16.02.2017).

154 Article 48 of the Treaty of Rome establishing the European Economic Community.

155 The first significant legislative act adopted in this field was Regulation (EEC) No 1612/68 of the Council of 15 October 1968 on freedom of movement for workers within the Community. OJ L 257 of 19 October 1968. Since it had been substantially amended several times, it was recently codified and repealed by Regulation (EU) No 492/2011 of the European Parliament and of the Council of 5 April 2011 on freedom of movement for workers within the Union. OJ L 141 of 27 May 2011. A selected list of CJEU cases on free movement of workers can be found on the website of the European Commission: http://ec.europa.eu/social/main.jsp?catId=953&langId=en (accessed 16.02.2017).

156 Article 20(2) (a) TFEU.

157 Article 20(1) TFEU.

158 Article 18 TFEU.

3.2. THE RIGHT TO HEALTH(CARE)

The right to health is a highly complex legal issue, the exact meaning of which is somewhat unclear.[159] It is generally categorised as a second-generation human right,[160] also called *socio-economic human right*. As opposed to first-generation civil and political rights promoting equal treatment of individuals and prohibiting state interference (also called *negative* rights), second-generation economic, social and cultural rights provide equal opportunity and evoke active measures of the state (also called *positive* rights).[161]

The right to health – the term most often used on international level[162] – was first[163] formulated in the Weimar Constitution[164] in Germany in 1919, and throughout the 20th century it appeared in numerous national constitutions and human rights treaties. On an international level, it was introduced by the Charter of the United Nations in 1945, which stipulates that 'the United Nations shall promote [...] solutions of international economic, social, health, and related problems'.[165] Shortly after, the World Health Organization (WHO) came to existence in 1946 and its Constitution gave a rather individual character to the right to health, defining it as the right to 'the enjoyment of the highest attainable standard' of physical, mental and social well-being, which is 'one of the fundamental rights of every human being without distinction of race, religion, political belief, economic or social condition'.[166] While the UN Universal

159 On the problem of its definition see B.C.A. Toebes, *The Right to Health as a Human Right in International Law*, Intersentia, Antwerp, Groningen, Oxford 1999, pp. 16–20.

160 On human rights issues related to the right to health see also E. Wicks, *Human Rights and Healthcare*, Hart Publishing, Oxford, Portland 2007.

161 J. Sári, *Alapjogok* (Fundamental rights), Osiris Kiadó, Budapest 2005, p. 19 and L. Trócsányi (ed.), *A mi alkotmányunk* (Our constitution), Complex Kiadó Kft., Budapest 2006, p. 474. On the distinction between positive and negative rights, see also T.L. Beauchamp and R.R. Faden, 'The Right to Health and the Right to Health Care' *The Journal of Medicine and Philosophy* 1979, vol 4 no 2, p. 120.

162 On the different terms concerning the right to health see Toebes, above n. 159, pp. 16–17.

163 Although a right to health was first adopted in the 20th century, Toebes is of the opinion that its roots can be found in the public health measures which have existed since the ancient civilisations. Toebes, above n. 159, p. 8.

164 The Weimar Constitution (*Die Verfassung des Deutschen Reichs* also known as *Weimarer Reichsverfassung*) was adopted on 11 August 1919 and governed Germany during the era of the Weimar Republic (1919–1933). In Article 161(1), it places the responsibility on the state to establish an insurance scheme, which, among others, aims to promote the conservation of the insured persons' health. http://www.documentarchiv.de/wr/wrv.html (accessed 17.02.2017).

165 Article 55(b) of the Charter of the United Nations.

166 Preamble of the Constitution of the World Health Organization.
This definition was reaffirmed by the Alma Ata Declaration in 1978. However, it goes further by stating that: 'governments have a responsibility for the health of their people which can be fulfilled only by the provision of adequate health and social measures'.

Declaration on Human Rights of 1948 lays down that 'everyone has the right to a standard of living adequate for the health and well-being of himself and the right to security in the event of [...] sickness',[167] Article 12 of the UN International Covenant on Economic, Social and Cultural Rights (1966) entirely corresponds to the wording of the WHO's Constitution as well as Article 14 of the Universal Declaration on Bioethics and Human Rights adopted by the UN Educational, Scientific and Cultural Organization (UNESCO) in 2005.

Similarly, on the European level the Council of Europe (COE) incorporated the right to health – either implicitly[168] or expressly – into its human rights treaties. The European Social Charter adopted in 1961 and revised in 1996 imposes exact tasks on the contracting parties to take appropriate measures to guarantee the right to the protection of health. These measures include the removal of the possible causes of ill health, the provision of advisory and educational facilities for the promotion of health and the encouragement of individual responsibility in matters of health and the prevention of epidemic, endemic and other diseases.[169] In 1997, the European Convention on Human Rights and Biomedicine (also called the Oviedo Convention) touched upon the right to health by prescribing that the 'parties [...] shall take appropriate measures with a view to providing [...] equitable access to health care of appropriate quality'.[170]

The Charter of Fundamental Rights of the European Union (CFREU), which was attached to the Treaty of Lisbon and became legally binding from 1 December 2009, also stipulates that:

> everyone has the right of access to preventive health care and the right to benefit from medical treatment under the conditions established by national laws and practices. A high level of human health protection shall be ensured in the definition and implementation of all the Union's policies and activities.[171]

Notwithstanding the possible legal consequences of failing to respect and guarantee this right, this provision is presumed to have a deeper political

---

167 Article 25(1) of the UN Universal Declaration of Human Rights.

168 Most authors agree that 'the right to healthcare is also indirectly supported by the more general right to life' (Article 2 of the Convention for the Protection of Human Rights and Fundamental Freedoms adopted by the COE in 1950). E. Rynning, 'The Ageing Populations of Europe – Implications for Health Systems and Patients' Rights' *European Journal of Health Law* 2008, vol 15, p. 303 and Wicks, above n. 160, pp. 13–14. See also A. Walus, 'National healthcare planning and the internal market: A conceptual view on the impact of EU law on Member States' regulatory autonomy in the field of healthcare' *European Journal of Social Security* 2015, vol 17 no 1, p. 53.

169 Article 11 of the European Social Charter.

170 Article 3 of the European Convention on Human Rights and Biomedicine.

171 Article 35 CFREU.

effect, namely by inspiring the institutions of the Union – especially the CJEU – 'to develop and embroider a new right to effective and speedy medical treatment'.[172]

At the same time, among the provisions on social security, it is expressly confirmed that: '(t)he Union recognises and respects the entitlement to social security benefits and social services providing protection in cases such as [...] illness, [...] in accordance with the rules laid down by Community law and national laws and practices'.[173] And similarly, '(e)veryone residing and moving legally within the European Union is entitled to social security benefits [...] in accordance with Community law and national laws and practices'.[174] One may wonder what this exactly means from the patients' point of view. Does it imply that a patient can establish a claim based on these provisions? Using the expression 'recognises and respects' in Article 34(1) softens the legal effect of the provision and does not place a responsibility on the Member States. Thus, it can be deduced that the Member States do not have any obligation to develop their healthcare schemes or offer healthcare benefits they did not offer before as long as their legislation is in conformity with Union law. So at the end of the day, the CFREU does not create any specific healthcare entitlement for patients.

Although these human rights treaties[175] clearly show that the right to health covers a wide range of health-related issues (e.g. the right to safe drinking water or adequate sanitation),[176] the focus of this book concerns only a part of it, namely the *right to healthcare*[177] or as it is formulated in the CFREU, *the right of access to healthcare*. It is of crucial importance for each person to have access to good quality health services, goods and facilities without any discrimination.[178] However, this individual right – as it can be seen from the wording of these treaties – evokes positive duties on the states' side: they are required to take all necessary measures to ensure access for all.[179] So the question should be raised whether the Member States of the European Union take all the measures

---

172 A. Kaczorowska, 'A Review of the Creation by the European Court of Justice of the Right to Effective and Speedy Medical Treatment and its Outcomes' *European Law Journal* 2006, vol 12 no 3, p. 346. On the evolution of the right to cross-border healthcare, see section 3.7. below.

173 Article 34(1) CFREU.

174 Article 34(2) CFREU.

175 The list of treaties dealing with the right to health is far from complete; I took the liberty to select those I find the most important. For a complete list consult World Health Organization, 'The Right to Health' Fact Sheet No. 31, http://www.ohchr.org/Documents/Publications/Factsheet31.pdf, 2008 (accessed 17.02.2017), p. 9.

176 WHO, above n. 175, p. 3.

177 Toebes, above n. 159, p. 19 and WHO, above n. 175, p. 1.

178 WHO, above n. 175, p. 4.

179 Barlow goes as far as to announce that the right to health is not a human right, since the fulfilment of this requirement 'would impose an intolerable burden on others,' namely to individual doctors, or hospital authorities, or governments. P. Barlow, 'Health care is not a human right' *British Medical Journal* 1999, vol 319, p. 321.

necessary to guarantee equal access for all, irrespective of the nationality of the person concerned. Nevertheless, Union law leaves this to the national legislatures.

3.3. THE RIGHT TO CROSS-BORDER HEALTHCARE

As can be concluded from the legal documents enumerated in the former sections, in the European Union both the right to free movement and the right to access to healthcare is guaranteed by Union law. However, the question still remains whether the coexistence of these rights is identical to the existence of the right to cross-border patient mobility. In the European Union, the right to access to healthcare across borders is rooted in the protection of the social security rights of migrant workers. It thus grew out of the coordination of European social security schemes. It was improved through the proactive approach of the CJEU,[180] and became a cross-cutting field between the areas of free movement, social security and public health.[181] The legislative basics of these fields are outlined in the section below.

In relation to patient mobility, the main question which must be raised concerning the relationship between the right to healthcare and patients' cross-border mobility is whether the right of access to healthcare extends beyond the borders of the state of affiliation.[182] Traditionally, in line with the *principle of territoriality*,[183] states cannot take the responsibility to ensure protection for all persons.[184] Therefore, they use territorial elements in order to define and organise their systems: they are free to use these territorial elements in defining the scope of their social security schemes, including healthcare systems.[185]

---

180 Greer states that 'the expansion of EU competencies into health' is an eminent example of *political spillover*, where European integration is 'driven by the EU institutions without democratic legitimacy or an obvious justification'. S.L. Greer, *The politics of European Union health policies*, Open University Press, Berkshire 2009, pp. 10–12.

181 I share Brook's opinion who writes that 'the Court has played and continues to play a crucial role in the development of EU public health policy, as well as in health services and broader social policy'. E. Brooks, 'Crossing borders: A critical review of the role of the European Court of Justice in EU health policy' *Health Policy* 2012, vol 105 issue 1, p. 33.

182 Palm and Glinos, above n. 124, p. 512.

183 Pennings defines the territoriality principle as '(t)he linking of the social system to the territory of the State'. F. Pennings, *European Social Security Law*, Intersentia, Antwerp 2010, p. 4.

184 In practice, it means that 'they cannot or do not wish to provide the same level of protection to migrants as to their own citizens'. WHO, above n. 175, p. 19.

185 R. Cornelissen, 'The Principle of territoriality and the Community regulations on social security (Regulations 1408/71 and 574/72)' *Common Market Law Review* 1996, vol 33, pp. 440–441; Pennings, above n. 183, p. 4 and N. Rennuy, 'Assimilation, territoriality and reverse discrimination: a shift in European social security law' *European Journal of Social Law* 2011, vol 1 no 4, p. 290.

Watson adds that '(t)he territorial basis of social security systems leads therefore to the non-recognition by the law of one country of social security rights acquired in other countries and to the non-availability of benefits outside the territory of the country under whose legal system the title to benefit is acquired'.[186] The principle of territoriality serves three basic objectives: controlling the quality of care, protecting the financial sustainability of the national system and ensuring adequate planning of healthcare infrastructure and capacity.[187]

However, 'patient mobility goes beyond conventional territorial logic'.[188] It deterritorialises national healthcare schemes and requires Member States to handle external elements within their healthcare systems. For example, a person covered may receive medical care in the territory of another Member State, or the Member State concerned may provide treatment for a person who is not affiliated to the state's healthcare system. The question is whether the above-mentioned objectives can still be achieved with a more open legal structure.

Since these matters are as old as the modern social insurance schemes themselves,[189] several legal instruments have been developed in the field of international social security in order to overcome the conflict of laws which occurs in such cases. These instruments aim to coordinate the social security systems of the individual states 'in such a way as to ensure that the migrant does not suffer any loss of rights'[190] due to practising his/her right to free movement. This function can be achieved by concluding bi-[191] or multilateral[192] agreements or by means of supranational legislation within the European Union. Despite their discrepancies, these legal tools are posited on the same logic based on the same principles: migrants must be treated equally with the citizens of the state concerned and may not be discriminated against on the grounds of their nationality (*principle of equal treatment*); migrants may claim benefits on the basis of their aggregated insurance period irrespective in which country they completed those periods (*principle of aggregation*); the territorial requirements of national social security systems must be removed, so the benefits granted

---

186 Watson, above n. 76, p. 35.

187 A.P. van der Mei, *Free Movement of Persons Within the European Community – Cross-Border Access to Public Benefits*, Hart Publishing, Oxford 2003, pp. 227–228.

188 Glinos et al., above n. 10, p. 1145.

189 Pennings, above n. 183, p. 3.

190 Watson, above n. 76, p. 8, 36.

191 It is remarkable that the very first bilateral agreement on the protection of social security rights of migrants was signed by France and Italy in 1904 and served as a sample later on. Watson, above n. 76, pp. 8–10. See also S. Roberts, 'A short history of social security coordination' in Y. Jorens (ed.), *50 years of Social Security Coordination: Past – Present – Future*, Publications Office of the European Union, Luxembourg 2010, p. 12.

192 For example, conventions of the ILO or the COE. J. Hajdú, *Az Európai Unió szociális joga, különös tekintettel a szociális biztonsági koordinációra* (Social law in the European Union, with special regard to the social security coordination), JATE Press, Szeged 2008, pp. 10–20 and Pennings, above n. 183, p. 6.

must be available for migrants in the territory of other states (*principle of exportability*); the conflict of laws must be prevented, so migrants are aware of which social security rules apply to them.[193]

As seen above, the right to healthcare is generally considered a positive right.[194] However, it is important to note that the right to cross-border healthcare appears in the case law of the CJEU as a rather negative right, in relation to which the Member States are obliged to remove all possible obstacles in order to guarantee the free movement of patients. It is regarded as 'a right promoting the individual's liberty',[195] namely the freedom to choose from which provider the patient wants to receive treatment regardless in which Member State the healthcare provider is established.

In each case, if a legal subject is observed, one of the first questions that should be posed is who has the legislative competence to regulate the matter in question.[196] This issue is especially crucial in Union law.[197] To understand the controversial legal nature of cross-border patient mobility, it is important to study how the legislation on EU level functions and complements national legislations in this field. Therefore, the intersection of different fields of the European Union's policy in which the current issue lies, are examined further below.

---

193 Watson, above n. 76, p. 35; R.C.A. White, *Workers, Establishment and Services in the European Union*, Oxford University Press, Oxford, New York 2004, p. 166 and Pennings, above n. 183, p. 7. More specifically on the principles of the social security Coordination Regulations in the EU, see Y. Jorens and F. Van Overmeiren, 'General principles of coordination in Regulation 883/2004' *European Journal of Social Security* 2009, vol 11 nos 1–2, pp. 47–79 and Rennuy, above n. 185.

194 See n. 161 above.

195 Palm and Glinos, above n. 124, p. 529.

196 See on the competence issues, among others, E. Randall, *The European Union and health policy*, Palgrave, New York 2001, pp. 12–22; Y. Jorens, M. Coucheir and F. Van Overmeiren, 'Access to health care in an internal market: impact for statutory and complementary systems' *Bulletin luxembourgeois des questions sociales* 2005, vol 18, p. 1; G. Berki, 'A betegmobilitás közösségi jogi keretei az Európai Unióban a szociális biztonsági koordináció nézőpontjából' (The legal framework of patient mobility within the European Union from the social security coordination's point of view) in G. Berki (ed.), *Opuscula Szegediensia 4*, Pólay Elemér Alapítvány, Szeged 2011, pp. 12–13.

197 The European Union is an extraordinary international association in the sense that the participating states have ceded some of their sovereign rights, their own competences to the EU's organs as to enable the Union to act independently. In exercising these powers, the EU is therefore able to issue sovereign acts which have the same force as laws in individual states. As Article 2(1) TFEU says: 'when the Treaties confer on the Union exclusive competence in a specific area, only the Union may legislate and adopt legally binding acts'. At the same time, as confirmed by Article 5(2) of the Treaty on European Union (TEU), the EU may act only within the framework of those competences which have been conferred on it in the Treaty. K.-D. Borchardt, *The ABC of European Union Law*, Publications Office of the European Union, Luxembourg 2010, p. 11.

3.4. LEGISLATION ON HEALTHCARE WITHIN THE EUROPEAN UNION

As McKee and Mossialos point out 'there is a paradox. Health systems in Europe are diverse, yet they are also interdependent. In themselves, they are exempt from European law, yet almost everything they do, and those elements that are essential for them to function, are governed by it.'[198]

The social security systems of the Member States are based on centuries of tradition. Each national social security legislation is unique,[199] the result of an organic development which is constantly taking place and reflects on the one hand the recent historical, social, economic, legal and political circumstances of the state and on the other hand the upcoming challenges. Therefore, although the Member States are highly autonomous to determine their social security – including healthcare – schemes and tend to defend this competence obstinately,[200] they face similar problems[201] some of which might be tackled more efficiently on supranational level.[202]

---

198 M. McKee and E. Mossialos, 'Health policy and European law: Closing the gaps' *Public Health* 2006, vol 120 issue 11, p. 16.

199 Many different classifications of welfare states exist. The most widely-known is Esping-Andersen's, who distinguished between three categories of welfare states, namely *liberal* (low degree of decommodification, means-tested assistance, modest universal transfers, modest social insurance plans, very limited social rights; countries with such system are e.g. the United States, Canada, Australia), *corporatist* (medium degree of decommodification, rights attached to status, conservative orientation and an ideological commitment to the family; countries with such system are e.g. Austria, Germany, France, Italy) and *universalist* (high degree of decommodification, universal coverage and generous social benefits; countries with such system are e.g. Scandinavian countries). G. Esping-Andersen, *The Three Worlds of Welfare Capitalism*, Polity Press, Cambridge 1990.
Another grouping may consist of the Scandinavian area, the English-speaking area, Continental Europe, and Southern Europe, where the continental type can be divided into a Bismarckian and a Christian-democratic type. S. Kuhnle, *Survival of the European Welfare State*, http://www.sv.uio.no/arena/english/research/publications/arena-working-papers/1994-2000/1999/wp99_19.htm, 1999 (accessed 17.02.2017).
See also, among others, M. Coucheir and Y. Jorens, *The European Legal Framework in Relation to Patient Mobility*, Europe for Patients Project 2005, p. 9 and M. Ferrera, 'Reconstructing the welfare state in Southern Europe' in S. Kuhnle (ed.), *Survival of the European Welfare State*, Routledge, London 2000, pp. 166–181.

200 P. Neroth, 'Can health survive the single market?' *The Lancet* 2005, vol 365 issue 9458, p. 461.

201 As regards European healthcare schemes, for example the adaption to constant developments in medical science, the aging of the European population and rising public expectations can be mentioned as potential challenges to tackle. European Commission, *Communication from the Commission. Follow-up to high level reflection process on patient mobility and healthcare developments in the European Union*, COM (2004) 301 final, 20.04.2004, p. 4.

202 Concerning the healthcare systems specifically, both Recital 5 of the Preamble of the PMD and the Council Conclusions on Common values and principles in European Union Health Systems provide that although there is a set of operating principles such as universality, access

In the field of social dimension, including healthcare, competences are split between the Member States and the Union. I share the opinion that in this regard the actions of the European Union can be grouped into two distinct categories. The first category consists of those actions which intend to implement the European Union's social and health policy, to improve the social schemes mainly by *harmonising* measures[203] and to encourage cooperation among the Member States.[204] The second set of tools aims to ensure the freedom of movement of persons by removing the potential social disadvantages related to migration within the European Union, such as impediments to access to healthcare in another Member State, by means of *coordination*.[205]

Before observing the exact provisions of the legislation, it is necessary to make a strict distinction between harmonisation and coordination within Union law.[206] While *harmonisation* intends to approximate the national laws and to reduce the disparities between them by introducing common values, targets, guidelines or a minimum level of standards, *coordination* links the systems of the individual Member States together without intervening in the national legislation in order to serve a purpose of the Union. On the one hand, according to Vogelaar's definition, 'harmonisation is the creation by the Community of the legal provisions required for its existence and development and which have at the same time an effect on national law in the sense that it will have to be modified or supplemented, i.e. adapted to the Community rule'.[207] In practice, this effect is achieved on EU level by adopting directives which must be implemented by the Member States. On the other hand, Pennings defines European social security coordination as a set of rules which 'intend to

to good quality care, equity and solidarity, that are shared by health systems throughout the Union, the practical ways in which these values and principles become reality vary significantly between Member States. However, the principle of *subsidiarity*, as stipulated by Article 5(3) TEU, requires that: 'in areas which do not fall within its exclusive competence, the Union shall act only if and in so far as the objectives of the proposed action cannot be sufficiently achieved by the Member States, either at central level or at regional and local level, but can rather, by reason of the scale or effects of the proposed action, be better achieved at Union level'. On the subsidiarity principle see S. Douglas-Scott, *Constitutional Law of the European Union*, Dorset Press, Dorchester 2002, pp. 173–183. She sheds light on the fact that although subsidiarity became a key issue in course of the drafting of the Maastricht Treaty, it was Pope Pius XI who developed subsidiarity as a substantial doctrine of canon law by including it into his papal encyclical entitled *Quadragesimo Anno* in 1931. Douglas-Scott, p. 174.

203 Article 153(2)(b) TFEU.

204 Article 153(2)(a) TFEU.

205 Watson, above n. 76, p. 30.

206 On this issue see, among others, Theodore W. Vogelaar, 'The Approximation of the Laws of Member States under the Treaty of Rome' *Common Market Law Review* 1975, vol 12 issue 2, pp. 211–216; Watson, above n. 76, pp. 30–34; Cornelissen, above n. 185, pp. 443–444 and Pennings, above n. 183, pp. 6–7.

207 Vogelaar, above n. 206, p. 216.

adjust social security schemes in relation to each other [...] in order to regulate transnational questions, with the objective of protecting the social security position of migrants'.[208] For this purpose, regulations are adopted.

Although their objectives and functioning mechanisms considerably differ from each other (summarised in Table 3 below), in certain cases it is not easy to make a distinction,[209] mainly because the definition of coordination within Union law is lacking and the Court has not taken the opportunity so far to provide a definition.[210] However, it dealt with the matter in numerous cases and repeatedly came to the conclusion that 'given the disparities between one Member State and another in matters of social security cover and the fact that the objective of social security coordination regulations is to coordinate the national laws but not to harmonise them, the conditions attached to a certain benefit in another Member State may, according to the circumstances, be to the insured person's advantage or disadvantage'.[211]

Table 3. The distinction between harmonisation and coordination

	Harmonisation	**Coordination**
Objective	To approximate national schemes	To link national schemes together
Effect on disparities between national legislations	Differences decrease or even cease	Differences remain to exist
Legal instrument	Directive	Regulation
Impact on national legislations	Member States must implement the directives through which the substance of national legislations might need to be changed	The regulations are directly applicable, they affect the sphere of operation of national legislations leaving the legal content untouched

Source: The author's own summary.

As will be shown in the next sections, in the field of healthcare legislation both types of instruments are used: patient mobility legislation 'oscillates between coordination and harmonisation'.[212]

208 Pennings, above n. 183, p. 6.

209 Lipstein considers the distinction even 'blurred'. K. Lipstein, *The Law of the European Economic Community*, Butterworths, London 1974, p. 18.

210 Cornelissen, above n. 185, p. 443; White, above n. 193, p. 165 and Pennings, above n. 183, p. 7.

211 See, among others, C-41/84 *Pinna*, 20; C-340/94 de *Jaeck*, 18; C-221/95 *Hervein I*, 16; Joined Cases C-393/99 and C-394/99 *Hervein II*, 50–52; C-211/08 *Commission v Spain*, 61; C-490/09 *Commission v Luxemburg*, 61.

212 K.M. Raptopoulou, 'The Directive on cross-border health care: signalling the coordination or the harmonisation of public health systems?' *European Journal of Social Law* 2012, vol 2 issue 3, p. 194.

3.5. LEGISLATION ON SOCIAL SECURITY AND PUBLIC HEALTH

As to the harmonising measures mentioned above, the Treaty stipulates among the provisions on social policy[213] that 'the Union shall support and complement the activities of the Member States', among others, 'in the field of social security and social protection of workers'.[214] This provision basically says that the Member States have most of the legislative power in this domain. The measures taken by the European Union in order to support and complement the Member States' activities are thus limited to the extent that the Member States have not exercised their competence.[215] This implies that 'in the absence of harmonisation at Community level, it is for the legislation of each Member State to determine, first, the conditions concerning the right or duty to be insured with a social security scheme and, second, the conditions for entitlement to benefits'.[216]

Moreover, the Treaty itself adds that the provisions adopted by the European Union 'shall not affect the right of Member States to define the fundamental principles of their social security systems and must not significantly affect the financial equilibrium thereof'.[217] This phrase constantly returns to the rulings of the Court on cross-border healthcare provision as well, which confirms that 'Community law does not detract from the powers of the Member States to organise their social security systems',[218] but at the same time, 'Member States must nevertheless comply with Community law when exercising those powers'.[219] Flear points out the contradiction between these assertions by saying

---

213 Title X. TFEU.

214 Article 153(1)(c) TFEU.

215 Article 2(5) TFEU.

216 See C-110/79 *Coonan*, 12; C-349/87 *Paraschi*, 15; Joined Cases C-4/95 and C-5/95 *Stöber and Piosa Pereira*, 36; C-120/95 *Decker*, 22; C-158/96 *Kohll*, 18; C-157/99 *Geraets-Smits and Peerbooms*, 45, 85; C-385/99 *Müller-Fauré and Van Riet*, 100; C-56/01 *Inizan*, 17; C-372/04 *Watts*, 92; C-444/05 *Stamatelaki*, 23; C-211/08 *Commission v Spain*, 53; C-173/09 *Elchinov*, 40, 57; C-512/08 *Commission v France*, 29; C-490/09 *Commission v Luxemburg*, 32.

217 Article 153(4) TFEU.

218 See C-238/82 *Duphar*, 16; C-159/91 and C-160/91 *Poucet and Pistre*, 6; C-70/95 *Sodemare*, 27; C-120/95 *Decker*, 21; C-158/96 *Kohll*, 17; C-157/99 *Geraets-Smits and Peerbooms*, 44; C-385/99 *Müller-Fauré and Van Riet*, 100; C-56/01 *Inizan*, 17; C-8/02 *Leichtle*, 29; C-372/04 *Watts*, 92, 146; C-444/05 *Stamatelaki*, 23; C-169/07 *Hartlauer*, 29; C-531/06 *Commission v Italy*, 35; Joined Cases C-171/07 and C-172/07 *Apothekerkammer des Saarlandes and Others*, 18; C-141/07 *Commission v Germany*, 22; Joined Cases C-570/07 and 571/07 *Blanco Pérez* and *Chao Gómez*, 43; C-211/08 *Commission v Spain*, 53, 75; C-173/09 *Elchinov*, 40, 57; C-490/09 *Commission v Luxemburg*, 16, 32.
Recital 10 and 35 of the Preamble of the Patient Mobility Directive also confirm that it fully respects 'the responsibilities of the Member States for the definition of social security benefits relating to health and for the organisation and delivery of healthcare and medical care and social security benefits, in particular for sickness'.

219 See the AG's Opinion in *Decker & Kohll*, 17–25; C-120/95 *Decker*, 23; 158/96 *Kohll*, 19; C-157/99 *Geraets-Smits and Peerbooms*, 46, 88; C-385/99 *Müller-Fauré and Van Riet*, 100;

that 'the ECJ flatters the Member States by asserting their sovereignty, only to deliver a legal conclusion that places them on the defensive'.[220]

In the field of healthcare, the competence of the European Union[221] is limited[222] to the completion of the national health policies concerning certain issues related to public health,[223] such as preventing physical and mental illness and diseases, obviating sources of danger to physical and mental health, reducing drug-related health damage,[224] safeguarding the quality and safety of organs and substances of human origin, blood and blood derivatives[225] and of medical products and devices,[226] combating the major cross-border health scourges, monitoring and early warning of and combating serious cross-border threats to health and reducing health damage in relation to tobacco and the abuse of alcohol.[227] The Treaty also emphasises that 'a high level of human health protection shall be ensured in the definition and implementation of all the Union's policies and activities'.[228]

Additionally to what was already mentioned above concerning the national competence in the field of social security, it is incorporated also with regard to healthcare that each:

> Union action shall respect the responsibilities of the Member States for the definition of their health policy and for the organisation and delivery of health services and medical care. The responsibilities of the Member States shall include the management of health services and medical care and the allocation of the resources assigned to them.[229]

C-56/01 *Inizan*, 17; C-372/04 *Watts*, 92; C-444/05 *Stamatelaki*, 23; C-169/07 *Hartlauer*, 29; C-531/06 *Commission v Italy*, 35; Joined Cases C-171/07 and C-172/07 *Apothekerkammer des Saarlandes and Others*, 18; C-141/07 *Commission v Germany*, 23; Joined Cases C-570/07 and 571/07 *Blanco Pérez* and *Chao Gómez*, 43; C-211/08 *Commission v Spain*, 53; C-173/09 *Elchinov*, 40; C-512/08 *Commission v France*, 29; C-490/09 *Commission v Luxemburg*, 16, 32.

220 Flear, above n. 86, p. 229.

221 An explicit legal basis for health was only introduced in Article 129 of the Treaty of Maastricht in 1992.

222 On the EU's competence on healthcare see T. Hervey and B. Vanhercke, 'Health care and the EU: the law and policy patchwork' in Mossialos et al., above n. 118, pp. 84–92.

223 These provisions were introduced by the Treaty of Maastricht in 1992 as Article 129.

224 Article 168(1) TFEU.

225 Article 168(4)(a) TFEU.

226 Article 168(4)(c) TFEU.

227 Article 168(5) TFEU.

228 Article 168(1) TFEU, which completely corresponds to Article 35 CFREU (see n. 171 above). See also Recital 1 of the Preamble of the PMD.

229 Article 168(7) TFEU. Similarly, Recital 4 and 19 of the Preamble of the PMD say that: 'Member States retain responsibility for providing safe, high quality, efficient and quantitatively adequate healthcare to citizens on their territory.'
In the course of the high level process of reflection on patient mobility and healthcare developments in the EU, six key areas of national responsibility were identified, namely: (1) how the health and social security system is financed (e.g. tax, social insurance etc) and

To sum up, from the observation above the following conclusion can be drawn: first, the Member States are principally free to determine their social security and healthcare schemes and secondly, the European Union may complement their national measures, but is not permitted to extend its actions beyond the limits of the competence which was conferred on it in the Treaty.

3.6. LEGISLATION ON THE PROTECTION OF MIGRANTS' SOCIAL RIGHTS

The significant discrepancies[230] between the Member States' national healthcare systems[231] pose a great threat to persons willing to use their right to free

overall organisation of the system including how prices are fixed; (2) internal allocations of resources (including human resources), through central or devolved mechanisms; (3) setting overall priorities for health expenditure, and the right of determining the scope of publicly funded care; (4) prioritisation of individuals' access to the system (if being paid for by the national scheme) with regard to clinical need; (5) management strategies within set budgets, for instance the use of evidence-based medicine – with allowance for national diversity in health policies and treatment patterns; (6) and issues of quality, effectiveness and efficiency of health care such as clinical guidelines. Council Conclusions, above n. 22, pp. 9–10.

230 Stiemer and Jorens note five main fields of differences between the various schemes, namely (1) the basis for the right to benefits (insurance-based and residence-based systems); (2) the financing of healthcare (tax-financed, contribution-financed and their combinations); (3) the institution providing healthcare; (4) the benefits involved; and (5) the way in which the benefits are provided (in kind and restitution systems). N. Stiemer, 'Sickness Insurance – Viewpoint of the EU-Member States' in Y. Jorens and B. Schulte (eds.), *Coordination of social security schemes in connection with the accession of Central and Eastern European States – "The Riga Conference"* la Charte, Brussels 1999, p. 227 and Y. Jorens, *European Integration and Health Care Systems: a Challenge for Social Policy EC Regulations 1408/71 between Status Quo and Upgrading.* http://www.ose.be/health/papers/jorenpaper2.pdf, 2001 (accessed 16.10.2012), p. 2.

231 For the purposes of this book, it seems necessary to briefly summarise the main typology of the European public healthcare schemes. Traditionally, a distinction is made between compulsory social insurance systems and national health services (also often referred to as Bismarckian and Beveridgian systems after their founding fathers). The main difference is that while '(c)ompulsory health insurance systems implement categorial protection (often extended to cover the whole population of a State), funded through social contributions and managed by the social partners', '(n)ational health services' (hereinafter also referred to as NHS) 'provide universal protection to all the residents of a country, by directly organising medical services, often of a public nature, which are financed mainly by tax revenue'. Further differentiation is needed between *reimbursement* and *benefit in kind* systems within the social insurance category, where the former is 'usually characterised by freedom on the part of the patients to choose their provider' and providing reimbursement for the medical costs and the latter 'guarantees access to health care through direct provision of benefits in kind, offered by medical providers contracted by health insurance bodies'. Palm et al., above n. 10, pp. 2–3.
On the typology of European healthcare systems see, among others, Y. Jorens, 'The Right to Health Care across Borders' in M. McKee, E. Mossialos and R. Baeten (eds.), *The Impact of EU Law on Health Care Systems*, P.I.E.-Peter Lang, Brussels 2002, pp. 83–84;

movement. Thus, unlike what is the case in the field of social policy and public health, as regards the promotion of free movement the European Union has legal permission to adopt coordination

> measures in the field of social security as are necessary to provide freedom of movement for workers; to this end, they shall make arrangements to secure for employed and self-employed migrant workers and their dependants: (a) aggregation, for the purpose of acquiring and retaining the right to benefit and of calculating the amount of benefit, of all periods taken into account under the laws of the several countries and (b) payment of benefits to persons resident in the territories of Member States.[232]

This part of the provision, 'deterritorialising social security',[233] remained basically unchanged[234] since the formulation of the Treaty of Rome (TEEC) in 1957[235] and serves as the legal basis for the social security Coordination Regulations thenceforth.[236]

It was clear for the Founding States that the desired flow of workers within the internal market could not be ensured without social security legislation measures,[237] since the workers could not be expected to move at the expense of losing their social rights.[238] As the European Commission articulated in the late 1990s, 'Community legislation on social security is a sine qua non for exercising the right to free movement of persons'.[239] The Coordination Regulations seek to

---

FLEAR, above n. 86, p. 209.; GY. NÉMETH, 'Az egészségbiztosítási rendszerekről – nemzetközi összehasonlításban I.' (Healthcare schemes – in international context) *Egészségügyi Gazdasági Szemle* 2007, vol 45 issue 5–6, pp.5–7; C. KARNER, 'Nemzetközi egészségügyi finanszírozási modellek és az állam szerepvállalása' (International models of healthcare financing and the role of the state) *Egészségügyi Gazdasági Szemle* 2008, vol 46 issue 2, pp. 3–9; ROBERTS et al., above n. 97, pp. 6–9 and K. FICSÓR, 'Az egészségügyi ellátórendszer finanszírozási modelljei – nemzetközi kitekintés' (Financial models of healthcare systems) in G. BERKI (ed.), *Opuscula Szegediensia 4*, Pólay Elemér Alapítvány, Szeged 2011.

232 Article 48 TFEU (Article 51 in the Treaty of Rome).

233 WATSON, above n. 76, p. 35 and CORNELISSEN, above n. 185, p. 446.

234 There is a remarkable change, though, in relation to the regime of legislative procedure. Whereas under Article 51 of the Treaty of Rome unanimity was required in the Council, according to the Treaty of Lisbon the Parliament and the Council must adopt the social security coordination measures acting *in accordance with the ordinary legislative procedure* (ex-codecision). Article 48 TFEU. This change indeed not only strengthens the EP's position in social security questions, but also facilitates the smoother legislative work in this field.

235 However, the history of social security coordination within Europe goes far beyond the date of birth of the European Communities. See n. 191 above. ROBERTS argues that '(t)he need for coordination can be traced back [...] to 1648 when the Treaty of Westphalia brought the Thirty Years War to an end' ROBERTS, above n. 191, p.8.

236 WHITE, above n. 193, p. 166.

237 On this issue, see V. PASKALIA, *Free movement, social security and gender*, Hart Publishing, Oxford, Portland 2007, pp. 54–55.

238 PENNINGS, above n. 183, p. 3 and WATSON, above n. 76, p. 35.

239 European Commission, *Proposal for a Council Regulation (EC) on coordination of social security systems*, COM (1998) 779 final, 21.12.1998.

prevent a person being penalised, facing disadvantages or losing social security rights as a result of moving across borders.[240]

The relevance of the issue at stake is shown by the fact that the first set of Coordination Regulations, Regulation (EEC) No 3/58[241] and 4/58,[242] were among the first legal instruments ever adopted by the Community.[243] Recently, the third generation of social security Coordination Regulations, i.e. Regulation (EC) Nos 883/2004 and 987/2009,[244] entered into force. These were the result of a lengthy and highly ponderous legislative procedure[245] and replaced Regulation Nos (EEC) 1408/71[246] and 574/72[247] on 1 May 2010. The latter regulations were used for almost forty years, during which they were amended almost yearly[248] and consequently became 'infamous for [their] complexity'.[249] Although one of

---

240 Y. Jorens, B. de Schuyter and C. Salamon, *Towards a rationalisation of the EC Co-ordination Regulations concerning Social Security?* Academia Press, Ghent 2007, p. 11.

241 Regulation No 3 of the Council concerning social security for migrant workers. OJ 30 of 16 December 1958.

242 Regulation No 4 of the Council laying down detailed rules for implementing and supplementing the provisions of Regulation No 3 concerning social security for migrant workers. OJ 30 of 16 December 1958.

243 On the first generation of social security Coordination Regulations see R. Cornelissen, '50 years of social security coordination' *European Journal of Social Security* 2009, vol 11 issue 1–2, pp. 11–13. See also Lipstein, above n. 209, pp. 94–111; Watson, above n. 76, pp. 28–29 and F. Pennings, 'Introduction: Regulation 883/2004 – the third coordination regulation in a row' *European Journal of Social Security* 2009, vol 11 issue 1–2, p. 4.

244 See n. 15 above.

245 On the legislative process see H. Verschueren, 'The EU social security co-ordination system: A close interplay between the EU legislature and judiciary' in P. Syrpis (ed.), *The Judiciary, the Legislature and the EU Internal Market*, Cambridge University Press, New York 2012, p. 180.

246 Regulation (EEC) No 1408/71 of the Council of 14 June 1971 on the application of social security schemes to employed persons, to self-employed persons and to members of their families moving within the Community. OJ L 149 of 5 July 1971.

247 Regulation (EEC) No 574/72 of the Council of 21 March 1972 fixing the procedure for implementing Regulation (EEC) No 1408/71 on the application of social security schemes to employed persons and their families moving within the Community. OJ L 74 of 27 March 1972.

248 Verschueren, above n. 245, p. 178. See also B. Spiegel, 'Die neue europäische Sozialrechtskoordinierung. Wie neu ist die Verordnung 883/2004? Allgemeine Überlegungen' (The new European social security coordination. How new is the Regulation 883/2004? General considerations) in F. Marhold (ed.), *Das neue Sozialrecht der EU* (The new social law of the EU), Linde Verlag, Wien 2005, p. 13.

249 F. Pennings, 'The European Commission Proposal to Simplify Regulation 1408/71' *European Journal of Social Security* 2001, vol 3 issue 1, p. 45. Pennings explains that the complexity was mainly caused by the many exceptions to the main rules, which were often the result of a political compromise; the extended amount of CJEU rulings interpreting the regulation provisions in a way which compelled the legislature to amend the Regulation; and the lack of an explanatory memorandum to the Regulation which left room for different interpretations both on the Member States' and the CJEU's sides.
Jorens and his colleagues described the Regulations 'as a patchwork, in which special rules exist for different categories of persons and whereby different principles are applied to different risks'. Jorens et al., above n. 240, p. 6. See also Verschueren, above n. 245, p. 178.

the main objectives of the proposal for a new Coordination Regulation[250] was to modernise and to simplify the former one, some scholars complain that the new regulations did not fully meet expectations.[251] This is especially true for the coordination of healthcare benefits, as will be shown below.[252]

One of the most innovative and ambitious ideas of the new Regulations was that the traditional, paper-based communication between Member States was to be replaced by a more modern, speedy and efficient communication system, named the Electronic Exchange of Social Security Information (EESSI). EESSI is an IT system that aims to help social security bodies across the Union to exchange information more rapidly and securely. By computerising the application of European law on social security coordination and replacing paper-based E-forms with electronic documents, it is expected to shorten processing times and speed up both the settlement of claims and the calculation and payment of benefits. Throughout the implementation of EESSI, numerous technical and organisational difficulties have occurred, which resulted in the continuous postponement of the operational deadline. Nevertheless, once it functions, the electronic exchange of data will bring benefits to border-crossing patients as well.[253]

As one of the main developments, the personal scope of coordination was extended,[254] making Regulations 883/2004 and 987/2009 applicable to both all the EU citizens[255] and nationals of third countries.[256] Moreover, the Regulations

---

250 COM (1998) 779, above n. 239.

251 M. Sakslin, 'Social Security Co-ordination – Adapting to Change' *European Journal of Social Security* 2000, vol 2 issue 2, p. 172; Pennings, above n. 249, p. 58; Spiegel, above n. 248, p. 21 and F. Marhold, 'Modernisation of European coordination of sickness benefits' *European Journal of Social Security* 2009, vol 11 issue 1–2, p. 131.

252 See section 3.7. below in this chapter.

253 See Administrative Commission Decision No E4 of 13 March 2014 concerning the transitional period as defined in Article 95 of Regulation (EC) No 987/2009 of the European Parliament and of the Council. OJ C 152 of 20 May 2014.

254 Regulation 1408/71 was subject to much criticism due to its restricted personal scope, which was originally limited to economically active persons. In this respect, Regulation 883/2004 is definitely considered as a step forward, since it is applicable to both active and non-active persons. Article 2 BR. F. Pennings, 'Conclusion: Simplification, Modernisation and Regulation 883/2004' *European Journal of Social Security* 2009, vol 11 issue 1–2, p. 237.

255 According to Article 20 TFEU, 'every person holding the nationality of a Member State shall be a citizen of the Union. Citizenship of the Union shall be additional to and not replace national citizenship'.

256 The personal scope of Regulation 883/2004 was extended to third country nationals (TCN) by Regulation (EU) No 1231/2010 of the European Parliament and of the Council of 24 November 2010 extending Regulation (EC) No 883/2004 and Regulation (EC) No 987/2009 to nationals of third countries who are not already covered by these Regulations solely on the grounds of their nationality. OJ L 344 of 29 December 2010.
Regulation 1408/71 was also applicable to TCNs after adopting Council Regulation (EC) No 859/2003 of 14 May 2003 extending the provisions of Regulation (EEC) No 1408/71

not only cover the European Union itself, but are also applicable in relation to the countries of the European Economic Area (EEA), Iceland, Liechtenstein and Norway from 1 June 2012,[257] and in relation to Switzerland from 1 April 2012.[258]

A slight change can be seen in the material scope as well, as paternity benefits and pre-retirement benefits were included, so that the coordination mechanism now covers ten branches of social security,[259] among others, sickness benefits.[260]

3.7. EVOLUTION OF THE LEGISLATION ON EUROPEAN CROSS-BORDER PATIENT MOBILITY

As Raptopoulou aptly recaps, 'patient mobility as a normative corpus emerged from the lacunae of secondary law, was developed into a solid case law edifice, subsequently acquired a quasi-compulsory character capable of generating sanctions in case of improper implementation, and, eventually, after many trials and turbulences, it was crystallised into secondary law'.[261]

As said above, patient mobility can be considered as a crossroads between healthcare legislation and the rules on free movement. Accordingly, the legal instruments in this field are complex and different in nature. The current instruments governing cross-border patient mobility can be grouped into three main categories: the coordination scheme approaching patient mobility from the free movement of persons' point of view, generally referred to as the *Regulation-based approach*; the rulings of the CJEU considering healthcare as subject to the Treaty rules on free movement of services, developing a *case law based approach*;

and Regulation (EEC) No 574/72 to nationals of third countries who are not already covered by those provisions solely on the grounds of their nationality. OJ L 124 of 20 May 2003.
The main idea concerning extending the scope of coordination to TCNs remained unchanged: the Regulations are applicable to them if they fulfil two conditions, namely they are legally resident in the territory of the European Union; and they are in a situation which is not confined in all respects within a single Member State. Article 1 of Regulation 1231/2010.

257 Decision of the EEA Joint Committee No 76/2011 of 1 July 2011 amending Annex VI (Social security) and Protocol 37 to the EEA Agreement. OJ L 262 of 6 October 2011.

258 Decision No 1/2012 of the Joint Committee established under the Agreement between the European Community and its Member States, of the one part, and the Swiss Confederation, of the other, on the free movement of persons of 31 March 2012 replacing Annex II to that Agreement on the coordination of social security schemes. OJ L 103 of 13 April 2012.

259 Article 3 BR: 'This Regulation shall apply to all legislation concerning the following branches of social security: (a) sickness benefits; (b) maternity and equivalent paternity benefits; (c) invalidity benefits; (d) old-age benefits; (e) survivors' benefits; (f) benefits in respect of accidents at work and occupational diseases; (g) death grants; (h) unemployment benefits; (i) pre-retirement benefits; (j) family benefits.'

260 Title III, Chapter I of the Basic Regulation and Title III, Chapter I of the Implementing Regulation.

261 Raptopoulou, above n. 212, p. 193.

and the *Patient Mobility Directive* aiming to create a coherent legal framework on cross-border healthcare.

The first group of instruments consists of social security coordination measures based on the principle of promoting free movement of persons: the social security Coordination Regulations themselves,[262] the decisions of the Administrative Commission for the Coordination of Social Security Systems (AC)[263] and the explanatory notes from the European Commission.[264] The basic logic behind this regulatory framework[265] is to ensure access to healthcare for insured persons moving across borders within Europe in any state covered by the geographical scope of the coordination[266] other than the country of affiliation, as if they were covered by the healthcare scheme in that country. Under the current coordination mechanism a strict distinction is made between necessary care occurring unexpectedly during a temporary stay in another Member State and deliberate patient movements, the express purpose of which is to receive planned care abroad. The opportunity to obtain non-planned medical care during a temporary stay abroad was already offered by the very first set of Coordination Regulations,[267] whereas – as a rather progressive step at that time and that level of European integration – provisions on planned care were introduced in 1972 by Regulation 1408/71.[268]

Until the mid-1990s, the social security Coordination Regulations were the sole legal source governing cases of cross-border patient mobility.[269] Since the Member States held considerable discretionary powers concerning

262 See n. 15 above.

263 The Administrative Commission is one of the bodies set up to guarantee the smooth functioning of the coordination mechanism. It is, among other tasks, primarily responsible for handling any question of interpretation arising from the provisions of the Coordination Regulations. Articles 71–72 BR.

264 For instance, the European Commission services have made remarkable efforts concerning the clarification of the relationship between the Social Security Coordination Regulations and the Patient Mobility Directive, which is one of the most delicate issues in the field at stake. See the *Guidance note of the Commission services on the relationship between Regulations (EC) Nos 883/2004 and 987/2009 on the coordination of social security systems and Directive 2011/24/EU on the application of patients' rights in cross-border healthcare*, AC 246/12, 21 May 2012.
Although these documents are not legally binding, they have played a significant role in the course of applying and developing the EU's legislation on cross-border patient mobility, since they promote the coherent, EU-compatible application of the provisions of the Coordination Regulations in the Member States by providing interpretation on problematic coordination issues and concepts.

265 The legal base of these legal tools is Article 48 TFEU.

266 Currently, the 28 Member States, Norway, Iceland, Liechtenstein and Switzerland are covered by the geographical scope of the social security Coordination Regulations. See n. 258 and 259 above.

267 See n. 241 and 242 above.

268 See especially Articles 22(1)(c) and 22(2) of Regulation 1408/71.

269 R. Cornelissen, 'Achievements of 50 years of European Social Security Coordination' in Jorens, above n. 191, p. 68.

the authorisation of scheduled treatments, speaking about free movement of patients at the time sounds like a slight exaggeration.[270] Nevertheless, in 1998 the Court took the lead and provided a completely new perspective for border-crossing patients.[271]

In the second category, the Court's healthcare rulings can be found, commencing with the landmark cases *Kohll*[272] and *Decker*,[273] which have been followed by a whole series of judgments[274] dealing with different aspects of obtaining healthcare abroad.[275] The novelty of this case law lies in the fact that the Court based its argumentation directly on the Treaty provisions[276] by revealing that healthcare services are considered services in the meaning of the Treaty and are thus subject to the rules on free movement of services. Therefore, any national measures resulting in making the provision of services between Member States more difficult than the provision of services purely within one Member State[277] breach primary law unless properly justified. Starting from this basis, the Court has systematically demolished the (discretionary) power of the Member States in the field of healthcare. Each case before the Court proved to be another dent and to open the door wider for the application of internal market rules to healthcare services. 'In effect a freedom of movement for patients was created, reinforcing and shaping the development of an internal

---

270 van der Mei notes that throughout the last decade of the 20th century, the Coordination Regulations increasingly became the subject of criticism due to 'the limited degree to which EC Regulations 1408/71 and 574/72 and the relevant national rules enable patients to obtain medical care in other Member States'. A.P. van der Mei, 'Cross-Border Access to Medical Care within the European Union – Some Reflections on the Judgments in Decker and Kohll' *Maastricht Journal of European and Comparative Law* 1998, vol 5, p. 277.

271 The CJEU has had a considerable role in the development of European legislation on many fields, including European patient mobility: it has found creative ways to expand the Union's competence and 'conquer' areas which were considered entirely national 'territory'. As Stone Sweet points out aptly, '(t)oday, the ECJ has no rival as the most effective supranational judicial body in the history of the world'. A. Stone Sweet, 'European Integration and the Legal System' in T.A. Börzel and R.A. Cichowski (eds.), *The State of the European Union Law, Politics and Society*, Oxford University Press, New York 2003, p. 18.
On the Court's approach towards cross-border patient mobility, see also V. Hatzopoulos and T. Hervey, 'Coming into line: the EU's Court softens on cross-border health care' *Health Economics, Policy and Law* 2013, vol 8 issue 1, pp. 1–5.

272 C-158/96 *Raymond Kohll v Union des caisses de maladie* [ECLI:EU:C:1998:171].

273 C-120/95 *Nicolas Decker v Caisse de maladie des employés privés* [ECLI:EU:C:1998:167].

274 See n. 17 above.

275 As Footman and her colleagues describe, 'the law developed in a piecemeal fashion, based on precedents derived from individual and often quite atypical cases'. K. Footman, C. Knai, R. Baeten, K. Glonti and M. McKee, *Cross-border health care in Europe*, http://www.euro.who.int/__data/assets/pdf_file/0009/263538/Cross-border-health-care-in-Europe-Eng.pdf, 2014 (accessed 18.02.2017) p. 6.

276 The Court referred to Articles 59 and 60 TEC (now Articles 56–57 TFEU).

277 C-381/93 *Commission v France*, 17; C-158/96 *Kohll*, 33; C-368/98 *Vanbraekel*, 44; C-157/99 *Geraets-Smits and Peerbooms*, 61; C-8/02 *Leichtle*, 37; C-372/04 *Watts*, 94; C-444/05 *Stamatelaki*, 25; C-211/08 *Commission v Spain*, 55; C-490/09 *Commission v Luxemburg*, 16, 33.

health care market and transgressing territoriality more deeply',[278] Flear says. In the patient mobility case law a clear trend could be seen as the Court proceeded to develop a new route for patient mobility:[279] on the one hand, it was extending (or – others might say – clarifying) the scope of application of the Treaty rules[280] 'in an incremental manner'[281] and on the other hand, it added interpretive remarks on various aspects of patient mobility situations[282] (Table 4 below).

As a first step,[283] even before the famous *Kohll* and *Decker* rulings, the Court made two important statements, which served as preconditions in regard to further development. It was first declared in the *Luisi and Carbone* case[284] that on the one hand, a healthcare service must be regarded as a service within the

278 Flear, above n. 86, p. 210.

279 On the phases of patient mobility case law, see Flear, above n. 86, pp. 210–212 and Kaczorowska, above n. 172, pp. 347–359.

280 The rules concerned are the rules on free movement of goods regulated by Articles 28–37 TFEU (especially Articles 34 and 36 TFEU; in the case law reference is usually made to Articles 30 and 36 TEC) and the rules on free movement of services regulated by Article 56–62 TFEU (especially Articles 56 and 57 TFEU; in the case law reference is usually made to Articles 59 and 60 TEC).

281 Flear, above n. 86, p. 210.

282 The aim of this section is to demonstrate the line of evolution of the right to cross-border healthcare and the legislative body governing it. Therefore, mainly the first dimension of the evolution of the case law, namely the clarification of the application of the internal market rules is examined here, whereas the further clarifications from the Court are to be analysed later in this book.

283 In fact, the very first cameo was presented by the CJEU at the end of the 1970s through the surprising outcome of the *Pierik I* and *II* cases, which concerned a Dutch national who worked and lived in the Netherlands, but went to Germany in order to receive hydrotherapy treatment there. Upon return, she requested a refund of the costs she had incurred. The sickness fund, however, refused to pay the costs on the grounds that the treatment in question was not included into the benefit package, thus not covered by the Dutch health insurance. C-117/77 *Bestuur van het Algemeen Ziekenfonds Drenthe-Platteland v G. Pierik (I)* [ECLI:EU:C:1978:72] and C-182/78 *Bestuur van het Algemeen Ziekenfonds Drenthe-Platteland v G. Pierik (II)* [ECLI:EU:C:1979:142]. The judgments implied that patients could have the right to obtain authorisation for types of treatment which had been deliberately excluded from the national insurance package on medical, ethical or financial grounds. C-182/78 *Pierik II*, 13.
Although the decisions were very favourable for the patients, the rulings caused remarkable opposition from the Member States, which as a countermeasure pushed through a modification of the then wording of the Coordination Regulation and inserted a condition to the rules on planned care, authorising the Member States to refuse to reimburse the costs of treatments which are not included into the benefit basket of the competent Member State. van der Mei, above n. 270, pp. 285–286.
Kaczorowska refers to this action of the Member States as something which 'stopped, neutralised, or reversed' the activism of the CJEU, when it went too far with broadening the interpretation of the EU rules in favour of patients. Kaczorowska, above n. 172, p. 353.

284 The joined cases concerned two Italian nationals, Graziana Luisi and Guiseppe Carbone, who travelled abroad (to France and to Germany) for medical and touristic purposes. While doing so, the amount of foreign currency they purchased exceeded the maximum amount permitted by Italian national law. During the trial the Court dealt not only with the free movement of capital but also with the notion of service provision. Joined Cases C-286/82 and C-26/83 *Graziana Luisi and Guiseppe Carbone v Ministero del Tesoro* [ECLI:EU:C:1984:35].

meaning of the Treaty,[285] consequently making the rules on free movement of services applicable to healthcare;[286] and on the other hand, that the freedom to provide services includes the freedom for the recipients of services, including persons in need of medical treatment, to go to another Member State in order to receive those services there.[287]

Although the baseline was established in the 1980s,[288] the breakthrough was delayed for another decade, when *Decker*[289] and *Kohll*[290] 'brought down a

---

285 Joined Cases C-286/82 and C-26/83 *Luisi and Carbone*, 16; C-159/90 *Society for the Protection of Unborn Children Ireland*, 18; C-158/96 *Kohll*, 29; C-368/98 *Vanbraekel*, 41; C-157/99. *Geraets-Smits and Peerbooms*, 53; C-385/99 *Müller-Fauré and Van Riet*, 38; C-56/01 *Inizan*, 16; C-8/02 *Leichtle*, 28; C-372/04 *Watts*, 86; C-444/05 *Stamatelaki*, 19; C-211/08 *Commission v Spain*, 47; C-173/09 *Elchinov*, 36; C-512/08 *Commission v France*, 30; C-490/09 *Commission v Luxemburg*, 16, 34.
On the controversy related to the application of Treaty provisions on free movement of services on healthcare, see the recent analysis of Rieder, above n. 52, pp. 3–10.
Healthcare services also belong to the broader notion of *social services of general interest* (SSGI). Although the special characteristics of healthcare as a service have been dealt with (see n. 22 above), the wide discussion about SSGI is beyond the scope of this research. On this topic, see, among others, European Commission, *Communication from the Commission to the European Parliament, the Council, the European Economic and Social Committee and the Committee of the Regions. Accompanying the Communication on 'A single market for 21st century Europe.' Services of general interest, including social services of general interest: a new European commitment*, COM (2007) 725 final, 20.11.2007; European Commission, *Communication from the Commission to the European Parliament, the Council, the European Economic and Social Committee and the Committee of the Regions. A Quality Framework for Services of General Interest in Europe*, COM (2011) 900 final, 20.12.2011; and also, J.W. van de Gronden, 'Social Services of General Interest and EU Law' in E. Szyszczak, J. Davies, M. Andenæs, T. Bekkedal (eds.), *Developments in Services of General Interest*, T.M.C. Asser Press, The Hague 2011 and U. Neergaard, E. Szyszczak, J.W. van de Gronden, M. Krajewski, *Social Services of General Interest in the EU*, T.M.C. Asser Press, The Hague 2013.

286 It must be added that the Court made it clear that 'the special nature of certain services does not remove them from the ambit of the fundamental principle of freedom of movement'. C-33/74 *van Binsbergen*; C-279/80 *Webb*, 10; C-158/96 *Kohll*, 20; C-368/98 *Vanbraekel*, 42; C-157/99 *Geraets-Smits and Peerbooms*, 54.

287 Joined Cases C-286/82 and C-26/83 *Luisi and Carbone*, 16; C-294/97 *Eurowings Luftverkehr*, 33–34; C-243/01 *Gambelli and Others*, 55; C-372/04 *Watts*, 87; C-444/05 *Stamatelaki*, 20; C-211/08 *Commission v Spain*, 48–50; C-173/09 *Elchinov*, 37; C-512/08 *Commission v France*, 31; C-490/09 *Commission v Luxemburg*, 35.
The CJEU holds the same about other types of services as well. See, among others, C-398/95 *SETTG*, 8 (touristic services) and C-55/98 *Vestergaard*, 20 (organisation of professional training courses).

288 As Hatzopoulos and Hervey phrase it, '(t)he revolution started without anybody realizing it'. Hatzopoulos and Hervey, above n. 271, p. 1.

289 Mr Decker, a Luxembourg national, requested reimbursement of the cost of a pair of spectacles with corrective lenses purchased from an optician established in Arlon, Belgium, with a prescription from an ophthalmologist established in Luxembourg. The Health Insurance Fund refused to reimburse him for the cost of those spectacles, on the grounds that they had been purchased abroad without its prior authorisation. Mr Decker contested the decision of the Fund, relying in particular on the Treaty rules on the free movement of goods. C-120/95 *Decker*, 2–4.

290 Mr Kohll, a Luxembourg national, requested prior authorisation for his daughter, who was a minor, to receive treatment from an orthodontist established in Trier, Germany. The request

first wall in the compartmentalised structure of medical care in the European Union'.[291] The main message of these judgments can be summarised as follows: the determination of the national social security schemes falls within the competence of the Member States alone;[292] medical goods and treatments are subject to the Treaty rules on free movement of goods[293] and services;[294] the prior authorisation (PA) scheme implemented in the national legislation is considered a barrier to free movement;[295] and this restriction of free movement cannot be justified.[296] In these cases the Member States came up with four possible grounds of justification, consistently rejected by the CJEU one by one.

On the control of the health expenditure, the Court held that aims of a purely economic nature cannot justify a barrier to the fundamental principle of the free movement.[297]When the Member States used the argument of safeguarding the financial balance of the social security system, the CJEU admitted that the risk of seriously undermining the financial balance of the social security system may constitute an overriding reason in the general interest capable of justifying a barrier of that kind. However, since the health insurance system in Luxembourg provided a flat-rate reimbursement, the CJEU affirmed that reimbursement at a flat rate of the cost of medical goods purchased or treatment obtained in another Member States has no effect on the financing or balance of the social security system.[298]

---

was rejected by the Health Insurance Fund on the grounds that the proposed treatment was not urgent and that it could be provided in Luxembourg. Mr Kohll appealed against the decision, arguing that the provisions relied on were contrary to the Treaty provisions on the free movement of services. C-158/96 *Kohll*, 2–4.

291 P. Cablar, 'Cross-border medical care in the European Union – bringing down a first wall' *European Law Review* 1999, vol 24 issue 4, p. 387.

292 C-120/95 *Decker*, 21–23; C-158/96 *Kohll*, 17–19. See also n. 216, 218 and 219.

293 C 120/95 *Decker*, 24. See also C-238/82 *Duphar*, 18.

294 C-158/96 *Kohll*, 21.
Furthermore, the Court added that 'the fact that the national rules (in these cases the legislation of Luxembourg) fall within the sphere of social security cannot exclude the application of the Treaty rules on free movement'. C-120/95 *Decker*, 25; C-158/96 *Kohll*, 21. See also C-368/98 *Vanbraekel*, 42; C-157/99 *Geraets-Smits and Peerbooms*, 54.

295 C-120/95 *Decker*, 36; C-158/96 *Kohll*, 35. The argument of the Court was that authorisation mechanisms 'encourage insured persons to purchase medical products in the competent MS rather than in other Member States or deter insured persons from approaching providers of medical services established in another Member State'. See also Joined Cases C-286/82 and C-26/83 *Luisi and Carbone*, 16; C-18/84 *Commission v France*, 16; C-204/90 *Bachmann*, 31; C-368/98 *Vanbraekel*, 45; C-157/99 *Geraets-Smits and Peerbooms*, 69; C-385/99 *Müller-Fauré and Van Riet*, 44, 103; C-56/01 *Inizan*, 18, 53; C-8/02 *Leichtle*, 30; C-372/04 *Watts*, 98; C 173/09 *Elchinov*, 41; C-512/08 *Commission v France*, 32; C-490/09 *Commission v Luxemburg*, 41.

296 C-120/95 *Decker*, 39–45; C-158/96 *Kohll*, 53.

297 C-398/95 *SETTG*, 23; C-120/95 *Decker*, 37–39; C-158/96 *Kohll*, 37, 41; C-385/99 *Müller-Fauré and Van Riet*, 72.

298 C-120/95 *Decker*, 39–40; C-158/96 *Kohll*, 38–42; C-368/98 *Vanbraekel*, 47; C-157/99 *Geraets-Smits and Peerbooms*, 72; C-385/99 *Müller-Fauré and Van Riet*, 73–74; C-145/03 *Keller*, 68;

To the argument of protecting public health by supplying goods and providing services by persons authorised by law to pursue the profession, the CJEU answered that since the conditions for taking up and pursuing regulated professions have been harmonised on Community level, the provision of a treatment by a healthcare provider established in another Member State provides guarantees equivalent to those provided by a healthcare practitioner established in the national territory.[299]

Finally, the CJEU closed the debate on the justification by stating that the rules on prior authorisation are not necessary to provide a balanced medical and hospital service accessible to all.[300]

Undoubtedly, the merit of *Kohll* and *Decker* is that they unequivocally strengthened the patients' position by declaring that 'the reimbursement of the cost of medical products and services obtained in other Member States is no longer to be regarded as a privilege given by the competent insurance organ, but rather as an enforceable individual right which can only in some cases be (partly) limited'.[301] However, both judgments concerned the consumption of a medical good or service provided outside of a hospital environment – a pair of glasses in the *Decker* case and an orthodontic treatment in the *Kohll* case. Furthermore, in both proceedings, the legislation of Luxembourg, operating a reimbursement system, was challenged. These facts gave many the impression that the application of internal market rules is highly limited:[302] they apply only to purchasing medical goods and to outpatient[303] medical services within the national healthcare schemes based on a reimbursement principle, whereas inpatient care and social security systems without reimbursement rates[304] are left intact by the activist approach of the European Court of Justice.[305]

C-372/04 *Watts*, 103; C-444/05 *Stamatelaki*, 30; C-173/09 *Elchinov*, 42; C-490/09 *Commission v Luxemburg*, 43.

299 C-215/87 *Schumacher*, 20; C-62/90 *Commission v Germany*, 18; C-120/95 *Decker*, 41–45; C-158/96 *Kohll*, 44–49; C-145/03 *Keller*, 50, 52; C-444/05 *Stamatelaki*, 37.

300 C-158/96 *Kohll*, 50–52; C-368/98 *Vanbraekel*, 48–49; C-157/99 *Geraets-Smits and Peerbooms*, 73–74; C-385/99 *Müller-Fauré and Van Riet*, 67; C-372/04 *Watts*, 104–105; C-444/05 *Stamatelaki*, 31–32; C-173/09 *Elchinov*, 42; C-490/09 *Commission v Luxemburg*, 43.

301 van der Mei, above n. 270, p. 293.

302 Flear, above n. 86, p. 211.

303 Hereinafter, outpatient care, extramural care and non-hospital care are used as synonyms, as well as inpatient care, intramural care and hospital care.

304 These are the Member States with national health services (e.g. the United Kingdom and Spain) and the ones with social insurance systems providing benefits in kind (e.g. the Netherlands and Hungary). On the classification of the European healthcare schemes, see n. 231 above.

305 C.G. De Cortazar, 'Kohll and Decker, or That is Somebody Else's Problem. The Challenge Facing Spain' *European Journal of Health Law* 1999, vol 6, p. 398.

In the *Vanbraekel*[306] and *Geraets-Smits and Peerbooms*[307] rulings, the Court made it clear that this is not the case, and expressly extended the application of the rules on free movement of services to benefit-in-kind schemes[308] and inpatient healthcare services.[309] Whereas the Member States operating a national health service were still convinced that these judgments did not concern them,[310] after the *Watts*[311] ruling, no doubt was left that the Treaty rules

306 Ms Descamps, a Belgian national residing and insured in Belgium, suffered from bilateral gonarthrosis. She sought authorisation from the competent healthcare fund to undergo orthopaedic surgery in France, to be paid for by the fund. The authorisation was refused on the grounds that the request was not adequately supported, since Ms Descamps had not produced the opinion of a doctor practising in a national university institution. Despite this decision, Ms Descamps went ahead with the operation in France and subsequently brought an action against the healthcare fund before the national court for reimbursement of the cost of that treatment. Ms Descamps died in the course of the proceedings, but her heirs pursued the action. C-368/98 *Vanbraekel*, 11–13.

307 The judgment concerns two Dutch nationals insured under Dutch law. Mrs Geraets-Smits suffered from Parkinson's disease. She requested the healthcare fund to reimburse the costs of care received at the Elena-Klinik in Kassel in Germany for specific, multidisciplinary treatment of that disease. That method involves, among others, examinations and treatment to determine the ideal medical treatment, physiotherapy and ergotherapy and sociopsychological support. The fund rejected to cover the costs of the treatment on the grounds that satisfactory and adequate treatment for Parkinson's disease was available in the Netherlands, and that the specific clinical treatment provided at the Elena-Klinik provided no additional advantage. The latter implies that there was no medical necessity justifying treatment in that clinic. C-157/99 *Geraets-Smits and Peerbooms*, 25–26.

Mr Peerbooms fell into a coma following a road accident. He was taken to hospital in the Netherlands and then transferred in a vegetative state to the University Clinic in Innsbruck in Austria. The Innsbruck clinic gave Mr Peerbooms special intensive therapy using neurostimulation. In the Netherlands, that technique is used only experimentally at two medical centres and patients over the age of twenty-five years are not allowed to undergo this therapy. It is therefore common ground that if Mr Peerbooms had remained in the Netherlands, he would not have been able to receive such treatment. Mr Peerbooms's neurologist requested the Dutch healthcare fund to pay the costs of the treatment at the University Clinic in Innsbruck. That request was rejected on the grounds that adequate treatment could have been obtained in the Netherlands. C-157/99 *Geraets-Smits and Peerbooms*, 31–34.

308 In the Court's opinion, 'it must be accepted that a medical service provided in one Member State and paid for by the patient should not cease to fall within the scope of the freedom to provide services guaranteed by the Treaty merely because reimbursement of the costs of the treatment involved is applied for under another Member State's sickness insurance legislation which is essentially of the type which provides for benefits in kind'. C-157/99 *Geraets-Smits and Peerbooms*, 55. See also C-385/99 *Müller-Fauré and Van Riet*, 39, 103; C-372/04 *Watts*, 89; C-444/05 *Stamatelaki*, 21; C-211/08 *Commission v Spain*, 47; C-490/09 *Commission v Luxemburg*, 36.

309 The Court stated that 'medical activities fall within the scope of the Treaty rules on free movement of services, there being no need to distinguish in that regard between care provided in a hospital environment and care provided outside such an environment'. C-368/98 *Vanbraekel*, 41; C-157/99 *Geraets-Smits and Peerbooms*, 53. See also n. 286 above.

310 De Cortazar argues that 'in States with a national health service, like Spain, there is no free competition among the healthcare providers within the framework of social security, and therefore the same restrictions operating internally could and should operate externally'. De Cortazar, above n. 305, pp. 398–399.

311 Mrs Watts, a UK national covered by the British NHS, suffered from arthritis of the hips and made enquiries of the competent institution into the possibility of her undergoing surgery

on free movement of services affect the social security system of each Member State irrespective of how it is organised and financed.[312]

Whereas in the *Kohll* case the Court seemed to refuse each possible ground for justification for the restriction of free movement by the Member States maintaining a prior authorisation system, it proved to be more indulgent when it was confronted with the 'planning argument' for hospital treatments in the *Geraets-Smits and Peerbooms* case. The Court acknowledged that 'the number of hospitals, their geographical distribution, the mode of their organisation and the equipment with which they are provided, and even the nature of the medical services which they are able to offer, are all matters for which planning must be possible'.[313] For the purpose of planning and 'to prevent any wastage of financial, technical and human resources, a requirement that the assumption of costs, under a national social security system, of hospital treatment provided in another Member State must be subject to prior authorisation appears to be a measure which is both necessary and reasonable'.[314] Thus, another parallelism was introduced (and confirmed with the *Müller-Fauré and Van Riet*[315] judgment)

abroad. She was seen by a UK consultant and her case was classified as 'routine', which meant a wait of approximately one year for surgery in a local hospital. On the grounds that the treatment in a local hospital is available 'within the government's NHS Plan targets' and therefore 'without undue delay', Mrs Watts's request was refused. She challenged the decision before the Administrative Court and in the meantime went to see a consultant in France. She was told that her need for surgery was becoming more urgent because of deterioration in her state of health. Mrs Watts was re-examined by the UK consultant, and was now categorised as a patient requiring surgery 'soon', in an intermediate category between the most urgent cases and the routine cases. That meant that she would be operated on within three or four months. Consequently, the competent institution repeatedly refused to authorise her treatment abroad. Nevertheless, Mrs Watts underwent a hip replacement operation in Abbeville, France. She paid the fees for that surgery and continued with her application for permission to apply for judicial review of the refusal decision, claiming in addition reimbursement of the medical fees incurred in France.

312 On financing the medical costs incurred abroad, see Chapter 3. Financial Affordability.

313 C-157/99 *Geraets-Smits and Peerbooms*, 76, 78–80. On this issue see also C-385/99 *Müller-Fauré and Van Riet*, 77–81; C-56/01 *Inizan*, 56; C-145/03 *Keller*, 62; C-372/04 *Watts*, 108–110; C-173/09 *Elchinov*, 43; C-512/08 *Commission v France*, 33–42.

314 See n. 313 above.

315 While on holiday in Germany, Ms Müller-Fauré, a Dutch national insured in the Netherlands, underwent dental treatment involving the fitting of six crowns and a fixed prosthesis on the upper jaw. The treatment was provided without recourse to any hospital facilities. When she returned from her holiday, she applied to the competent healthcare fund for reimbursement of the costs of the treatment. The fund refused reimbursement on the basis of the opinion of its advisory dental officer and argued that insured persons are entitled only to treatment itself and not to reimbursement of any related costs, except in exceptional circumstances which did not exist in this case. C-385/99 *Müller-Fauré and Van Riet*, 20–22.

Ms Van Riet, another Dutch national, had been suffering from pain in her right wrist. An authorisation was requested to enable her to have an arthroscopy performed in Deurne hospital in Belgium, where that examination could be carried out much sooner than in the Netherlands. The healthcare fund rejected the request on the grounds that the test could also be performed in the Netherlands. In the meantime, Ms Van Riet had already had the

in the system: whereas receiving extramural care abroad did not impose the obligation on the patient to request a prior authorisation from the competent institution, to obtain intramural care, the Member States could legitimately require patients to apply for permission in advance.

After the inclusion of inpatient care and also national healthcare schemes basically functioning without reimbursement rates,[316] the Court's endeavour was completed in this dimension: the rules on free movement of services became applicable to both types of care and to each type of healthcare system.

Table 4. The evolution of CJEU case law on patient mobility[317]

Dimension 1: Clarification of the scope of application of the Treaty rules on free movement of goods and services to health services	**Patient mobility case law of the ECJ**	**Dimension 2:** Clarification of conditions of the application of internal market rules to health services	
Phase 0	Medical service: a service within the meaning of the Treaty	C-26/83 *Luisi and Carbone*	
Phase 1	Prior authorisation: a barrier to free movement of goods and services, and this restriction cannot be justified	C-120/95 *Decker*; C-158/96 *Kohll*	– Potential grounds of justification for restriction of free movement
Phase 2	Extension of internal market rules also to benefit-in-kind systems and inpatient care	C-368/98 *Vanbraekel*	– Additional reimbursement – Post-factum authorisation

(continued)

arthroscopy in Deurne hospital and, following that examination, the decision was taken to carry out an ulnar reduction to relieve the patient's pain. Care before and after the treatment, and the treatment itself, were provided in Belgium, partly in hospital and partly elsewhere. The fund refused to reimburse the cost on the grounds that there was no emergency nor any medical necessity such as to justify Ms Van Riet receiving treatment in Belgium, since appropriate treatment was available in the Netherlands within a reasonable period. C-385/99 *Müller-Fauré and Van Riet*, 25–26.

316 The Court is of the opinion that: 'there is no need, from the perspective of freedom to provide services, to draw a distinction by reference to whether the patient pays the costs incurred and subsequently applies for reimbursement thereof or whether the sickness fund or the national budget pays the provider directly'. C-385/99 *Müller-Fauré and Van Riet*, 103.

317 Advocate General (AG) Mergozzi similarly highlights the evolutionary steps of the development of the healthcare case law in his opinion delivered on 25 February 2010 in C-211/08 *European Commission v Kingdom of Spain* [ECLI:EU:C:2010:340]. 37–41.

Table 4 ***continued***

		C-157/99 *Geraets-Smits and Peerbooms*	– Acceptance of the 'planning-argument' as justification in case of inpatient care – Procedural requirements – Necessity on medical grounds, availability of the same or equally effective treatment – Determination of benefits covered – Undue delay
		C-385/99 *Müller-Fauré and Van Riet*	– Distinction between outpatient and inpatient care
Phase 3	Extension of internal market rules also to national health services	C-372/04 *Watts*	– The relation between undue delay and waiting lists
Phase 4	Full application of the rules on free movement of services to both types of care and each type of healthcare scheme		Further clarification of the issues mentioned above and also other ones such as – Distinction between scheduled care and unscheduled care – Coverage of ancillary costs etc.

Source: The author's own summary.

While Coordination Regulations 1408/71 and 574/72 absorbed only a few drops of this case law, high expectations were expressed towards the new set of regulations to abolish the duality of the system by incorporating the conclusions of the Court into secondary law.[318] However, to the disappointment of many, the Member States missed this regulatory moment to transform the patient mobility legislation, simplify it and adapt it to the needs of the patients. Instead, the new Coordination Regulations maintained the 'coexistence of two separate "coordination methods", [...] which were difficult to reconcile'.[319] Despite

[318] 'The bulk of case law on the national authorisation procedures with regard to cross-border health care was so closely linked to the coordination of sickness benefits that an integration of it into the text of the regulation was to be expected.' Jorens and Van Overmeiren, above n. 193, p. 59. See section 3.7.

[319] Jorens and Van Overmeiren, above n. 193, p. 59.

the generally passive attitude of the Member States towards the case law,[320] a remarkable modification was made to the Regulations[321] concerning the second condition attached to the situation in which Member States *may not refuse* to authorise a treatment abroad. In Regulation 1408/71 'a factual, administrative criterion'[322] was included which was based on the time normally necessary for obtaining the treatment in question in the Member State of residence[323] and which provided Member States with a significant discretionary power.[324] This condition was slightly transformed, so that the current wording of Regulation 883/2004 implies that the authorisation *shall be accorded* if the treatment in question cannot be given to the patient 'within a time limit which is medically justifiable'.[325] This rephrasing can be seen as a positive improvement, since it serves the interest of the patients better[326] and limits the discretionary power of the competent Member State: the condition is personalised, and requires the competent institutions to take due account of the medical circumstances of the person concerned instead of basing their decisions mainly on abstract administrative standards.

To the question why the Member States mostly ignored the findings of the Court and failed to gradually reform the legal landscape of patient mobility, different answers can be given. Marhold holds that 'the Court [...] introduced harmonising elements into the coordination of sickness benefits'[327] through its case law and since it can be very much interpreted as reaching beyond the European Union's competence in the field of social security, the Member States were reluctant to include 'further harmonisation-promoting provisions relating to medical treatment in Regulation 883/2004'.[328] Without saying that this reason might not have played a role,[329] it must be noted that refusing to codify the case law did not alter the fact that the findings of the Court concern each Member

320 Marhold, above n. 251, p. 128.

321 On this issue, see, among others, E. Felten, 'Patientmobilität im Spiegel des primären und sekundären Gemeinschaftsrecht' (Patient mobility in the mirror of the primary and secondary Community law) *Das Recht der Arbeit* 2008, issue 1, pp. 89–90 and Jorens and Van Overmeiren, above n. 193, p. 60.

322 Cornelissen, above n. 185, p. 464.

323 Article 22(2) of Regulation 1408/71.

324 Cornelissen is of the opinion that 'such a discretionary power on the part of the competent institution is too wide'. Cornelissen, above n. 185, p. 464).

325 Article 20(2) BR.

326 It was the European Parliament that articulated the needs of the patients nicely during the legislative procedure and insisted on this amendment in its position on the first reading of the proposal. European Parliament, *European Parliament legislative resolution on the proposal for a European Parliament and Council regulation on coordination of social security systems*, P5_TA (2003) 0365, 3.09.2003.

327 Marhold, above n. 251, p. 127.

328 Marhold, above n. 251, p. 128.

329 It is well known that the Member States act highly sensitively in relation to the competence debate. Protecting their autonomy could thus have been a motivating factor.

State and that they must apply the rules declared by the Court in practice. In fact, the reform of secondary law offered the Member States an ideal opportunity to reverse the activism of the CJEU, if they wished, as they did as a reaction to the *Pierik* judgments.[330]

Nevertheless, instead of taking effective countermeasures, they left the legislation in question mostly intact, so there might have been something else behind their reluctance. In my opinion, at the time of drafting the new basic regulation[331] the Member States could not yet clearly see the far-reaching effects of the case law, since the Court clarified the scope of the 'second way' of patient mobility step-by-step at the end of the 1990s and the beginning of the 2000s. Moreover, as shown above, some of the Member States were firmly convinced that the healthcare case law was not applicable to them. In the Commission's proposal on the renewal of the Coordination Regulations, the intention to incorporate the findings of the Court was not present[332] and although attempts were made, especially during the Danish presidency in the second half of 2002, to reflect on the case law, they all failed due to the lack of unanimity in the Council.[333] This argumentation is supported by the fact that after the Court completed the extension of the case law based approach by the middle of the last decade,[334] the Member States reached a compromise and incorporated at least some elements of the case law into Implementing Regulation 987/2009, such as the rules on additional reimbursement,[335] the reimbursement of ancillary costs[336] and the referrals by the Member State of treatment.[337]

Although from the patients' point of view a one-track system would have been more desirable instead of the maintenance of the separate paths of patient mobility, 'their disunion'[338] was codified with the adoption of the Patient Mobility Directive.

---

330 See n. 283 above.
However, notably in the *Pierik* cases the Court interpreted secondary law, namely Article 22(1)(c) and (2) of Regulation 1408/71, whereas in the patient mobility case law national legislation was confronted with primary law, namely the Treaty provisions on free movement of services.

331 Strictly interpreted, it was an approximately six-year legislative work commencing with the Commission's proposal at the end of 1998 until the adoption of the Basic Regulation on 30 April 2004. Nevertheless, the preparatory works started way earlier, since social security coordination was one of the areas involved in the SLIM project, launched after the Edinburgh European Summit in 1992. The project on 'Simpler Legislation for the Single Market' aimed 'not only at elimination of legislation that has become superfluous or invalid, but also at the improvement and adaptation of existing legislation'. L. Senden, *Soft Law in European Community Law*, Hart Publishing, Oxford 2004, p. 19. See also Spiegel, above n. 248, p. 14.

332 Comment on Article 18, COM (1998) 779, above n. 239, p. 8.

333 See n. 234 above.

334 See the process of extension in Table 4 above.

335 C-368/98 *Vanbraekel* incorporated into Article 26(7) IR.

336 C-8/02 *Leichtle* and C-466/04 *Acereda Herrera* incorporated into Article 26(8) IR.

337 C-145/03 *Keller* incorporated into Article 26(5) IR.

338 Jorens and Van Overmeiren, above n. 193, p. 60.

The third, newest element of this trichotomous system of patient mobility legislation (Figure 1 below) is the Patient Mobility Directive.[339] The Directive has a rather long history which dates back to the time of drafting the so-called Services Directive[340] in 2004. Although the proposal for the Services Directive[341] did include medical services as well,[342] after lengthy negotiations healthcare was withdrawn[343] from the scope of the Services Directive due to its special characteristics.[344] It was decided to adopt a separate legal instrument on the cross-border provision of healthcare services.[345] The Proposal of the Patient Mobility Directive[346] also evolved remarkably during the legislative negotiations and it incorporated uneasy compromises.[347] As a result, the Directive – in certain respects at least – falls short of the prior expectations of many.[348]

Figure 1. The coexistence of legal instruments in the field of European cross-border patient mobility

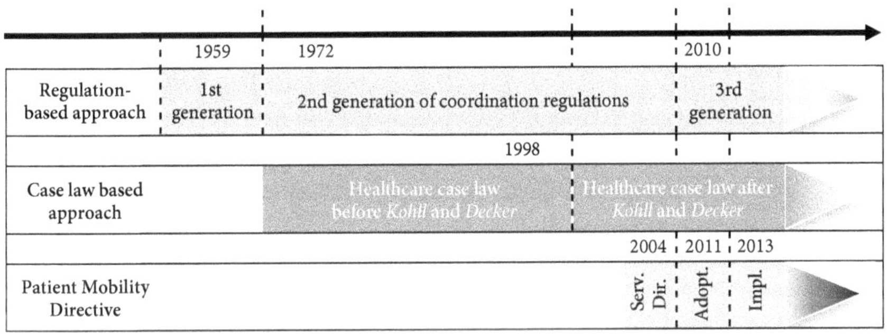

Source: The author's own summary.

---

339 See n. 20 above.

340 See n. 21 above.

341 European Commission, *Proposal for a Directive of the European Parliament and of the Council on services in the internal market*, COM (2004) 2 final, 05.03.2004.

342 Article 23 of the Proposal for Directive 2006/123.

343 European Parliament, *European Parliament legislative resolution on the proposal for a directive of the European Parliament and of the Council on services in the internal market*, P6_TA (2006) 0061, 16.02.2006.

344 See n. 22 above.

345 See n. 23 above.

346 European Commission, *Proposal for a Directive of the European Parliament and of the Council on the application of patients' rights in cross-border healthcare*, COM (2008) 414 final, 02.07.2008.

347 In the course of the discussions, a tension was built up 'between the Council of Ministers, which tends to see itself as a guardian of national health systems, and the European Parliament, which tends to see itself as a voice of Europe's citizens (and potential patients)'. H. Legido Quigley, I. Passarani, C. Knai, R. Busse, W. Palm and M. Wismar, 'Cross-border healthcare in Europe: clarifying patients' rights' *British Medical Journal* 2011, vol 342, p. 367.

348 European Patients Forum (EPF), EU *Directive 2011/24/EU on the application of patients' rights in cross-border healthcare: Legislation Guidance for Patient Organisations*, http://www.eu-patient.eu/Documents/Policy/Cross-borderHealthcare/2013%2011%2018_CBHC_guidance-final.pdf, 2013 (accessed 18.01.2014), p. 5.

The Patient Mobility Directive reaches far beyond patient mobility per se:[349] its ambition was not only to incorporate the findings of the Court on the provision of healthcare services[350] and to clarify its relationship with the existing framework of social security coordination, but also to facilitate cooperation between the Member States.[351] Consequently, the measures incorporated into the Directive target two main fields of cross-border healthcare: on the one hand the questions directly related to the *free movement of patients*, such as the reimbursement of medical costs, the requirement of prior authorisation and administrative procedures regarding cross-border patient mobility;[352] and on the other hand, measures promoting *inter-country cooperation*, such as mutual assistance, the recognition of prescriptions issued in another Member State, the development of European reference networks, cooperation in relation to the diagnosis and treatment of rare diseases and cooperation on eHealth and health technology assessment.[353]

As both the Council Conclusions and the Patient Mobility Directive state, a clear, coherent legal framework must be ensured for Union citizens about their rights and entitlements when they move from one Member State to another, in order to ensure legal certainty.[354] However, with the new Directive a complex, multi-functional, mixed source was created, which once again, instead of simplifying the legislation on European cross-border patient movements, added to the unanswered questions.

4. CONCLUSION

The main finding of this chapter is that European citizens have the right – if they fulfil some exact conditions – to obtain certain healthcare benefits abroad on behalf of their health insurance. However, this has not always been the case: the current form of the regulatory framework on patient mobility is the result of a long progress, which – in my opinion – has not yet ended.

The coexistence of three separate legal tools, which are very different in nature, has generated abundant discussions both at national and EU level, since

349 E. Jelfs and R. Baeten, *Simulation on the EU Cross-Border Care Directive. Final Report*, http://www.uems.net/uploads/media/CrossBorderHealthcareSimulation_FinalRep_0905 2012.pdf, 2011 (accessed 02.09.2013), p. 8 and Peeters, above n. 114, p. 29.

350 See n. 24 above.

351 Article 1(1) PMD.

352 Chapter III PMD.

353 Chapter IV PMD.

354 Recital 9 of the Preamble of the Patient Mobility Directive.

their relation to each other is still unclear to some extent, despite the apparent efforts from the European legislature's side to clarify it. The uncertainties, doubts, questions and conflicting rules surrounding the issue result, as will be shown below, in serious difficulties which patients are facing when using their European citizenship rights in practice to access healthcare in a Member State other than the Member State where they reside. On this point, the aim is clear: ceasing legal uncertainty in order to enable European patients to rely on the rights conferred on them by the European Union.

CHAPTER 2
LEGAL COMPLEXITY

The European legislation governing intra-EU patient movements across the Member States is in itself very complex. In this book, two dimensions of the legal complexity are identified: the complexity of legal rules applicable to the various scenarios of cross-border patient mobility and the complexity of the simultaneous application of legal tools. On the one hand, access to healthcare outside the Member State of residence includes three different situations to which different rules apply: access to healthcare *in the competent Member State when residing outside* the competent Member State; access to *necessary healthcare* during a temporary stay outside the Member State of residence; and access to *planned healthcare* outside the Member State of residence. On the other hand, these situations are currently regulated by two (if counting the case law as well, three) separate sets of rules:[355] the *social security coordination mechanism* and the case law-based *Patient Mobility Directive*, which partly overlap and partly conflict with each other, creating doubts and legal uncertainty.

These two dimensions of legal complexity are scrutinised in the next sections to show which difficulties border-crossing patients face and how these difficulties could be tackled. The rules applicable to various scenarios of cross-border patient mobility are analysed, synthesising the provisions of the different legal tools alongside the administrative requirements and procedures which must be followed in the different scenarios. For each scenario, the starting point is the body of the Regulation. The picture is completed with what the Court concluded in its case law and the Patient Mobility Directive added to the legal framework. Without any doubt, the legislation on cross-border healthcare provision is not the only challenge for patients, the related administrative procedures are often lengthy, time-consuming and ponderous. Through these formal processes, patients are confronted with a complex legal framework and they might be easily discouraged by the administrative burden or the conditions attached to the different forms of patient mobility. Therefore, the examination of the administrative conditions and procedures cannot be left out of this analysis.

At the end of the chapter, the conflicts and defects of the recent legal and administrative framework are pointed out.

---

355 On the multipillar legislative system, see section 3.7. in Chapter 1. Setting the scene, above.

1. ACCESS TO HEALTHCARE IN THE COMPETENT MEMBER STATE WHEN RESIDING OUTSIDE THAT MEMBER STATE

If someone resides in the competent state, it is self-evident that if he/she is insured, this implies that he/she is entitled to sickness benefits in kind in that country according to its national legislation. In this case, we do not speak of cross-border healthcare, since no borders are crossed and there is no need to refer to the European legislation.[356] This is an entirely national matter and all related questions are answered by the national legislation of this state. However, if the person resides in a Member State other than the competent Member State, supranational legislation comes into play.

1.1. THE COORDINATION REGULATIONS' ROUTE

Under the coordination rules, a distinction is made between certain groups of people in relation to their entitlements: in addition to the general rules, special rules on frontier workers and pensioners are in place. In principle, a person residing in a Member State other than the competent Member State is entitled – if he/she fulfils the entitlement conditions under the national legislation of the competent Member State[357] – to sickness benefits in kind in the Member State of residence,[358] meaning that the healthcare benefits are provided in the latter state. One may wonder, though, how it can be decided which one of the countries involved is considered the Member State of residence, since in certain cross-border cases it is not always obvious.

---

356 Nevertheless, if the competent Member State requires a certain length of qualifying period in order to ensure the right to sickness benefits in kind, the competent institution must take into account the qualifying periods completed in other Member States as well. Jorens et al., above n. 240, p. 22. See also van der Mei, above n. 187, p. 236.
However, this exact provision is no longer incorporated in the sickness chapter of the Regulation, as it was under Article 18 of Regulation 1408/71; 'it is now applicable through the general principles of aggregation of periods and assimilation of facts (Articles 6 and 7 of Regulation 883/2004), which fully apply to sickness benefits'. Y. Jorens, J.-P. Lhernould and S. Roberts, *Handbook on European Social Security Law*, http://www.sgk-kap.org/en/database/db/B2_C8_717.pdf, 2011 (accessed 05.12.2011), p. 267.

357 'The question as to whether the claimant has the right to benefits in kind is [...] always assessed on the basis of the legislation of the competent country, where he/she is insured.' Jorens et al., above n. 240, p. 24.

358 Article 17 Basic Regulation (BR).

1.1.1. *Determination of the Place of Residence*

When a person uses his/her right to free movement, potentially more than one Member State is involved. The legal collision can lead to either a positive[359] or a negative conflict[360] of laws, both of which are undesirable under European law. Conflicting rules have the potential to impede free movement, and therefore need to be avoided.[361] One of the main principles of the Coordination Regulations is that in every given situation only *a single legislation can be applied*, which means that there is always one, but strictly not more than one country whose legislation must be applied.[362] The Coordination Regulations define a set of rules which are designed to avoid the complications occurring when different legislations collide and to designate the applicable legislation.[363]

Under the Coordination Regulations, in each case the first thing that has to be defined is which country is competent for the social security benefits in question. The competent Member State is that in which a person is covered by the social security system, including the healthcare system and which is responsible for the financing of the sickness benefits, even if obtained in another Member State. The Basic Regulation (BR) provides that according to the *lex loci laboris* principle, the competent Member State is usually the Member State of pursuing working activity.[364] In the case of inactive persons, not carrying out a professional activity or working as civil servants, not receiving unemployment benefits or serving in the armed forces in one of the Member States, the legislation of the Member State of residence applies (*lex loci domicilii*).[365] When obtaining healthcare, it is of utmost importance to establish which country is the competent Member State and which country can be identified as the place of residence. However, this issue is sometimes far from simple.

The following definition is given in the Basic Regulation: residence is the place where a person *habitually resides*.[366] However, no other criterion was originally added,[367] so it was the Court of Justice of the European Union (CJEU)

---

359 It results in the application of the legislation of multiple Member States at a time and potentially leads to double taxation and overlapping of benefits.

360 The national laws involved mutually exclude each other, thus the person concerned is not covered by either legislation at the time, leading to the possibility to escape social security obligations, but also to lack of benefits.

361 Jorens et al., above n. 240, p. 17.

362 Article 11(1) BR.

363 Title II BR.

364 Article 11(3) (a) BR.

365 Article 11(3)(e) BR.

366 Article 1(j) BR.

367 On the concept of residence see M. Coucheir (ed.), M. Sakslin (ed.), S. Giubboni, D. Martinsen and H. Verschueren, *The relationship and interaction between the coordination Regulations and Directive 2004/38/EC*, trESS Network, Ghent 2008; and European Commission, *Practical guide on the applicable legislation in the European Union (EU), the European Economic Area (EEA) and Switzerland*, 2014, pp. 41–49.

that described the circumstances which shall be taken into account when determining the Member State of residence, in particular: the migrant person's family situation; the reasons which have led him/her to move; the length and continuity of the residence; the fact that he/she is in stable employment; and his/her intention as it appears from all the circumstances.[368] These criteria were then incorporated into the Implementing Regulation (IR), which now provides for a kind of two-limb test.

It stipulates that if the Member States involved cannot agree on the determination of the Member State of residence, they must establish *the centre of interests of the person* concerned, based on an overall assessment of all available information relating to relevant facts, especially the duration and continuity of presence on the territory of the Member States concerned[369] and the person's situation.[370] If this assessment does not result in an agreement, the person's intention, as it appears from such facts and circumstances, especially the reasons that led the person to move, shall be considered to be decisive for establishing that person's actual place of residence.[371] These elements of the residence-test are detailed below.

Concerning the *length of the stay* abroad, it should be emphasised that Union law does not make a distinction between *temporary stay and residence* according to their lengths. As the CJEU has said, all the circumstances have to be evaluated carefully on a case-by-case basis. So according to my understanding, a two years' stay may be considered a temporary stay if it is clear from the circumstances that the person intends to return to his/her Member State (for example a temporary labour contract, temporary accommodation abroad, family remaining in the Member State of origin), whereas a four-week long stay may be considered residence if the person intends to habitually reside in that Member State. In fact, the CJEU stated in its judgment in *Swaddling* that 'the length of residence in the Member State cannot be regarded as an intrinsic element of the concept of residence'.[372]

The CJEU's recent judgment reaffirmed this interpretation.[373] Mr I, an Irish resident who performed a professional activity in Ireland and the United Kingdom, was holidaying in Germany when he was admitted as an emergency patient to the university hospital in Düsseldorf. He was soon diagnosed with a rare, bilateral infarct to his brain stem, which resulted in severe quadriplegia and

368 C-76/76 *Silvana di Paolo v Office national de l'emploi* [ECLI:EU:C:1977:32] 17–21; C-102/91 *Doris Knoch v Bundesanstalt für Arbeit* [ECLI:EU:C:1992:303] 19–24; C-90/97 *Robin Swaddling v Adjudication Officer* [ECLI:EU:C:1999:96], 29 and C-255/13 *I v Health Service Executive* [ECLI:EU:C:2014:1291], 44–45. See also Lhernould et al., above n. 93, p. 11.

369 Article 11(1)(a) IR.

370 Article 11(1)(b) IR.

371 Article 11(2) IR.

372 C-90/97 *Swaddling*, 30.

373 C-255/13 *I v Health Service Executive* [ECLI:EU:C:2014:1291].

loss of motor function. Later he was found to have a genetic mutation affecting the composition of his blood and was diagnosed with cancer. Ever since he had been admitted to hospital, he remained gravely ill, wheelchair-bound and his health status required constant monitoring and treatment. As the Irish High Court pointed out, he was compelled to live in Germany due to his medical condition and the necessity of continuous treatment. During the legal proceedings, Mr I confirmed that he was willing to return to Ireland and was not attempting to integrate into German society. To illustrate the point, he stressed that he kept contact with his family living in Ireland, that he had not opened a bank account or did not own any properties in Germany and that he did not speak German. In its decision, the CJEU declared that the simple fact that such a person has remained in a Member State, even continuously over a long period, does not necessarily mean that he resides in that State within the meaning of Regulation 883/2004 and for the purpose of determining a person's habitual centre of interests, *all relevant factors must be taken into account*, among which no hierarchy exists. Consequently, although Mr I had lived in Germany for a long time (more than eleven years), this situation did not reflect a personal choice on his part. Hence, he must be regarded as staying in Germany, not residing there.[374]

With regard to *the person's situation*, a broad scale of various circumstances must be taken into account: the nature and the specific characteristics of any activity pursued, in particular the place where such activity is habitually pursued, the stability of the activity, and the duration of any work contract;

---

374 On this case, see M. Cousins, *Habitual residence: fact or (legal fiction)? Case C-255/13, I v. Health Service Executive*, https://works.bepress.com/mel_cousins/82/, 2014 (accessed 23.02.2017) and G. Berki, 'Az Európai Bíróság ítélete egy "egészségügyi menekült" ügyében: A tartózkodás és a lakóhely fogalmi dilemmája egészségügyi szolgáltatás külföldi igénybevétele esetén' (The CJEU's decision in the case of a 'healthcare refugee': the dilemmas of the place of stay and the place of residence in relation to obtaining healthcare abroad) *Jogesetek Magyarázata* (*Case Law Review*) 2015, vol 6 issue 4, pp. 55–61.
However, it is worth noting that different rules apply to residence situations of up to three months and to those of more than three months. The rules are included in Directive 2004/38/EC of the European Parliament and of the Council of 29 April 2004 on the right of citizens of the Union and their family members to move and reside freely within the territory of the Member States (hereinafter also referred to as the Residence Directive). OJ L 158 of 30 April 2004.
The different concepts of residence in Regulation 883/2004 and Directive 2004/38 create numerous implementation problems. The main difference between the views is that the Regulation refers to an EU-wide notion which was further clarified by the CJEU based on a factual situation, whereas in the Residence Directive no residence definition was included, which means that it can be interpreted extremely widely covering short-term residence periods as well. See Coucheir et al., above n. 367, p. 26; and European Commission, DG Employment, Social Affairs and Inclusion, *Explanatory notes on modernised social security coordination – Relationship between Regulation (EC) No 883/2004 and Directive No 2004/38/EC*, 2011, p. 4.
It is also remarkable that whereas Regulation 883/2004 distinguishes between *stay* [Article 1(k)] and *residence* [Article 1(j)], the Patient Mobility Directive lacks this distinction.

his/her family status and family ties; the exercise of any non-remunerated activity; in the case of students, the source of their income; his/her housing situation, in particular how permanent it is; and the Member State in which the person is deemed to reside for taxation purposes.

The *intention of the person* concerned must be assessed as it appears from all the circumstances, meaning that it must be supported by factual evidence. The mere declaration that a person considers or wants to have his/her residence in a specific place is not sufficient. The question of intention occurs when the institutions involved cannot establish the place of residence based on the assessment of the circumstances detailed earlier, thus the intention of the person acts as a 'tie breaker'.

This is not the only situation in which the Regulations order the national institutions to make a legal decision based on the intention of the person concerned – a similar logic is used when making a distinction between planned and unplanned care and the intention of the person concerned is the decisive factor.[375] Although it is true that in most situations the factual circumstances reveal more or less clearly what the person's intention might be, this is not always so, and when doubts arise it is highly complicated to investigate and prove a mental condition such as intention behind a certain action. Mr. I's case was a good illustration of this.

1.1.2. General Rules

It is important to note that the benefit is provided in the Member State of residence in accordance with the legal regulations of that country.[376] This rule might seem illogical considering that the costs of the treatment must be borne by the competent Member State.[377] However, from a practical point of view this is the only acceptable solution, since it is unrealistic to expect the healthcare provider to be familiar with the legislation of another Member State.[378] Nevertheless, as a result of the application of this rule, it is of no relevance

375 Strban et al, above n. 5, pp. 35–39.

376 Article 17 BR.

377 It is obvious that the medical treatment is provided at the expense of the competent Member State, since the health contributions must be paid in that country. van der Mei, above n. 187, p. 236. However, this provision also implies that the patient 'is entitled to a package of sickness benefits in kind in accordance with the legislation of a Member State to whose social security he or she does not contribute financially'. H. Verschueren, 'Financing Social Security and Regulation (EEC) 1408/71' *European Journal of Social Security* 2001, vol 3 issue 1, p. 14.

378 'It might therefore have been thought logical to require the institution of the place of residence to provide benefits in accordance with the legislation administered by the competent institution, which will after all have to meet the cost. Such a solution would not, however, be practical, since it would require an institution to apply the legislation of another Member State. That doubtless explains why the authors of the regulation decided

whether the required sickness benefits in kind are included in the insurance package of the competent Member State, because the legislation of the Member State of residence determines the available benefits and the rules of provision.[379] Thus, it may happen that the competent Member State is obliged to reimburse the cost of a treatment provided in another Member State; a medical cost which it would not cover if the treatment was provided on its own territory. Or, conversely, an insured person might not be entitled to a certain benefit in the Member State of residence, irrespective of the fact that he/she pays health contributions for that in the competent Member State.[380] However, this latter case should not cause a problem, since the insured persons have the right to benefits in kind in the competent Member State (where they are covered by the national healthcare scheme) as well when staying there.[381]

As the main rule, the Basic Regulation provides that the healthcare benefits must be given to the insured persons in the Member State of residence *as though they were insured under the said legislation.*[382] The *full integration*[383] of these persons into the healthcare system of the Member State of residence has several consequences. One concerning the applicable healthcare basket could be seen above. Looking at this from the obligations' side, however, it has to be noted that these persons are required to make the same forms of payment as the nationals of that state do.[384] The same rules apply to the insured person's family members[385] residing outside the competent Member State.

---

instead that benefits in kind should be provided by the institution of the place of residence in accordance with the provisions of the legislation administered by that institution as though the person concerned were insured with it. The obvious practical advantage of that solution is that the institution which provides benefits in kind does so in accordance with the only legislation that it can be expected to be familiar with, namely its own legislation.' Opinion of AG Jacobs in C-451/93 *Claudine Delavant v Allgemeine Ortskrankenkasse für das Saarland* [ECLI:EU:C:1995:176] 16.

379 Jorens et al., above n. 240, p. 25. See also Coucheir and Jorens, above n. 199, p. 19 and Pennings, above n. 183, p. 157.

380 Verschueren, above n. 377, p. 14 and van der Mei, above n. 187, p. 238.

381 Article 18(1) BR.

382 Article 17 BR.

383 This comes from the rule on equal treatment as well, since 'the persons to whom [the] Regulation applies shall enjoy the same benefits and be subject to the same obligations under the legislation of any Member State as the nationals thereof'. Article 4 BR.

384 See an example on drug provision Pennings, above n. 183, p. 157. Chapter 3. Financial affordability gives a deeper insight into financing medical treatments abroad.

385 The definition of family members under the coordination rules can be found in Article 1(i) BR, which is detailed further with regard to sickness benefits in kind in Article 1(i) (1)(ii) 'as any person defined or recognized as a member of the family or designated as a member of the household by the legislation of the Member State in which he/she resides'. So here again the Member State (MS) of residence's legislation applies. However, if under the national legislation of the MS of residence the concerned person's family members are not entitled to sickness benefits in kind, the legislation of the competent MS applies. C-451/93 *Claudine Delavant v Allgemeine Ortskrankenkasse für das Saarland* [ECLI:EU:C:1995:176] 19: '[...] when a worker resides with the members of his family in the

1.1.3. Special Rules on Frontier Workers

The Regulations do create a specific category of workers who most likely – but not necessarily – live close to frontiers, and special rules apply to them in relation to access to healthcare. Frontier workers[386] gained a unique position in this respect under the rules of the former coordination regulation, i.e. Regulation (EEC) No 1408/71. The specialty of their status was based on the frequent (at least weekly) return to the Member State of residence, while working outside of that Member State (the competent MS). It is argued that there is a strong link with the competent Member State and with the Member State of residence at the same time.[387] Therefore, these persons had the unconditional *freedom of choice* where they intended to obtain healthcare benefits in kind: they could receive them in the Member State of residence, or in the competent Member State while staying there.[388]

Regulation 883/2004 provides the right to *double access* to *each insured person* and his/her family members residing outside the competent Member State,[389] erasing frontier workers' special status in this respect. At the same time,

---

territory of a Member State other than the Member State in which he works, under whose legislation he is insured by virtue of the regulation, the conditions for entitlement to sickness benefits in kind for members of that person's family are also governed by the legislation of the State in which that person works in so far as the members of his family are not entitled to those benefits under the legislation of their State of residence.' See also Jorens, above n. 231, p. 88. The different family concepts of the Member States are especially relevant, for example, when determining the social security status of non-married partners, same sex couples and children during the adoption procedure.

386 Article 1(f) BR defines frontier workers as follows: 'any person pursuing an activity as an employed or self-employed person in a Member State and who resides in another Member State to which he/she returns as a rule daily or at least once a week'. It is legally irrelevant whether the Member State of residence and the Member State of the working activity are neighbouring countries. Therefore, Calnan's definition, which says that 'frontier workers [...] are those who live on the frontiers of two countries and live in one country but work in another', is lacking the condition of frequent return on the one hand and excludes those frontier workers who commute between non-neighbouring countries, on the other. Calnan et al., above n. 12, p. 26.

387 Frontier workers have enjoyed a privileged position concerning social security coordination: specific – mostly more beneficial – rules apply to them not only for sickness benefits but, for example, for unemployment benefits as well (Article 65a BR).
However, in certain situations these special rules might prove to be less favourable, as demonstrated in relation to unemployment benefits for wholly unemployed frontier workers by the judgment of the Court in C-443/11 *F.P. Jeltes, M.A. Peeters, J.G.J. Arnold v Raad van bestuur van het Uitvoeringsinstituut werknemersverzekeringen* [ECLI:EU:C:2013:224].

388 In this case, the 'benefits in kind shall be provided by the competent institution and at its own expense, in accordance with the provisions of the legislation it applies, as though the persons concerned resided in that Member State'. Article 20 of Regulation 1408/71.
Workers residing outside of the competent Member State and their family members also had this right under Article 21 of Regulation 1408/71 while staying in the competent Member State.

389 Article 18(1) BR.

the new Coordination Regulations replaced numerous bilateral agreements that existed between the Member States ensuring the freedom of choice for the family members of frontier workers.[390] However, some Member States restrict this right of frontier workers' family members and apply the same rules to them as they do to temporary visitors.[391] Consequently, when Denmark, Ireland, Croatia, Finland, Sweden or the United Kingdom[392] is the competent Member State, the family members of frontier workers are entitled only to sickness benefits in kind necessary on medical grounds while staying on the territory of this country.[393] In my opinion, the reasoning behind these exceptional rules is questionable.[394] According to the current legislation, the category of frontier workers represents a special group of migrant workers, who – thanks to their 'unique situation' – are provided with special coordination rules.[395] However, if the Member States apply the same rules on migrant workers and their family members, I see no legally justifiable reason not to apply the same rules to frontier workers and their family members. In this regard, I share Pennings's opinion that it would be preferable to remove these rules.[396]

Another debated issue in the course of drafting the new Coordination Regulations was whether the right to choose should be maintained when the former frontier worker retires. This was not the case under the former regulation: the freedom to choose the country of healthcare provision ended as

---

390 Such agreements existed, for example, between Belgium and France, Belgium and Luxembourg and Luxembourg and Germany. See Jorens et al., above n. 240, p. 30.

391 Article 18(2) BR.

392 Listed in Annex III BR; the restriction is not limited in time, but is to be reviewed no later than 31 October 2014. Article 87(10b) BR.
Estonia, Spain, Italy, Lithuania, Hungary and the Netherlands were also listed in Annex III BR; but the restriction concerning these MSs was applicable only until 30 April 2014, the end of the transitional period. Article 87(10a) BR.
In the trESS European Report a specific problem was noted concerning the family members of frontier workers who work in the Netherlands. Until 1 May 2014, they were entitled to claim only necessary care during a temporary stay in the Netherlands. However, this did not create problems in practice, since '(o)n the basis of bilateral agreements with the neighbouring countries, family members of frontier workers are entitled to claim benefits in kind in the Netherlands on the condition that they have an MVG 111 form, which can be obtained from a particular insurance company. […] In practice, this may complicate the position of frontier workers since they may have to deal with four institutions.' Y. Jorens and J.-P. Lhernould, *European Report 2013*. trESS Network, Ghent 2013, p. 28.
Nevertheless, this difficulty has been solved since 1 May 2014.

393 Pennings states that this rule was the result of a political compromise made by the drafters of the Regulation 883/2004, since a certain number of Member States were reluctant to allow choosing for the family members in fear of extra costs. Pennings, above n. 183, p. 158.

394 I find this reasoning improper to justify such a limitation of the freedom of the family members to choose where they wish to obtain medical treatment. Irrespective of whether the healthcare is provided for the family members in the MS of residence or the MS of working activity, it is the competent MS which must bear the costs. So one may wonder how much extra cost it would cause if this restriction were abolished.

395 See n. 387 above.

396 Pennings above n. 183, p. 158.

soon as the frontier worker stopped pursuing his/her former working activity.[397] Nevertheless, this rule could result in a treatment that began in the competent Member State being discontinued, because the retired frontier worker became subject to the healthcare scheme of the Member State of residence. To overcome this problem, Regulation 883/2004 introduced a new rule according to which:

> a frontier worker who has retired because of old-age or invalidity is entitled in the event of sickness to continue to receive benefits in kind in the Member State where he/she last pursued his/her activity as an employed or self-employed person, in so far as this is a continuation of treatment[398] which began in that Member State.[399]

More advantageous rules were adopted with regard to pensioners who 'in the five years preceding the effective date of an old-age or invalidity pension have been pursuing an activity as an employed or self-employed person for at least two years as a frontier worker'.[400] Their healthcare protection was greatly strengthened by providing them with the right to entitlement to sickness benefits in kind in the Member State of the former working activity, provided that one condition is met: both the Member State of the former working activity and the Member State of residence opted for this.[401]

The question is rightfully raised why *the right to continuity of treatment* is only provided to frontier workers and not extended to any migrant person. It can be argued that it might be unfavourable to anyone to have to suspend an ongoing medical treatment due to a shift between national healthcare regimes. The very existence of the social security coordination mechanism is based on the idea that migrant persons should not suffer from social disadvantages because they used their right to free movement.[402] In my opinion, it would serve the interest of European patients very well to grant the right to continuity of treatment to everyone[403] who falls under the scope of the Coordination Regulations.

---

397 Between certain Member States agreements were conducted to prolong this right of the frontier workers even after they were retired. See the example of Belgium and Luxembourg in Jorens et al., above n. 240, p. 29.

398 Continuation of treatment includes: continued investigation, diagnosis and treatment of an illness for its entire duration. Article 28(1) BR.

399 Article 28(1) BR. The same rule applies to the family members of the retired frontier worker unless the competent MS is listed in Annex III of the Regulation.

400 Article 28(2) BR.

401 Member States listed in Annex V of the Regulation are Belgium, Germany, Spain, France, Luxembourg, Austria and Portugal. If both MSs are one of these countries, the freedom to choose remains even after retirement.

402 This is the core of the so-called *Petroni principle*, worked out by the CJEU in a case related to the payment of pensions to employed persons and the successors of a migrant worker. C-24/75 *Teresa et Silvana Petroni v Office national des pensions pour travailleurs salaries* [ECLI:EU:C:1975:129], 13.

403 The Patient Mobility Directive takes a small, but remarkable step in this regard, namely as part of the responsibility of the Member State of treatment it stipulates that 'in order to

Although one of the main aims of the new generation of Coordination Regulations was to simplify the legislation,[404] it maintained and even developed the rules applicable to frontier workers and their family members. However, the question may be raised whether these rules are still justified, whether maintaining the category of frontier workers is still desirable. Does the requirement of weekly return establish a link that is stronger compared to migrant workers who do not meet this requirement? For instance, does a migrant worker who frequently spends four weeks in the competent Member State and then two consecutive weeks in the Member State of residence have a less strong link on the grounds that he/she does not meet the requirement of weekly return compared to a frontier worker who spends one and a half days in the Member State of residence each weekend? And in a borderless Europe, how can the fulfilment of the weekly-return requirement be verified? In my opinion, this categorisation is rather vague and hardly justifiable. It would thus be worth considering whether the category of frontier workers is still needed within the coordination of social security schemes as an exception to the general rules applicable to insured persons.

1.1.4. *Special Rules on Pensioners*

In addition to the special rules applicable to frontier workers and their family members, special rules also apply to pensioners and their family members residing outside the competent Member State.[405] If the pensioner receives his/her pension from only one Member State and he/she resides in this state, he/she is obviously entitled to sickness benefits in kind in this country – if he/she fulfils the conditions of entitlement under the national legislation.

ensure continuity of care, patients who have received treatment are entitled to a written or electronic medical record of such treatment, and access to at least a copy of this record'. Article 4(2)(f) Patient Mobility Directive (PMD). This provision imposes the obligation on the healthcare practitioners to provide patients with data which might be essential for their further treatment, and is thus a relevant addition to cross-border patients' rights.

404 See section 3.7. in Chapter 1. Setting the scene.

405 An interesting aspect of healthcare entitlements for pensioners residing in a MS other than the competent MS was highlighted by the CJEU's ruling in the *van Delft* case. C-345/09 *J. A. van Delft and Others v College voor zorgverzekeringen* [ECLI:EU:C:2010:610].
The appellants in the main proceedings were Dutch nationals, receiving statutory pensions from the Netherlands while residing in other Member States. Due to a change to national legislation, the Dutch competent institution started to deduct from the pensions paid to the appellants the contributions for benefiting from the compulsory statutory sickness insurance scheme. The appellants contested the decision of the competent institution and argued that in accordance with the Coordination Regulation they must be provided with the opportunity to choose whether they wish to receive benefits in kind in the MS of residence or to conclude an insurance contract privately (as they did before the change to the Dutch legislation). In the latter case the Netherlands does not have the right to deduct the contributions since it does not bear the costs of healthcare. In this case, the CJEU interpreted the Coordination Regulations as not precluding such a national legislation.

However, if the old-age, invalidity or survivors' benefits come from more than one Member State, the situation is slightly more complicated. If one of the pension paying Member States is the Member State of residence, the pensioner and his/her family members are entitled to sickness benefits in kind in this country as though the pension was payable solely under the legislation of that Member State.[406] Consequently, the entire medical cost is borne by the Member State of residence. This provision has been subject to intense discussion for about a decade, since it

> does not guarantee a sufficiently fair distribution of the burden of benefits between the States liable to pay pensions, as it is sufficient for the State of residence to be liable to pay a small pension for the entire burden to fall upon it, even though the person concerned may have been active almost entirely in another State and be entitled to a commensurate pension from that State.[407]

Roberts and his colleagues share a French proposal in this respect, the point of which is the distribution of the financial burden among the pension-paying Member States in proportion to the periods completed in each of the Member States involved. This would certainly increase the fairness and prevent some of the current disproportions.[408] Nevertheless, this rule remained unchanged[409] so far and it seems that the European Commission has just missed another legislative opportunity to revise this article.[410]

If the pensioner receives his/her pension from more than one Member State, but the Member State of residence is not one of them, the pensioner and his/her family members have the right to obtain healthcare benefits in the Member State of residence 'in so far as he/she would be entitled thereto under the legislation of the Member State[411] or of at least one of the Member States[412] competent in respect of his/her pensions'.

---

406 Article 23 BR.

407 Roberts et al., above n. 97, p. 4.

408 See the statistical data from Luxembourg, Austria and Switzerland. De Wispelaere and Pacolet, above n. 9, p. 34.

409 Different scenarios were discussed, such as deleting the Regulation articles concerned; distributing the healthcare costs based on the ratio of insurance periods; and apportioning responsibility in line with the longest insurance history. Each of them was refused either because they would reduce mobile pensioners' healthcare rights or because they 'would introduce greater administrative complexity which might, at least partly, reduce the gains of a fairer distribution of costs'. Roberts et al., above n. 97, pp. 26–27.

410 No suggestions concerning this provision was included into the Commission's recent *Proposal for a Regulation of the European Parliament and of the Council amending Regulation (EC) No 883/2004 on the coordination of social security systems and regulation (EC) No 987/2009 laying down the procedure for implementing Regulation (EC) No 883/2004*. COM (2016) 815 final, 13.12.2016.

411 The medical cost has to be borne by this MS. Article 24(2)(a) BR.

412 The medical cost has to be borne by the MS to whose legislation the person concerned has been subject for the longest period of time. Article 24(2)(b) BR.

It must be added, however, that if the Member State of residence and the competent Member State which allocates the pension differ from each other (e.g. the pensioner worked and thus receives his/her entire pension from one Member State, but resides in another), the competent Member State (the one paying the pension benefit) is free to opt for ensuring the pensioner the sickness benefits in kind while staying on its territory.[413] The different entitlements of the different groups under the Regulation are summarised in Table 5 below.

Table 5. Entitlement to sickness benefits in kind for people residing outside the competent MS

Persons residing outside the competent MS	in the MS of residence	in the competent MS	
1) Insured persons	entitled to healthcare benefits in kind	entitled to healthcare benefits in kind	*Double access: unconditional freedom of choice*
2) Family members of insured persons	entitled to healthcare benefits in kind	entitled to healthcare benefits in kind	
3) Frontier workers	entitled to healthcare benefits in kind	entitled to healthcare benefits in kind	
4) Family members of frontier workers	entitled to healthcare benefits in kind	in certain Member States entitlement is limited to *necessary care*	MSs listed in Annex III BR
5) Retired frontier workers	entitled to healthcare benefits in kind	entitled to *continuation of treatment*	
6) Family members of retired frontier workers	entitled to healthcare benefits in kind	entitled to *continuation of treatment*, unless the MS of last activity listed in Annex III BR	
7) Pensioners	entitled to healthcare benefits in kind	entitled to healthcare benefits in kind if MS listed in Annex IV BR. If MS is not listed in Annex IV, entitlement is limited to necessary care.	determination of competent MS is based on which MS is responsible for paying the pension or pensions
8) Family members of pensioners	entitled to healthcare benefits in kind	entitled to healthcare benefits in kind if MS listed in Annex IV BR. If MS is not listed in Annex IV, entitlement is limited to necessary care.	

Source: The author's own summary.

413 Article 27(2) BR. The Member States ensuring this additional right are listed in Annex IV BR: Belgium, Bulgaria, the Czech Republic, Germany, Greece, Spain, France, Cyprus, Luxembourg, Hungary, the Netherlands, Austria, Poland, Slovenia and Sweden.

Lately, the UK's Brexit-decision[414] has revived interest in access to healthcare for pensioners.[415] Notably, an estimated 1.2 million British citizens live in another EU country,[416] a considerable share of them pensioners, who decided to move abroad, for example to a more attractive climate in Spain or France, after retirement.[417] According to administrative data based on the number of so-called PD S1,[418] at least 125,000 British pensioners live in the EU outside of the UK, along with another 20,000 family members. In line with the Coordination Regulations' full integration model,[419] Britons are treated in the exact same fashion as the nationals of the Member States they live in.[420] However, if they do not receive a pension from the Member State of residence, the costs of medical treatments must be reimbursed by the competent Member State.[421]

For instance, most of the British pensioners living in Spain have never worked there, but draw a pension solely from the UK, thus – although they reside abroad – the UK remains competent for covering the costs of healthcare.[422] The coordination mechanism does not only guarantee access to local healthcare facilities and equal treatment for elderly British patients, but also clarifies the financial settlements between the countries involved. At this stage of the negotiations, it is extremely hard to predict what these pensioners can expect after the UK leaves the EU, but it can be confidently stated without the coordination mechanism, their position might be significantly more complicated.

---

414 On a referendum held on 23 June 2016, the United Kingdom voted in favour of leaving the European Union.

415 Among others, the issue came up in the recent sessions of the Health Committee in the House of Commons in January and February 2017. See http://data.parliament.uk/writtenevidence/committeeevidence.svc/evidencedocument/health-committee/brexit-and-health-and-social-care/oral/46148.html and http://data.parliament.uk/writtenevidence/committeeevidence.svc/evidencedocument/health-committee/brexit-and-health-and-social-care/oral/47484.pdf (accessed 27.02.2017).

416 O. Hawkins, *Migration Statistics*, Briefing Paper, Number SN06077, House of Commons Library, London 2017, p. 26.

417 Administrative data shows that in 2015, about 58,000 UK pensioners holding a PD S1 were residing in Spain. J. Pacolet and F. De Wispelaere, *The entitlement to and use of sickness benefits by persons residing in a Member State other than the competent Member State*, FMSSFE, Leuven 2016, pp. 21–22.

Other sources indicate much higher numbers (the reason of the difference might be that they do not refer only to the number of pensioners, but the whole British population living in Spain), like an article which cited the Spanish foreign minister saying that about 800,000 Brits live in his country. 'Spain: Brexit Britain must pay for expats' healthcare' *The Local*, 04.10.2016, http://www.thelocal.es/20161004/spain-britain-pay-expat-healthcare-brexit, (accessed 27.02.2017).

418 See section 1.3. below.

419 See n. 383 above.

420 Article 24(1) BR.

421 Article 24(2) BR.

422 The article of The Local (above n. 417) estimates the cost 223 million English pounds in 2014–2015.

In my opinion, if the UK does not agree with the EU to continue to apply the Coordination Regulations, the EU countries will no longer be bound by EU legislation and thus will not be required to treat Britons equally with their own nationals. The UK could prevent such complications by negotiating new bilateral agreements.[423]

1.2. THE DIRECTIVE'S ROUTE

The Patient Mobility Directive does not, however, apply to situations in which a patient residing outside of the competent State receives healthcare in the Member State of residence. The Patient Mobility Directive is applicable to cross-border healthcare, which – by definition – involves healthcare provision in a Member State other than the Member State of affiliation.[424] According to the wording of the Directive, the Member State of affiliation is 'the Member State competent to grant to the insured person a prior authorisation to receive appropriate treatment outside the Member State of residence'.[425] Since in this case, no treatment is obtained outside the Member State of residence, the Commission argues that under the Directive's rules, 'such a scenario is considered as lacking a cross-border element' and therefore falls outside of the scope of the Patient Mobility Directive.[426]

However, if the healthcare is obtained in the competent Member State instead of the Member State of residence, the Directive might be applicable. In order to apply the Directive's rules, two conditions must concurrently be met in addition to the fact that the healthcare is provided in the competent Member State, namely the treatment is not subject to prior authorisation under the Directive's regime and the treatment is provided in accordance with the Directive instead of in accordance with the sickness benefit chapter of the Coordination Regulation. Among these circumstances, the Directive stipulates that the medical costs have to be assumed by the competent Member State.[427]

---

423 See also H. McKenna, 'Five big issues for health and social care after the Brexit vote', https://www.kingsfund.org.uk/publications/articles/brexit-and-nhs, 2016 (accessed 27.02.2017)

424 Article 3(e) PMD.

425 Article 3(c)(i) PMD.

426 AC 246/12, above n. 264, p. 19.
In 2013, an appendix was added summarising the answers to the most significant questions that arose in relation to the Guidance note. Administrative Commission for the Coordination of Social Security Services, *Appendix to the interpretative note of the Commission on the relationship between Regulations (EC) Nos 883/2004 and 987/2009 on the coordination of social security systems and Directive 2011/24/EU on the application of patients' rights in cross-border healthcare*, AC 270/13, 28 May 2013.

427 Article 7(2)(b) PMD.

As to the first condition, whether or not the treatment in question is subject to prior authorisation, the Member States have the freedom to determine within the limits of the Directive[428] which elements of their national benefit baskets require a prior authorisation for the cross-border healthcare costs to be reimbursed.

The fulfilment of the second condition, however, is related to the patient, who cannot or does not want to use the coordination route and opts for the Directive's route instead. The persons who do not have full entitlement to healthcare in the competent Member State can benefit from the Directive to gain access to the healthcare which they are not entitled to under the Regulations.[429] These persons are the family members of frontier workers if the competent Member State is listed in Annex III of the Basic Regulation[430] and pensioners and their family members if the competent Member State is not listed in Annex IV of the Basic Regulation.[431] However, also other persons who have full entitlement in the competent Member State can voluntarily decide to get reimbursed in accordance with the Directive, if they wish to receive healthcare under circumstances which would exclude the healthcare provision from the scope of the Regulation, for instance at a non-contracted healthcare provider. The scenarios examined in this section are summarised in Table 6 below.

Table 6. Access to healthcare when residing outside the competent MS

MS of treatm. / MS of res.	MS of residence	competent MS
competent MS	When a person **resides** in the competent MS and **is treated** in that MS: *the national legislation of the competent MS* applies	
MS other than the competent MS	When a person **resides** in a MS other than the competent MS and **is treated** in the **MS of residence**: *Coordination Regulations* apply (Art. 17 BR): the person concerned is – as a principle – entitled to healthcare in the MS of residence as though he/she were *insured* in that state. *Patient Mobility Directive* does not apply (cross-border element is lacking).	When a person **resides** in a MS other than the competent MS and **is treated** in the **competent MS**: *Coordination Regulations* apply (Art. 18 (1) BR): the person concerned is – as a principle – entitled to healthcare in the competent MS as though he/she *resided* in that state. *Patient Mobility Directive* might apply (Art. 7(2)(b) PMD): the costs must be assumed by the competent MS.

Source: The author's own summary.

428 Article 8 PMD.
429 AC 246/12, above n. 264, p. 23.
430 Article 18(2) BR and Article 7(2)(b) PMD. See n. 392.
431 Article 27(2) BR and Article 7(2(a) PMD. See n. 413.

1.3. ADMINISTRATIVE FORMALITIES WHEN ACCESSING HEALTHCARE IN THE COMPETENT MEMBER STATE AND RESIDING OUTSIDE OF THAT MEMBER STATE

People residing outside the competent Member State need to meet certain administrative requirements to obtain their benefits in good order in the Member State of residence. First, the insured person and his/her family members have to register themselves at the institution of the place of residence.[432] Second, they have to provide proof of insurance under the sickness scheme of the competent Member State. For this purpose, an *S1 form*[433] has to be requested from the competent institution.[434] This document states that the person concerned fulfils the conditions for entitlement to healthcare benefits in kind in accordance with the competent Member State's national legislation. In the framework of their obligation to cooperate, both the competent institution and the institution of the place of residence have to inform the other one in the event of registration, change or cancellation of registration.[435]

If insured persons or their family members wish to obtain medical treatments in the competent Member State, they are free to do so under the same conditions as the persons residing there. However, if family members of frontier workers[436] or pensioners and their family members[437] whose access to healthcare in the competent Member State is restricted intend to obtain planned healthcare in the competent Member State, they are required – under the Coordination Regulations – to request a prior authorisation.[438]

In 2015, '(a)pproximately 1.4 million persons reside in a Member State other than the competent Member State, and are registered for healthcare in their Member State of residence by means of a PD S1. This implies that on average 0.3% of insured persons reside in a Member State other than the competent Member State.'[439] Luxembourg is the absolute leader of this list with one-fifth (22.5 per cent) of its insured population living in another Member State. Furthermore, Belgium, Austria, the Netherlands and Liechtenstein are over

---

432 Article 24(1) IR.

433 The S1 form is a portable document (PD) under the new coordination regime replacing the former E 106 form.

434 Article 24(1) IR.

435 Article 24(2) IR.

436 On the rules of access to healthcare for family members of frontier workers see section 1.1.3. of this chapter.

437 On the rules of access to healthcare for pensioners and their family members see section 1.1.4. of this chapter.

438 The rules on the prior authorisation procedure for planned care when residing outside the competent MS are discussed in section 3. of this chapter.

439 De Wispelaere and Pacolet, above n. 9, p. 32. See also J. Pacolet and F. De Wispelaere, above n. 417, p. 12.

the one per cent threshold, whereas all the other countries reported less than one per cent of their insured persons holding a PD S1.[440]

Several Member States apply an alternative procedure instead of exchanging S1 forms. For instance, the cooperation of the Nordic countries (Denmark, Finland, Sweden, Norway and Iceland) does not involve exchange of such documents. Similarly, the reimbursement of medical costs is based on bilateral agreements between Ireland and the UK, the UK and Malta, France and Belgium, Belgium and Luxemburg.[441]

So far, the situation was observed in which the Member State of residence and the competent Member State differ from each other and in which the required healthcare benefit was provided in one of these states. In the next sections, those cases are dealt with in which the healthcare is provided in a third state other than the Member State of residence or the competent Member State. In this sense, *necessary or unplanned* and *planned or scheduled* care should be distinguished from each other.

2. ACCESS TO NECESSARY HEALTHCARE DURING A TEMPORARY STAY OUTSIDE OF THE MEMBER STATE OF RESIDENCE

People can have plenty of reasons to take a temporary visit abroad: for instance, going on holiday, visiting friends or family members, going on a business trip, studying abroad, participating in training or a conference or taking up short-term employment. The obvious interest of the person who becomes in need of healthcare during a temporary stay is to obtain the necessary treatment as quickly as possible; therefore the European Union's continuing intention is to guarantee the entitlement to benefits in kind for temporary visitors in the Member State where they are staying at the given moment.

2.1. THE COORDINATION REGULATIONS' ROUTE

Under the social security coordination rules two categories of temporary stay must be clearly distinguished. The first category is the temporary stay which is based on any other reason than obtaining healthcare in another Member State, meaning that the reason of the stay is legally irrelevant. The only requirement

---

440 'On average 0.3% of the insured persons reside in a Member State other than the competent Member State.' J. Pacolet and F. De Wispelaere, above n. 417, pp. 14–15. See also De Wispelaere and Pacolet, above n. 9, pp. 32–33.

441 J. Pacolet and F. De Wispelaere, above n. 417, p. 11.

is that *the temporary visitor becomes in need of healthcare while abroad*. The second category is the temporary stay which is based on the patient's (expressed) intention *to obtain healthcare after crossing the border(s)*. So once again, the decisive criterion is the intention of the person concerned, although, as already noted, in certain cases it is far from simple to determine.[442] Since different rules apply to these two cases, they are observed separately. First, after a brief analysis of their discrepancy, the temporary visitors' necessary healthcare is scrutinised further in this section, while the rules on planned healthcare, which is considered as the narrow concept of patient mobility,[443] will then be detailed.[444]

2.1.1. Distinction between Unplanned and Planned Care

The Regulation has traditionally applied this distinction since the beginning of the 1970s, when the rules on planned healthcare were introduced.[445] To date, different rules apply to these two scenarios, while the decisive criterion between unplanned and planned healthcare is the (initial) intention of the patient. Unlike in case of unplanned or occasional care, where the need for healthcare cannot be foreseen and it manifests itself unexpectedly during a temporary stay abroad, healthcare is considered as planned or scheduled when a patient travels to another Member State with the intention to receive medical treatment there. Nevertheless, the intention of the patient is not always as explicit as not to raise the question how it can be investigated among real life circumstances.

The CJEU faced this dilemma in the case of a chronically ill patient who travelled to Germany to visit his son. During his temporary stay in Germany, he was admitted to a clinic in Munich for cardiovascular disease. His health insurance fund refused to reimburse his medical costs on the grounds that his hospital treatment in Germany had been planned. The CJEU ruled that when a person with a pre-existing pathology travels abroad, it cannot be automatically presumed that s/he intends to obtain medical treatment in that Member State.[446]

However, it can happen that a chronically ill patient or a pregnant woman who prefers to give birth abroad tries to make his or her medical travel look like a holiday – during which medical necessity occurred – and the authorities do not have many tools to prove otherwise. Austrian authorities also reported on

442 See section 1.1.1. above in this chapter.
443 On the definitions, see section 2.3. in Chapter 1. Setting the scene.
444 See section 3. below in this chapter.
445 See section 3.7. in Chapter 1. Setting the scene, especially n. 268.
446 C-326/00 *Idryma Koinonikon Asfaliseon (IKA) v Vasileios Ioannidis* [ECLI:EU:C:2003:101].

a problematic case of distinction between unplanned and planned healthcare which concerned an Austrian national who wanted to undergo a sex-change operation in Germany. The planned treatment was not authorised, but the patient obtained the desired healthcare anyway. However, after the operation, due to post-operative complications, further surgery was needed and he had to stay in the German hospital for another week. The patient argued that the latter operation was not planned and occurred as a necessary treatment, so he claimed for reimbursement of the related costs. The request for reimbursement was turned down and the Austrian authorities confirmed that '(w)hat is essential for the distinction between "planned" and "occasional" healthcare is the purpose of the stay abroad which led to healthcare'.[447] Thus, the question is not only how the intention of the patient can be investigated and proved when uncertain, but also at which moment in time the intention is decisive: is the question settled already in the moment of travel as can be seen in the Austrian argumentation based on the 'purpose of the stay', or may the intention of the patient change over time?

This latter issue can be demonstrated in cases where the patient receives treatments of different kinds. For example, if an insured person suffers an accident and breaks his or her leg and subsequently is operated on, the situation is rather clear. However, if – at the same time – his or her kidney stones are removed (and no prior kidney pain could be demonstrated, as a result of which necessity would be clearly present), the competent institution might question whether this service consumption was still unplanned. If we apply the Austrian authorities' interpretation, we might come to the conclusion that at the moment of the journey abroad, none of the medical interventions were planned, but it might happen that the patient who had to undergo surgery anyway, decided to fix another health problem at the same time.

It can be argued that this approach, namely applying a distinction between unplanned and planned healthcare, seeks to balance between the migrant person's right to access to healthcare and the competent Member State's interest in controlling resources. While in case of unplanned care the possible occurrence of healthcare provision, and thus the financing obligation of the competent Member State, is adventitious, in case of planned care the healthcare provision is the reason and the goal of the journey, and thus almost certainly evokes the financing obligation of the competent Member State. This logically explains why different administrative procedures are in place and unplanned care can be received simply by presenting an EHIC, whereas obtaining planned care under the Regulation's regime requires a prior authorisation from the competent institution in the form of a PD S2.

[447] Jorens and Lhernould, above n. 392, pp. 29–30.

2.1.2. *General Rules*

In principle, the insured persons and their family members who stay in a Member State other than the competent Member State are entitled to sickness benefits in kind which become necessary on medical grounds during their temporary stay in the Member State of stay.[448]

The same logic can be seen here as for persons residing outside the competent Member State,[449] namely the healthcare is provided by the Member State where the patient can be found at the moment of the need for healthcare, in this case the Member State of temporary stay; the healthcare is provided on behalf of the competent state, meaning that this state determines the conditions of entitlement and bears the medical costs; and the patient is *fully integrated* into the healthcare scheme of the Member State providing the treatment, meaning that the healthcare is provided in accordance with the legislation of that country and that the patient must be treated equally with patients insured in that country as though he/she was insured there as well.[450]

Currently, access to necessary healthcare benefits abroad is open to all who are entitled to these benefits in the competent Member State, although this was not always so. Before Regulation (EC) No 631/2004[451] entered into force on 1 July 2004 different levels of benefit coverage had been guaranteed to certain groups of people falling under the personal scope of Regulation 1408/71. The former legislation provided a highly limited circle of benefits for the employed and self-employed by saying that benefits abroad are available only for those 'whose condition necessitates immediate benefits during a stay in the territory of another Member State'.[452] The necessity of immediate care referred to a situation in which the provision of the appropriate treatment 'cannot be postponed without endangering the life or health of the person concerned'.[453] Healthcare

448 Article 19(1) BR. This article must apply *mutatis mutandis* to the pensioners and the members of their family as well. Article 27(1) BR.

449 See section 1. above in this chapter.

450 Article 19(1) BR. See also Jorens et al., above n. 240, p. 34.

451 Regulation (EC) No 631/2004 of the European Parliament and of the Council of 31 March 2004 amending Council Regulation (EEC) No 1408/71 on the application of social security schemes to employed persons, to self-employed persons and to members of their families moving within the Community, and Council Regulation (EEC) No 574/72 laying down the procedure for implementing Regulation (EEC) No 1408/71, in respect of the alignment of rights and the simplification of procedures. OJ L 100 of 6 April 2004.

452 Article 22(1)(a) of Regulation 1408/71 before 1 July 2004.

453 Decision No 135 of the Administrative Commission of 1 July 1987 concerning the granting of benefits in kind provided for in Article 17(7) and Article 60(6) of Regulation (EEC) No 574/72 and the concepts of urgency within the meaning of Article 20 of Regulation (EEC) No 1408/71 and of extreme urgency within the meaning of Articles 17(7) and 60(6) of Regulation (EEC) No 574/72. OJ C 281 of 4 November 1988, 4.

in conjunction with pregnancy and childbirth provided before the beginning of the 38th week of pregnancy was also regarded as immediately necessary care.[454]

At the same time, a more favourable scheme applied, for example, to pensioners and their family members, jobseekers and students who 'had a right to any benefits in kind which appeared necessary'[455] irrespective of the fulfilment of the urgency condition. When the European Council opted for the introduction of the European Health Insurance Card in 2002,[456] the stakeholders were unified in the opinion that certain changes were necessary to the rules on the coordination of healthcare benefits in kind. They agreed that:

> for greater protection for insured persons, provision should be made to bring into line the rights of all insured persons in respect of access to benefits in kind during a temporary stay in a Member State other than the State in which the person concerned is insured or resident.[457]

The amending regulation ended the above-mentioned difference by equalising the claim to healthcare and guaranteeing equal access to necessary care during a temporary stay.[458]

Nevertheless, defining the category of necessary care is still considered somewhat problematic in practice: the person holding the authority of deciding about the necessity of the healthcare on the one hand and the material scope of necessary care on the other have been subject to discussions.

2.1.3. The Scope of Necessary Care

A first question that arises is whose task it is to decide which benefits fall under the scope of necessary care. It should be pointed out that the necessity of the healthcare provision is evaluated on a case-by-case basis by the healthcare provider and that this must be determined in the light of 'the nature of the benefits and the expected length of the stay'.[459] The healthcare practitioner, who is – usually – in the physical proximity[460] of the patient, is in the optimal

454 Paragraph 1 of the Preamble of Decision No 195 of the Administrative Commission of 23 March 2004 on the uniform application of Article 22(1)(a)(i) of Council Regulation (EEC) No 1408/71 as regards healthcare in conjunction with pregnancy and childbirth. OJ L 160 of 30 April 2004.

455 Jorens et al., above n. 240, p. 34.

456 European Council, *Presidency Conclusions*, Barcelona, 15–16 March 2002, 34.

457 Paragraph 3 of the Preamble of Regulation 631/2004.

458 Article 1(1)(a) of Regulation 631/2004.

459 Article 19(1) BR.

460 The traditional doctor-patient relationship requires personal, face-to-face contact, although the application of ICT technologies may change – or at least influence – this in the future by a broad introduction of remote care delivery through telemedicine. 'Telemedicine involves the use of telecommunications and computer technology in the delivery of health

position to examine the person concerned, to estimate his/her health status and needs, and to decide whether the treatment is necessary. Therefore, the physician is in charge of taking the decision whether or not to provide the treatment as *necessary on medical grounds*. In accordance with the Regulation, this patient-specific assessment must be based on two concrete criteria: the medical status of the patient and the planned duration of his/her stay in the territory of the Member State concerned.[461] It is indeed a good solution to leave this decision to the healthcare professional who is able to provide the necessary treatment on the spot, but at the same time, it requires that each healthcare professional all over the European Union is aware of these rules. Whether this is the case, is questionable.

In my opinion, each Member State has the obligation – in order to abide by the Regulations – to train its healthcare professionals in this regard and to ensure that healthcare professionals practising in its territory are able and willing to provide foreign patients with healthcare in accordance with the EU legislation. The same goes, for instance, for the dissemination of information related to the proper application of the EHIC, in the course of which the providers also play a key role.[462] The Implementing Regulation confirms this opinion by stipulating that 'the competent authorities shall ensure that their institutions are aware of and apply all the Community provisions, legislative or otherwise, including the decisions of the Administrative Commission, in the areas covered by and within the terms of the basic Regulation and the implementing Regulation.'[463]

The second question is related to the content of the healthcare, namely which benefits are covered by the concept of *care necessary on medical grounds*. Necessary care is a broader concept than – although often mixed up with – *immediate or emergency care*, because it does not necessarily require the condition of immediate urgency of healthcare provision.[464] At the same time, certain treatments principally cannot be considered necessary within the meaning of the Regulation, because they do not serve the basic goal of necessary

services to enable provider-patient and provider-provider consultation across geographic boundaries.' E. A. Miller, *Telemedicine and the Provider-Patient Relationship: What We Know So Far*, Report Prepared for the Nuffield Council's Working Party on Medical Profiling and Online Medicine: The Ethics of 'Personalised' Medicine in a Consumer Age, 2010. See also n. 119.

461 European Commission, DG Employment, Social Affairs and Inclusion, *Explanatory notes on modernised social security coordination – Necessary care*, 2011, p. 3.

462 See section 2.3. below in this chapter.

463 Article 89(3) IR.

464 Therefore, the Austrian practice, namely that Austrian providers refused to accept EHICs on the grounds that the care was not deemed urgent, is incorrect and not in line with the Union legislation. M. Coucheir, *EHIC Report 2013*, trESS Network, Ghent 2013, p. 19.

care.[465] While defining this category, its aim has to be kept in mind: 'to enable the insured person to continue his/her stay under safe medical conditions, taking account of the planned length of the stay'[466] and 'to prevent an insured person from being forced to return, before the end of the planned duration of stay, to the competent Member State to obtain necessary care.'[467] Thus, the idea is to make available all benefits in kind which serve the purpose of avoiding the undesired interruption of the patient's stay abroad, but not exceeding this level of healthcare by providing benefits which can also be obtained in the patient's Member State of residence upon his/her arrival back home.[468]

It should be noted, though, that there are a few groups of specific benefits in kind to which these rules apply, the qualification of which has however been highly problematic[469] and needed to be clarified partly by the Court of Justice and partly by the Administrative Commission (AC): these are the healthcare benefits in kind in conjunction with *pregnancy and childbirth*; the healthcare benefits in kind in conjunction with *pre-existing and chronic diseases* and illnesses which require *continuous treatment and specialised medical infrastructure or environment.*

The first group, the healthcare benefits in kind in conjunction with pregnancy and childbirth, has already been mentioned above,[470] since under the former coordination regime this was considered immediate necessary care, although the legislation contained a time limit element, namely the beginning of the 38th week of pregnancy. This restriction is not in force any longer, so necessary care shall include all the benefits in kind in conjunction with pregnancy and childbirth.[471] One may wonder why the former limitation was left out from the revised AC decision. However, as far as I believe, the truth is that it was not: merely the formalisation of the rule was changed. The obvious logic behind the 38th week rule was to avoid the misuse of the legislation on the

---

465 An example can be aesthetic surgery. Although even aesthetic surgery can be considered necessary care, for example, as part of a complex facial reconstruction surgery after a car accident.

466 Decision No 194 of the Administrative Commission of 17 December 2003 concerning the uniform application of Article 22(1)(a)(i) of Council Regulation (EEC) No 1408/71 in the Member State of stay. OJ L 104 of 8 April 2004, 1.

467 Article 25(A)(3) IR.

468 For instance, the majority of dental treatments fall under this category, so dental care is rarely provided as necessary care. Coucheir and Jorens, above n. 199, p. 29.

469 Despite the efforts for clarification, problems repeatedly occur regarding these controversial groups of healthcare services. See examples in Coucheir, above n. 464, p. 21.

470 See n. 454 above.

471 Article 1 of Decision No S3 of the Administrative Commission of 12 June 2009 defining the benefits covered by Articles 19(1) and 27(1) of Regulation (EC) No 883/2004 of the European Parliament and of the Council and Article 25(A)(3) of Regulation (EC) No 987/2009 of the European Parliament and of the Council.

benefits in kind available during a temporary stay abroad and to prevent this procedure from being used at the end of the pregnancy for deliberate travelling to give birth in another Member State. Thus, this logic has remained within the legislation, which indicates that 'the benefits in kind in conjunction with childbirth are not covered by these provisions when the objective of the stay in another Member State is to receive these treatments'.[472] Consequently, in accordance with the current wording of the AC decision, it is still an exception to the necessary care provisions if someone travels abroad for the purpose of giving birth in that Member State, irrespective of whether she does so before or after the beginning of the 38th week of pregnancy. However, once again the question arises: how can the mother's intention be investigated? How can any competent institution prove that the objective behind the travel abroad was to give birth in that other Member State?

Nonetheless, in its explanatory notes on necessary care the European Commission takes it a step further by saying that 'this restriction must be applied carefully and assessed on a case by case basis'.[473] It also gives two concrete examples of situations in which the benefits provided must be considered as necessary care. These situations are: when the migrant woman wishes to go back to her home country in order to take advantage of the help offered by her family, or a woman wants to give birth in the State of residence of her husband or partner. Some problems concerning this interpretation should be pointed out. First of all, one cannot ignore the contradiction between, on the one hand, the original intentions of the Union legislature when creating the rules of necessary care and, on the other hand, the reasoning in the recent interpretation by the Commission. While the former is clearly declared as to ensure medical treatments which become necessary during a temporary stay abroad, where the purpose of this stay may be anything other than obtaining healthcare, the latter considers the purpose of the stay as twofold: giving birth and receiving support from the relatives before and after the birth of the child. Also, the Commission reveals that one of the purposes is to deliberately travel to give birth in another Member State. So why are these cases not considered planned care? If it is accepted that in an ageing society, among the current demographic prognoses pregnant women must enjoy a higher level of protection and be considered as an exceptional group receiving healthcare in accordance with this procedure even if they travel for medical purposes, how can these cases be distinguished from the ones where the family support element lacks and where a woman travels to another Member State to receive a better treatment, thereby 'misusing' this procedure? How can the Member State where the family support element exists be identified? Which Member State is meant by the 'home country' of the

472 Article 2 of AC Decision S3.

473 DG EMPL, above n. 461, p. 3.

pregnant women? And which Member State is to be considered as 'the State of the residence of her husband or partner'? Which residence concept applies? To sum up, the Commission's intention as indicated in the explanatory notes is appreciated, but this interpretation raises more questions than it answers. If the Commission insists on these exceptions, they will have to be clarified carefully and placed within the framework of planned care in order to sustain the consistency of legislation and implementation, because they completely contradict the elementary aim of necessary care.

To the second group, the healthcare benefits in kind in conjunction with pre-existing and chronic diseases, the same rules apply as a consequence of one of the Court's healthcare rulings, namely the above-mentioned *Ioannidis* judgment.[474] In this case, the Court faced the problem of determining the decisive criterion to decide between necessary care and planned care when there is a disease that was diagnosed before leaving the Member State of residence. The CJEU held that the Regulation provisions on necessary care cannot be interpreted

> as meaning that those benefits are limited solely to cases where the treatment provided has become necessary because of a sudden illness. In particular, the circumstance that the treatment necessitated by developments in the insured person's state of health during his temporary stay in another Member State may be linked to a pre-existent pathology of which he is aware, such as a chronic illness, cannot suffice to prevent him from enjoying the benefit of the Regulation provisions on necessary care.[475]

An interpretation which considers any treatment obtained by a patient with a chronic disease abroad as planned care irrespective of the original aim of the patient's temporary stay outside the Member State of residence greatly restricts the free movement of these persons. Therefore, AC Decision S3 clearly stipulates that sickness benefits in kind necessary on medical grounds 'include the benefits provided in conjunction with chronic or existing illnesses'[476] unless 'the objective of the stay in another Member State is to receive these treatments'.[477]

The third group contains certain concrete illnesses which require continuous treatment and a specialised medical infrastructure or environment. In these cases, in order to ensure that the treatment is available during a temporary stay abroad, for practical reasons a prior agreement has to be concluded with the specialised medical unit.[478] It is incumbent on the Administrative Commission

474 See section 2.1.1. above in this chapter.
475 C-326/00 *Ioannidis*, 41.
476 Article 1 of AC Decision S3.
477 Article 2 of AC Decision S3.
478 Article 19(2) BR and Article 3 of AC Decision S3.

to set up and frequently update the list of diseases that are subject to prior agreement between the person concerned and the institution providing the care.[479] Needless to say that despite the requirement to conclude a prior agreement these treatments are also considered necessary care; the prior agreement must not be confused with the prior authorisation required in case of planned treatment abroad.

The definition of necessary care is also dependent on the *length of temporary stay* which means that the circle of available treatments is not constant; besides the medical condition of the patient, the duration also plays an essential role. Since the goal is to avoid the temporary visitor having to suspend his/her stay and return to the country of residence to obtain healthcare there, it is not hard to imagine that the definition of necessary care might be different for a visitor on a three-day conference-trip and for an Erasmus student spending five months abroad. The example mentioned in the explanatory notes is a good illustration of this: if these two persons broke a leg, they both would be entitled to an operation to fix the broken bone, but the conference visitor would most possibly receive all further treatment in his/her Member State of residence upon return, whereas the student who is planning to stay for another couple of months, would start physiotherapy in the Member State of stay.[480]

However, since unplanned healthcare does not require prior authorisation and its coverage is not limited to the benefit basket of the competent Member State, if the basket of treatments is more generous in another Member State, some patients might see it as a 'back door' to receive healthcare in the latter country. Thus, patients might be tempted to take a short trip to this Member State and pretend to require an unforeseen treatment instead of embarking on a less attractive administrative process. The treating medical professional, who is in charge of deciding whether a treatment is necessary for the patient, might not be in the position to detect such techniques.[481] For example, in Spain dental coverage by the public healthcare system is limited to certain urgent treatments. An urgent dental extraction is covered, but dental filling is not. If a patient insured in Spain goes on holiday in Luxembourg for a month and has a toothache, he/she could visit any dentist working with the Luxembourg National Health Fund and should receive the same treatment as anyone insured in Luxembourg, considering the duration of the stay. If the doctor considers it

---

479 This non-exhaustive list is attached to the AC Decision S3 and currently includes the following treatments: kidney dialysis, oxygen therapy, special asthma treatment, echocardiography in case of chronic autoimmune diseases and chemotherapy.

480 DG EMPL, above n. 461, p. 3.

481 Concerning this kind of abuse, see Jorens et al., above n. 240, p. 139.

necessary to perform a dental cleaning and a filling, Spain should reimburse the invoice envisaged under Luxembourg social security law.[482]

To conclude, the medical practitioner assesses all the relevant circumstances as indicated above and decides in the first instance whether the treatment may be considered necessary care. In this respect, I share the opinion that '(t)he relevant factor is the place where the illness occurs, i.e. the Member State where a person resides temporarily or the Member State where he or she is insured'.[483] It is therefore essential whether the healthcare component or the cross-border mobility component of patient mobility occurs first, or in other words, when and where the need for healthcare manifests itself. However, as shown above, this question is often not easy to answer.

Nevertheless, the scope of necessary care and its distinction from planned care remains a sensitive subject and calls for further clarification from the European institutions.[484]

The healthcare decisions of the CJEU[485] have mostly concerned planned care. However, an infringement procedure against the Kingdom of Spain offered the opportunity for the Court to clarify its views on unplanned care as well.[486] Although the Court mainly dealt with financial matters in this judgment,[487] there is an issue which should be underlined here, namely that necessary healthcare as well as planned healthcare is classified as 'a service within the meaning of the Treaty'[488] and therefore the application of the Regulations does not exclude the simultaneous application of the Treaty provisions. On the contrary, the Court reiterated what was already stated on several occasions:[489] the fact that a national legislation is in conformity with the Coordination Regulations does not result in that legislation being removed from the scope of the Treaty provisions.[490]

---

482 Dental care is reimbursed in Luxembourg at the rate of 88 per cent. Specific reimbursement rates and conditions apply for dental prostheses. Example published in Strban et al., above n. 5, p. 37.

483 Jorens, above n. 231, p. 89.

484 The Member States complained that 'the concept is not defined in a sufficiently accurate way, [...] precise guidelines are lacking. [...] As a result, the interpretation varies between countries and between providers within the same country.' Coucheir, above n. 464, p. 22.

485 See n. 17 above.

486 C-211/08 *European Commission v Kingdom of Spain* [2010 Page I-05267].
The infringement procedure was based on a complaint from a French citizen resident at the material time in Spain and insured under the Spanish national health system. On returning to Spain after being admitted to hospital during a stay in France, under cover of form E 111 (predecessor of the European Health Insurance Card), that person met with refusal on the part of the Spanish institution to reimburse the portion of the hospitalisation costs which, in accordance with the French legislation, the French institution had left him to pay.

487 The questions related to financing are dealt with in Chapter 3. Financial affordability.

488 See n. 285. C-211/08 *Commission v Spain*, 47–50.

489 C-120/95 *Decker*, 27; C-158/96 *Kohll*, 25; C-372/04 *Watts*, 46–47. See also C-173/09 *Elchinov*, 38.

490 C-211/08 *Commission v Spain*, 45.

2.2. THE DIRECTIVE'S ROUTE

Directive 2011/24/EU does not differentiate between planned and unplanned types of medical treatments. The reason for this is that – as already mentioned – unlike the Coordination Regulations, which are based on the free movement of persons, the Directive grew out of the case law of the CJEU on the free movement of healthcare services. This case law repeatedly emphasised not only that medical treatments are subject to the Treaty rules on free movement of services,[491] but also that the freedom to provide services includes the freedom for the recipients of services (including persons in need of medical treatment) to go to another Member State in order to receive those services there.[492] That being said, it will come as no surprise that the material scope of the Patient Mobility Directive also covers both unplanned and planned care.[493] However, it was indeed rather unexpected when this came to the surface, because from the proposal of the Directive exactly the opposite could be deduced. In the proposal, the Commission indicated that the new directive 'would allow patients to seek any healthcare in another Member State'.[494] The expression *seek* unequivocally implies that the original intention was to 'put in place an alternative mechanism based on the principles of free movement and building on the principles underlying decisions of the Court of Justice',[495] which at that time exclusively concerned planned care abroad. Moreover, the preamble of the proposed Directive expressly stated that '(t)his Directive does not address the assumption of costs of healthcare which become necessary on medical grounds during a temporary stay of insured persons in another Member State'[496] and similarly, in Chapter III the proposal referred to 'insured persons travelling to another Member State with the purpose of receiving healthcare there or seeking to receive healthcare provided in another Member State'.[497] One may wonder how – after all – the material scope of the Directive was extended to cover the provision of necessary care as well.

---

491 See n. 294 above.

492 See n. 287 above.

493 This point is still disputed. Both Bieback and Strban argue that the Directive exclusively applies to planned medical treatment. I on the other hand support the argument – as shown below – that the standpoint of the Court and the current wording of the Directive (especially Article 1(2) PMD) allows the conclusion that the Directive has to be applied to unplanned care too. Nevertheless, the issue is far from clear, so it leaves room for a converse interpretation. What is even more problematic is that it is a potential source of diverse implementation and thus legal uncertainty. K.-J. Bieback, 'Rechtlinie 2011/24/EU – Patientenrechtlinie' in M. Fuchs (ed.), *Europäisches Sozialrecht*, Nomos, Baden-Baden 2013, p. 656 and Strban, above n. 126, p. 398.

494 COM (2008) 414, above n. 346, p. 4.

495 Ibid.

496 Recital 20 of the Preamble, COM (2008) 414, above n. 346, p. 25.

497 Article 6(1), COM (2008) 414, above n. 346, p. 36.

In my opinion, the above mentioned argumentation of the Court might be – at least partly – responsible for this change of view. Since healthcare services were, as a principle, acknowledged as falling under the scope of the Treaty provisions on free movement of services, no legitimate reason can be found to argue that necessary care has to be exempted from this rule. At the same time, the exclusion of unplanned care from the scope of the Directive could have been based on the argument that the provision of necessary healthcare during a temporary stay abroad has been efficiently coordinated by the coordination mechanism and no major failures of the system made it reasonable to apply a new legal instrument to these situations.

Nevertheless, the adopted version of the Directive is less clear-cut on this point, and leaves the door open for a more extensive interpretation. Whereas in the Preamble it still provides that the 'Directive should apply to individual patients who decide to seek healthcare in a Member State other than the Member State of affiliation',[498] where the words *decide* and *seek* suggest that the Directive was basically constructed to cover only planned care, both the definition of cross-border healthcare[499] and of patient[500] are abstract enough to be interpreted as covering planned as well as unplanned care. The Commission's interpretive note finally erased the doubts by pointing out that 'both the Regulations and the Directive apply to planned and unplanned healthcare'.[501] Although the note itself is not legally binding, the Member States did implement the Directive accordingly. Either way, whether it was the original intention of the European legislature to include unplanned care in the scope of the Directive, remains debateable. This, however, not only leads to administrative pitfalls, but also raises the question when it can be more beneficial for the patient to opt for the Directive instead of the Regulations when obtaining necessary care.

The Coordination Regulations cover the Member States' compulsory healthcare schemes and the healthcare providers which concluded an agreement with the competent institution of the country they are established in. On the coordination route of patient mobility, medical costs are only reimbursed if the healthcare is obtained at a contracted healthcare provider.[502] On the route of the Directive, however, this restriction does not exist; Member States are obliged to reimburse the costs for treatments obtained either at contracted or at non-contracted providers.[503] Therefore, if necessary care is provided by a non-contracted provider, the Directive ensures a higher level of protection for

498 Recital 11 of the Preamble of the Patient Mobility Directive.
499 Article 3(e) PMD. See n. 112.
500 Article 3(h) PMD. See n. 91.
501 AC 246/12, above n. 264, p. 4.
502 Member States have the freedom, of course, to reimburse costs of treatments provided by non-contracted or private providers, but they are not obliged to do so.
503 AC 246/12, above n. 264, p. 4.

patients. In any other case, the Regulations seem to offer a more satisfactory solution.

The lack of distinction between unplanned and planned care in the Directive has both advantages and disadvantages. A good side is that neither different rules must be applied, nor must the intention of the patient be taken into account. The lack of distinction annuls the problem that the difference in the administrative procedures under the Regulation's regime might be a source of fraudulent use of patients' mobility rights. Moreover, dilemmas related to some specific groups of patients, such as pregnant women and chronically ill persons, in case of which the investigation of the patient's intention can be even more problematic due to a pre-existent medical condition,[504] are irrelevant.

As a disadvantage, applying the same set of rules to each healthcare provision can result in paradoxical situations. This is especially true when we apply the Directive's authorisation rules consistently in each situation regardless of whether the healthcare service required is unforeseen. Since the Directive permits Member States to provide for a system of prior authorisation for the reimbursement of certain costs of cross-border healthcare services, theoretically it would be possible that a Member State refuses to reimburse the costs of unplanned hospital treatment obtained without a prior authorisation at a purely private provider. For instance, suppose an insured person suffers a ski accident during a skiing holiday abroad and the emergency helicopter takes him or her to the nearest private clinic located in the ski resort. In this case, the application of the Regulations does not even come into play, since purely private providers operating outside the statutory healthcare system are excluded from their scope.[505] Under the Directive's rules, the patient can request reimbursement of the medical costs based on the domestic tariffs in the Member State of affiliation. However, since the Directive allows – as is shown later in this chapter[506] numerous Member States used this possibility – to make the reimbursement of hospital costs dependent on prior authorisation, the competent Member State is free to refuse the reimbursement due to the lack of prior authorisation. Although it was not reported that any Member State would apply this exact method, the reality of this problem is proven by the fact that this question was expressly addressed in the Administrative Commission. The Secretariat of the AC was of the view that a treatment should be reimbursed if it becomes necessary during a temporary stay and prior authorisation cannot be requested.[507] Undeniably,

---

504 See section 2.1.3 above in this chapter.

505 However, sometimes this kind of private coverage could be reimbursed under the Regulations, but only in some Member States and always considering their own tariffs. Article 25(B)(7) IR.

506 See section 3 below in this chapter.

507 Administrative Commission for the Coordination of Social Security Services, *Minutes of the Working Party of the Administrative Commission on Patients' mobility*, AC 332/11, 4 October 2011.

this interpretation is perfectly logical and realistic – in case of an accident (i.e. urgency or immediate necessity) it is unrealistic to expect the patient to request an ex ante authorisation under the Directive just in case he/she suffers an accident and is admitted to a private facility. However, it is not entirely in line with the current wording of the Directive, which does not even recognise the notion of medical necessity in this respect. Additionally, the interpretation given by the Secretariat is not binding for the Member States either.

Although the Directive undoubtedly strengthens European patients' right to access to unplanned healthcare abroad since it opens up the general possibility to be reimbursed for treatments obtained from private providers outside of the statutory scheme, it would be desirable to expressly codify into the Directive that the reimbursement of costs of medical services which become necessary during a temporary stay abroad cannot be made dependent on a prior authorisation of any kind, including the requirement of a referral from a medical doctor. Nevertheless, this change would necessitate the introduction of certain – not completely unproblematic – terms as well, such as necessary care[508] or temporary stay.[509]

2.3. ADMINISTRATIVE FORMALITIES WHEN OBTAINING NECESSARY HEALTHCARE

Under the traditional regime of the Coordination Regulations, in order to obtain *necessary healthcare* in a Member State other than the Member State of residence during a temporary stay in that Member State on the account of the patient's health insurance in the competent Member State, three basic requirements must be met: the person concerned must be entitled to sickness benefits in kind in the competent Member State; the person concerned must be able to prove his/her entitlement to the foreign healthcare provider he/she intends to obtain treatment from; and the healthcare must be obtained from a public healthcare provider.

First, the person concerned must be *entitled to sickness benefits in kind* under the national legislation of the Member State where he/she is covered by the compulsory health insurance scheme.[510] The formalisation of the entitlement rules is the sole responsibility of the Member States, although if these requirements are met, the healthcare basket provided in the Member State of stay determines the benefits available as necessary care during a temporary stay abroad.[511]

---

508 See section 2.1.3. above in this chapter.

509 See section 1.1.1. above in this chapter.

510 See n. 357 above.

511 See n. 379 above.

Secondly, the patient must be able to present a *proof of entitlement* to the sickness benefits in kind issued by the competent institution for the healthcare provider in the Member State of stay.[512] For this purpose, the E 111 form was used until it was progressively – in three stages[513] – replaced by the European Health Insurance Card (EHIC).[514] The aim of this action was to simplify procedures without changing the existing rights and obligations.[515] The Administrative Commission published its decision aimed at introducing the European Health Insurance Card[516] in 2003, in which decision it also adopted the basic provisions concerning the application of the EHIC. The target of the adoption of a uniform health insurance card was twofold: on the one hand, the Union legislature intended to simplify the access to healthcare during a temporary stay abroad by introducing the EHIC initially 'in a format in which the data necessary for the provision of health care and reimbursement of the costs can be read with the naked eye';[517] on the other hand, the EU legislature wanted to ensure that the insured persons can use their right to healthcare benefits in kind through this card 'on the same terms as those applicable to persons insured under the legislation of the Member State of stay'.[518] This is the practical implementation of the equal treatment principle in the healthcare provision.[519]

512 Article 25(A)(1) IR.

513 Paragraph 1 of the Preamble of Decision No 191 of the Administrative Commission of 18 June 2003 concerning the replacement of forms E 111 and E 111 B by the European health insurance card. OJ L 276 of 27 October 2003.

514 The European Council decided on the replacement of the paper forms with the European Health Insurance Card at its Barcelona Summit in March 2002 and asked the European Commission to present a proposal before the Spring European Council held in March 2003. The Commission's proposal was presented in the form of a communication: *Communication from the Commission concerning the introduction of a European health insurance card*, COM (2003) 73 final, 17.02.2003.

515 See n. 456 above.

516 Decision No 189 of the Administrative Commission of 18 June 2003 aimed at introducing a European health insurance card to replace the forms necessary for the application of Council Regulations (EEC) No 1408/71 and (EEC) No 574/72 as regards access to health care during a temporary stay in a Member State other than the competent State or the State of residence. OJ L 276 of 27 October 2003.

517 Paragraph 3 of the Preamble of AC Decision 189.
On the design and specifications of the European health insurance card see Decision No 190 of the Administrative Commission of 18 June 2003 concerning the technical specifications of the European health insurance card (OJ L 276 of 27 October 2003). See also the revised decisions of the Administrative Commission on these matters, namely Decision No S1 of the Administrative Commission of 12 June 2009 concerning the European Health Insurance Card (OJ C 106 of 24 April 2010) and Decision No S2 of the Administrative Commission of 12 June 2009 concerning the technical specifications of the European Health Insurance Card (OJ C 106 of 24 April 2010).

518 Article 25(A)(2) IR.

519 See n. 383 above.

The EHIC is an individual plastic card[520] that contains a certain set of data[521] which can be easily recognised in any Member State and enables patients to turn directly to the healthcare providers in case of need for healthcare in another Member State. The card is issued by the competent Member State, which must also determine the validity period of the document.[522] The length of the validity periods differs widely in the Member States from several months (e.g. in Poland the EHIC is valid for six months principally) to several years (e.g. in Italy EHIC is valid for six years, in the Czech Republic for five years, in Ireland for four years).[523] Both very short and very long validity periods can raise concerns. On the one hand, the need for a regular change of EHICs due to a short-term validity constitutes a relatively big administrative burden, whereas on the other hand, long validity increases the possibility of fraudulent usage if the insurance status of the person concerned changes during the time of validity.

The national determination of the length of the validity period may also be subject to discussion, since in this way, the Member States can indirectly influence the length of temporary stay abroad. One could question why an expiry date is actually needed. In my opinion, the aim of preventing fraud and misuse cannot be accepted as a reason, since they should be stopped by strengthening the cooperation among the competent institutions and not by forcing patients to request a new card – in some Member States – after just a few months. Using the analogy of the national health insurance cards, the EHIC could be issued for an unlimited period of time and if any changes occur in the insurance status of the patient, the institutions involved should have the obligation to inform each other as they are obliged to do so under the validity period.[524] Alternatively, the competence of determining the length of the validity period could be transferred to the Union and universal validity period(s) could be set up throughout the EU. The problem with the latter solution is that the EHIC is ultimately manifesting entitlement based on national law, the determination of which belongs to the sole competence of the Member States.

The fact that the only proof of entitlement to sickness benefits in kind is the EHIC may raise concerns. Unlike on a national level, where the existence of healthcare entitlements can be checked on some kind of database,[525] on a

---

520 Article 2 of AC Decision No S1.

521 Detailed in AC Decision No S2.

522 Article 3 of AC Decision No S1.

523 Different validity periods might be applicable to different groups such as pensioners. See J. Pacolet and F. De Wispelaere, *The European Health Insurance Card*, Network Statistics FMSSFE, Leuven 2016, pp. 15–16.

524 Article 24(2) IR.

525 For instance, in Hungary, a colour code system was introduced in relation to entitlement checks. When a patient presents his/her national social security card (TAJ kártya) to a healthcare provider, the provider is obliged to check his/her social security status in the online database. If the system gives a *green signal*, it means that the card is valid and the

European level no such controlling mechanism is in place. The provider to whom an EHIC is presented is bound by Union legislation – if the criteria are met – to provide the patient with necessary care, lacking any means to check the entitlement. This might lead to the fraudulent consumption of healthcare services and legal disputes in relation to the reimbursement of the costs of these services. Although it does not seem realistic nowadays, in the long run it would be highly desirable to set up a European database, an online verification system (maybe as an integral part of the EESSI)[526] which would enable providers to check patients' social security status, and thus prevent the misuse of the EHIC procedure.[527]

The card can be requested free of charge, although when exceptional circumstances occur such as theft, loss of the card or an urgent travel, and these situations prevent an EHIC from being issued, the competent institution must issue a provisional replacement certificate (PRC) with a limited validity period.[528]

Thirdly, the costs of necessary care are reimbursed only if the healthcare was provided by a *public healthcare provider*,[529] meaning that under the Regulation's regime, reimbursement cannot be claimed for medical treatment provided by private healthcare providers functioning beyond the scope of the public healthcare system.[530] This restriction can very well be seen as a budget control tool: the Member States intend to avoid being obliged to reimburse the definitely higher private charges. By doing so, they do reduce patients' freedom of choice. What is worse is that patients do not always seem aware that they can expect their medical costs to be reimbursed under the Regulation only if they obtain treatment at a public provider. In this respect, I share the opinion of the German healthcare insurance institutions, which suggest an easy way to tackle this source of misunderstanding: each healthcare provider that functions under the scope of the Regulation and thus accepts the EHIC in the course of providing necessary care, should be obliged to display an EU-wide, universal,

social security status of the patient is settled (rendezett). A *red signal* is received when – despite the card being valid – there is a problem regarding the patient's social security status (nem rendezett). A *blue signal* is for those who became insured in another country, making their card temporarily invalid (átmenetileg érvénytelen). *Brown* is for those whose card is deemed invalid for some other reason.

526 See n. 253 above.

527 In this respect, work has been in progress at EU level for years now. The *NETC@RDS for e-EHIC ID project* aims at enabling the health practitioners to check foreign patients' entitlement to health care. http://netcards-project.com/web/frontpage, (accessed 28.02.2017) See also COM (2003) 73, above n. 514, p. 8.

528 Article 5 of AC Decision No S1.

529 In most of the cases this implies that the provider has a contract with the responsible institution of the MS of stay.

530 However, these costs can be reimbursed under the PMD's regime. Further details on the inclusion of private providers can be found in this section below.

easily recognisable symbol in their entrance area.[531] I agree that a similar scheme could be followed as for credit card symbols: it is nowadays common that restaurants, bars and hotels indicate somewhere around their entrance which types of credit cards are accepted for payment.[532] This practice results in a clear situation on both sides and prevents later difficulties. A similar solution could be applied to the EHIC. Moreover, it would not require any considerable investment, but would completely solve the above-mentioned problem and certainly improve patients' feeling of certainty in such situations.

In recent years, the EHIC grew to be a very important and useful tool in the Union's healthcare policy. Data show that in 2013 already almost 200 million EHICs were in circulation,[533] which makes the EHIC one of the most visible EU tools for EU citizens and 'surely the most well-known tool for healthcare abroad'.[534] Currently, the EHIC covers about forty per cent of the insured population in the EU.[535]

Nevertheless, the practical functioning of the EHIC remains a subject of constant discussion and many problems of ill-application are reported.[536] The main problems can be grouped into three categories, namely *improper usage* of the EHIC by patients; *non-acceptance* of the EHIC by healthcare providers in the Member State of stay; and *invoice rejection* based on the usage of the EHIC by competent institutions.

The inappropriate or fraudulent use of the EHIC is not a widespread problem. Rarely did cases occur in which the EHIC was used to obtain planned care, the treatment predated the issue of the EHIC or the EHIC was not used by the insured person to whom the EHIC was issued.[537]

However, it is a more frequent problem that healthcare providers refuse to accept the EHIC presented to them or to follow the procedure applicable to the provision of necessary care. The reasons behind this are multifarious. On the one hand, illegitimate refusals are, for example, based on a lack of knowledge regarding the EHIC and its procedures; concerns or reluctance regarding extra paper work and red tape associated with the EHIC;[538] and concerns regarding

---

531 Jorens and Lhernould, above n. 392, p. 29 and Coucheir, above n. 464, p. 25. See also Pacolet and De Wispelaere, above n. 523, p. 27.

532 See also point 39 of A6-0173/2007, above n. 23.

533 J. Pacolet and F. De Wispelaere, *The European Health Insurance Card*, Network Statistics FMSSFE, Leuven 2014, p. 4.

534 Lhernould, above n. 8, p. 184.

535 Pacolet and De Wispelaere, above n. 523, p. 12.

536 Jorens and Lhernould (2013: 29.), Pacolet and De Wispelaere, above n. 533, pp. 15–18, Pacolet and De Wispelaere, above n. 523, pp. 25–29.

537 Coucheir, above n. 464, p. 18. See also Pacolet and De Wispelaere, above n. 523, pp. 25–26.

538 Providers often prefer private insurance over the EHIC or refer foreign patients to private providers. Neither of these practices complies with EU law.

late or non-payment by the competent institution;[539] on the other hand, legitimate refusals are based on the fact that one or more of the above conditions to use the EHIC to obtain healthcare abroad are not met, especially when the patient turns to a private, non-contracted provider that falls outside of the scope of EHIC procedures; or the patient aims to obtain planned care instead of necessary care.

Invoice rejections are not unknown either. Once again, '(a) multitude of reasons are reported as to why countries fail to accept forms E125[540] or SED S080[541] for treatment obtained by their insured persons'.[542] Most often the problems occur either in relation to the use of the EHIC or the invoice.[543] In 2015, '(t)he share of rejected invoices compared to the total claims of reimbursement received is on average 1%'.[544]

In my opinion, the main risk beyond these practices is that they hold a significant potential to undermine the public trust towards the EHIC itself[545] and towards EU tools in general. Therefore, it is very important to pay due attention to such claims and to develop techniques which are able to tackle the most typical problems. In general, better controlling and monitoring mechanisms should be introduced both on the national and European level. The claims coming either from patients, providers or competent institutions should be promptly investigated and if deemed necessary, legal action should be taken against any person or entity who may not comply with Union legislation. Moreover, further active, awareness-raising initiatives should be carried out both among patients and healthcare providers.[546] Although 'many countries stress that information is continuously kept available through a variety of channels,'[547]

539 Coucheir, above n. 464, p. 19. See also Pacolet and De Wispelaere, above n. 523, p. 26.

540 E125 is a paper-based form, an individual statement of the costs of the medical treatment a person received in another Member State. Although E-forms were abolished by the new set of Coordination Regulations, they are still in use in several Member States.

541 SED is the abbreviation for structured electronic document. SEDs were designed to replace the former E-forms and make communication of data between institutions easier and more efficient. SED S080 serves as a replacement of E125 and is used for claiming reimbursement.

542 Coucheir, above n. 464, p. 23.

543 If, for instance, the form is incomplete or completed incorrectly. Coucheir, above n. 464, p. 23. See also Pacolet and De Wispelaere, above n. 523, pp. 28–29.

544 Pacolet and De Wispelaere, above n. 523, p. 29.

545 Coucheir, above n. 464, p. 3, 20.
For instance, a few years back, the notorious non-acceptance practices of South-European touristic areas were very bad marketing for the EHIC. See, among others, T. Hunter, 'Holidaymakers warned as Spain blocks EHIC usage' *The Telegraph*, 31.03.2013 and H. Meyer, 'Spain's Ehic refusal prompts legal action from European Commission' *The Guardian*, 30.05.2013.

546 Most countries do not take active measures to raise awareness concerning the EHIC either among patients or among providers. Coucheir, above n. 464, pp. 12–13. See also Pacolet and De Wispelaere, above n. 533, p.6.

547 Coucheir, above n. 464, p. 12.

the above-mentioned problems show that more active measures should be implemented. In my view, this is a shared responsibility of the Member States and the Union,[548] where best practices should be exchanged. The problems analysed above and some possible solutions suggested are summarised in Table 7.

Table 7. Ill-application of the European Health Insurance Card

Nature of ill-application		Examples of ill-application	Possible solutions to tackle ill-application
improper usage of the EHIC by patients	patient acting in good faith	the validity period of the EHIC expired	awareness-raising among patients in various forms (e.g. through general practitioners, media)
		unaware of the legislation, the patient intends to obtain planned care with the EHIC	
		not covered by the healthcare scheme of the MS that issued the EHIC	facilitating more efficient inter-institutional communication
	patient acting maliciously (fraudulent usage of the EHIC)	the treatment predates the issue of the EHIC	indicating the starting date of the validity/date of issue on the EHIC
		the patient maliciously intends to obtain planned care with the EHIC	developing controlling and monitoring mechanisms and taking legal steps if necessary
		usage of fake, forged EHIC	
		the EHIC is used by someone other than the person it was issued to	
non-acceptance of the EHIC by healthcare providers	illegitimate practices of non-acceptance	lack of knowledge about EHIC and its procedures	awareness-raising among healthcare providers in various forms (e.g. in the framework of general healthcare education, specialised trainings, journals, circular letters)
		concerns regarding extra paper work and red tape	improving administrative procedures

548 The European Commission has made serious efforts to spread information on and promote the EHIC: it launched an online campaign with videos which were published on the most common video sharing sites; a smartphone application was designed, available in 25 languages, which provides a guide on how to use the EHIC in the 32 countries and includes general information about the card, emergency phone numbers, covered treatments and costs, how to claim reimbursement and who to contact if you have lost your card; it continuously provides information in the form of different leaflets, booklets, press releases, and through its website.

Nature of ill-application		Examples of ill-application	Possible solutions to tackle ill-application
		concerns regarding late or non-payment	improving cooperation between competent institutions, speeding up reimbursement mechanisms by more efficient inter-institutional communication, taking legal steps in the event of delayed or non-payment
	legitimate practices of non-acceptance	private provider	applying an EU-wide, universal symbol to providers that accept EHIC
		requested healthcare falls outside of the notion of necessary care	providing clearer guidelines on the scope of necessary care
		usage of invalid EHIC	
invoice refusal by competent institutions	EHIC related problems	improper use of the EHIC (see above)	
	invoice related problems	incomplete or incorrectly completed document	facilitating more efficient inter-institutional communication

Source: The author's own summary.

Although I firmly believe that the EHIC holds great opportunities, the EU is far from using its full potential. It seems to me that the expectations about the EHIC are only partly met and there is still a long way to go to its full implementation. The replacement of the paper-based E-forms[549] with the EHIC should be considered a first step. A second step would be an improved version of the EHIC which is able to electronically store healthcare data safely,[550] not to mention that that the original idea was to combine the EHIC with the national health insurance cards.[551] This has not happened yet in many countries, although in the long run it could replace these national cards.[552]

I share the opinion that the '*electronification*' of the EHIC is the direction in which the European Union should move towards.[553] The EHIC could function as a 'European healthcare passport' incorporating both national and European healthcare rights of the person concerned, enabling healthcare providers to

549 The following E-forms were progressively replaced: E111 (for holidays), E128 (for posting), E110 (for international road transport), E128 (for study) and E119 (for job seeking). COM (2003) 73, above n. 514, p. 4.

550 COM (2003) 73, above n. 514, p. 5.

551 COM (2003) 73, above n. 514, p. 12.

552 The EHIC carries a free area which *is an area located on the reverse side of the European card and available for national purposes.* Point 3.3.4. of Annex 1 to AC Decision S2. This free area could be used to integrate the national healthcare card into the EHIC.

553 COM (2003) 73, above n. 514, pp. 15–16.

verify his/her entitlements and storing medical data. However, it must be understood that the implementation of such a system requires considerable future investments and raises numerous problems.[554]

Under the Directive's regime, from the three conditions detailed above only one remained, namely that costs are only reimbursed *if the healthcare in question is among the benefits to which the insured person is entitled in the Member State of affiliation.*[555] Subsequently, Member States are not obliged to reimburse the costs of treatments which are not covered by or are expressly excluded from the benefit basket of the Member State of affiliation. It must be pointed out though, that this is not entirely the same condition as in the Regulation, because when necessary care is received under the coordination mechanism, the rules on the benefit coverage of the Member State of treatment apply.[556] It is indeed the competent Member State which defines whether or not the person is entitled to healthcare services under its own legislation, but if he/she is so entitled and obtains occasional care in another Member State, the available benefits are defined by the legislation of the latter country.[557] The Directive's provision is not necessarily disadvantageous for the patient. Yet, he/she must be aware that if he/she obtains a medical treatment which is normally provided in the Member State of stay as a benefit included into its benefit package but is not covered by the benefit package of the Member State of affiliation, reimbursement cannot be claimed under the Directive.

Unlike under the Regulation, patients are not required to present a proof of their entitlement to healthcare services to the healthcare providers, since the healthcare provider is no longer interested whether the patient's social security status checks out, whether he/she really is entitled according to the national healthcare legislation. The provider receives the full payment for the treatment from the patient, so it does not participate in the posterior reimbursement procedure between the patient and the competent institution. If the patient proves not to be entitled to the healthcare obtained, on the grounds of Article 7(1) of the Patient Mobility Directive the competent institution can legitimately refuse to reimburse the medical costs, which in the end remain at the expense of the patient.

Similarly, the restriction regarding the accessible providers is not applicable either. The Directive covers both public and private providers, which obviously extends the patient's possibility to choose. Therefore, this can be seen as a beneficial development from the patient's point of view.[558] However, some providers

554 Among others – as in any application where ICT is involved – it raises serious concerns regarding data protection and confidentiality of sensitive medical data.

555 Article 7(1) PMD.

556 According to the full integration principle, the person is treated as though he/she were insured under the legislation of the MS of stay. Article 19(1) BR and Article 25(A)(3) IR.

557 This issue is dealt with in details in section 2.1.2. above in this chapter.

558 However beneficial the inclusion of private providers is, it raises a serious concern in relation to equal treatment and might result in reverse discrimination. On reverse discrimination see n. 909 below.

have already been reported to abuse the extended opportunities offered by the Directive, inviting patients with an EHIC to pay upfront (even though domestic patients do not pay on the spot) or directing them to private providers instead of public ones which function under the scope of the Regulation.[559] These practices are illegitimate and do not serve the interest of patients. Therefore, such cases should be notified to the responsible authorities which can take the necessary measures to prevent such cases from happening again.

Table 8 shows the discrepancies of the administrative conditions between the Regulation's and the Directive's provisions when obtaining unplanned care.

Table 8. Administrative formalities related to unplanned care

Administrative condition	Coordination Regulation	Patient Mobility Directive
(1) entitlement to healthcare services	✓	✓
	the patient must be entitled to healthcare services under the legislation of the competent MS	the patient must be entitled to healthcare services under the legislation of the competent MS AND the healthcare must be among the benefits provided by the MS of affiliation
(2) presentation of proof of entitlement to healthcare services to the healthcare provider	✓	✗
	the patient must hold an EHIC or a PRC	no need to present proof of entitlement
(3) restriction on the accessible healthcare providers	✓	✗
	only public providers are covered	both public and private providers are covered
(4) prior authorisation	✗	?
	no need to request PA (in exceptional cases a prior agreement with the healthcare provider might be required)	*in theory*, MSs can refuse to reimburse the costs of treatments subject to PA, but obtained as necessary care without a PA

Source: The author's own summary, based on the legislation.

As a last possible scenario, in the next section the rules applicable to planned care are examined in detail.

[559] Coucheir, above n. 464, p 20.

3. ACCESS TO PLANNED HEALTHCARE OUTSIDE OF THE MEMBER STATE OF RESIDENCE

Healthcare is of high priority for most people. Thus, if they suffer from a serious illness, every possible solution is carefully assessed in order to receive proper medical attention, which includes the opportunity to travel to obtain treatment outside the country where they reside.

The European Union has guaranteed the – rather limited – right to planned treatment abroad for decades in the framework of social security coordination. However, the legal rules related to scheduled healthcare were completely redefined by the European Court of Justice, when it applied the fundamental principles of the free movement of services and goods for the sector of healthcare in two milestone cases in the late 1990s.[560] The Court made it clear that despite the limited EU competence in the field of social security,[561] healthcare provision is not 'an island beyond the reach of Community law'.[562]

3.1. THE COORDINATION REGULATIONS' ROUTE

As described above, the Coordination Regulations distinguish two different cases of obtaining treatment while temporarily staying abroad. The rules on *necessary healthcare* have already been scrutinised,[563] so hereinafter solely the diverse legal rules applicable to *planned healthcare* are dealt with.

3.1.1. General Rules

What is typical of planned healthcare is that the expressed aim of leaving the Member State of residence and entering another Member State is to receive a certain medical treatment, preferably at the expense of the health insurance of the person concerned. So here the need for healthcare precedes the intention of travelling abroad as opposed to necessary care, which requires that the need for healthcare occurs after crossing the border(s). As already mentioned, while in the latter case the possibility of need for healthcare is a risk which might occur during the insured person's visit abroad, in the former case the healthcare provision is why the insured person travels abroad. Accordingly, this right of patients[564] is highly limited under the coordination regime: patients 'travelling to another Member State with the purpose of receiving benefits in

560 See section 3.7. in Chapter 1. Setting the scene.
561 See section 3.5. in Chapter 1. Setting the scene.
562 Jorens et al., above n. 196, p. 2.
563 See section 2. above in this chapter.
564 These rules apply to the insured persons and the members of their family. Article 20(3) BR.

kind during the stay shall seek authorisation from the competent institution'.[565] The authorisation is therefore the sole competence of the competent Member State, which is completely understandable taking into account that this state must bear the costs of the treatment. However, its discretion is fairly restricted: if two criteria are simultaneously met, the competent institution must accord the authorisation without evaluation. This two-limb test consists of the following conditions: the requested treatment is *included into the benefit package* (vector of treatment) of the Member State of residence; and this benefit in kind cannot be provided to the patient *within a medically justifiable time limit, taking into account his/her current state of health and probable course of his/her illness* (vector of time).[566] These criteria, if satisfied, render it mandatory to grant the patient prior authorisation.

Notwithstanding, similar rules apply to the provision of the medical treatment itself as in the event of necessary care described above:[567] the healthcare is provided in the Member State of stay in accordance with the provisions of the legislation it applies, as though the patient were insured under the said legislation.[568] It cannot be doubted that the European legislature supports the idea of full integration in order to ensure the highest possible protection for the migrant persons in these sensitive situations. Additionally, pensioners and their family members are entitled to planned care under the same conditions outside the Member State of residence.[569]

Although the full integration model seems to be patient-friendly and clear, the conditions included in the Coordination Regulations connected to (1) the *benefit coverage* and (2) the *medically justifiable time limit* are far from obvious. They have already offered the Court several opportunities for clarification and interpretation. It is thus worth analysing them here. It must be noted that it is the Court itself which can be held responsible for the very existence of these conditions in the first place, since their introduction was merely a response from the Member States to the two *Pierik* judgments.[570] As mentioned above, in these decisions the Court 'had virtually recognized a free movement of patients', but at the same time it 'had almost fully ignored the Member States' health care interests'.[571] Consequently, however welcomed the rulings were from the patients' perspective, the Court went a step too far when granting the right to obtain treatment that is not included in the benefit package of the home state. By doing so, the Court seemingly lost sight of the sensitive balance between the interests of the Member States and the patients in a field which is very

565 Article 20(1) BR.
566 Article 20(2) BR. See RIEDER, above n. 52.
567 See section 2.1.2. above in this chapter.
568 Article 20(2) BR.
569 Article 27(3) BR.
570 See n. 283 above.
571 VAN DER MEI, above n. 270, p. 286.

delicate from both sides.[572] As a consequence, the Member States used the most effective way to neutralise the Court's initiative: they modified the secondary EU legislation.[573] They inserted rules into Regulation 1408/71 that expressly allowed Member States to deny authorisation if the treatment required was not 'among the benefits provided for by the legislation of the Member State on whose territory the person concerned resided'.[574]

3.1.2. *Determination of the Applicable Benefit Basket*

As to this first condition, the benefit baskets[575] provided by the statutory healthcare schemes as well as the methods used to determine the available healthcare benefits differ from each other in the various Member States.[576] As Coucheir and Jorens point out, 'it has to be well understood that the definition of the benefits package forms an integral part of Member States' autonomy'.[577] In most cases, the Member States set up a list, a benefit catalogue, enumerating the healthcare benefits which can be received in the framework of the public health insurance in the Member State concerned.[578] The Court summarised the possible solutions as follows: to list precisely the treatments or treatment methods; or to state more generally the categories or types of treatments or treatment methods.[579] The first solution is less flexible, but it provides more certainty, while the second one 'insert[s] some flexibility by using "open" criteria in order to adapt to the constantly and rapidly changing developments in medical circles'.[580]

---

572 Although the intention of the CJEU was commendable and served the best interest of patients, it is false not to take into account the economic reality that Member States might not be able to finance treatments abroad which their healthcare system does not cover. This was the case in the 1970s and this statement is even more correct in the enlarged Union. Whatever solution might occur to enhance patient mobility, the competences and capabilities of the Member States should be respected.

573 See van der Mei, above n. 270, pp. 284–287 and A. Bosco, 'Are national social protection systems under threat? Observations on the recent case law of the Court of Justice' *European Issues* 2000, no 7, p. 19.

574 Article 22(2) of Regulation 1408/71.

575 'The term "benefits basket" refers to the totality of services, activities and goods reimbursed or directly provided by a publicly funded SHI [Social Health Insurance] or NHS [National Health Service] system.' R. Busse, E. Van Ginneken, J. Schreyögg and M. Velasco Garrido, 'Benefit baskets and tariffs' in Wismar et al., above n. 4, p. 92.

576 Busse et al., above n. 122, p. 14.

577 Coucheir and Jorens, above n. 199, p. 93. The CJEU also confirms in its Elchinov judgment that 'it is for each Member State to decide which medical benefits are reimbursed by its own social security system'. C-173/09 *Elchinov*, 59.

578 Busse et al., above n. 575, p. 92.

579 C-173/09 *Elchinov*, 59.

580 A.P. van der Mei, 'Case C-512/08, Commission v. France, Judgment of the European Court of Justice (Grand Chamber) of 5 October 2010 and Case C-173/09, Georgi Ivanov Elchinov v. Natsionalna zdravnoosiguritelna kasa, Judgment of the Court of Justice (Grand Chamber) of 5 October 2010' *Common Market Law Review* 2011, vol 48 issue 4, p. 1304.

In the case of scheduled treatment this issue is highly relevant, since patients have the right to receive a prior authorisation only if the benefit in question is included into the benefit package of the Member State of residence.[581] Although the Court has confirmed numerous times that the Member States have the liberty to organise their healthcare systems[582] including the determination of the healthcare benefit baskets, this national autonomy was undermined on several occasions by the European Court of Justice itself.

First, the European Court of Justice touched upon the benefit package question in its *Geraets-Smits and Peerbooms* judgment,[583] in which it evaluated the conditions required by the Dutch healthcare system. Under the national legislation, which does not provide a pre-established list of types of healthcare benefits in kind covered by the social insurance system, two conditions must be satisfied in order to receive medical treatment funded by the social insurance:[584] the treatment in question must be capable of being regarded as a qualifying benefit, meaning that it is considered *normal in the professional circles concerned*, not experimental;[585] and the treatment in question must be *necessary*,[586] meaning that no similar treatment is available without undue delay in the Netherlands.[587] The first condition is related to determining the benefit package, whereas the second one can be linked to the question of availability, which will be discussed later in this section.

Concerning the normality of the treatment,[588] the Court pointed out that – keeping in mind that each Member State has the competence to organise its own national social security system and in particular to determine the conditions governing the entitlement to benefits[589] – 'it is not in principle incompatible with Community law for a Member State to establish, with a view to achieving its aim of limiting costs, limitative lists excluding certain products from reimbursement under its social security scheme'.[590] Thus, the national

581 Article 20(2) BR, C-56/01 *Inizan*, 42; C-372/04 *Watts*, 56; C-173/09 *Elchinov*, 54.

582 See the settled case law of the CJEU on this matter under n. 218.

583 See n. 307 above.

584 C-157/99 *Geraets-Smits and Peerbooms*, 22.

585 C-157/99 *Geraets-Smits and Peerbooms*, 23. The experimental nature of treatments was also dealt with in Joined Cases E-11/07 and E-1/08 *Olga Rindal* (Case E-11/07); Therese Slinning, represented by legal guardian Olav Slinning (Case E-1/08) and The Norwegian State, represented by the Board of Exemptions and Appeals for Treatment Abroad.

586 In this case, the phrase 'necessary' may not be confused with the treatment necessary on medical grounds in the event of occasional treatment abroad.

587 C-157/99 *Geraets-Smits and Peerbooms*, 24.

588 Mrs Geraets-Smits was insured under the Dutch health insurance scheme and received treatment in Germany. In this case, the main proceeding was about a multidisciplinary treatment of Parkinson's disease. (C-157/99 *Geraets-Smits and Peerbooms*, 25).
Mr Peerbooms, also insured in the Netherlands, was subject to a special intensive therapy using neurostimulation in Austria, which was considered experimental in the Netherlands. (C-157/99 *Geraets-Smits and Peerbooms*, 32).

589 C-157/99 *Geraets-Smits and Peerbooms*, 85.

590 C-157/99 *Geraets-Smits and Peerbooms*, 86. See also C-238/82 *Duphar*, 17.

competence for healthcare organisation includes the liberty to exclude certain benefits from the benefit package. Moreover, the Court added that 'Community law cannot in principle have the effect of requiring a Member State to extend the list of medical services paid for by its social insurance system'.[591]

However, it is not the extension, but the means of exclusion at stake here, namely whether the Member State must set up limitative lists *expressly* enumerating the benefits excluded from the reimbursed benefit coverage, or whether it may apply special conditions which *indirectly* limit the circle of benefits reimbursed. The Court did not explicitly answer this in its judgment, although it made it clear that whatever method is used to determine the content of the benefit basket, it must be based on objective, non-discriminatory criteria, without reference to the origin of the treatment in question.[592] According to the Court's arguments, in the exact case 'to allow only treatment habitually carried out on national territory and scientific views prevailing in national medical circles to determine what is or is not normal will make it likely that Netherlands providers of treatment will always be preferred in practice'.[593] The Court also offered a possible solution to make the Dutch condition more objective and in compliance with EU rules by extending it 'in such a way that, where a treatment is sufficiently tried and tested by international medical science,[594] the authorisation cannot be refused on that ground'.[595] So no distinction is made between the treatment being provided in the competent Member State or outside of its territory.[596]

Although this condition lacks any discriminatory implications, it also induces certain questions, which were left open by the Court. For example, what can be considered as 'sufficiently tried and tested'? Whose responsibility is it to decide about it? What kind of assessment has to be used in the course of this decision-making?[597] On top of that, the global view of 'normality' conveyed by

---

591 C-157/99 *Geraets-Smits and Peerbooms*, 87. See also C-385/99 *Müller-Fauré and Van Riet*, 98; C-173/09 *Elchinov*, 58. In relation to this matter, one could also raise the question whether the possible exclusion of certain medical treatments might breach Union law.

592 C-157/99 *Geraets-Smits and Peerbooms*, 89. See also C-238/82 *Duphar*, 21.

593 C-157/99 *Geraets-Smits and Peerbooms*, 96.

594 In this regard, 'all the relevant available information, including, in particular, existing scientific literature and studies, the authorised opinions of specialists and the fact that the proposed treatment is covered or not covered by the sickness insurance system of the Member State in which the treatment is provided' must be taken into consideration when deciding on whether the criterion of 'normality' is met. C-157/99 *Geraets-Smits and Peerbooms*, 98.

595 C-157/99 *Geraets-Smits and Peerbooms*, 97.

596 See F. Pennings, 'Overview of Recent Cases Before the European Court of Human Rights and the European Court of Justice' *European Journal of Social Security* 2001, vol 3 issue 3, p. 280; Pennings, above n. 183, p. 171 and Coucheir and Jorens, above n. 199, pp. 92–101.

597 Standing Committee of European Doctors, *Free movement of patients: When is a treatment sufficiently tried and tested – How to decide?* http://cpme.dyndns.org:591/adopted/CPME_AD_Brd_290303_9_EN_fr.pdf, 2003 (accessed 02.03.2017).

the Court seems to set aside the disparities in the medical treatment patterns in the different Member States,[598] and theoretically implies that a Member State might be obliged to reimburse the costs of a treatment which is not only not available in that country but also not accepted or even opposed by the healthcare professionals of the Member State concerned.[599]

Coucheir and Jorens point out that putting the national policies of determining the scope of healthcare coverage into an international perspective might not only be seen as a threat to the autonomy of the Member States, but as 'an occasion to share best practices, which, in the long run, could result in a converging of national health care baskets'.[600] Although this approach is very innovative, it seems to be slightly over-optimistic: on the one hand, Member States react very sensitively to any actions which have the potential to affect their healthcare competence, and on the other hand, extending benefit coverage in the Member States might require serious financial investments. This converging is thus very much dependent on the financial potential of the individual Member States. Nevertheless, setting up a standardised package of healthcare offered across the European Union,[601] although this will, realistically, not happen very soon, would be a ground-breaking achievement of the Union's healthcare policy.

Secondly, the CJEU was confronted with this issue of benefit packages in the *Elchinov* case,[602] in which the question of the method to determine the circle of benefits covered was raised with regard to one of the new Member States, namely Bulgaria.[603] Although – as Murphy noted correctly[604] by referring to the opinion

598 For certain treatments, the approaches of the different States vary significantly. Steyger mentions delivering babies at home, hormone replacement treatment and dispensing medicines as examples. E. Steyger, 'National Health Care Systems Under Fire (but not too heavily)' *Legal Issues of Economic Integration* 2002, vol 29 issue 1, p. 106.

599 Steyger, above n. 598, p. 106 and Coucheir and Jorens above n. 199, p. 99.

600 Coucheir and Jorens, above n. 199, p. 98.

601 P. Kanavos, M. McKee and T. Richards, 'Cross border health care in Europe. European court rulings have made governments worried' *British Medical Journal* 1999, vol 319 issue 7192, p. 1158.

602 C-173/09 Georgi Ivanov *Elchinov* v Natsionalna zdravnoosiguritelna kasa [ECLI:EU:C:2010:581].

603 For a detailed analysis of the case, see G. Berki, 'Az Európai Bíróság újabb ítélete az egészségügyi szolgáltatás tervezett külföldi igénybevételének tárgyában. A tagállami ellátási csomag tartalmának kérdése' (Another CJEU ruling on scheduled treatment abroad: the question of the content of benefit baskets) *Jogesetek Magyarázata* (*Case Law Review*) 2012, vol 3 issue 2, pp. 39–47; T. Sokol, 'Rindal and Elchinov: A(n) (Impending) Revolution in EU Law on Patient Mobility' *Croatian Yearbook of European Law and Policy* 2010, vol 6 no 6, pp. 167–208; M. Eliantonio and C. Backes, 'Taking constitutionalization one step too far? The need for revision of the Rheinmühlen case law in the light of the AG Opinion and the ECJ's ruling in Elchinov' *Maastricht Faculty of Law Working Paper* 2010/9; C. Murphy, 'An Effective Right to Cross-Border Healthcare? On Patients, Primacy and Procedural Autonomy: Comment on Elchinov' *European Law Review* 2011, No 4, pp. 542–557; and van der Mei, above n. 580.

604 Murphy, above n. 603, p. 543.

of Advocate General Cruz Villalón[605] – each question[606] referred to the Court could have been answered according to the existing case law, 'the accession to the European Union of new States with different healthcare systems, both in terms of their organisation and their financial resources, raises uncertainties about the applicability of case-law which was conceived and correspondingly developed in an era preceding that expansion'.[607]

In the case concerned, the competent national institution refused to give the patient[608] the prior authorisation on the grounds that the treatment in question was not included in the domestic healthcare benefit basket.[609] Unlike under the Dutch legislation, the benefits covered by the Bulgarian compulsory health insurance scheme were listed comprehensively and definitively in the law on health insurance. Accordingly, the legal uncertainty at stake was not based on the discretionary power of the competent institution. Instead – despite the clear attempt of the legislature to set out an objective, transparent and non-discriminatory system – the lower court and the Supreme Administrative Court disagreed on the scope of the benefit coverage, namely whether one of the categories[610] listed in the law included the treatment concerned.[611] It must be kept in mind that the outcome of this assessment is decisive from the Regulation's point of view: if the treatment is theoretically covered by the health insurance scheme but cannot be provided in the territory of the Member State, the competent institution is obliged to issue the S2 form enabling the patient to receive the treatment abroad. If it is not covered, the Member State has no obligation to finance the medical costs.

The Bulgarian Supreme Administrative Court was of the opinion 'that the fact that it is impossible to provide the treatment in issue in Bulgaria, even though it is referred to in the national legislation, establishes a presumption that it is not

605 Opinion of AG Cruz Villalón in C-173/09 *Georgi Ivanov Elchinov v Natsionalna zdravnoosiguritelna kasa* [ECLI:EU:C:2010:581], 2.

606 The national court's questions concerned two topics. Apart from the patient mobility issues, it challenged the settled *Rheinmühlen* case law of the CJEU (C-166/73 *Rheinmühlen-Düsseldorf v Einfuhr- und Vorratsstelle für Getreide und Futtermittel* [ECLI:EU:C:1974:3]) on the relationship between the CJEU and national courts. The latter issue is not dealt with in this book, but analysis can be found in the articles referred to in n. 603.

607 Opinion of AG Villalón in *Elchinov*, 2.

608 Mr Elchinov, a Bulgarian citizen covered by the compulsory healthcare insurance system in Bulgaria, suffered from a malignant oncological disease of the right eye. He was recommended to undergo a specialised treatment, which was not available in his Member State of residence. Therefore, he requested prior authorisation to travel to Germany and receive the required medical care in a special clinic for eye diseases in Berlin. C-173/09 *Elchinov*, 10–11.

609 C-173/09 *Elchinov*, 12.

610 There were two categories on the list which potentially absorb the treatment concerned: under number 136 'other operations on the eyeball' and, under number 258 'high-technology radiotherapy for oncological and non-oncological conditions'. C-173/09 *Elchinov*, 11.

611 Opinion of AG Villalón in *Elchinov*, 58.

included among the benefits that are lawfully payable'.[612] The CJEU held that if the list of reimbursed medical benefits does not expressly and precisely specify the treatment method applied but defines types of treatment, an application for prior authorisation cannot be rejected on the grounds that the required treatment is not provided within the territory of the Member State of residence, since such a ground, if it were accepted, would imply an unjustified restriction on the scope of the coordination rules on planned medical care.[613]

In my opinion, the Court – once again – went a bit too far on this point. It acknowledged that the national legislature took obvious efforts to create an objective, transparent and non-discriminatory framework, but it did not seem to respect the presumptive legislative intention not to cover benefits which are not provided in the Member State concerned and dismissed the restrictive interpretation of the national higher court. This extensive interpretation, however, may warn Member State – especially the ones with a relatively limited healthcare budget – to formalise their benefit catalogues even more carefully in order to avoid the possibility that they might be required to pay for advanced treatments which go beyond the financial limits of these Member States. However, taking into account the current state of medicine and the rapid improvement of medical research, it is highly doubtful whether it is possible to define an exhaustive list. As Newdick notes, '(a) "positive" or "white" list of approved treatments would need to be very responsive to advances in clinical and pharmaceutical developments. If the system is too slow or bureaucratic, it could deprive patients of beneficial new treatments available elsewhere.'[614] Moreover, the Court's standpoint in the *Elchinov* judgment may motivate the Member States to set up negative or black lists and clearly indicate those benefits which are excluded from the benefit coverage.[615] This may increase the level of legal certainty but decrease the level of protection, resulting in exactly the reverse effect than the one the Court intended to reach.[616]

Recently, the Swedish legislation was reported to be somewhat problematic with regard to the determination of the benefit basket, where – instead of having an explicit list in terms of what is covered by the healthcare system – the concept of 'science and evidence-based medicine' is used. Although research results and comprehensive clinical experience should guide the delivery of healthcare, the concept was criticised for being vague.[617]

---

612 C-173/09 *Elchinov*, 14.

613 C-173/09 *Elchinov*, 62 and 73. See also Pennings, above n. 8, p. 429.

614 C. Newdick, 'The European Court of Justice, transnational health care and social citizenship – Accidental death of a concept?' *Wisconsin International Law Journal* 2009, vol 26 issue 3, pp. 861–862.

615 Murphy, above n. 603, p. 554.

616 van der Mei, above n. 580, p. 1306 and Berki, above n. 603, p. 46.

617 Strban et al., above n. 5, p. 53.

To sum up, the first condition of Article 20(2) is satisfied if the treatment required is explicitly or implicitly included in the benefit package of the Member State of residence. If the result of the assessment is affirmative, the second criterion will be observed, namely whether the treatment required, which is proven to be covered by the compulsory healthcare scheme of the Member State of residence, can be provided within a medically justifiable time limit.

3.1.3. *Medically Justifiable Time Limit*

While the first condition attached to prior authorisation remained intact and Article 20(2) of Regulation 883/2004 echoes exactly the same phrase as Article 22(2) of Regulation 1408/71, a remarkable change was implemented with regard to the second condition. As already mentioned,[618] the old Regulation imposed the obligation of granting authorisation when the treatment required could not be given 'within the time normally necessary for obtaining the treatment in question in the Member State of residence taking account of the patient's current state of health and the probable course of the disease'.[619] This rather administrative criterion, which was based on the impersonal, generalised, *normally necessary time limit*, was slightly rephrased in the new Regulation into a more personal medical condition based on 'a time limit which is medically justifiable'.[620] The discrepancy – although it might seem small – is significant, as can be deducted from Cornelissen's example illustrating the practical side:

> under the [...] wording of Article 22(2) Regulation 1408/71, authorisation may be refused to a person requiring surgery which, if carried out within three months might prevent the risk of irreversible aggravation of health or even death, if the 'time normally necessary for obtaining the treatment' in question in the competent State is six months.[621]

Under the wording of the new Regulation, however, the time limit is individualised taking due account of the medical circumstances of the person concerned. This development is also rooted in the case law of the CJEU. The Court dealt with the interpretation of the second condition in numerous rulings. Its findings in this regard can be summarised as follows: the requirement of medical necessity is in practice satisfied only when the *same or equally effective* treatment cannot be obtained *without undue delay* in the territory of the Member State of residence; while assessing the necessity of the treatment, the national

---

618 See section 3.7. in Chapter 1. Setting the scene.

619 Article 22(2) of Regulation 1408/71. See also C-56/01 *Inizan*, 44; C-372/04 *Watts*, 57; C-211/08 *Commission v Spain*, 59; C-173/09 *Elchinov*, 54.

620 Article 20(2) of Regulation 883/2004.

621 Cornelissen, above n. 185, p. 464.

authorities are required to have regard to *all the relevant circumstances of each specific case*; the mere existence of *waiting lists* in the territory of the Member State concerned cannot constitute a justified ground to refuse to grant prior authorisation.

First, the CJEU was asked to give its opinion about the second condition for mandatory authorisation in the above cited *Geraets-Smits and Peerbooms* judgment,[622] when it needed to interpret the Dutch requirement of medical necessity in the light of the Regulation and of the Treaty. Under the legislation of the Netherlands, to grant authorisation allowing the assumption of the costs of a medical treatment provided outside of the country is subject to the condition that it is proven that the insured person's state of health requires the treatment.[623] In the course of the proceedings, it turned out that 'in practice this condition often appears to be interpreted as meaning that the provision of such treatment is not to be authorised unless it appears that appropriate treatment cannot be provided without undue delay in the Netherlands'.[624] However, this interpretation immediately leads to two further questions, namely what can be considered 'appropriate treatment' and what does 'undue delay' mean. The answers are decisive on this point, but the Court was reluctant to give a full interpretation of either of them. Still, it added that the condition concerning the necessity of the treatment is satisfied if the *same or equally effective treatment* can be obtained without undue delay.[625] 'Furthermore, in order to determine whether equally effective treatment can be obtained without undue delay, the national authorities are required to have regard to all the circumstances of each specific case and to take due account not only of the patient's medical condition at the time when authorisation is sought but also of his past record'.[626]

Consequently, it can be concluded that the same or equally effective treatment is considered appropriate. However, this does not seem to solve the problem: neither guidelines were given on the interpretation of the expression 'equally effective treatment', nor was the meaning of 'undue delay' established. For lack of an EU-wide interpretation, the competent Member State has to decide whether the treatment requested to undergo abroad is equally effective as the ones provided in its own territory, and has the authority to evaluate whether the patient has to wait too long for the treatment.[627] Therefore, it is still unclear under which circumstances the competent institution may not refuse to grant

622 See n. 307 above.

623 C-157/99 *Geraets-Smits and Peerbooms*, 64 and 99. See also C-385/99 *Müller-Fauré and Van Riet*, 42.

624 C-157/99 *Geraets-Smits and Peerbooms*, 101.

625 C-157/99 *Geraets-Smits and Peerbooms*, 103. See also C-385/99 *Müller-Fauré and Van Riet*, 89; C-56/01 *Inizan*, 45, 59; C-372/04 *Watts*, 61; C-173/09 *Elchinov*, 65, 67; C-268/13 *Petru*, 31.

626 C-157/99 *Geraets-Smits and Peerbooms*, 104. See also C-385/99 *Müller-Fauré and Van Riet*, 90; C-56/01 *Inizan*, 46; C-372/04 *Watts*, 62, 68; C-173/09 *Elchinov*, 66; C-268/13 *Petru*, 32.

627 Kesteloot et al., above n. 92, p. 47.

prior authorisation: its discretionary power is very extensive and the right of the patient is rather uncertain. A whole series of Court cases have sought to clarify these matters.

The Court proceeded its observation of the Dutch legislation in the *Müller-Fauré and Van Riet* case,[628] in which the referring court asked the Court to explain specifically what is meant by 'without undue delay' and, in particular, whether that condition must be assessed on a strictly medical basis, regardless of the waiting time normally necessary for the treatment in question.[629] Despite the obvious and expressed need for clarification, the Court once again avoided describing the notion of undue delay by simply repeating its own statement in the *Geraets-Smits and Peerbooms* case.[630]

What it did, however, is extend the list of factors that must be taken into account by the competent institution when determining whether the treatment which is equally effective for the patient can be obtained without undue delay in the territory of the Member State of affiliation. Besides the patient's medical condition at the time authorisation is sought and his/her medical history, 'where appropriate, also the degree of pain or the nature of the patient's disability which might, for example, make it impossible or extremely difficult for him to carry out a professional activity' must be taken into consideration.[631] By saying this, the Court peremptorily switched to *medically justifiable time limit*, which is again a considerable improvement in favour of patients. Moreover, as Flear noted correctly, '(t)his clearly goes beyond an assessment of the patient's medical need alone'.[632] The fact that the potential effect on the patient's employment status may be taken into consideration shows that the Court opts for an extensive evaluation process. Although the usage of the expression 'for example' indicates that the list given by the Court is not exhaustive, it leaves open the question what kind of other circumstances may play a role.

Recently, the *Petru* case[633] added an interesting new aspect to the interpretation of the second condition. The CJEU pointed out that one of the

---

628 C-385/99 *V.G. Müller-Fauré v Onderlinge Waarborgmaatschappij OZ Zorgverzekeringen UA and E.E.M. van Riet v Onderlinge Waarborgmaatschappij ZAO Zorgverzekeringen* [ECLI:EU:C:2003:270] Ms. Müller-Fauré underwent dental treatment in Germany, while Ms. Van Riet requested authorisation to obtain arthroscopy and ulnar reduction treatment in Belgium. In both cases, the sickness funds refused to bear the costs of the medical care on the grounds that the medical necessity of the treatments was not proved. See n. 315 above.

629 C-385/99 *Müller-Fauré and Van Riet*, 35.

630 C-385/99 *Müller-Fauré and Van Riet*, 89.

631 C-385/99 *Müller-Fauré and Van Riet*, 90.

632 Flear, above n. 86, p. 227.

633 C-268/13 *Elena Petru v Casa Judeţeană de Asigurări de Sănătate Sibiu and Casa Naţională de Asigurări de Sănătate* [ECLI:EU:C:2014:2271]. Elena Petru, a Romanian national who resides in Transylvania, suffered from a serious cardiovascular disease. In 2007 she had suffered a myocardial infarction and needed surgery. When her condition deteriorated in 2009, she had to be admitted to a clinic specialised in cardiovascular diseases in Timisoara.

circumstances that the competent institution must take into account may, in a specific case, be the lack of medication and basic medical supplies and infrastructure.[634] Although this circumstance clearly has the potential to make it impossible to provide healthcare without undue delay, the CJEU underlined that it is for the national court to determine whether the treatment could have been carried out in another domestic hospital in due time.[635] In line with this logic, the CJEU gave a cautious answer to a politically sensitive question[636] and

---

Ms Petru's condition required an operation involving open heart surgery to replace the mitral valve and insert two stents. (C-268/13, 9.) Upon her stay at the Romanian hospital, she noticed that the local hospital infrastructure was far from adequate: according to her claim, medication and basic medical commodities were lacking, such as painkillers, antiseptic/disinfectant, absorbent cotton wool or sterile dressings, and the number of beds was insufficient, resulting in a situation with – on average – three times more patients than beds. (C-268/13, AG Opinion, 6).

She proceeded to request a prior authorisation (E-112 form) from the competent institution to undergo the complex surgical procedure in Germany. Her application was refused on the grounds that – taking into account the nature of the treatment requested, the patient's state of health and the probable course of the disease – the healthcare service sought could be provided in a medical establishment in Romania within a reasonable length of time. Thus, there was no indication to give authorisation to receive the treatment abroad. (C-268/13, 11.). Nevertheless, Ms Petru did approach a German clinic, where the operation was successfully performed and it cost – including the post-operational hospital stay – almost 18,000 euros in total. (C-268/13, 10).

Following her surgery, Ms Petru brought a civil action against the competent institution and demanded the reimbursement of the medical expenses incurred in Germany. Her action was dismissed at first instance, but she appealed. The court of second instance acknowledged that the parties disagreed as to the interpretation of the provisions of national and EU law applicable to the dispute before it, and that the outcome of the case depended upon the interpretation given to Article 22 of Regulation No 1408/71. (C-268/13, 16–17).

634 C-268/13, *Petru* 32–33.

635 C-268/13, *Petru* 34–35.

636 The story behind the legal proceedings is an unfortunately familiar one in numerous Eastern European Member States. Interestingly enough, the CJEU did not follow the line of argumentation of the AG who differentiated between *occasional, localised and incidental shortages of resources* and *structural, generalised and prolonged deficiency*, and came to the conclusion that a Member State struggling with the latter problem would be – by definition – unable to meet the costs that resulted from the mass health-related exodus of insured patients. (C-268/13, AG Opinion, 31).

In his opinion, Member States with structural and prolonged deficiencies can decline to authorise planned care abroad, even if this may effectively mean that certain healthcare services cannot be provided. (C-268/13, AG Opinion, 38.). This approach might have been politically more feasible than the CJEU's final conclusion, but it would have raised serious concerns in relation to European citizens' (equal) right to adequate healthcare services based on Article 35 of the Charter of Fundamental Rights of the European Union. See section 3.2. in Chapter 1. Setting the scene.

On the one hand, it is commendable that the CJEU's clarification provided European patients with the entitlement to receive healthcare abroad when facing insufficient medical circumstances in their home state; on the other hand though, this entitlement might cause serious headache to certain Member States if they do not develop their hospital facilities in the near future. Whether they can be required and/or are able to do so, opens up a whole different debate.

declared that inadequate medical infrastructure can indeed result in a situation in which a Member State cannot refuse to authorise planned care abroad, but did not go as far as to decide whether this was the case in Romania.[637]

The issues adumbrated above again arose in the *Inizan*[638] ruling, but it did not facilitate the understanding of the aforementioned phrases either. The question what 'undue delay' means still remained.

However, an important step was taken in *Watts*,[639] where the Court elucidated the relationship between the concept of undue delay and the setting up of waiting lists[640] in the Member States. The question of waiting lists had already been touched upon in the Müller-Fauré and Van Riet case, where the government of the United Kingdom drew attention to the fact that 'in practice authorisation for treatment in another Member State is generally given in the United Kingdom when there is a delay for treatment beyond the maximum waiting times'. Additionally, it emphasised that 'national waiting lists take account of the different needs of different categories of patients and permit the best possible allocation of hospital resources. The lists are flexible so that if a patient's condition suddenly deteriorates, he can be moved up the waiting list and treated more quickly'.[641] Consequently, one may wonder whether undue delay means a delay beyond the maximum waiting times. Can the Member States be obliged to determine maximum waiting times for certain types of treatments? If a Member State defines a maximum waiting time, does that mean that the non-provision of the required treatment within this period ensures the right for the patient to obtain the treatment abroad at the expense of

---

[637] C-268/13, *Petru* 36.

[638] C-56/01 *Patricia Inizan v Caisse primaire d'assurance maladie des Hauts-de-Seine* [ECLI:EU:C:2003:578] The main proceedings took place between Ms Inizan, a French national who intended to undergo a multidisciplinary pain treatment in Germany, and the French health insurance fund, which rejected her request for reimbursement on the grounds that the requirements for planned care under the Regulation rules had not been satisfied. Paragraphs 43–50 and 59 of the judgment deal with the interpretation of the second condition.

[639] C-372/04 *The Queen, on the application of Yvonne Watts v Bedford Primary Care Trust and Secretary of State for Health* [ECLI:EU:C:2006:325] Mrs Watts's request for prior authorisation for a hip replacement operation was refused twice on the grounds that she was placed on the waiting list and that there was no undue delay. See n. 311.

[640] 'The waiting list is a formal record of patients identified as needing non-emergency appointment to a hospital for assessment or treatment. It is used to progress the appropriate procedures of review, selection and admission to ensure that none of those patients become lost or inadvertently overlooked. Waiting lists are a statement of known demand that quantifies, at any point in time, the number of patients waiting for assessment or treatment.' C.M. de Pancorbo and L. Moral, 'Improving Waiting List Information Systems' in HOPE, *Waiting lists and waiting times in health care – Managing demand and supply*, http://www.hope.be/05eventsandpublications/docpublications/60_waiting/60_waitinglists_2001.pdf, 2001 (accessed 09.11.2012), p. 4.

[641] C-385/99 *Müller-Fauré and Van Riet*, 58.

his/her health insurance automatically? Moreover, could not the European Union itself determine a general maximum waiting time?

The Court indicated in its *Müller-Fauré and Van Riet* judgment – and confirmed in *Watts* – that setting up waiting lists is not per se incompatible with Union law. It is part of the Member States' autonomy concerning the organisation of their healthcare schemes,[642] but 'a refusal to grant prior authorisation which is based not on fear of wastage resulting from hospital overcapacity but solely on the ground that there are waiting lists on national territory for the hospital treatment concerned, without account being taken of the specific circumstances attaching to the patient's medical condition' cannot be accepted and a 'waiting time which is too long or abnormal' would be more likely to serve as a ground for compulsory authorisation.[643] However, this interpretation is still rather vague, and does not provide legal certainty, either for the competent institutions or for the patients.

As a consequence, in the *Watts* case, the Court was asked directly to shed light on whether the criteria for the interpretation of the phrase 'within the time normally necessary for obtaining the treatment in question' are the same as those used to define the term 'without undue delay'.[644] Answering the question, the Court pointed out again that the refusal to grant prior authorisation can be based only on an objective medical assessment which takes due account of all the relevant factors identified in the case law of the Court. Therefore, the competent institution is entitled to refuse the authorisation on the grounds of non-satisfaction of the criterion in regard to waiting time only if it does not exceed the period which is acceptable in the light of an objective medical assessment of the clinical needs of the person concerned in the light of his/her medical condition; and the history; and probable course of his/her illness; the degree of pain he/she is in and/or the nature of his/her disability at the time the authorisation is sought.[645] Still, it is remarkable that – unlike in the *Müller-Fauré and Van Riet* ruling – in *Watts* the Court failed to make reference to the potential impact of the patient's medical status to her employment status, which evokes the question whether factors other than the ones of a purely medical nature must be taken into consideration. Interestingly enough, in the *Elchinov* judgment, the reference to the impact on professional activity appeared again.[646]

---

642 'Where the demand for hospital treatment is constantly rising, primarily as a consequence of medical progress and increased life expectancy, and the supply is necessarily limited by budgetary constraints, it cannot be denied that the national authorities responsible for managing the supply of such treatment are entitled, if they consider it necessary, to institute a system of waiting lists in order to manage the supply of that treatment and to set priorities on the basis of the available resources and capacities'. C-372/04 *Watts*, 67.

643 C-385/99 *Müller-Fauré and Van Riet*, 92; C-372/04 *Watts*, 63.

644 C-372/04 *Watts*, 51.

645 C-372/04 *Watts*, 68, 70.

646 C-173/09 *Elchinov*, 66.

It is also clearly shown that the setting of waiting times is expected to be done *flexibly and dynamically*, so that the period initially notified to the person concerned may be reconsidered in the light of any deterioration in his/her state of health occurring after the first request for authorisation,[647] as in Mrs Watt's case. Furthermore, the Court firmly dismissed the UK's arguments according to which such an interpretation would be

> liable to undermine the national competent authorities' power to manage the available hospital capacity in their territory by the use of waiting lists, provided that the existence of such lists does not prevent the taking account in each individual case of the medical circumstances and the clinical needs of the person concerned when he requests authorisation to receive hospital treatment in another Member State at the expense of the system with which he is registered.[648]

To sum up, according to the rules of the Regulation as interpreted by the CJEU a three-step assessment process can be drawn up in regard to the prior authorisation requirement. This is illustrated below in Table 9. If the two criteria of Article 20(2) BR are cumulatively satisfied, the competent institution has no liberty to decide whether to accord the prior authorisation, since it cannot fulfil its obligation to provide the requested treatment, which is included in the benefit package of the Member State concerned, within a medically justifiable time limit.

Table 9. Assessment under Article 20(2) BR

<table>
<tr><td rowspan="2">Benefit coverage</td><td colspan="4">Question No1: Is the treatment in question among the benefits provided for by the legislation in the Member State where the person concerned resides? (Article 20(2) BR)</td></tr>
<tr><td colspan="3">YES</td><td>NO</td></tr>
<tr><td rowspan="3">Availability</td><td colspan="3">Question No2: Can the person concerned be given such treatment within a time limit which is medically justifiable? (Article 20(2) BR)</td><td rowspan="6">The first condition of Article 20(2) BR is not met, thus the competent MS is not obliged to accord the authorisation.</td></tr>
<tr><td colspan="3">Question No2 Part1: Is the same or equally effective treatment available in the Member State of residence? (ECJ)</td></tr>
<tr><td colspan="2">YES</td><td>NO</td></tr>
<tr><td rowspan="3">Waiting time</td><td colspan="2">Question No2 Part2: Is the same or equally effective treatment available in the Member State of residence without undue delay? (ECJ)</td><td rowspan="3">The conditions of Article 20(2) BR are met, thus the competent MS is obliged to accord the authorisation.</td></tr>
<tr><td>YES</td><td>NO</td></tr>
<tr><td>The second condition of Article 20(2) BR is not met, thus the competent MS is not obliged to accord the authorisation.</td><td>The conditions of Article 20(2) BR are met, thus the competent MS is obliged to accord the authorisation.</td></tr>
</table>

Source: The author's own summary.

[647] C-372/04 *Watts*, 69.
[648] C-372/04 *Watts*, 75.

Notably, a few Member States defined *legal maximum waiting times* and introduced *waiting time guarantees*, meaning that if the treatment in question cannot be provided for the patient within the waiting time specified in the national legislation, a prior authorisation shall be granted. In Spain, a prior authorisation is granted automatically if the expected waiting time exceeds the maximum legal waiting times established at a national level regarding some specific treatments. In Sweden, it is guaranteed by the law that a patient shall have instant contact with the healthcare system for consultation, seeing a GP within seven days, consulting a specialist within ninety days, and waiting for no more than ninety days after being diagnosed to receive treatment; if the waiting time guarantee is not upheld, the request for prior authorisation cannot be rejected. Similarly, in Slovenia, if at the time of registration the waiting time which exceeds the longest admissible waiting time was set and there is no other healthcare provider in the country where the waiting time is not exceeded, the patient has the right to healthcare in another EU or EFTA State. From the patients' point of view, setting reasonable maximum waiting times can be seen as a source of safety and certainty, and must therefore be considered a good practice.[649]

In my opinion, it could be argued that *introducing a general maximum waiting time* (MWT) in Union law would ensure a higher level of protection for patients. That is to say, if a Member State cannot provide the patient, who is covered by the statutory healthcare system of that Member State, with the requested healthcare, which is included in the benefit package of the Member State in question, it fails to fulfil its obligation that is based on the legal entitlement of the person. Thus, the Member State is obliged to grant a permission to the said person to obtain the requested healthcare in another Member State, if the patient opts for it.

Setting a maximum waiting time would not solve all the problems related to undue delay, but could possibly motivate the Member States to keep waiting times low, ensure timely healthcare provision and manage waiting lists more efficiently. In theory, this would require just a slight modification of the text of the Basic Regulation.[650] However, in practice, one might suspect that Member

649 Strban et al., above n. 5, p. 54.

650 The sentence 'the authorisation shall be accorded where the treatment in question is among the benefits provided for by the legislation in the Member State where the person concerned resides and where he/she cannot be given such treatment within a time limit which is medically justifiable, taking into account his/her current state of health and the probable course of his/her illness' should be completed by adding the maximum time limit, for instance 'he/she cannot be given such treatment within a time limit which is medically justifiable, *and which is not longer than X days from the submission of the request for authorisation*'.
Of course, generally it is not a legal issue to elaborate how long this MWT should be, but it is for the healthcare experts to decide what is, on the one hand, realistic and feasible within the European healthcare systems and, on the other hand, serves the purpose of providing patients with timely healthcare within the EU at the same time.

States would heavily oppose the introduction of such a rule in the fear that it would considerably reduce their autonomy and discretionary power[651] on the one hand, and on the other, it would require significant investment in the healthcare sector in certain Member States in order to achieve short waiting times. Therefore, in today's circumstances it is not very likely that such an amendment would be supported by the required majority in the Council.[652] Since this initiative is of a harmonising nature and goes beyond the current competences of the Union in this respect, the introduction of a maximum waiting time cannot be imagined without the common support of the Member States themselves.

Nevertheless, in the long run this is a desirable direction for legislation, since it would not only improve the social protection of migrants but would serve the interest of every single patient EU-wide by inducing the decrease of waiting times in healthcare in general.

3.2. THE DIRECTIVE'S ROUTE

The coordination mechanism on planned care had been long in place when 'a handful of dissatisfied patients, some seeking redress at the European Court of Justice by invoking the principles of free movement of goods and services'[653] offered the Court the opportunity to change the landscape of Union legislation on planned care.[654] As said above, in the proceedings before the Court national legislations have been challenged, which more or less followed the Coordination Regulations' path, and the Court consistently held that the national authorisation systems constitute an obstacle to the free movement.

Since the steps taken by the Court from the limited patient mobility of the coordination mechanism towards the 'liberalisation of patient mobility' within Europe have already been outlined, just a few things will be underlined here. The Court's main consideration was that healthcare services are not different from any other services which move freely within the Union.[655] Therefore, any national measures and legislative arrangements which hinder patients, as the recipients of these services,[656] to obtain medical treatments abroad must be seen as a barrier to free movement[657] and as breaching Union law

[651] Such a measure would clearly go beyond coordination of social security systems, which is why Member States might argue that the Union overreaches its competence.

[652] On the legislative procedure related to social security coordination measures, see n. 234.

[653] M. McKee, R. Busse, R. Baeten and I. Glinos, *Cross-border healthcare collaboration in the European Union: Placing the patient at the centre*, Eurohealth 2013, vol 19 no 4, p. 4.

[654] On the CJEU's approach see section 3.7. in Chapter 1. Setting the scene.

[655] See n. 285 and 286 above.

[656] See n. 287 above.

[657] See n. 295 above.

unless properly justified.[658] The main breakthrough of this concept was the following: whereas the basic principle of planned care under the coordination system was that prior authorisation from the competent institution was required,[659] under the case law the main rule was that no prior authorisation could be prescribed. The cases in which the requirement of prior authorisation was accepted were exceptional cases where Member States could justify the existence of the authorisation system.[660] Besides the numerous grounds of justification which were refused by the Court,[661] there were two reasons which actually turned out capable of serving as a legitimate ground for restricting patient mobility by setting up or maintaining a prior authorisation system. Both of them were based on the *necessity of planning* within healthcare systems: hospital planning[662] and planning concerning the use of major medical equipment.[663]

Concerning planning requirements, the Court first acknowledged that the number of hospitals, their geographical distribution, the mode of their organisation and the equipment with which they are provided, and even the nature of the medical services which they are able to offer, are all matters for which planning must be possible. The possibility of planning serves two basic aims: on the one hand, it seeks to achieve that there is sufficient and permanent access to a balanced range of high-quality hospital treatment in the State concerned; and on the other hand, it assists in meeting a desire to control costs and to prevent, as far as possible, any wastage of financial, technical and human resources.[664]

---

658 See n. 296 above.

659 Article 20(1) BR: 'Unless otherwise provided for by this Regulation, an insured person travelling to another Member State with the purpose of receiving benefits in kind during the stay shall seek authorization from the competent institution.'

660 'Although Community law does not in principle preclude a system of prior authorisation, the conditions attached to the grant of such authorisation must nonetheless be justified with regard to the overriding considerations examined and must satisfy the requirement of proportionality'. C-157/99 *Geraets-Smits and Peerbooms*, 82; C-385/99 *Müller-Fauré and Van Riet*, 83; C-372/04 *Watts*, 113–114; C-173/09 *Elchinov*, 41.
The settled case law of the CJEU was confirmed by a rather recent order of the Court, which says: that 'Article 49 EC and Article 22 of Regulation (EEC) No 1408/71 [...] do not, in principle, preclude legislation of a Member State which makes the entitlement to full reimbursement of expenses incurred in respect of hospital treatment provided in another Member State subject to obtaining prior authorisation. On the other hand, those provisions preclude such legislation which is interpreted as excluding, in all cases, full reimbursement by the competent institution for hospital treatment given without prior authorisation.' C-430/12 *Elena Luca v Casa de Asigurări de Sănătate Bacău* [ECLI:EU:C:2013:467].

661 See n. 296 above.

662 This argument first occurred in the *Geraets-Smits and Peerbooms* judgment, and was then confirmed at several occasions. C-157/99 *Geraets-Smits and Peerbooms*, 76, 78–80; C-385/99 *Müller-Fauré and Van Riet*, 77–81; C-56/01 *Inizan*, 56; C-145/03 *Keller*, 62; C-372/04 *Watts*, 108–110; C-173/09 *Elchinov*, 43; C-512/08 *Commission v France*, 33–42.

663 The question of the prior authorisation requirement when the treatment is provided outside of a hospital environment and involves the use of major medical equipment was raised in the course of an infringement procedure against France. C-512/08 *Commission v France*.

664 See n. 662 above.

It is indeed a valid argument that in certain cases planning is not only desirable, but even inevitable in order to ensure the sustainability of European healthcare schemes.[665] However, the question in which cases planning is truly necessary and therefore maintaining a prior authorisation system is a justified national measure is highly contentious. Not surprisingly, a discussion emerged from this question.[666] In this respect, the Court added important points of clarification in its *Müller-Fauré and Van Riet*[667] and *Commission v France*[668] judgments. In the former, it concluded that:

> the distinction between hospital services and non-hospital services may sometimes prove difficult to draw. In particular, certain services provided in a hospital environment but also capable of being provided by a practitioner in his surgery or in a health centre could for that reason be placed on the same footing as non-hospital services.[669]

This argumentation clearly shows the Court's intention to interpret the notion of hospital treatment restrictively. However, it does not provide a specific ground on which a distinction can be made between inpatient care, where the requirement of prior authorisation is tolerated, and outpatient care, where the requirement of prior authorisation cannot be justified. In the latter judgment, the Court accepted the arguments of France and declared that planning objectives might not only relate to hospital environment, but also to major medical equipment, 'regardless of the setting, hospital or otherwise, in which it is intended to be installed and used'.[670] However, once again, no further specification of the definition of major medical equipment was offered by the Court. Thus, although the legal status of border-crossing patients was strengthened by the

---

[665] The CJEU emphasises that a borderless, uncontrolled patient flow carries the potential to jeopardise 'all the planning which goes into the system of agreements in an effort to guarantee a rationalised, stable, balanced and accessible supply of hospital services'. C-157/99 *Geraets-Smits and Peerbooms*, 81; C-385/99 *Müller-Fauré and Van Riet*, 82; C-372/04 *Watts*, 111.

[666] It is not difficult to see that on this point, the Member States wish to stay in control and interpret this ground of justification widely, whereas the European Union attempts to protect or even extend patient's rights (and the principle of free movement) by limiting the discretionary power of the national institutions.

[667] C-385/99 *Müller-Fauré and Van Riet*. See n. 315.

[668] The baseline of the infringement procedure against France was that the Commission argued that the requirement of prior authorisation for the purpose of responsibility for payment by the competent institution for treatment available at a general practitioner's surgery in another Member State and requiring the use of major medical equipment constituted a restriction of the freedom to provide services, whereas the French government held that the Court's case law must be interpreted as allowing – for the sake of overall planning objectives – to require prior authorisation in regard to medical treatments calling for the use of major medical equipment outside hospital infrastructures, having regard to the very high costs of that equipment and to its impact on the budget of social security systems. C-512/08 *Commission v France*, 20 and 25.

[669] C-385/99 *Müller-Fauré and Van Riet*, 75; C-512/08 *Commission v France*, 35.

[670] C-512/08 *Commission v France*, 37.

opportunity to obtain healthcare without prior authorisation, the lack of well-defined boundaries of the Member States' discretion left patients uncertain and hesitant about which treatments could and could not be reimbursed when the patient was not granted authorisation beforehand.

The Directive follows this logic of the case law by stipulating that – as a principle – 'the Member State of affiliation shall not make the reimbursement of costs of cross-border healthcare subject to prior authorisation' except in cases set out in the Directive itself.[671] The Union permits the Member States to restrict free mobility of patients by applying authorisation schemes within a limited scope. This limitation must be based 'on overriding reasons of general interest, such as planning requirements relating to the aim of ensuring sufficient and permanent access to a balanced range of high-quality treatment in the Member State concerned or to the wish to control costs and avoid, as far as possible, any waste of financial, technical and human resources'.[672]

It can therefore be concluded that the main principle of the Directive is that no prior authorisation is required. However, a few exceptions exist when the restriction of free movement by applying the prior authorisation requirement is lawfully justified. These exceptions, which grant the competent institutions the right to make the reimbursement of medical costs abroad subject to prior authorisation, can be divided into two groups: they partly concern the *planning requirement*[673] and partly *medical quality and safety issues*.[674]

When transposing the Directive, the Member States could choose whether or not they opt for introducing a scheme of prior authorisation under the Directive. Most of them did choose to restrict the free movement of patients in this way. Only the Czech Republic, Estonia, Finland, Lithuania, the Netherlands, Norway and Sweden do not currently have a prior authorisation scheme under the Directive's regime. All the rest of the EU countries (and Iceland) do apply either, but mostly both, of the above restrictive scenarios.[675]

3.2.1. *Planning Requirement*

The grounds for planning which already appeared in the case law of the Court are repeated in the Directive:[676] healthcare may be subject to prior authorisation

---

671 Article 7(8) PMD.

672 Article 7(9) PMD. On healthcare capacity planning see R. Baeten and W. Palm, 'The Compatibility of Health Care Capacity Planning Policies with EU Internal Market Rules' in J.W. van de Gronden, E. Szyszczak, U. Neergaard and M. Krajewski (eds.), *Health Care and EU Law*, T. M. C. Asser Press, The Hague 2011, pp. 389–411.

673 Article 8(2)(a) PMD.

674 Article 8(2)(b) and (c) PMD.

675 Strban et al., above n. 5, p. 56.

676 Pennings points out a tiny wording difference with less tiny consequences: whereas the case law referred to the two objectives of planning as cumulative aims (see n. 662), the

if it 'involves overnight hospital accommodation of the patient in question for at least one night'[677] or it 'requires use of highly specialised and cost-intensive medical infrastructure or medical equipment.'[678] Although the grounds are the same, they appear slightly more specified as when observed in the judgments of the Court: the Directive attempted to fine-tune these provisions.

Hospital treatments only fall within the category of justified restriction of free movement as far as they require the patient to stay at least one night in hospital. In this respect, medical protocols might be decisive, since they define those types of treatments which normally necessitate in-hospital stay and also suggest the approximate length of the stay.[679] The downside of this approach is that it leaves no room for individually influencing factors and personal assessment, whereas it can easily happen that a medical intervention has diverse effects on diverse persons: one person might need in-hospital stay afterwards (or beforehand), whereas another does not. Introducing this condition seems to answer the question whether out-patient care or one-day surgery, which can be performed only in a hospital setting, might be subject to an authorisation requirement: they cannot unless they fall under the second category, requiring the usage of highly specified or cost-intensive medical infrastructure or medical equipment. However, one may wonder whether overnight hospital stay requires considerably more planning than daytime hospital stay. For example, if a person is treated in a hospital setting during the day but is allowed to spend the nights at his/her home, the above condition is not met, although it can be rightfully argued that this treatment requires a comparable scale of planning.

Whereas in most of the Member States the determination of the exact scope of this situation is lacking, it is worth noting that Belgian law defines hospitalisation by reference to whether overnight stay is required in the State of treatment, and not whether that is required in Belgium. In Romania, overnight stay implies hospitalisation that exceeds twenty-four hours. The Commission's report on the operation of the Directive drew attention to the phenomenon that several Member States require prior authorisation if the healthcare provision involved overnight stay in the Member State of treatment.[680] That is, however,

---

Directive – by using the word '*or*' in Article 7(9) – treats them as alternatives. Thus, even one of them (e.g. the desire to control costs) can be enough to lawfully justify the existence of an authorisation scheme. Pennings says that '(t)he requirements of the Directive may, thus, be less strict than those of the case law' and '(a)s a result, the formula of the Directive can lead to legal uncertainty and incoherence between case law and the Directive'. Pennings, above n. 8, p. 440.

677 Article 8(2)(a)(i) PMD.

678 Article 8(2)(a)(ii) PMD.

679 A. Clarke and R. Rosen, 'Length of stay – How short should hospital care be?' *European Journal of Public Health* 2001, vol 11 issue 2, pp. 166–170.

680 European Commission, *Report from the Commission to the European Parliament and the Council, Commission report on the operation of Directive 2011/24/EU on the application of patients' rights in cross-border healthcare*, COM (2015) 421 final, 04.09.2015.

not in line with the current wording and the intention behind the adoption of the Directive. The prior authorisation scheme based on initial planning serves the purpose of ensuring sufficient and permanent access to a balanced range of high-quality treatment, of controlling costs and of avoiding the wastage of financial, technical and human resources in the Member State of affiliation.[681] It is thus desirable to determine precisely which treatment does fall into this category and which does not. This categorisation shall be made by the Member State of affiliation and shall not be dependent on the Member State of treatment or on the way the treatment is provided in that Member State.[682]

A similar flaw can be discovered in the event of the use of highly specialised and cost-intensive medical infrastructure or medical equipment. This category is more sophisticated than its predecessor in the case law, but neither the notion of *highly specialised* infrastructure or equipment, nor the notion of *cost-intensive* infrastructure or equipment are circumscribed.[683] The question might be raised whether specification and cost-intensiveness can be defined according to Member States' national standards taking into account that the local differences or international medical science must indicate which cases fall under this category as seen in *Geraets-Smits and Peerbooms*.[684] It is, however, a development that – unlike in the case law – it is acknowledged that not only medical equipment but also necessary medical infrastructure, such as specialised services and facilities, can constitute grounds of planning.

Concerning treatments requiring the use of highly specialised and cost-intensive medical infrastructure or medical equipment, numerous Member States set a list of treatments which necessitate a prior authorisation on these grounds. This technique is used by Belgium, Spain, France, Croatia, Hungary, Luxemburg, Malta, Poland, Portugal, Romania, Slovenia, Slovakia and the United Kingdom.[685]

To sum up, the aim of the legislature to make the above categories more concrete is appreciated. However, it is crucial to indicate clearly the limits of

---

681 Article 8(2)(a) PMD.

682 Strban et al., above n. 5, p. 57.

683 In 2014, a study attempted to induce common understanding of these notions by creating the following definitions: 'Medical equipment or infrastructure is cost-intensive if: 1. its life time equipment costs (LEC), i.e. the sum of acquisition costs and life time service costs, are high relative to health expenditures per capita (affordability criterion); and 2. its fixed costs are high relative to its variable costs (cost-effectiveness criterion). Medical equipment or an intervention is highly specialised if: 1. its utilisation rate in a country is low; and either: 2. the technical complexity of the equipment, expressed in terms of the share of service costs to acquisition costs, is high; or 3. medical staff involved in the treatments with the medical equipment or infrastructure are scarce.' M. Versteegh, K. Weistra, W. Oortwijn, S. de Groot, K. Redekop, F. Rutten, P. Davis, *Literature-based approach to defining the concept of healthcare which requires 'highly specialised and costintensive medical infrastructure or medical equipment'*, Prepared for EC DG SANTE, Luxembourg 2014, p. 9.

684 See n. 593 and 594.

685 Strban et al., above n. 5, p. 57.

the Member States' discretionary power. In my opinion, this goal has not been achieved by the current wording of the Directive, which is rather vague, lacks precise definitions, and leaves too much room for arbitrary interpretation. Uncertainty on this essential point of the legislation is not in favour of the border-crossing patients, and thus these issues demand further clarification. Notwithstanding that it does not tackle the above-mentioned problems, it does reduce the uncertainty by obliging the Member States to specify the categories of healthcare the planning objectives of which justify the existence of the prior authorisation scheme.[686]

3.2.2. Protection of Public Health

The protection of public health by means of prior authorisation is a new element in the Patient Mobility Directive. The protection of public health did appear earlier in the case law of the Court several times as a possible ground for restricting patient mobility, but the Court consistently held that 'since the conditions for taking up and pursuing regulated professions have been harmonised on Community level,[687] the provision of a treatment by a healthcare provider established in another Member State provides guarantees equivalent to those provided by a healthcare practitioner established in the national territory'.[688] The drafters of the Directive did not seem to fully agree with this argument and included quality and safety reasons which can justify prior authorisation under the Directive's regime. Concerns might appear both in relation to treatments which might 'present a particular risk for the patient or the population';[689] and healthcare providers that might 'give rise to serious and specific concerns relating to the quality or safety of the care'.[690]

It is true that the variety of national healthcare systems manifests itself also in the different approaches to certain treatments. In particular, medical interventions which are heatedly debated from a bioethical point of view[691] are treated differently in the Member States of the European Union. Home birth services are a good example in this respect. Whereas it is rather liberally ruled in certain Member States, in others very strict rules apply to such situations.[692] Hungary, for example, belongs to the latter group: intense political and legal

---

686 Article 8(2) PMD.

687 See n. 118 on the mutual recognition of qualifications.

688 See n. 299 above.

689 Article 8(2)(b) PMD.

690 Article 8(2)(c) PMD.

691 See n. 56 above.

692 On the different legislations in some of the Member States, see E. Declercq, R. DeVries, K. Viisainen, H.B. Salvesen and S. Wrede, 'Where to give birth? Politics and the Place of Birth' in R. DeVries, S. Wrede, E. van Teijlingen and C. Benoit (eds), *Birth by Design: Pregnancy, Maternity Care, and Midwifery in North America and Europe*, Routledge, New York, London 2002, pp. 7–27.

debate has been taking place about whether and under which conditions a woman is legally entitled to give birth outside a hospital environment. The severity of the current legislation[693] might drive women to another Member State with a more permissible law.[694] Therefore, a Member State with a stricter legislation could argue that the treatment concerned presents a particular risk for the patient or the population[695] and make that treatment subject to prior authorisation under the scope of the Patient Mobility Directive. The Member States are required to officially declare which treatments are considered risky in this relation and 'make publicly available which healthcare is subject to prior authorisation for the purposes of this Directive'.[696] However, in the effort to reduce uncertainty, it is highly advisable to extend the obligation of prior notification towards the Commission to this category as well.[697]

Moreover, the Member States are not only permitted to make these treatments subject to prior authorisation, but may also refuse to grant prior authorisation on the grounds that 'the patient will be exposed with a reasonable certainty to an unacceptable patient-safety risk'[698] or 'the general public will be exposed with reasonable certainty to a substantial safety hazard as a result of the cross-border healthcare in question'.[699] It would have been helpful, though, if the legislature had given a hint about who is in charge of deciding whether a safety risk is still acceptable[700] or what is to be understood by *reasonable certainty*.[701]

---

693 See Governmental Decree No 35/2011 (III. 21.) on the Rules, Conditions and Excluding Reasons of Childbirth Outside of Hospital Environment.

694 The same goes, for example, to palliative care and end-of-life treatments.

695 In the case of home birth, studies show that there is a considerably higher health risk both for the mother and for the newborn compared to hospital birth, so this might be a valid argument. See, among others, A. de Jonge, B.Y. van der Goes, A.C.J. Ravelli, M.P. Amelink-Verburg, B.W.J. Mol, J.G. Nijhuis, J. Bennebroek Gravenhorst, S.E. Buitendijk, 'Perinatal mortality and morbidity in a nationwide cohort of 529 688 low-risk planned home and hospital births' *An International Journal of Obstetrics & Gynaecology* 2009, vol 116 issue 9, pp. 1177–1184 and N.M. Daysal, M. Trandafir and R. van Ewijk, 'Saving lives at birth: The impact of home births on infant outcomes' *Discussion Paper Series* 2012, Forschungsinstitut zur Zukunft der Arbeit, No. 6879.

696 Article 8(7) PMD.

697 See n. 686 above.

698 Article 8(6)(a) PMD.

699 Article 8(6)(b) PMD.

700 According to Article 8(6)(a) PMD, a clinical evaluation must take place. However, it is not indicated whose opinion is decisive concerning the acceptability of the safety risk. Is it the patient, who might be willing to take higher risks since he/she requested prior authorisation for the healthcare (e.g. in the case of home birth)? Is it the competent institution, which might not be willing to authorise any healthcare considered risky? Or is it the health practitioner, who might form an impartial professional opinion; however, who might not be willing to approve any treatment which possibly induces medical liability issues.

701 In this case, the burden of proof lies with the competent institution which ought to justify the refusal of the request for prior authorisation. Yet, it is an interesting question how the presence of an unacceptable safety risk can be proven with a reasonable certainty.

The quality and safety concerns in relation to certain *healthcare providers* are more difficult to deal with. According to Article 3(g) of the Patient Mobility Directive, a healthcare provider must be understood as 'any natural or legal person or any other entity legally providing healthcare on the territory of a Member State'. Consequently, the following question arises: how can a healthcare provider that gives rise to serious and specific quality or safety concerns legally provide healthcare services within the European Union. To answer this question, first it must be noted that healthcare professions[702] are regulated professions[703] in the European Union and – as the Court has underlined[704] – the rules according to which healthcare professions can be accessed and pursued in the territory of the European Union are harmonised. Thus, in my opinion, two scenarios are possible here: safety concerns that arise about a healthcare provider that performs his/her activity legally in the territory of a Member State but falls outside of the scope of Directive 36/2005;[705] or a healthcare provider that falls within the scope of the said Directive and pursues his/her activity legally, but does not meet certain national standards or guidelines, such as provisions on supervision.[706] For the sake of legal certainty and in order to avoid the arbitrary 'exclusion' of healthcare providers, clear and transparent indicators are needed to identify which healthcare providers are considered unadvisable, meaning not only that the provider can be made subject to prior authorisation[707] but that this authorisation may also be refused.[708]

Besides the grounds of refusal mentioned above, the Directive also stipulates that authorisation may be lawfully refused if the requested healthcare can be provided on the territory of the Member State of affiliation within a time limit which is medically justifiable, taking into account the current state of health and the probable course of illness of each patient concerned.[709] This provision of the Patient Mobility Directive fully corresponds with the relevant provision of the Coordination Regulation,[710] which was analysed earlier in this section. Similarly, the Directive echoes the Regulation by adding that 'the Member State of affiliation may not refuse to grant prior authorisation when the patient is entitled to the healthcare in question, and when this healthcare cannot be

---

702 Under the scope of Directive 2005/36, harmonised healthcare professions are: doctors of medicine, nurses responsible for general care, dental practitioners, veterinary surgeons, midwives and pharmacists.

703 See Article 3(1)(a) of Directive 2005/36 on the recognition of professional qualifications.

704 See n. 687 above.

705 A medical masseur or a physiotherapist might be a good example.

706 In this case, Member States are free to refuse to grant prior authorisation to the patient concerning healthcare provided by such a healthcare provider. Article 8(6)(c).

707 Article 8(2)(c) PMD.

708 Article 8(6)(c) PMD.

709 Article 8(6)(d) PMD.

710 Article 20(2) BR.

provided on its territory within a time limit which is medically justifiable'.[711] It is actually not quite clear why the Directive repeats in Article 8(6)(d) what can be deduced already from Article 8(5).[712]

Both routes of patient mobility apply prior authorisation schemes when a person intends to receive scheduled healthcare abroad. Nevertheless, whereas in the framework of the coordination mechanism prior approval from the competent institution is required, under the Patient Mobility Directive prior authorisation is considered an obstacle to free movement. Therefore, the scope of the justified application of such measures is limited by law. As can be deduced from the above analysis, the unique legal tools themselves contain numerous problematic points, such as the determination of the benefit baskets, the definition of, among others, the medically justifiable time limit, undue delay, highly specialised and cost-intensive medical infrastructure and medical equipment, reasonable certainty and the specification of the conditions for introducing prior authorisation and refusing to grant one. In relation to the national transposition of prior authorisation rules,[713] several questions arose in the last years. Numerous Member States implemented the Directive in such a restrictive way that it raised concerns about the EU-conformity of national prior authorisation schemes.[714] The picture is even more complex if these tools are examined in an administrative context.

3.3. ADMINISTRATIVE FORMALITIES WHEN OBTAINING PLANNED HEALTHCARE

As the Member States' entitlement to require prior authorisation regarding planned care has already been analysed, in this section those rules

---

711 Article 8(5) PMD. The decision whether a time span is medically justifiable from an individual patient's point of view must be 'based on an objective medical assessment of the patient's medical condition, the history and probable course of the patient's illness, the degree of the patient's pain and/or the nature of the patient's disability at the time when the request for authorisation was made or renewed'. This list of factors to be taken into account is broader than the one in Article 20(2) BR, which enumerates only the patient's current state of health and the probable course of the illness. The other factors codified in the Directive can be traced in the case law. See n. 631 and 632. However, unlike in the judgments of the Court, in the Directive no reference is made to the possible effect of the illness to the employment status of the patient. See also PENNINGS's remark on this, above n. 8, p. 442.

712 In my opinion, Article 8(6)(d) could simply have been erased from the text, which would not have changed the content of the legislation.

713 See Y. JORENS and J. DE CONINCK, *Reply to an ad hoc request for comparative analysis of national legislations. Administrative procedures for cross-border healthcare*, FreSsco Network, Ghent 2015.

714 W. PALM, 'The cross-border care Directive: implementation status' *Eurohealth* 2016, vol 22 no1, p. 21.

are highlighted which are applicable to the procedures through which authorisations are granted or requests refused. Here as well, an evolution of legislation can be observed, since first only the Regulation's authorisation procedure existed, then subsequently certain points of which were interpreted and clarified by the CJEU and certain requirements regarding these procedures were stressed, and then the Directive created its own, separate authorisation system applicable to cross-border healthcare in general and codified the case law of the Court as well.

The Coordination Regulation provides that 'an insured person travelling to another Member State with the purpose of receiving benefits in kind during the stay shall seek authorisation from the competent institution'.[715] Notably, the competent institution is bound to issue the requested permission, if two well-known conditions are met, namely that the treatment is included in the benefit package provided for by the Member State of residence and that the said treatment cannot be provided in this country within a medically justifiable time limit.[716]

While limiting the discretionary power of the competent institutions in terms of refusing to issue prior authorisation, Article 20(2) of the Basic Regulation does not in any sense intend to prevent the Member States from entitling their citizens to be reimbursed for medical costs incurred abroad even if the criteria referred to in that article are not met. As the Court repeatedly confirmed,

> the sole purpose of that provision is to identify the circumstances in which the competent national institution is precluded from refusing authorisation sought on the basis of [the Regulation]. That provision is not designed to limit the circumstances in which such authorisation may be granted. It follows that, where permission is granted on the basis of a national rule which provides that authorisation is to be granted where it is established that hospital treatment can be provided under better medical conditions abroad, such permission constitutes an authorisation within the meaning of [the Regulation].[717]

This provision basically indicates that the Member States are free to authorise treatments abroad even if – lacking the fulfilment of the said conditions – they are not legally obliged to do so.[718]

---

715 Article 20(1) BR.

716 Article 20(2) BR. These criteria are dealt with in section 3.1. above.

717 C-368/98 *Vanbraekel*, 31; C-56/01 *Inizan*, 41, 50; C-173/09 *Elchinov*, 39, 53.

718 On the different practices of the Member States see Kesteloot et al., above n. 92, pp. 47–48; Coucheir and Jorens, above n. 199, pp. 22–23; J. Hajdú, 'Cross border health care under the 1408/71 EC Regulation' *Studia Juridica Caroliensia*, vol 3, Károli Gáspár Református Egyetem Állam- és Jogtudományi Kar, Budapest 2008 and van der Mei, above n. 580, p. 1301.

Concerning the prior authorisation scheme of the coordination mechanism, which in practice materialises into the issuing of the so-called *S2 form*,[719] the Court defined some minimum requirements in its case law.

First, the Court pinpointed that 'a scheme of prior authorisation cannot legitimise discretionary decisions taken by the national authorities which are liable to negate the effectiveness of provisions of Community law'.[720] Therefore, the administrative procedure must be based 'on objective, non-discriminatory criteria which are known in advance',[721] 'in such a way as to circumscribe the exercise of the national authorities' discretion, so that it is not used arbitrarily';[722] and 'on a procedural system which is easily accessible and capable of ensuring that a request for authorisation will be dealt with objectively and impartially within a reasonable time and refusals to grant authorisation must also be capable of being challenged in judicial or quasi-judicial proceedings'.[723] Furthermore, 'refusals to grant authorisation, or the advice on which such refusals may be based, must refer to the specific provisions on which they are based and be properly reasoned in accordance with them. Likewise, courts or tribunals hearing actions against such refusals must be able to seek the advice of wholly objective and impartial independent experts'.[724]

Each of these requirements (which are summarised in Table 10 below) aim to limit the Member States' discretionary power, to guarantee an impartial and objective evaluation of the requests and to ensure transparency of the procedures in order to strengthen the patients' feeling that they are not exposed to an uncontrollable, untraceable bureaucratic mechanism. However, some

719 The S2 form is a PD under the new Regulation, which replaced the paper-based E 112 form but continued to function as a proof of entitlement to scheduled treatment abroad. According to Article 26(A)(1) IR, 'for the purposes of the application of Article 20(1) BR, the insured person shall present this document issued by the competent institution to the institution of the place of stay'. The CJEU also confirmed in *Keller*, that 'forms E 111 and E 112 are intended to assure the institution of the Member State of stay and the doctors authorised by that institution that the holders of those forms are entitled to receive in that Member State, during the period specified in the form, treatment whose cost will be borne by the competent institution'. C-145/03 *Keller*, 49.

720 Joined Cases C-286/82 and C-26/83 *Luisi and Carbone*, 34; Joined Cases C-358/93 and C-416/93 *Bordessa and Others*, 25; Joined Cases C-163/94, C-165/94 and C-250/94 *Sanz de Lera and Others*, 25; C-205/99 *Analir and Others*, 37; C-157/99 *Geraets-Smits and Peerbooms*, 90; C-385/99 *Müller-Fauré and Van Riet*, 84; C-372/04 *Watts*, 115.

721 Article 22(1) IR lay the charge on the Member States to 'ensure that any necessary information is made available to insured persons regarding the procedures and conditions for the granting of benefits in kind'.

722 C-205/99 *Analir and Others*, 38; C-157/99 *Geraets-Smits and Peerbooms*, 90; C-385/99 *Müller-Fauré and Van Riet*, 85; C-56/01 *Inizan*, 57; C-372/04 *Watts*, 116; C-173/09 *Elchinov*, 44; C-512/08 *Commission v France*, 43.

723 C-157/99 *Geraets-Smits and Peerbooms*, 90; C-56/01 *Inizan*, 48, 57; C-372/04 *Watts*, 116; C-512/08 *Commission v France*, 43.

724 C-56/01 *Inizan*, 49, 57; C-372/04 *Watts*, 117.

of the requirements are rather vaguely phrased and may thus not have the desired result. For instance, the criterion which says that the factors assessed in the authorisation procedure are to be known in advance does not concretise how or by means of what platform and where this information must be published or how much in advance this has to be communicated towards the insured persons.[725] Similarly, it is not quite clear what can be considered *reasonable time* concerning the decision-making. Also, no consequence is attached to the scenario if the authority fails to make its decision within the above period of time.

With regard to the latter problem, several Member States apply a so-called *positive silence* or *automatic authorisation rule* meaning that that in case the request of the insured person is not decided within the procedural time limit, this can be considered a decision in favour of the person in question. For instance, in Belgium, the patient submits a demand of authorisation accompanied by a medical report by the specialist doctor to the advising doctor of his/her sickness fund. The advising doctor decides within forty-five calendar days; if no reply is received within that period, the authorisation is deemed to be granted and an S2 form is issued. In Spain, the same time limit is applied with the same legal consequence, whereas in Poland the decision must be made not later than thirty days.

Nevertheless, these deadlines – thirty and forty-five days – seem rather long taking into account the specific nature of the issues at stake in these procedures. It is certainly left to the Member States to define their administrative procedures and the processing times thereof, but the interest of patients should motivate them to reply to requests as soon as possible, thus not applying general administrative processing times but setting much shorter deadlines. For instance, in Slovenia an administrative decision concerning a prior authorisation should be issued within thirty days, but in practice it is usually made within several days, if necessary under twenty-four hours.[726]

What could further increase the level of legal certainty in favour of patients is the introduction of an EU-wide maximum processing time (MPT), including the automatic authorisation rule. However, the arguments put forward with regard to the maximum legal waiting time for treatments above are valid in this case as well.

---

[725] One may raise the question, for example, whether it is appropriate to inform the insured person about these rules only right before he/she submits his/her request for a treatment abroad.

[726] STRBAN et al., above n. 5, p. 55.

Table 10. Requirements concerning a prior administrative authorisation scheme in accordance with the case law of the CJEU

(1) Requirements concerning the criteria of the assessment	objective, non-discriminatory
	known in advance
	capable of preventing arbitrary decisions
(2) Requirements concerning the procedural system	easily accessible
	capable of ensuring objectivity and impartiality
	capable of ensuring a decision within a reasonable time
	capable of being challenged in judicial or quasi-judicial proceedings.
(3) Requirements concerning administrative decisions and courts or tribunal hearing actions	must refer to the specific provisions on which they are based
	must be properly reasoned

Source: The author's own summary.

In principle, the competent institution is responsible for assessing all the relevant information in each case and for deciding about the provision of prior authorisation. This rule is completely reasonable taking into account that the competent institution has to bear the costs of the scheduled treatment.[727] However, there is an exception when the institution of the place of residence plays a significant role in this procedure, namely if the insured person does not reside in the competent Member State and is willing to obtain treatment in a third Member State.

In this case, the person concerned has to request the authorisation from the institution of the place of residence, which certifies whether the conditions set out in the second sentence of Article 20(2) BR are met in its own territory. At the same time, the request has to be forwarded to the competent institution without delay and this institution decides whether or not to grant the authorisation. It may refuse to grant the authorisation if the said conditions are not met in the Member State of residence or if the competent Member State itself can provide the required treatment within a medically justifiable time limit.[728] Since this process involves lengthy administrative decision-making in two Member States, it can be – in practice – highly time-consuming, which is very likely to be disadvantageous for the patient in need of medical care. Therefore, the Union legislature implemented two provisions in favour of the patient to ensure the timely provision of the treatment. First, 'in the absence of a reply within the deadlines set by its national legislation, the authorisation shall be

727 Article 26(A)(1) IR.
728 Article 26(A)(2) IR. On the issue of the medically justifiable time limit, see section 3.1.3. above in this chapter.

considered to have been granted by the competent institution'.[729] As can be seen, the automatic authorisation rule is not unknown in the patient mobility legislation, although is explicitly codified only in relation to this specific case. Secondly, if the patient needs urgent vitally necessary treatment, and 'the authorisation cannot be refused in accordance with the second sentence of Article 20(2) BR, the authorisation shall be granted by the institution of the place of residence on behalf of the competent institution, which shall be immediately informed by the institution of the place of residence'.[730]

Both solutions seek to avoid the patient having to wait for an administrative decision for an unreasonably long time. The first solution approximates to my idea on guaranteeing legal certainty for patients by setting a deadline or maximum processing time for administrative decision-making. Yet, instead of national processing times, I support the introduction of a universal, European deadline set out by the Regulation. The second solution was inspired by the *Keller* case,[731] which is detailed below.

The administrative procedure can result either in granting the authorisation or in refusing the request for authorisation.[732] However, after an authorisation has been granted, another crucial issue is the scope of the authorisation, namely where the limits lie of the entitlement covered by the authorisation issued by the competent Member State. The *Keller* case also served as a proper opportunity for the Court to take its stand on this question. In this case, the patient, who was entitled by the competent institution to receive medical care in Germany,

---

729 Article 26(A)(2) IR.

730 Article 26(A)(3) IR.

731 C-145/03 *Heirs of Annette Keller v Instituto Nacional de la Seguridad Social (INSS)* [ECLI:EU:C:2005:211] The case concerned a German national, who resided in Spain and was affiliated to the Spanish healthcare system. While on a temporary visit in Germany, she was hospitalised and diagnosed with a malignant tumour, sufficiently serious to be likely to cause her death at any time. Since she wished to be able to continue receiving the medical treatment necessitated by the condition affecting her in Germany, Ms Keller requested authorisation from the Spanish competent institution. The authorisation was issued to her, because – taken due account to the serious nature of her state of health – a transfer to Spain was not advisable. Following numerous examinations and a thorough analysis of the various possibilities of treatment available, the doctors of the German hospital considered that, in view of its extremely delicate nature and the special expertise it required, the surgical operation which was immediately and vitally necessary for Ms Keller could only be performed in a specialised clinic in Switzerland.

732 In 2013, 3.7 per cent, in 2014, 8.2 per cent, in 2015, 7 per cent of the requests for prior authorisation were refused. The two major issues on the grounds of which most requests were refused were the fact that the treatment requested was not included in the benefit package of the competent Member State and that the treatment could be delivered in the competent Member State within a medically justifiable time limit.
See data in J. Pacolet and F. De Wispelaere, *Planned cross-border healthcare*, Network Statistics FMSSFE, Leuven 2014, pp. 13–14; J. Pacolet and F. De Wispelaere, *Planned cross-border healthcare*, Network Statistics FMSSFE, Leuven 2015, pp. 10–11; and De Wispelaere and Pacolet, above n. 54, pp. 19–20.

was transferred and operated on in Switzerland due to the decision of the German doctors. The competent institution was reluctant to bear the costs of the treatment in the latter country, because in its opinion medical treatment provided in a non-member country would have required express permission, so the authorisation issued did not cover such an arrangement.[733] The Court proved its commitment to the principle of *shared responsibilities*. From this principle, it follows that by issuing a prior authorisation, the competent institution is dependent on the decision of the doctors authorised by the institution of the Member State of stay. They are called on to treat the insured person in that country, and the competent institution is obliged to accept and recognise the findings and choices of treatment made by them.[734] Since 'the doctors established in the Member State of stay are clearly best placed to assess the state of health of the person concerned and the immediate treatment required by that state',[735] they are free to choose the treatment they find the most appropriate in accordance with the current state of medical knowledge, which also includes the possibility to choose to transfer the patient to another state where the treatment required can be provided.[736] In this regard, it is not relevant whether that state is one of the Member States of the European Union.[737] At the same time, the institution of the place of stay must keep the competent institution informed and provide it with the relevant data if it appears medically appropriate to supplement the treatment covered by the existing authorisation.[738]

Although according to the settled case law the person concerned, provided with a prior authorisation, cannot be required to return to the competent Member State to undergo a medical examination there, when doctors authorised by the institution of the Member State of stay consider that his/her state of health requires urgent vitally necessary treatment,[739] the competent institution must retain the right – at any time during the procedure granting the authorisation – to have the insured person examined by a doctor of its own choice in the Member State of stay or residence.[740] The latter issue opens up the question of *fraud*

733 C-145/03 *Keller*, 19. One may wonder though, whether the situation would have been different if Ms Keller had been operated on in another Member State. In my opinion, this was a very weak argument from the competent Member State.

734 C-145/03 *Keller*, 50. This can be considered as a confirmation of a finding which showed up several times in the case law of the CJEU: see by analogy, in the context of medical findings concerning the incapacity for work, C-22/86 *Giuseppe Rindone v Allgemeine Ortskrankenkasse Bad Urach-Münsingen* [ECLI:EU:C:1987:130], 15; C-45/90 *Alberto Paletta (I) and others v Brennet AG* [ECLI:EU:C:1992:236], 28 and C-206/94 *Brennet AG v Vittorio Paletta (II)* [ECLI:EU:C:1996:182], 24–28.

735 C-145/03 *Keller*, 51.

736 C-145/03 *Keller*, 54.

737 C-145/03 *Keller*, 55.

738 Article 26A(5) IR.

739 C-22/86 *Rindone*, 21; C-145/03 *Keller*, 56.

740 Article 26A(4) IR.

and abuse: what possibilities does the competent institution have if doubts are raised in relation to the medical findings on which the administrative decision is based. The Court dealt with the matter of abuse in its *Paletta* judgments.[741] In *Paletta I*, the Court ruled that 'the competent institution is bound in fact and in law by the medical findings made by the institution of the place of residence or temporary residence, when it does not have the person concerned examined by a doctor of its choice, as it may do under' the Coordination Regulations.[742] This implies that if the competent institution does not exercise its right offered by the Regulations, it must rely on the institution of the place of stay or residence. However, as pointed out in this case, sometimes the competent institution is simply 'not able to make good use of this possibility',[743] because it might not be aware of the insured person's exact place of stay and even if it does know, the competent institution might not have any consultant doctor in the given area. Nevertheless, when its opinion on fraudulent use of the coordination rules was expressly asked for in *Paletta II*, the Court reminded that 'Community law cannot be relied on for the purposes of abuse or fraud'.[744] If reasonable doubts are raised in relation to the veracity of the facts on which a prior authorisation is based, the Member States involved must cooperate in accordance with the procedure set out by Article 5 of the Implementing Regulation. Therefore, in order to fight and prevent fraud and abuse, it is essential that the competent institutions in the various Member States have direct contacts and support each other.

If the competent institution refuses to provide the patient with a prior authorisation, the patient has the right to challenge the decision. The outcome of the review is either that the administrative decision of the first instance is affirmed and the authorisation denied, or that as a result of new facts (e.g. a deterioration in the claimant's health status) or due to the re-assessment of the

---

741 C-45/90 *Alberto Paletta (I) and Others v Brennet AG* [ECLI:EU:C:1992:236] and C-206/94 *Brennet AG v Vittorio Paletta (II)* [ECLI:EU:C:1996:182]. Both decisions concerned the members of an Italian family who were employed in Germany and reported to have fallen sick while on a leave in another country. The competent institution (that happened to be their employer in this case) refused to provide benefits on the grounds that it did not consider itself bound by the medical findings made abroad, the veracity of which it had serious reasons to doubt. C-45/90 *Paletta I*, 2–4.

742 C-45/90 *Paletta I*, 28. See also C-22/86 *Rindone*, 15.

743 C-45/90 *Paletta I*, 26. This statement is all the more valid when the competent institution is not a social security authority, but an employer.

744 C-206/94 *Paletta (II)*, 24. See also, in particular, regarding the *freedom to provide services*, C-33/74 *van Binsbergen*, 13; and C-23/93 *TV10 SA v Commissariaat voor de Media* [ECLI:EU:C:1974:131], 21; regarding the *free movement of goods*, C-229/83 *Association des Centres distributeurs Édouard Leclerc and others v SARL 'Au blé vert' and others* [ECLI:EU:C:1985:1], 27; regarding the *freedom of movement for workers*, C-39/86 *Sylvie Lair v Universität Hannover* [ECLI:EU:C:1988:322], 43; (3) and regarding the *Common Agricultural Policy*, C-8/92 *General Milk Products v Hauptzollamt Hamburg-Jonas* [ECLI:EU:C:1993:82], 21.

situation, the authorisation is granted. In this respect, the question had to be answered how it should be evaluated if the patient – after the refusal – in the meantime underwent the desired treatment abroad without an authorisation. The *Vanbraekel* case[745] shed light on the Court's position, among others, on *post factum authorisation*. Both here and in the *Elchinov* judgment,[746] where the question appeared again, the Court firmly held that

> where the request of an insured person for authorisation has been refused by the competent institution and it is subsequently established, either by the competent institution itself or by a court decision, that that refusal was unjustified, that person is entitled to be reimbursed directly by the competent institution in an amount equivalent to that which it would ordinarily have borne if authorisation had been properly granted in the first place.[747]

This case law provides patients with the certainty that if they fulfil the conditions for planned care required by the Regulation, they are entitled to the permission and as a consequence to be reimbursed according to the coordination regime even if the competent authorisation refuses their authorisation first. However, due to several loopholes accompanying the conditions for planned care (e.g. unclearly defined benefit coverage or dilemmas in relation to the medically justifiable time limit), it is often not easy for patients to guess whether they might fulfil the requirements. Thus, obtaining treatment abroad without an authorisation in the hope that the authorisation will be granted *a posteriori* carries the risk that if the permission is not granted after all, the financial burden remains on the patient unless he/she can claim reimbursement under the Patient Mobility Directive.

There are a couple of Member States which explicitly implemented this point of the case law into their national legislation and/or practice, such as Belgium, where the authorisation can be granted ex post facto when the patient could not wait for the reply before leaving the country, or in case of force majeure; Finland, where a patient who has been treated abroad without prior authorisation, can apply for it and for full reimbursement of the costs afterwards; Slovakia, where the insured person may also request the issuance of retroactive authorisation no later than within one year from the day on which the treatment was provided if the conditions for granting the authorisation are fulfilled; and the United Kingdom where, generally, reimbursement or the issuing of an authorisation will not usually be retrospectively authorised where the patient should have applied for prior authorisation but did not do so – unless exceptional reasons apply in

745 See n. 306 above.

746 See n. 608 above.

747 C-368/98 *Vanbraekel*, 34; C-326/00 *Ioannidis*, 61; C-8/02 *Leichtle*, 55; C-145/03 *Keller*, 69; C-173/09 *Elchinov*, 48. See also A.P. van der Mei, 'Cross-Border Access to Health Care within the European Union: Some Reflections on Geraets-Smits and Peerbooms and Vanbraekel' *Maastricht Journal of European and Comparative Law* 2002, vol 9 issue 2, p. 211.

a particular case, for example, circumstances where it was not possible for the patient to have applied for prior authorisation before receiving the treatment abroad. This would be determined on a case-by-case basis, taking account of the facts of the case. Retrospective authorisation and reimbursement will be given in cases where the initial decision to refuse authorisation or reimbursement is overruled on review or appeal.[748]

Most of the rules laid down by the Court were codified in the Patient Mobility Directive. At the same time, the Directive created its own, genuine authorisation system.

Interestingly enough, the authorisation scheme of the Patient Mobility Directive grew out of the idea that prior authorisation cannot be required in relation to healthcare services because it constitutes a barrier to free movement.[749] Soon it became clear however, that in certain cases prior authorisation is a necessary and justified measure, on the one hand because an uncontrollable patient flow has the potential to jeopardise healthcare planning and thus result in wastage of financial, technical and human resources and endanger the Member States' healthcare systems in general;[750] and on the other hand because in some cases the patient's safety is at stake.[751]

The grounds of justification[752] and the possible reasons for refusal[753] are not analysed here again. The focus is set on the procedural requirements included in the Directive, which provides that:

> the system of prior authorisation, including the criteria and the application of those criteria, and individual decisions of refusal to grant prior authorisation, shall be restricted to what is necessary and proportionate to the objective to be achieved, and may not constitute a means of arbitrary discrimination or an unjustified obstacle to the free movement of patients.[754]

It is apparent from the wording of the Directive that its aim is to limit the scope of prior authorisation schemes as much as possible. Whereas the European institutions tend to focus on keeping the requirement of authorisation as an *ultima ratio*, the Member States consider it as one of the last remaining safeguards to protect their healthcare systems.[755] The Member States might

---

748 Strban et al., above n. 5, p. 53.

749 See n. 295. See also Recital 38 of the Preamble of the Patient Mobility Directive and Article 7(8) PMD.

750 See Recital 40 of the Preamble of the Patient Mobility Directive.

751 Recital 43 of the Preamble of the Patient Mobility Directive.

752 Article 8(2) PMD. This issue is detailed in section 3.2. above in this chapter.

753 Article 8(6) PMD. This issue is detailed in section 3.2. above in this chapter.

754 Article 8(1) PMD.

755 It can also be said that prior authorisation is looked at as a 'means of restricting, or at least rationalizing, "exodus" from the national welfare system towards other Member States'

therefore implement the Directive in a way which allows them to use prior authorisation schemes permitted by the Directive to their full potential. Whether these measures will be accepted as necessary and proportionate[756] is a question for the future. In regard to this, one may ask whether all the national measures which make healthcare subject to prior authorisation based on one of the justifying reasons incorporated in the Directive should necessarily be seen as proportionate. Are there really no less restrictive measures that can be applied which are able to achieve the objectives in a similar way? For instance, could a prior notification system[757] not fulfil the same role? In a possible prior notification system the patient could unilaterally inform both the competent institution and the institution where he/she intends to obtain the treatment. Thus both institutions could reckon with this need in their planning,[758] and if concerns arise regarding to the protection of public health,[759] the competent institution would be in charge of informing the patient about the risk, who would be free to consider whether he/she is willing to take the risk or not.

The provisions which say that 'the administrative procedures shall be based on objective, non-discriminatory criteria'[760] and that they 'shall be easily accessible and capable of ensuring objectivity and impartiality'[761] are true reflections of the case law.[762] Similarly, nothing new is added to the requirement that the decisions resulting from these procedures must be 'properly reasoned, subject to review and capable of being challenged in judicial proceedings'.[763]

However, an interesting new element is that the Directive expressly imposes the obligation on the Member States to deal with the requests for cross-border healthcare within a reasonable period of time. Moreover, these national

---

facilities'. V. Hatzopoulos and T.U. Do, 'The case law of the ECJ concerning the free provision of services: 2000–2005' *Common Market Law Review* 2006, vol 43, p. 941.

756 The requirement of the *necessity and proportionality* of the restricting measures is also rooted in the case law of the CJEU, which on several occasions held that 'the conditions attached to the grant of an authorisation must satisfy the requirement of proportionality' [C-157/99 *Geraets-Smits and Peerbooms*, 82; C-385/99 *Müller-Fauré and Van Riet*, 83; C-372/04 *Watts*, 113–114; C-173/09 *Elchinov*, 41] and that they must 'not exceed what is objectively necessary for that purpose and that the same result cannot be achieved by less restrictive rules' [C-205/84 *Commission v Germany*, 29; C-180/89 *Commission v Italy*, 18; C-106/91 *Ramrath*, 31; C-157/99 *Geraets-Smits and Peerbooms*, 75; C-385/99 *Müller-Fauré and Van Riet*, 68; C-8/02 *Leichtle*, 43; C-372/04 *Watts*, 106; C-444/05 *Stamatelaki*, 34; C-173/09 *Elchinov*, 44].

757 The idea of a prior notification system is included in the Directive, but only as a voluntary option to receive in return a written confirmation of the amount to be reimbursed. Article 9(5) PMD.

758 Justifying reasons based on planning are included in Article 8(2)(a) PMD.

759 Justifying reasons based on the protection of public health are included in Article 8(2)(b)–(c) PMD.

760 Article 9(1) PMD.

761 Article 9(2) PMD.

762 See n. 721–723 above.

763 Article 9(4) PMD. See also n. 724.

standards of time must be made public in advance.[764] Nevertheless, the problem is that this rule requires that the requests are – as the Directive phrases it – *dealt with*, not *decided about* within this timeframe. This difference is apparently not just a matter of word choice, but sets a deadline for the start of the administrative procedure, not for the end of it. Of course, it is important for patients to know that their requests enter the evaluation phase in due time, but it is even more important to know when they can expect the result on which the reimbursement of medical costs depends. As I have already mentioned, the introduction of a universal maximum processing time could greatly contribute to the protection of patients' rights.[765]

It is worth noting that the Directive requires the Member States to take into account three factors when considering a request, namely the specific medical condition,[766] the urgency and individual circumstances.[767] It is most evident that the patient's state of health influences the decision as well as the timeliness of the treatment. However, no reference is made to what those individual circumstances are that have to be assessed. They could be a whole range of things, such as the medical history, the refusal of former requests, the ability to carry out a professional activity or even non-health-related determinants. On this point, the Member States are free to decide which circumstances they want to include into their implementing laws.

The above mentioned procedural requirements are categorised in Table 11 below.

Table 11. Requirements concerning a prior administrative authorisation scheme in accordance with the Patient Mobility Directive

(1) Requirements concerning the system of PA in general	necessary
	proportionate
	may not constitute a means of arbitrary discrimination
	may not constitute an unjustified obstacle to the free movement of patients
(2) Requirements concerning the criteria of the assessment	objective, non-discriminatory
	necessary and proportionate
(3) Requirements concerning the procedural system	easily accessible
	related information publicly available at the appropriate level
	capable of ensuring objectivity and impartiality

764 Article 9(3) PMD.
765 See the idea of MPT earlier in this section.
766 Article 9(3)(a) PMD.
767 Article 9(3)(b) PMD.

	requests must be dealt within a reasonable period of time
	the specific medical condition, the urgency and individual circumstances must be taken into account
(4) Requirements concerning administrative decisions	must be properly reasoned
	must be subject to review
	capable of being challenged in judicial proceedings

Source: The author's own summary.

There is an exceptional rule applicable to patients with rare diseases.[768] 'When a patient affected, or suspected of being affected, by a rare disease applies for prior authorisation, a clinical evaluation may be carried out by experts in that field.'[769] Since one of the specificities of rare diseases is the scarcity of relevant knowledge and expertise,[770] it is possible that there are no experts in the Member State of affiliation who are familiar with the rare disease in question, in which case it is highly advisable[771] to seek scientific opinion in another Member State. In the course of this exercise, the newly invented European reference networks[772] are supposed to play a significant role in the future.[773] Through these provisions, the European Union took a small, but important step towards 'ensuring effective and efficient recognition, prevention, diagnosis, treatment, care, and research for rare diseases in Europe'.[774]

It must be acknowledged that the case law compliant codification of the procedural safeguards is indeed a step forward. However, the Directive does not do much more than that: it does not go 'beyond the existing precedents in recognising additional rights for the patient'.[775] Quite the contrary, by creating an authorisation mechanism parallel with the Coordination Regulations, it makes the European legal framework on cross-border patient mobility even more difficult to handle for patients. Some potential sources of difficulties hiding in the legislation are scrutinised in the next section.

---

768 'Rare diseases are those that meet a prevalence threshold of not more than five affected persons per 10000, in line with Regulation (EC) No 141/2000 of the European Parliament and of the Council of 16 December 1999 on orphan medicinal products, and they are all serious, chronic and often life threatening.' Recital 55 of the Preamble of the Patient Mobility Directive.

769 Article 8(4) PMD.

770 European Commission, *Communication from the Commission to the European Parliament, the Council, the European Economic and Social Committee and the Committee of the Regions on Rare Diseases: Europe's challenges*, COM (2008) 679 final, 11.11.2008, p. 2.

771 It is not phrased in the Directive as an obligation, but rather as an opportunity for the Member States.

772 On the provisions related to European reference networks, see Article 12 PMD.

773 Article 13(a) PMD.

774 COM (2008) 679 final, above n. 770, p. 3.

775 S. de la Rosa, 'The Directive on Cross-Border Healthcare or the art of codifying complex case law' *Common Market Law Review* 2012, vol 49, p. 34.

4. SIMULTANEOUS APPLICATION OF LEGAL TOOLS ON EUROPEAN CROSS-BORDER PATIENT MOBILITY

What patients are likely to find very confusing about the Union's legislation on cross-border patient mobility is that different legal tools (partly) cover the same issues (such as authorisation and reimbursement) and while also applying different rules to the same issues under their own, individual regimes. In the absence of a well-defined hierarchy among the simultaneously applicable legal institutions, patients can easily get lost in the labyrinth of legal provisions. This section aims to mark some of the main crossroads of this maze and attempts to offer an itinerary to find a way through.

Many of the issues which are shared by or differ in the Regulations and the Directive have already been discussed in the above sections. Therefore, here a comparative approach is used to highlight the discrepancies of the different legal tracks.[776] Four (plus one) criteria of comparison are taken into account in this section, namely (1) objective and legal basis, (2) scope, (3) approach towards authorisation schemes and (4) administrative procedure. (5) The difference between the reimbursement regimes is touched upon only briefly because their in-depth analysis is carried out in a separate chapter.[777] After the comparison the relationship of the two pillars of patient mobility are examined.

4.1. OBJECTIVE AND LEGAL BASIS

As already said,[778] the mechanisms of the Coordination Regulations and the Patient Mobility Directive, which is based on the case law of the Court, emerged from different ideas, and are thus rooted in different legal bases. Whereas the Coordination Regulations were adopted in accordance with Article 48 of the Treaty[779] to enhance the free movement of workers and to ensure that they do not lose social entitlements while using their right to move freely within the Union,[780] the baseline for both the case law and the Patient Mobility Directive

[776] The main focus is certainly on the differences between the Coordination Regulations and the Patient Mobility Directive, but reference is made also to those points where the Directive diverges from the case law.

[777] On the financial regimes, see Chapter 3. Financial affordability.

[778] On the coexistence of different legal tools in the field of European cross-border patient mobility, see section 3.7. in Chapter 1. Setting the scene.

[779] Article 48 Treaty on the Functioning of the European Union (TFEU) was numbered as Article 42 Treaty Establishing the European Union (TEC) and was originally codified as Article 51 in the Treaty of Rome. See also n. 232.

[780] On the aim of the coordination of social security schemes within the EU, see section 3.6. in Chapter 1. Setting the scene.

has been that healthcare constitutes a service within the meaning of the Treaty[781] and therefore any restriction of healthcare provision is considered a barrier of the free movement of services[782] unless properly justified.[783] Both the underlying logic and the legislative competence are different in the two fields.

While analysing questions that fall under the broad scope of healthcare, a principle that cannot be overlooked is that the organisation and the delivery of healthcare in the European Union primarily belong to the responsibility of the Member States.[784] Therefore, each time a European legal tool is dealt with, the question will be posed whether the Union has the legislative power to rule the field concerned.

The competence question is rather simple to answer for the Coordination Regulations where the Treaty expressly assigns the legislative bodies of the Union to 'adopt measures in the field of social security as are necessary to provide freedom of movement for workers'.[785] The Regulations aim to ensure access to healthcare for insured persons in various situations through the logic of coordination, and thus lacks the slightest attempt to intervene into the Member States' national social security legislations. Instead, it provides supranational rules which connect the national systems. This mechanism undoubtedly facilitates the free movement of persons in today's Europe and has great contributions for border-crossing patients as well. However, it does not necessarily cover each cross-border patient movement[786] and limits the patient flow by posing rather rigid conditions.[787]

For the Directive, the answer to this question is less clear-cut. The Directive itself refers to two different provisions of the Treaty as its legal bases. On the one hand, it points at Article 114 on the approximation of laws, which provides the EU institutions with permission to 'adopt measures for the approximation of the provisions laid down by law, regulation or administrative action in Member States which have as their object the establishment and functioning of the internal market'.[788] This provision is a clear reflection of the revolutionary innovation of the patient mobility case law, which puts healthcare services in the territory of the free movement of services.[789] The question of whether

781 See n. 294 above.
782 See n. 295 above.
783 See n. 296 above.
784 Article 168(7) TFEU. See also n. 217–218 and 229.
785 Article 48 TFEU.
786 One of its defects is that private healthcare provision falls outside of its scope.
787 These conditions are dealt with in detail in sections 1–3. above in this chapter.
788 Article 114(1) TFEU.
789 On the approach of the Court, see section 3.7. in Chapter 1. Setting the scene, especially n. 271. The Directive itself argues that: 'Article 114 is the appropriate legal basis since the majority of the provisions of this Directive aim to improve the functioning of the internal market and the free movement of goods, persons and services.' Recital 2 of the Preamble of the Patient Mobility Directive. The Directive also adds that: 'while recognising their specific

healthcare can be considered a service under Union law has triggered heated discussions both on the political and the academic level.[790] Among the various components of this debate, there is also an aspect related to legislative competence. Whereas in the field of social security the latitude of the Union is limited to coordination measures, in the field of service provision it is allowed to harmonise national rules. Not surprisingly, the Member States reacted very negatively to the activist approach of the Court[791] and labelled the patient mobility case law as an 'unwarranted incursion into Member State's autonomy to organise their social security system'.[792] So although both the case law[793] and the Directive[794] confirm that they do respect the Member States' national competencies in organising and delivering healthcare, they very likely erode the national health powers by extending Union competence beyond the boundaries of national healthcare legislations.

The Directive also refers to Article 168 of the Treaty on public health. In my opinion, this is where the Patient Mobility Directive's true added value for

---

nature, all types of medical care fall within the scope of the TFEU'. Recital 6 of the Preamble of the Patient Mobility Directive.

790 There has not been a full agreement on whether the special characteristics of healthcare services lift them out of the circle of services of an economic nature. See n. 22. Even within the Court, there have been different views. A good example is AG Ruiz-Jarabo Colomer's Opinion in *Geraets-Smits and Peerbooms*, who went as far as to question 'whether the treatment provided by medical practitioners and health-care institutions may be regarded as a service within the meaning of the Treaty, in view of the fact that the person for whom the service is provided does not receive it in return for remuneration'. Opinion of AG Ruiz-Jarabo Colomer delivered on 18 May 2000 in C-157/99 *B.S.M. Geraets-Smits v Stichting Ziekenfonds VGZ and H.T.M. Peerbooms v Stichting CZ Groep Zorgverzekeringen*, 26.
On the same day another AG opinion was delivered in *Vanbraekel*. Similarly to AG Ruiz-Jarabo Colomer, AG Saggio – in conjunction with the opposing governments – argued that the findings in the C-263/86 *Humbel* case in relation to publicly funded education should be applied to public healthcare schemes and services which, on the one hand, are an integral part of the public health-care system, in the sense that they are established and organised by the State, and, on the other hand, are financed by public funds, must be excluded from the provisions on freedom of movement. Opinion of AG Saggio delivered on 18 May 2000 in C-368/98 *Abdon Vanbraekel and Others v Alliance nationale des mutualités chrétiennes*, 21.

791 The preoccupation of the Member States can 'be appreciated by the fact that all the (old) Member States have occasionally intervened in the proceedings before the Court in this field, and essentially with positions opposed to those finally adopted by the Court'. Hatzopoulos and Do, above n. 755, p. 937. Obermaier supports this statement with numbers: he counted in total seventy-four observations from the Member States in the first ten patient mobility cases. A.J. Obermaier, 'Fine-tuning the Jurisprudence: The ECJ's Judicial Activism and Self-restraint' *Institute for European Integration Research*, Working Paper No. 02/2008, p. 24.

792 Murphy, above n. 603, p. 552. See similarly Kaczorowska, above n. 172, p. 352 'The issue arises whether the Court of Justice, when it decided that medical services provided in the context of national social security schemes were within the scope of Articles 49 and 50 EC, extended the scope of the fundamental principles of the internal market beyond acceptable limits, and thus encroached on the sovereign powers enjoyed by Member States.'

793 See n. 292 above.

794 Article 1(1) PMD.

patients lies. It exceeds the 'hard core' social security topics such as access to healthcare and financing, and takes some – maybe slightly dispirited – steps towards the creation of a 'common healthcare area' within the European Union. Although there is still a long way to go in order to achieve the latter, the initiatives, such as the creation of European reference networks,[795] the recognition of prescriptions[796] and cooperation on eHealth innovations,[797] are heading into a right direction. However, the European institutions do not have very powerful entitlements in most of these matters, so their action is mainly limited to supporting national activities and to facilitating cooperation. As a consequence, although many of these provisions can be considered innovative and valuable, they cannot be expected to ensure prompt benefits on the patients' behalf.[798] In the long run though, the cooperation measures have the potential to reshape the cross-border healthcare market – as Golynker writes, '[t]he individual and collective interests can be brought together by the regulation which transforms cross-border healthcare from reimbursement transactions to cooperation partnerships'.[799] It is desirable that in the coming years both the Member States and the EU institutions pay more attention and put more effort into this cooperation.

As a conclusion, it is worth underlining that whereas the Social Security Coordination Regulations do not intend to achieve more than ensuring smooth access to healthcare for those who practice their right to move freely within the Union, the Patient Mobility Directive 'engages into a competition' with the Regulations in the social security issues by stating that patients must be considered as recipients of services on the common market. Yet, it also regulates some public health issues to enhance cross-border care which are not touched by the Regulations.

---

795 Article 12 PMD.

796 Article 11 PMD. See on this issue R. Baeten and L. San Miguel, 'Cross-border recognition of medicines prescriptions: Results from a mystery shopping experiment' *Eurohealth* 2013, vol 19 no 4.

797 Article 14 PMD.

798 This is not true for all of the public health provisions in the Directive. For instance, the obligation of the Member States to ensure that prescriptions issued in another Member State are recognised results in an instant development of patients' social protection. Article 11 PMD. In order to ensure the uniform application of this provision of the Patient Mobility Directive, another Directive was adopted, namely Commission Implementing Directive 2012/52/EU of 20 December 2012 laying down measures to facilitate the recognition of medical prescriptions issued in another Member State. OJ L 356 of 22 December 2012. See D. van den Steen, 'Cross-border health care: Common rules on medical prescriptions when travelling to another EU country' *Eurohealth* 2013, vol 19 no 4.

799 O. Golynker, 'Patient Mobility and healthcare in the EU' in F. Pennings and G. Vonk (eds.), *Research Handbook on European Social Security Law*, Edward Elgar Publishing, Cheltenham 2015, p. 512.

4.2. SCOPE

The former point already shed light on the fact that the scope of the two tools is different. The Coordination Regulations cover the whole spectrum of social security, not only healthcare benefits, whereas as well as individual healthcare matters the Directive infiltrates public health as well. The point is that the two instruments have a common zone which they share and both impose rules on. However, they do so according to different philosophies, in different ways. Therefore, it is important to clarify where the borders lie within this shared area. Concerning the scope, two factors can be identified which are regulated differently, namely to which type of healthcare the legal tools apply and to which healthcare providers the legal tools apply.

The Regulations coordinate – among other social security branches[800] – sickness benefits both in cash and in kind. Concerning healthcare, however, their scope focuses on three situations, namely when insured persons reside outside of the country where they are covered by the national healthcare scheme,[801] when insured persons temporarily stay outside of the country where they are covered,[802] and when insured persons travel to another Member State with the express purpose to receive healthcare in that country.[803] The Directive, however – as its title shows – deals solely with cross-border healthcare, meaning that neither other social security benefits, nor cash benefits are dealt with. The Directive intends to break with the strict – and not always clear[804] – categorisation of the Regulations and thus imposes rules on cross-border healthcare[805] in general.[806] This implies that the same rules govern the above-mentioned situations, since each healthcare provision is considered service provision within Union legislation. This might seem as providing greater freedom for patients, but as shown above, applying the same rules for instance to planned and unplanned care might result in controversial situations.[807]

A similar difference of approach can be seen also in relation to the question which healthcare providers are covered by the different legal tools: the Regulations are more restrictive than the Directive, which intends to broaden the scope. Whereas under the Coordination Regulations healthcare can be received only

800 See n. 259 above.

801 Article 17–18 BR, Article 24 IR.

802 Article 19 BR, Article 25 IR.

803 Article 20 BR, Article 26 IR.

804 On the problematic cases related to the distinction between necessary care and planned care, see section 2.1.1. above in this chapter.

805 On the definition of cross-border healthcare, see n. 112.

806 It must be noted, though, that certain health-related services are expressly excluded from the material scope of the Patient Mobility Directive, such as long-term care, organ transplantation and vaccinations. Article 1(3) PMD.

807 See the relation of necessary care and prior authorisation under the Directive in section 2.2. above in this chapter.

from providers within the statutory system,[808] the Patient Mobility Directive requires the Member States to reimburse medical costs occurred both at private and public providers.[809] This is also an important development in patients' protection, since before the adoption of the Directive they could not expect any reimbursement for treatments obtained outside the public system. This is thus one of the scenarios where the Directive is obviously more advantageous for the patient than the Regulations. However, since in many Member States, like Poland or Hungary, treatments obtained at such providers are not reimbursed when it takes place within the competent country, the obligation to reimburse them in cross-border situations gives rise to reverse discrimination.[810]

To sum up, while both planned and unplanned care are covered by both instruments, healthcare provided by non-contracted healthcare providers is covered only by the Patient Mobility Directive.

4.3. APPROACH TOWARDS AUTHORISATION SCHEMES

One of the most visible discrepancies between the two tracks of patient mobility is their relation to prior authorisation for medical treatments. The issue of authorisation was indeed the crucial point when the Court departed from the Regulations towards a new path of patient mobility, which does not require prior authorisation for health services. The Court has never asserted that the Regulation itself restricts the freedom of service provision. Nevertheless, in the *Kohll* judgment[811] it declared a national legislation – which was in line with the Regulation[812] – being in violation of Community law by making the reimbursement of the costs of a health service subject to prior authorisation.[813]

This duplicity still exists. Whereas the principle of the Coordination Regulation is that planned healthcare abroad must be approved by the competent institution,[814] the Directive – in conformity with the case law – is driven by the idea that authorisation is required only in exceptional cases listed in the Directive.[815] These exceptions, which must be interpreted restrictively, concern situations in which overriding reasons of general interest, such as planning

808 Pennings, above n. 8, p. 426.

809 Article 1(2) PMD. During the legislative debate on the PMD in the Council, the inclusion of non-contracted providers was a major outstanding issue. I. Kowalska-Bobko, A. Mokrzycka, A. Sagan, W.C Włodarczyk, M. Zabdyr-Jamróz, 'Implementation of the Cross-Border Healthcare Directive in Poland: How Not to Encourage Patients to Seek Care Abroad?' *Health Policy* 2016, vol 120 issue 11, p. 1234.

810 See n. 558 above and n. 909 below. See also Kowalska-Bobko et al., above n. 809, p. 1234.

811 See n. 272 above.

812 C-158/96 *Kohll*, 25. See also n. 489 and 490.

813 C-158/96 *Kohll*, 54.

814 Article 20(1) BR.

815 Article 8(2) PMD.

objectives and the protection of public health, justify the limitation of the free movement of services.[816]

The legal tools concur on the point that a request for prior authorisation cannot be refused (or must be issued) when two criteria are conjunctively met, namely that the patient is entitled to the healthcare in question and that it cannot be provided to him/her in a medically justifiable time limit.[817] A slight difference is that whereas the Regulation takes the benefit basket of the Member State of residence as a basis to decide whether the patient is entitled to the treatment concerned, the Directive refers to the benefit package of the Member State of affiliation, which is not necessarily the Member State of residence. Also, the Directive – codifying the case law – describes a longer list of factors which must be taken into account when assessing the length of the medically justifiable time limit.[818] However, the exact definition of medically justifiable time limit is still lacking, which leaves room for different interpretations on the part of Member States. Introducing a universal maximum waiting time would therefore considerably decrease national discretion on this point.

4.4. ADMINISTRATIVE PROCEDURES

The main source of complexity with regard to the administrative procedures is that both the Regulations and the Directive have their separate procedures, with their own set of administrative requirements, documents to fill in and attach, and administrative steps to follow. It is crucial for patients to be aware of all the relevant information on the procedures themselves, their entitlements under the two legal tools and the implications of the outcomes of these procedures. For instance, it is of utmost importance to inform the patient what the difference is between being granted prior authorisation under the Regulations or under the Directive.

First of all, the Member States were not obliged but permitted to introduce a prior authorisation procedure for treatments obtained in accordance with the Patient Mobility Directive. This means that those Member States which opted for no authorisation scheme[819] had to set up only a reimbursement procedure when implementing the Directive. However, those countries which chose to use the opportunity to restrict patient movements had to decide on the new authorisation system. In its Guidance note,[820] the Commission suggested to the Member States to consider 'whether they wish to create one unified system of

816 See section 3.2. above in this chapter.

817 Article 20(2) BR and Article 8(5) PMD.

818 See under section 3. above in this chapter. Moreover, the Directive regulates legitimate reasons of refusal which are not included in the Regulations.

819 Currently these states are the Czech Republic, Estonia, Finland, Lithuania, the Netherlands, Norway and Sweden.

820 See n. 264 above.

prior authorisation, which deals with requests for authorisation under both the Regulations and the Directive, or whether they have two separate systems'.[821]

As a result of the transposition, in terms of administrative procedure and requirements attached to the right to reimbursement, numerous patterns can be identified among the Member States. On the one hand, most of the Member States which apply a prior authorisation requirement created a uniform procedure where the authorisation process under the Regulation and under the Directive are merged and go through the same steps. This is what Austria, Belgium, Bulgaria, Germany, Greece, France, Croatia, Hungary, Iceland, Luxemburg, Latvia, Poland, Portugal, Slovenia, Slovakia and the United Kingdom decided to do. On the other hand, some Member States, such as Cyprus, Denmark, Spain, Ireland, Italy, Malta and Romania decided to keep the procedures under the two different legal tools entirely separated.[822] In some of these states, the separate authorisation procedures belong to the competence of different divisions of the same institution, or even to different institutions like in Spain.[823] Finding the competent institution might prove to be challenging for some patients, especially if the lack of information is added to the picture.

As a matter of illustration, I hereby briefly describe the Hungarian authorisation scheme. In Hungary, the administrative procedure concerning healthcare obtained under the scope of the Regulations or the Directive is not fully integrated but the two routes share some common points. In each case, the starting point of the formal procedure is the submission of a standardised request for authorisation[824] by the insured person, in case of minors his/her legal representative or the physician involved, with the medical documentation of the patient attached.[825] The patient needs to declare in case he/she intends to obtain healthcare from a provider falling outside of the scope of the Regulation, expressly opts for not using the Regulation's mechanism for any other reasons or wishes to be provided with an authorisation without indicating the authorised provider on it, in which cases the Directive's rules and procedure are applicable.[826] Consequently, if the patient does not make any of the above statements, the Regulation's procedure is applied.

Either way, the procedure continues with an assessment phase. The first part of the assessment is shared by the two routes. First, it must be examined – within eight days from the submission – as to whether the requested treatment is covered by the Hungarian social insurance system.[827] If it is not, the

821 AC 246/12, above n. 264, p. 8.

822 Strban et al., above n. 5, p. 57.

823 In Spain, the prior authorisation under the Regulations is granted by the National Social Security Institution (INSS), whereas under the Directive, by the Regional Healthcare Services.

824 The form can be found in Annex II to Governmental Decree No 340/2013.

825 Article 3(2) of Governmental Decree No 340/2013.

826 Article 7(1) of Governmental Decree No 340/2013.

827 Article 5(1) of Governmental Decree No 340/2013.

Regulations do not impose the obligation on the Member State to accord an authorisation, but under the Hungarian legislation the patient can request authorisation on the grounds of equity.[828] If it is covered by the national scheme, then it shall be investigated – within another fifteen days – whether the requested treatment can be provided by a contracted, Hungarian provider within the medically justifiable time limit indicated on the request by the patient's physician.[829] If it can, the Hungarian Healthcare Fund (NEAK) refuses to grant authorisation to receive healthcare abroad, since it can meet its obligation within the territory of the country. At the same time, it makes a suggestion on a domestic provider that has the capacity to provide the patient with the requested treatment.[830] If the treatment cannot be provided in the territory of the country within the time limit defined by the patient's physician, the authorisation mechanism can be continued in different ways depending on whether the Regulation's or the Directive's route is chosen by the patient.

If the Regulation's rules are followed, the competent authority proceeds to evaluate whether the provider indicated in the request meets the requirements concerning quality, safety[831] and cost-efficiency.[832] In case these criteria are fulfilled, the NEAK enquires the foreign provider indicated in the request whether it has the capacity to carry out the requested medical intervention and when this could take place. If the provider replies in the affirmative, the NEAK proceeds to according the authorisation as indicated in the patient's request – within eight days from when it was confirmed that the treatment could not be provided at a Hungarian contracted provider[833] – and the reimbursement will take place in accordance with the Coordination Regulations.[834] However, if the foreign provider does not meet any of the above requirements, the NEAK makes a suggestion to obtain the requested treatment at another provider established within the EEA or Switzerland. If the patient accepts this advice, the permission is issued accordingly,[835] but if the patient does not accept this advice and intends

[828] Article 9(1) of Governmental Decree No 340/2013. Since the European legislation does not apply in this case, this procedure is not detailed further in this book.

[829] Article 5(2) of Governmental Decree No 340/2013.

[830] Article 5(3) of Governmental Decree No 340/2013.

[831] Notably, this quality and safety check element is missing from the procedure under the Directive, whereas the Patient Mobility Directive itself puts a great emphasis on the quality and safety of the providers and concerns in that respect are accepted as justified reasons to refuse to grant authorisation. Article 8(6)(a)–(c) PMD. See section 3.2.2. above in this chapter and especially n. 698. This has not been implemented in the Hungarian authorisation system.

[832] Article 5(4) of Governmental Decree No 340/2013. The cost-efficiency requirement is met if the cost of the medical treatment abroad is maximum 30 per cent higher than the domestic cost of the same treatment if provided in Hungary.

[833] Article 5(5) of Governmental Decree No 340/2013.

[834] Article 5(7) of Governmental Decree No 340/2013.

[835] Article 5(6) of Governmental Decree No 340/2013.

to receive healthcare in another Member State of the Union, he/she is redirected to the Directive's route.[836]

As already said, the Directive's rules are applicable either if the patient expressly requests it at the beginning of the procedure,[837] or if he/she refuses to obtain the requested healthcare at the provider the NEAK suggested[838] or if the healthcare is not subject to prior authorisation.[839] In these cases, an authorisation is issued – without further evaluation – after the recognition that the requested treatment cannot be provided in Hungary within the medically justifiable time limit, and medical costs are reimbursed in accordance with the Directive. This procedure is summarised in Table 12 below.

Hungary – like numerous other EU-countries[840] – seems to insist on a rather strict authorisation policy, using the legitimate possibilities to keep patient movements – and thus healthcare expenditure – under control as far as possible.

Table 12. Hungarian administrative procedures in relation to planned healthcare abroad

<table>
<tr><td colspan="3">Step No1: Submission of the request for planned treatment abroad</td></tr>
<tr><td colspan="3">Question No1: Does the patient
(1) intend to obtain healthcare from a provider falling outside of the scope of the Regulation or
(2) expressly opt for not using the Regulation's mechanism for any other reasons or
(3) wish to be provided with an authorisation without indicating the authorised provider on it</td></tr>
<tr><td>NO → Coordination Regulations' mechanism is applicable</td><td colspan="2">YES → Patient Mobility Directive's mechanism is applicable</td></tr>
<tr><td colspan="3">Step No2: Assessment of the request</td></tr>
<tr><td colspan="3">Question No1: Is the requested treatment covered by the Hungarian social insurance? (The issue shall be examined within 8 days.)</td></tr>
<tr><td>NO → no obligations under European law, but the patient can claim for authorisation on the ground of equity</td><td colspan="2">YES → both the Regulations or the Directive can be applicable, the assessment proceeds</td></tr>
<tr><td></td><td colspan="2">Question No2: Can the requested treatment be provided by a contracted, Hungarian provider within the medically justifiable time limit indicated on the request by the patient's physician? (The issue shall be examined within another 15 days.)</td></tr>
<tr><td></td><td>YES → the NEAK refuses the request and makes a suggestion on a domestic provider to obtain the treatment at</td><td>NO → the assessment proceeds</td></tr>
</table>

(continued)

836 Article 7(2) of Governmental Decree No 340/2013.

837 See n. 825 above.

838 Article 7(3) of Governmental Decree No 340/2013.

839 Article 8(1) of Governmental Decree No 340/2013.

840 Similarly, in Poland, the legislation implementing the Directive is very restrictive, the goal of which is 'to either defer the public payer's expenses into the future or to discourage patients from seeking care abroad or from seeking care altogether'. Kowalska-Bobko et al, above n. 809, p. 1233.

Table 12 *continued*

<table>
<tr><td colspan="3">Step No3: The two routes diverge</td></tr>
<tr><td colspan="2">Regulation's route</td><td>Directive's route</td></tr>
<tr><td colspan="2">Question No1: Does the provider meet the NEAK's requirements concerning quality, safety and cost-efficiency?</td><td rowspan="2">If the prior assessment reveals that the requested treatment is covered by the Hungarian social insurance but cannot be provided at a contracted Hungarian provider within the medically justifiable time limit indicated by the physician of the patient, the NEAK issues an authorisation within the scope of the Directive if the patient declared in advance that he/she

(1) intends to obtain healthcare from a provider falling outside of the scope of the Regulation or
(2) expressly opts for not using the Regulation's mechanism for any other reasons or
(3) wishes to be provided with an authorisation without indicating the authorised provider on it
OR
(4) refuses to obtain the treatment at the provider suggested by the NEAK.</td></tr>
<tr><td>NO → the NEAK makes a suggestion to another provider within the EEA or Switzerland that meets the above requirements and issues the authorisation accordingly.

If the patient refuses to obtain the treatment at the suggested provider, the NEAK issues an authorisation under the scope of the Directive.</td><td>YES → the NEAK enquires the foreign provider indicated in the request whether it has the capacity to provide the patient with the requested healthcare and when the treatment could take place → the NEAK issues the authorisation (within 8 days from when it was confirmed that the patient cannot be provided with the treatment in Hungary).</td></tr>
</table>

Source: The author's own summary.

In my opinion, the patients' best interest is to have an administrative procedure which is easily accessible, quick, transparent and as simple as possible. Therefore, I would support the introduction of an integrated administrative scheme in each Member State, in which patients can get all the necessary information and can make all the necessary arrangements at the same time. I think that the national contact points (NCP), which have been designed to provide patients with information about cross-border healthcare, are the best positioned to play the main role in this integrated system and act as mediators between the patient and the other parties (insurers, providers) involved. A unified authorisation system would enable the patients to benefit from the most advantageous option to obtain healthcare abroad. Similarly, from the patients' point of view it would be highly desirable to define a universal *maximum procedural time*, which would set a limit to the circuitous administrative processes.

4.5. REIMBURSEMENT REGIMES

The enumeration of the differences between the various paths of patient mobility and of the sources of complication would not be complete without referring briefly to the discrepancy between the reimbursement regimes. Since the regimes are analysed in the next chapter, the main point I would like to highlight here is that both the level and the mechanism of reimbursement are genuinely different in the Regulations and in the Directive. Whereas – in principle – the Regulations offer a reimbursement of medical costs up to the level of the costs in the Member State of treatment and prioritise inter-institutional reimbursement, under the Directive reimbursement can be claimed up to the level of cost coverage in the Member State of affiliation and patients need to advance the medical costs. Thus, the latter might put a considerable financial burden on the patient, who must be aware of the nature of reimbursement in advance.

4.6. THE LEGISLATIVE PUZZLE

After this comparison, which is briefly summarised in Table 13 below, the following question presents itself: how do these pieces of the legislative puzzle fit together? What is the current relationship of the two (plus one)[841] pillars of patient mobility, and how could it be developed in favour of the patients? Instead of stating that the Regulation is inconsistent with the Treaty, the Court emphasised in its case law that the mechanisms included in the Regulations and in the case law complement each other. This attitude can be seen in the Directive as well, which unambiguously states in its Preamble that 'for patients the two systems should be coherent; either this Directive applies or the Union regulations on the coordination of social security systems apply'.[842]

When observing the current relationship of the Regulations and the Directive, Article 2(m) of the Directive should be taken as a starting point, which indicates that the Directive should apply without prejudice to the Coordination Regulations. This implies that they are applicable in parallel and that there is no priority between them. One may wonder, though, whether it is good that there is no hierarchy between the two instruments. From the patients' point of view, the order of priority is rather simple, since if the conditions of the Regulations are met, more favourable rules apply both to the level and to the

841 It must be kept in mind that despite the Directive's intention to codify the case law, the case law still exists, is applicable and is expected to be developed by the Court in the future. Pennings warns that 'the risk exists that the Directive will be overruled by new case law [...] since there are differences between the approach of the Court and the Directive'. Pennings, above n. 8, p. 436. Similarly, Murphy is of the opinion that 'the case law of the CJEU will continue to be of relevance for "mobile" patients'. Murphy, above n. 603, p. 557.

842 Recital 30 of the Preamble of the Patient Mobility Directive.

mechanism of reimbursement. This fact is – at least partly – acknowledged by the Directive, which provides that:

> with regard to requests for prior authorisation made by an insured person with a view to receiving cross-border healthcare, the Member State of affiliation shall ascertain whether the conditions laid down in the Coordination Regulation have been met. Where those conditions are met, the prior authorisation shall be granted pursuant to that Regulation unless the patient requests otherwise.[843]

It is worth pointing out that this provision looked slightly different in the Commission's original proposal. It was phrased as follows:

> when the circumstances under which an authorisation to go to another Member State in order to receive appropriate treatment under the Coordination Regulation must be granted are met, the provisions of that Regulation shall apply and the provisions of this Directive shall not apply.[844]

To my understanding, there are two points where the change of the wording adversely affects the patients. On the one hand, the current wording of the Directive refers to *requests for prior authorisation made by an insured person*, indicating that if the request is not submitted in advance, like in the case of necessary care[845] or post-factum authorisation,[846] there is no obligation to apply the more beneficial rules of the Regulation. On the other hand, the adopted version of the Directive puts the choice into the hands of the patients by saying that the rules of the Regulation must be applied *unless the patient requests otherwise*. This provision would be fully acceptable if patients could be expected to act as informed customers, one hundred per cent aware of their entitlements, possibilities, options to choose from and the consequences of their choice. Can this be expected from today's cross-border patients in the current circumstances? Doubts can be raised here.[847] Moreover, one might wonder in which case it would be more advantageous to apply the Directive's regime, if the Regulation can be applied too. If the Regulation cannot be applied, then of course the Directive might offer a solution for the patient, but if the insured person is entitled under both legal instruments, I see no reason not to pinpoint that the Regulation has an absolute priority as it is more beneficial for the patient. This does not exclude that the patients could still be provided with the right to expressly refuse to use the Regulation's mechanism for instance in the case

---

843 Article 8(3) PMD.

844 Article 3(2) of the Proposal for the Patient Mobility Directive, COM (2008) 414, above n. 346.

845 See section 2. above in this chapter.

846 See section 3.3. above in this chapter.

847 Jorens and Lhernould, above n. 392, p. 30.

of planned outpatient care, which can be obtained without prior authorisation in accordance with the Directive, if they confirm that they are aware of the implications of this decision on their entitlements.

Table 13. Discrepancies between the simultaneously existing mechanisms of European cross-border patient mobility

	Coordination Regulations	Patient Mobility Directive
Legal base	*Article 48 TFEU* (ex Article 42 TEC) in the framework of free movement of workers	*Article 114 TFEU* (ex Article 95 TEC) on the approximation of laws in the field of the functioning of the internal market *Article 168 TFEU* (ex Article 152 TEC) on public health
Material scope	sickness benefits in kind in various legal scenarios	cross-border healthcare (long-term care, organ transplantation and vaccination programmes against infectious diseases are expressly excluded)
	providers within the statutory system	providers within and outside of the statutory system
Approach towards authorisation	in the case of planned care, PA must always be requested *compulsory grant of authorisation*: if the benefit is included in the benefit package of the MS of residence, but cannot be provided within a medically justifiable time limit	*principle*: cross-border healthcare cannot be made subject to PA *exception*: PA scheme justified by an overriding reason of general interest *refusal*: may be based on justified reasons listed in the PMD, among which a request can be refused if the benefit is included in the benefit package of the Member State of affiliation and can be provided within a medically justifiable time limit
Administrative procedures	separate or unified authorisation procedures (in certain MSs no authorisation procedures under the Directive's regime)	
Reimbursement mechanism	reimbursement up to the level of cost coverage in the MS of treatment complemented, where appropriate, up to the level of cost coverage in competent MS inter-institutional reimbursement	reimbursement up to the level of cost coverage in the MS of affiliation patients advance the costs
The current relationship between the Regulations and the Directive	no clear priority between the Regulations and the Directive *With regard to requests for prior authorisation made by an insured person with a view to receiving cross-border healthcare, the Member State of affiliation shall ascertain whether the conditions laid down in the Coordination Regulation have been met. Where those conditions are met, the prior authorisation shall be granted pursuant to that Regulation unless the patient requests otherwise.*	

Source: The author's own summary.

As to the possible further development of the legal framework on European patient mobility, I firmly believe that the duplicity of the legislation must cease, since – for now – it is a very complex structure, where the interrelations of the legal tools are challenging to handle both for the patients and for the other participants (healthcare authorities, insurers, providers etc). In my opinion, there are two options to deal with this problem. A less radical solution is what was suggested above and which is basically what the Commission originally intended to codify into the Directive, namely that with rather small changes a clear hierarchy could be established which focuses on the patient's best interest and obliges the Member States to automatically apply the more beneficial provisions of patient mobility from the patients' point of view.[848] However, in my opinion, a more drastic change is needed and one set of rules should be applicable to European border-crossing patient movements, implemented into one single legal instrument. The rules, which are currently included in various legislative instruments, should not be evaluated separately, since they aim to regulate the same phenomenon. My idea is to genuinely simplify this system by erasing each and every overlapping issue from the Patient Mobility Directive and incorporating them into the Coordination Regulations.[849] Nevertheless, the Directive should remain and further concretise the public health aspects of patient mobility; this would not interfere in the Regulation rules.

In my view, the integrated patient mobility legislation should synthesise the high level of protection provided by the Regulations and the more liberal approach of the Directive. The establishment of the integrated system in the framework of the Regulations would solve the problem of diverse transposition in the various Member States and enable the European institutions to monitor the application of the rules more easily. Last, but not least, a mono-track system – especially if combined with an accessible and patient-friendly network of national contact points – would significantly decrease the legal uncertainty and administrative burden on the patients' side.[850]

5. CONCLUSION

It was already affirmed that European patients are legally entitled to receive medical treatment outside of the Member State of residence within the EU, if they fulfil certain conditions required by EU legislation. The main finding of this

848 See also Pennings, above n. 8, pp. 446–447.

849 The core of this idea is not a recent one. The inclusion of the case law into the Coordination Regulations occurred both when the new set of Regulations was drafted (See section 3.7. in Chapter 1. Setting the scene, especially n. 327 and 328.) and after healthcare services were excluded from the Services Directive. See Wismar et al., above n. 8, pp. 5–6. The attempts failed and left room for the adoption of the Patient Mobility Directive. The idea appeared also in course of the dialogue in the Administrative Commission. AC 332/11, above n. 507, p. 6.

850 The idea of an integrated legal and financial system is elaborated as a part of my *de lege ferenda* suggestions in Chapter 5. Conclusions and suggestions.

extensive chapter on the realisation of access to healthcare across borders is that although the right to cross-border care is granted, in practice European patients encounter serious legal difficulties when they intend to exercise this right.

It was found that the different legal routes based on different legal bases have been functioning next to each other for numerous years and the joint application of these systems continued to raise questions. Although years of political debate and public consultation led to the adoption of a new piece of legislation, the Patient Mobility Directive was rightfully designated to be 'one of the most controversial pieces of European healthcare legislation in recent years',[851] which left many questions unanswered. I would even go so far as saying that it raised some additional questions. I see the solution to the core of this problem in a pair of interrelated arrangements. On the one hand, the more patient-friendly coordination mechanism is to be strengthened and liberalised by opening up the system for private providers as well and by reinforcing the monitoring of the application of the Regulations' rules. On the other hand, the duplicity of the legislation is to be ceased by erasing the overlapping social security issues from the Directive, which would keep governing the – rather innovative, but still improvable – public health-related questions of cross-border healthcare, while the social security issues would be united under the scope of the Coordination Regulations. The one-track system would not only bring transparency and simplicity, but would take due account of the patient's best interest by insuring timely administrative decisions based on an objective assessment of clear legal conditions.

In the next two, shorter chapters two further fields of potential problems are scrutinised briefly, namely, the financing of cross-border healthcare and the issue of information on cross-border healthcare.

[851] Jelfs and Baeten, above n. 349, p. 8, 30.

CHAPTER 3

FINANCIAL AFFORDABILITY

Financing healthcare is one of the main concerns of patients.[852] Therefore, special attention must be paid to the financial aspect of cross-border patient movements, and the dedication of a separate chapter to these issues aims to emphasise their utmost importance in patients' decisions. In this chapter, the main question to be answered is how cross-border medical treatments can be financed based on the healthcare entitlements of the patients in the Member State of affiliation.

When a patient receives healthcare in his/her 'normal setting', in the Member State where he/she resides, and is familiar with the healthcare system and aware of the basic functioning of that system, he/she is more or less confident about when, how much and under what procedure he/she may expect to pay for healthcare. However, healthcare financing structures, as well as healthcare systems in general,[853] vary greatly between the various Member States of the Union.[854] Consequently, if the patient obtains healthcare abroad, the question of financing instantly arises. At the same time, the level of medical costs and especially cost-sharing arrangements can motivate patients to obtain

852 According to a survey that was monitoring the reasons behind unmet needs for healthcare within the European Union, '(i)n the EU27, on average, 30% of those reporting an unmet need for medical treatment or examination referred to the cost of the examination or treatment as the reason for this. [...] Significantly more people in the EU12 cited costs as the reason (40%) than in the EU15 (25%). In almost half of Member States (13 out of 27), the cost of treatment was the most important single reason for unmet need and in 9 of them (Belgium, Greece, Italy, Portugal, Ireland, Bulgaria, Cyprus, Latvia and Romania) around half or more referred to this as the main reason. In Romania almost three-quarters of those with an unmet need cited the treatment being too costly.' T. Ward and E. Ozdemir, *Disparities in access to essential services*, Research note 2012/8, Prepared for the use of the European Commission DG EMPL, pp. 9–10.

853 See n. 231 above.

854 On general models of healthcare financing, see Karner, above n. 231. On healthcare financing in the Member States of the European Union, see, among others, M. Huber, 'Health Care Financing in European Union Member States. An Initial Perspective Based on Recent OECD Work on Overall Social Trends' in R. Leidl (ed.), *Health Care and its Financing in the Single European Market*, IOS Press, Amsterdam 1998, pp. 59–71 and S. Thomson, T. Foubister and E. Mossialos, *Financing health care in the European Union: Challenges and policy responses*, World Health Organization, Copenhagen 2009, pp. 23–48.

healthcare in another country[855] where the prices imposed on patients are more beneficial.[856]

There are numerous methods of financing medical costs which might play a role in cross-border situations. Below, the following such methods are further scrutinised: out-of-pocket payments, payments through specialised insurance for travelling purposes and payments through healthcare schemes.

Out-of-pocket payments should be understood as those situations where the patient uses his/her own financial means to pay for healthcare services abroad without the prospect of reimbursement. This usually is the case if the patient lacks healthcare coverage within a statutory system or intends to 'buy' a medical treatment which is not included in the benefit basket provided for by the competent Member State (e.g. dental treatments, cosmetic surgical interventions).[857] These patients are certainly free to receive the treatment of their choice in the Member State of their choice if the treatment requested is available in that country. Since this healthcare service consumption is independent from the social security coverage, neither the Coordination Regulations, nor the social security provisions of the Patient Mobility Directive (PMD) apply. However, these patients can also benefit from those provisions of the Directive which affect cross-border patients in general, such as rules on information rights and Member States' responsibilities[858] or cross-border cooperation.[859]

Travel insurance is a unique combination of insurance services[860] designed especially for travel purposes. Since these insurance packages usually contain a medical coverage element, they can also be considered as an alternative to finance healthcare costs abroad, although they only cover the costs of necessary

---

855 On the determinants of cross-border patient movements, see section 2.1. in Chapter 1. Setting the scene.

856 'Cost-sharing [...] is an important consideration for patients [...]; predictably, patients' cost-sharing requirements are given as a reason for the existence of cross border arrangements only in a handful of "other arrangements", e.g. where providers attract patients from other countries where the services in question require significant cost-sharing and where providers can offer them considerably cheaper than in the home country (prime example: dental care in Hungary for patients from Austria). Policy-makers need to be aware that such a diversion of care to other countries may increase inequities as those most suffering from cost-sharing can often not afford travel costs.' Busse et al., above n. 122, p. 5.

857 For these purposes, voluntary health insurance schemes may also serve as a satisfying solution. On private health insurance, see, among others, A. Maynard and A. Dixon, 'Private health insurance and medical savings accounts: theory and experience' in Mossialos et al., above n. 62 and E. Mossialos and S.M.S. Thomson, 'Voluntary health insurance in the European Union' in Mossialos et al., above n. 62. The examination of the private health insurance schemes is beyond the scope of this research.

858 Chapter II PMD.

859 Chapter IV PMD.

860 Most travel insurance packages include – for instance – emergency medical and evacuation assistance, non-stop assistance service, and cover the costs of lost, stolen or damaged baggage, cancellation and travel delay, and legal and funeral expenses.

treatment. The exact scope and level of healthcare coverage is specified in the insurance contract itself. Compared to the current solutions of the European legislation for reimbursement of necessary care, travel insurance has the advantage that it may offer a broader scale of services than the patient's health insurance. For example, numerous health insurance schemes exclude benefits for health injuries related to extreme sports from their scope,[861] which would leave the patient unprotected against such risks. An appropriate travel insurance on the other hand can fill this gap. Furthermore, this private insurance can provide coverage in the event of an EHIC refusal,[862] a requirement of co-payment or the usage of private medical facilities. Consequently, the role of travel insurance – although mostly supplementary – is important for European cross-border patients.

Healthcare schemes all over Europe – irrespective of how they are organised and financed – do have extraterritorial elements such as the reimbursement of costs of healthcare obtained abroad. However, within the framework of European legislation, each Member State applies different rules on cost coverage for cross-border medical care. Therefore, the next sections discuss those common rules which impose a universal reimbursement obligation on the Member States.

It is an old, well-known (and proven) cliché that 'money makes the world go round'. This is equally true for healthcare systems: healthcare budgets constitute a fundamental unit of national budgets,[863] so anything which has the potential to genuinely affect healthcare expenditures is a politically sensitive area. Not surprisingly, when the first cases of cross-border patient mobility ended up before the Court of Justice of the European Union, the Member States did not hold back from expressing their concerns about the correspondence between free patient movements and possibly increasing healthcare costs, which carries 'the risk of seriously undermining the financial balance of the social security system'.[864] The Court eased the tension by introducing a new reimbursement regime which gradually differs from the Coordination Regulations' financing mechanism and '*has no effect on the financing or balance of the social security system*'.[865] This dichotomy still exists, since the Court's solution lives on in the

861 This is the case, among others, in Hungary. In 2007, a new law implemented a – heavily attacked – provision into the Compulsory Health Insurance Act (Ebtv.), resulting in the exclusion of any benefits provided in connection to accidents which occurred in the course of extreme sport activities from statutory healthcare financing. Article 18(6)(e) Ebtv.

862 On the refusal of EHICs, see section 2.3 in Chapter 2. Legal complexity.

863 On national healthcare expenditure, see Eurostat, *European social statistics. 2013 edition*, Publications Office of the European Union, Luxembourg 2013, pp. 88–91.

864 C-120/95 *Decker*, 39–40; C-158/96 *Kohll*, 38–42. On the same matter, see also C-368/98 *Vanbraekel*, 47; C-157/99 *Geraets-Smits and Peerbooms*, 72; C-385/99 *Müller-Fauré and Van Riet*, 73–74; C-145/03 *Keller*, 68; C-372/04 *Watts*, 103; C-444/05 *Stamatelaki*, 30; C-173/09 *Elchinov*, 42; C-490/09 *Commission v Luxembourg*, 43.

865 Ibid.

Patient Mobility Directive. However, it must be recognised that 'the demarcation line between these two systems of legislation appears to have been blurred by the Community legislature'[866] since certain findings of the Court made their way into the Regulations.

Nevertheless, the distinctness of the financing mechanisms under the different legal tools profoundly defines patients' legal status and their capacity and willingness to use their cross-border healthcare rights, making it reasonable to examine those two reimbursement systems alongside the case law.

1. THE FINANCIAL REGIME OF THE COORDINATION REGULATIONS

The basic idea behind the Coordination Regulations is to protect the European migrants' acquired social rights and facilitate their free movement within the Union. In order to fulfil this mission in the field of cross-border healthcare, the Regulations are based on the principle that the costs of medical treatments provided by the Member State of residence or of temporary stay must be *fully reimbursed* by the competent Member State.[867] Notably, notwithstanding that the health contributions were paid in accordance with the legislation of the competent Member State, since the hosting Member State's rules apply to the healthcare provision,[868] the costs are calculated in accordance with the tariffs of the latter country.[869]

The reimbursement procedure between the institutions involved can take place in various forms, namely reimbursement based on actual costs, reimbursement based on fixed amounts (lump-sum)[870] and a mutual waiver agreement.[871]

First, the financial transfer can be based on proof of the *actual expenditure* as shown in the accounts of the institution that provided the healthcare benefits

[866] Opinion of AG Mergozzi in C-211/08 *European Commission v Kingdom of Spain* [ECLI:EU:C:2010:88], 71.

[867] Article 35(1) Basic Regulation (BR). See also Paragraph 1 of the Preamble of Decision No S4 of the Administrative Commission (AC) for the Coordination of Social Security Systems of 2 October 2009 concerning refund procedures for the implementation of Articles 35 and 41 of Regulation (EC) No 883/2004 of the European Parliament and of the Council. OJ C 106 of 24 April 2010.
This has been repeatedly confirmed also by the Court. See C-368/98 *Vanbraekel*, 33; C-56/01 *Inizan*, 20; C-145/03 *Keller*, 66; C-372/04 *Watts*, 126.

[868] Articles 17, 19(1), 20(2) BR.

[869] See n. 377 above. When a Member State imposes relatively low health contributions and is obliged to pay the bill of a medical treatment provided in a Member State with high medical costs, this can mean a serious burden for the health financing system of the former state.

[870] Article 35(2) BR.

[871] Article 35(3) BR. See also C-326/00 *Ioannidis*, 54.

in kind.[872] This claim for a refund must be introduced to the debtor Member State (competent Member State) 'within 12 months of the end of the calendar half-year during which those claims were recorded in the accounts of the creditor institution' (in the Member State of the healthcare provision).[873] In principle, the claims must be paid 'within 18 months of the end of the month during which they were introduced to the institution of the debtor Member State'.[874] It must be underlined at this point that higher rates than those applicable to the benefits concerned in the Member State of treatment may not be taken into account in the reimbursement.[875] This rule is another reflection of the ever-present equal treatment principle.[876]

Secondly, if the first method is not appropriate,[877] reimbursement can be made on the basis of *fixed amounts*.[878] This payment method can, however, only be used in very specific cases, namely when the healthcare is provided for family members who do not reside in the same Member State as the insured person[879] or for pensioners and members of their family residing outside the competent Member State.[880] This fixed amount shall be as close as possible to actual expenditure.

In this case,

> the inventory shall be presented to the debtor Member State by the end of the year following the reference year, and the claims based on this inventory shall be introduced as soon as possible following the publication in the Official Journal of the European Union of the annual fixed amounts per person, but latest within the 12-month period following the month during which the average costs for the year concerned were published.[881]

Here as well, the claim must be paid to the creditor by the debtor within eighteen months of the end of the month during which it was introduced.[882]

Thirdly, the Regulation allows the Member States to agree on any other method of reimbursement or the institutions involved can even mutually waive

872 Article 62(1) Implementing Regulation (IR).
873 Article 67(1) IR, see also Article 1 of AC Decision S4.
874 Article 67(5) IR, see also Article 1 of AC Decision S4.
875 Article 62(3) IR.
876 See n. 383 above.
877 The Member States claiming the reimbursement of the cost of benefits in kind on the basis of fixed amounts are the following: Ireland, Spain, Cyprus, the Netherlands, Portugal, Finland, Sweden and the United Kingdom. This list can be found in Annex III IR.
878 Article 35(2) BR and Article 63(1) IR.
879 Article 17 BR and Article 63(2)(a) IR.
880 Articles 24–26 BR and Article 63(2)(b) IR.
881 Article 67(2) IR, see also Article 6 of AC Decision S4.
882 See n. 873 above.

all reimbursements coming under their jurisdiction.[883] For instance, Denmark has a waiver agreement with a number of countries, including Ireland, Portugal and the UK, and for certain groups in relations with Greece.[884]

Although claims for reimbursement between the Member States concerned have to be made as promptly as possible, similarly the Member States are obliged to reimburse claims as soon as possible.[885] It can be deduced from the above time limits, that even if the institutions meet the deadlines set up by the Regulations,[886] the procedures are very lengthy;[887] it can easily take years before a claim is settled. This problem – although it mostly manifests itself between the institutions – has an adverse effect on patients as well. They are the innocent third party here suffering the consequences of the system malfunctioning. Delayed payments and non-payments might drive providers to behaviour that is not compliant with EU law, such as not accepting EHICs and inviting patients to pay the invoice directly[888] instead of a posterior reimbursement by the debtor institute. These practices not only diminish the patients' rights but endanger the fruitful cooperation between the Member States and – in the long run – question the sustainability of the coordination mechanism. In my view, the only way to reverse this tendency is to urge – if necessary – the competent institutions to settle the claims more promptly and to monitor the application of the Regulations' rules more closely.

Another alternative to release the financial tension burdening the healthcare provider and to make the authority of the Member State of stay interested in the effective management of the reimbursement procedure could be obliging the latter to advance the costs of the treatment, as long as the costs are reimbursed by the competent Member State. This could reduce providers' fear of unpaid invoices and hopefully result in providers being less tempted not to comply with EU law. The authority on the Member State of stay would not only guard the procedure by preparing the documentation carefully in order to minimise contestations and keeping close contact with the authority of the competent

883 Article 35(3) BR.

884 See Annex 1 IR.

885 Article 66(1) IR.

886 If the creditor does not meet the deadline to introduce the claim, the claim will not be considered (Article 67(5) IR), whereas if the debtor does not meet the deadline to pay the claim, interest can be charged by the creditor (Article 68(1) IR).

887 In the Proposal for the Implementing Regulation, the Commission stood up for the setting of shorter deadlines, but due to the requirement of unanimity in the Council, those suggestions failed in the course of the negotiations. See European Commission, *Proposal for a Regulation of the European parliament and of the Council laying down the procedure for implementing Regulation (EC) No 883/2004 on the coordination of social security systems*, COM (2006) 16 final, 31.01.2006, Article 66 on pp. 43–44.

888 On the ill-application of the EHIC, see section 2.3 in Chapter 2. Legal complexity and especially n. 539 and Table 7.

Member State, but it would also be incited to speed up the reimbursement process. Patients could benefit from such arrangement.

On the one hand, the implementation of the equal treatment principle guarantees equal rights for migrants compared to the nationals of the State of treatment as though they were insured there.[889] On the other hand, however, it creates *equal obligations*.[890] Thus, if the nationals bear or advance all medical expenses or a certain part of them in the Member State of treatment, this legislation applies to the migrants as well; so they are also obliged to pay for the treatment in question. This might be especially unusual and unfavourable for those who are insured in a benefit in kind system, where they obtain the treatments free of charge. They may find themselves in a highly uncomfortable situation if they do not inform themselves of the local system applied in the Member State of stay in advance. Therefore, it is very important that both the Member States and the European institutions use all possible ways and tools at their disposal to raise patients' awareness of their rights and obligations.[891]

Although the basic full reimbursement principle is the same,[892] the Regulations provide special procedural rules on reimbursement for *necessary care* and *planned care*. These are briefly outlined below.

1.1. NECESSARY CARE

In the above-mentioned situation, when the patient has actually borne the costs of all or part of the necessary healthcare services during a temporary stay, and the legislation of the Member State of stay enables the reimbursement of those costs, the patient has two options to meet the medical expenses: the insured person may claim reimbursement at the institution of the place of stay;[893] or send an application for reimbursement directly to the competent institution.[894] In both cases the costs have to be reimbursed directly to the person concerned in accordance with the rates laid down by the legislation of the Member State of stay[895] and without exceeding the total cost of the care borne by

889 On the full integration idea, see n. 383.

890 Article 4 BR.

891 On the information rights of patients, see Chapter 4. Information obstacles.

892 See n. 866 above.

893 Article 25(B)(1) IR.

894 Article 25(B)(5) IR.

895 It is doubtful, though, whether the competent institutions really refund occasional care accordingly. For instance, the trESS European Report 2013 shed light on a Belgian practice which – in certain cases – 'deprives insured persons of the possibility to obtain reimbursement in accordance with the legislation of the country of stay;' it is thus not 'in keeping with the provisions of the Coordination Regulations'. JORENS and LHERNOULD, above n. 392, p. 29.

the patient.[896] The possibility to claim reimbursement at the institute of the place of stay is an especially beneficial rule from the patients' point of view, because it can considerably shorten the time before the patient receives reimbursement. In contrast, if the request is submitted to the competent institution, the coordination arrangements between the institutions in the different Member States which aim at defining the amount of the reimbursement might take longer. However, the patient might prefer to take the necessary administrative steps in the competent Member State, where he/she is more familiar and thus comfortable with the system.

Furthermore, in the case of substantial expenditure, the Implementing Regulation offers the legal opportunity to request an appropriate advance from the competent institution.[897] It is nevertheless problematic that no guidelines are given in the legislation about what should be considered substantial expenditure, and that the institutions are not obliged to provide an advance, but are free to do so.

Nevertheless, these provisions do not change the fact that the competent institution must fully reimburse all the costs incurred in the institution providing the healthcare[898] in accordance with the procedure detailed above.

1.2. PLANNED CARE

Concerning the reimbursement of the costs of *scheduled treatment*, the Implementing Regulation took over two remarkable points from the case law. It implemented on the one hand the so-called *Vanbraekel* supplement and on the other hand the obligation to reimburse ancillary costs.

1.2.1. Vanbraekel *Supplement*

In the *Vanbraekel* judgment[899] the applicable tariffs were the focus, since in this case, the tariffs applied by the Member State of treatment (France) were lower than the ones in the Member State of affiliation (Belgium).[900] Consequently, the question was raised which scheme had to be applied as a basis for the calculation of the amount reimbursed and whether the patient *can also claim*

896 Article 25(B)(8) IR. If the patient agrees or if the Member State of stay does not provide for reimbursement in the case concerned, the competent institution may undertake the reimbursement of the costs incurred within the limits of and under the conditions of the reimbursement rates laid down in its legislation. Article 25(B)(6)–(7).

897 Article 25(B)(9) IR.

898 Article 35 BR and Article 62 IR.

899 See n. 306 above.

900 C-368/98 *Vanbraekel*, 17.

extra reimbursement to cover the difference between the two systems.[901] Although the then rules of the Coordination Regulations did 'not have the further effect of requiring such additional reimbursement',[902] from the Treaty rules on the free movement of services, the Court deduced that:

> the fact that a person has a lower level of cover when he receives hospital treatment in another Member State than when he undergoes the same treatment in the Member State in which he is insured may deter, or even prevent, that person from applying to providers of medical services established in other Member States and constitutes, both for insured persons and for service providers, a barrier to freedom to provide services.[903]

Since such additional reimbursement does not impose any additional financial burden on the competent Member State and thus cannot be 'liable to have a significant effect on the financing of the social security system', the restriction of the free movement of services cannot be properly justified.[904] Consequently, the Court held that 'additional reimbursement covering the difference must be granted to the insured person by the competent institution'.[905]

This finding of the Court was codified in Article 26(B)(7) of the Implementing Regulation, which is rather unexpected considering that the Court formed this conclusion by interpreting the rules on freedom of services and that the Member States had been reluctant to incorporate the case law into the Regulations.[906] Therefore, this rule seems a bit extraneous in the Coordination Regulation, which serves to facilitate the free movement of persons. Even if the difference of legal bases[907] is set aside, the nature of this provision remains controversial. On the one hand, as van der Mei says, the right to additional reimbursement 'must be welcomed, because it promotes cross-border access to health care without imposing any additional financial burden on Member States and their sickness funds'.[908] On the other hand, though, the provision of the *Vanbraekel* supplement breaks with the full integration theory of the Regulations and does thus not comply with the principle of equal treatment.[909] As pointed out earlier in this section, the principle of equal treatment implies that both the rights and obligations of migrant persons and nationals of the Member State concerned are *equal*. Under the current Union legislation, the right to additional reimbursement

901 C-368/98 *Vanbraekel*, 35.
902 C-368/98 *Vanbraekel*, 37.
903 C-368/98 *Vanbraekel*, 45.
904 C-368/98 *Vanbraekel*, 52.
905 C-368/98 *Vanbraekel*, 53. See also C-173/09 *Elchinov*, 78; C-512/08 *Commission v France*, 51.
906 On this matter, see section 3.7. in Chapter 1. Setting the scene and especially n. 320.
907 On the difference of legal bases, see section 4.1. in Chapter 2. Legal complexity.
908 van der Mei, above n. 747, p. 212.
909 See n. 383 above.

enables cross-border patients to receive a refund for co-payments if the level of the cost coverage is higher in their Member State of insurance, whereas the domestic patients in the Member State of stay cannot claim reimbursement for those expenses. As a result, *reverse discrimination* occurs, because the migrants are in a more favourable situation than non-migrants. There is reverse discrimination when non-mobile patients enjoy a lower level of social protection than mobile patients. How could this unfair situation be solved? Of course, national law must comply with Union law, so eroding the rights of cross-border patients is not an option. A fair and legally correct solution could be 'to upgrade the legal position' of the 'non-mobile' patients to match that of mobile ones or to reconsider the Union law provision in question.[910]

Moreover, even within the group of migrants, there is a difference between the legal status of persons obtaining planned care abroad who have the right to additional reimbursement and of persons receiving occasional care abroad to whom the Regulation does not grant the right to additional reimbursement.[911] The Court acknowledged that the cases of unscheduled and scheduled treatment must be distinguished in this respect.[912] It points out in its reasoning that the patient – in many cases, when the need for healthcare arises unexpectedly – is not in a position to compare the medical costs of the two Member States involved and the circumstances leave no alternative but to provide the insured person with hospital treatment in the Member State of stay.[913] The Court agrees with the Commission's argument that in certain cases the deterioration in the insured person's health during a temporary stay in another Member State is not such as to deprive him or her of the choice between going to hospital in that state and an early return to the state of affiliation to receive the necessary hospital treatment there.[914] Nevertheless, it held that the non-provision of complementary reimbursement in case of unplanned care (as it was the case in the Spanish legislation) is not regarded as a restriction on cross-border healthcare services, and so it does not breach EU law.[915]

1.2.2. Ancillary Costs

When obtaining medical treatment outside of the patient's catchment area, the incurred costs exceed the *stricto sensu* medical costs; the patient must also reckon with the expenses related to travelling and accommodation, not only for him/herself but also for the accompanying persons if there are any. As a result,

---

910 See RENNUY, above n. 185, p. 316.
911 See also PENNINGS, above n. 8, p. 435.
912 C-211/08 *Commission v Spain*, 58, 60.
913 C-211/08 *Commission v Spain*, 64.
914 C-211/08 *Commission v Spain*, 66.
915 C-211/08 *Commission v Spain*, 72.

the Court was asked in the *Leichtle* case[916] how the Member States should treat these costs with regard to cross-border patient movements. The Court confirmed that 'expenditure in connection with board and lodging can be regarded as forming an integral part of the health cure itself'[917] and that although ancillary costs, such as travel costs and visitor's tax are 'not medical in character, and are not as a rule paid to health care providers, they none the less appear to be inextricably linked to the cure itself'.[918] Still, it cannot be inferred from these findings that the competent institution is required to reimburse these additional expenses in each case; the Court lays down a duty to apply the equal treatment principle and to grant reimbursement if such duty exists when these costs arise from movements within the Member State.[919] The Implementing Regulation echoes this rule in Article 26(C)(8), imposing the obligation on the competent institutions to assume 'the costs of travel and stay which are inseparable from the treatment of the insured person' both for that person and for the accompanying person, if the national legislation provides for the reimbursement of such costs.

To sum up,[920] the Coordination Regulations' financial regime is built upon the principle of full reimbursement between the institutions involved. As a rule, the patient cannot be required to advance the medical costs unless the nationals of the Member State of stay do the same. In the latter case, reimbursement can be claimed either in the Member State of treatment or the competent Member State. The institutions of the Member States must cooperate closely and settle the claims as quickly as possible. This, however, is often not the case, which rebounds on the patients themselves as well.

2. THE FINANCIAL REGIME OF THE PATIENT MOBILITY DIRECTIVE

As a result of the interpretation of the Treaty rules on the free movement of services, the reimbursement of medical costs in relation to cross-border

[916] Case C-8/02 *Ludwig Leichtle v Bundesanstalt für Arbeit* [ECLI:EU:C:2004:161].
Mr Ludwig Leichtle, a German civil servant, requested confirmation from the competent institution that the expenditure associated with a health cure which he proposed to take at Ischia, in Italy, would be covered. His request was rejected on the grounds that the care provided in Italy did not offer much greater prospects of success than the health cures available in Germany. Mr Leichtle underwent the thermal cure anyway and brought a legal action against the decision of the competent institution.
See on this case, A. den Exter, 'Patient Mobility in European Union: Health Spas in Ischia, Italy' *Croatian Medical Journal* 2005, vol 46 issue 2, pp. 197–200.

[917] Case C-8/02 *Leichtle*, 33.

[918] Case C-8/02 *Leichtle*, 35.

[919] C-372/04 *Watts*, 139–140; C-466/04 *Acereda Herrera*, 38.

[920] The basic points of the different financial regimes are compared in Table 14 below.

healthcare has always stood on a different footing than the Coordination Regulations. Already in the first judgments, the Court insisted that reimbursement must be provided in accordance with the tariffs of the State of insurance; thus, cross-border patient movements – even if they were not authorised in advance – have no effect on the financial equilibrium of the Member State concerned.[921]

The Patient Mobility Directive follows the same approach and provides that:

> the costs of cross-border healthcare shall be reimbursed or paid directly by the Member State of affiliation up to the level of costs that would have been assumed by the Member State of affiliation, had this healthcare been provided in its territory without exceeding the actual costs of healthcare received.[922]

It was reported though that several Member States adopted reimbursement practices whereby the reimbursement tariff for cross-border patients is based on the tariff that would be borne by the Member State of affiliation if the treatment concerned was received from a non-contracted provider on its territory – which is, of course, considerably lower than the rate for contracted providers.[923] Another questionable technique reported from Poland is that there is an annual reimbursement limit for cross-border healthcare meaning that when the annual financial reserve is depleted, reimbursement is postponed until next year or later.[924] Such practices are clearly not in line with either the wording or the intention of the Directive and must be investigated by the Commission.

The above rule, however, does not in any sense prevent the Member State of affiliation from reimbursing the full cost of the treatment, if it exceeds the level of reimbursement calculated on the basis of domestic tariffs.[925] If the Member States use this opportunity and transpose the Directive accordingly, it is a real advantage for border-crossing patients. If not, however, this financing mechanism proves to be less attractive for patients who come from countries with relatively low tariffs and intend to obtain healthcare in a Member State with

---

921 See n. 863 above.

922 Article 7(4) PMD. Reimbursement may never lead to the enrichment of the patient.

923 COM (2015) 421, above n. 680, p. 5. See also, Palm, above n. 714, p. 21. For instance, Finland implemented the Directive in a way that cross-border patients receive – under the Directive's regime – the same reimbursement as when using private healthcare services in Finland. This amount is usually only 20–30 per cent of the total costs incurred. M. Kattelus, 'Implementation of the Directive on the Application on Patient's Rights in Cross-border Healthcare (2011/24/EU) in Finland' *European Journal of Health Law* 2014, vol 21 issue 1, p. 32. I think that this approach is clearly not in compliance with EU law, highly limits the free movement of patients and thus was rightfully criticised by the European Commission.

924 Kowalska-Bobko et al, above n. 809, p. 1236.

925 Article 7(4) PMD. See also C-120/95 *Decker*, 29; C-158/96 *Kohll*, 27; C-368/98 *Vanbraekel*, 36; C-56/01 *Inizan*, 19; C-466/04 *Acereda Herrera*, 34.

higher medical prices, because the difference between the incurred costs and the reimbursed costs remains at the expense of the patient.[926]

2.1. ANCILLARY COSTS

With regard to the *ancillary costs*, the Patient Mobility Directive partly erodes and partly upgrades patients' legal status in comparison to the case law. On the one hand, not making it obligatory to reimburse those costs *inextricably linked to* the treatment abroad can be seen as a step backwards; whereas on the other hand, extending the scope of the reimbursement of additional costs to persons obtaining necessary care, and expressly including 'the extra costs which persons with disabilities might incur due to one or more disabilities when receiving cross-border healthcare'[927] are relevant improvements. Still, the lack of a compulsory nature results in a very vague guarantee for the patients, which is not in line with the case law of the Court. This is one of those critical points of the Directive which apparently do not comply with the findings of the Court[928] and can thus be easily overruled by new case law.[929] For example, if a Member State provides reimbursement for travel costs in accordance with its national law to patients travelling for treatment within the country, the case law – on the grounds of equal treatment – imposes the obligation to do the same if the travel is related to cross-border healthcare.[930] As a result, if this Member State – while implementing the Directive – did not choose to reimburse ancillary costs, as it has the freedom to so decide, the patient can challenge this provision in a judicial proceeding.

In my opinion, the wording of Article 7(4) of the Directive concerning the reimbursement of additional costs is incorrect and should be altered to guarantee expressly the equal treatment of domestic and cross-border patients, similar to the corresponding article of the Coordination Regulations.[931] Even more so, since the next paragraph of the same article allows the Member States to adopt provisions in accordance with the Treaty on the Functioning of the

---

926 'Some reports express concerns about the flow of patients between countries with "high fees" and countries with "low fees" and towards countries providing excellent medical care.' Jorens and Lhernould, above n. 392, p. 30.

927 The European Parliament demanded in its first reading of the Proposal to make this provision mandatory, but it was not supported by the Council. See Article 6(3) of European Parliament, *European Parliament legislative resolution of 23 April 2009 on the proposal for a directive of the European Parliament and of the Council on the application of patients' rights in cross-border healthcare*, P6_TA (2009) 0286, 23.04.2009.

928 See n. 918 above.

929 See n. 840 above.

930 See section 1.2.2. above in this chapter and especially n. 918.

931 Article 26(C)(8) IR.

European Union aimed at ensuring that patients enjoy the same rights when receiving cross-border healthcare as they would have enjoyed if they had received healthcare in a comparable situation in the Member State of affiliation. However, this provision also only gives the Member States permission instead of imposing the obligation on them to apply the principle of equal treatment with domestic patients.

In my view, the *two dimensions of equal treatment* are equally important and should be safeguarded by European legislation, by the Patient Mobility Directive in this case. Whereas the non-discrimination between domestic patients and patients coming from other Member States is satisfactorily ensured in the Directive,[932] the equal treatment between patients obtaining domestic healthcare services and those who share the same nationality but use their cross-border healthcare rights is left to the discretion of the Member States. This aspect of non-discrimination should be improved further. For instance, in Hungary, the national legislation is not clear about whether Hungarian patients are entitled to obtain necessary care at non-contracted providers in another Member State under the Directive's regime. One could argue that the Hungarian healthcare system does not cover treatments at private providers within the country,[933] thus it can do the same when the provider is established in another Member State. However, the Directive is unambiguous on the point that the Member State of affiliation shall ensure the costs incurred by an insured person who receives cross-border healthcare are reimbursed, if the healthcare in question is among the benefits to which the insured person is entitled in the Member State of affiliation.[934] So the counter-argument is that it is the treatment in question which decides whether the costs shall be reimbursed, not the status of the provider. The current legislation accepts the latter argument, because it provides that if an insured person obtains unplanned, medically necessary treatment at a provider that does not fall under the scope of the Regulations but is established within the European Union, the costs shall be reimbursed.[935]

---

932 *The principle of non-discrimination with regard to nationality shall be applied to patients from other Member States.* Article 4(3) PMD.
However, there is one exception to the general application of non-discrimination on the grounds of nationality, namely Member States are free to *adopt measures regarding access to treatment aimed at fulfilling their fundamental responsibility to ensure sufficient and permanent access to healthcare within their territory* if those measures are justified by overriding reasons of general interest. This provision opens up the door for restricting arrangements based on rather vaguely defined arguments, so that even the wish to control costs might be enough to reason such a limitation. See n. 676. However, the Member States' latitude is narrowed down by the requirements that *such measures shall be limited to what is necessary and proportionate and may not constitute a means of arbitrary discrimination and shall be made publicly available in advance.*

933 Article 9 Ebtv.

934 Article 7(1) PMD.

935 Article 8(1) of Governmental Decree No 340/2013.

Nevertheless, this right of patients is neither expressly declared in the national legislation, nor communicated to the public. In my opinion, this constitutes *reserve discrimination*, where non-mobile patients enjoy a lower level of social protection, since their domestic private medical expenses are not reimbursed, than mobile patients, whose private medical expenses, which occurred abroad, are (at least partly) reimbursed.

The principle of *equal treatment* plays a crucial role in the Directive's financing mechanism. It is applied both in relation to the chargeable healthcare fees and the eligibility criteria and administrative formalities.

2.2. CHARGEABLE HEALTHCARE FEES

Besides the above-mentioned general requirement of non-discrimination,[936] the Directive specifies that:

> Member States shall ensure that the healthcare providers on their territory apply the same scale of fees for healthcare for patients from other Member States, as for domestic patients in a comparable medical situation, or that they charge a price calculated according to objective, non-discriminatory criteria if there is no comparable price for domestic patients.[937]

This rule undoubtedly offers cross-border patients an important guarantee that they cannot be required to pay higher healthcare fees than the nationals of the Member State where they obtain a treatment.[938] However, the phrasing of this provision evokes some questions, such as what the expression 'in a comparable medical situation' means and how the Member States can monitor and enforce the application of this rule.

From the point of view of the Directive's financial regime it is a fundamental question whether there is a price list for medical treatments calculated in advance.

---

936 See n. 931 above.

937 Article 4(4) PMD. This provision does not deprive the healthcare providers of the right to set their own prices, as long as they do it without discriminating against foreign patients.

938 Pennings, above n. 8, p. 445. This can also be seen as codification of the Court's findings, since in C-411/98 *Ferlini*, the Court declared that the unilateral application to patients not affiliated to the domestic healthcare schemes of scales of fees for medical care (which in this case occurred in relation to the birth of Mr Ferlini's child in Luxembourg, who was employed by the European Commission, thus – together with his family – affiliated to the Joint Scheme) which are higher than those applicable to residents affiliated to the national social security scheme constitutes discrimination on the grounds of nationality prohibited under the provisions of the Treaty, in the absence of objective justification in this respect. C-411/98 *Angelo Ferlini v Centre hospitalier de Luxembourg* [ECLI:EU:C:2000:530], 62. See also Strban, above n. 126, p. 399.

If there is, the fees applicable to domestic patients can be invoiced to cross-border patients, if they are in a comparable medical situation. One may wonder whether this implies that they should have the same diagnoses or whether they can only be considered being in a *comparable medical situation* if they receive exactly the same treatment. At the same time, the price a domestic patient is required to pay does not only necessarily depend on his/her medical status but also on his/her *insurance status and entitlements.* How could this be taken into account while calculating the price for cross-border patients? Should foreign patients be treated as uninsured domestic patients? If there are different scales for domestic patients, can foreign patients be automatically charged the highest one? Since the healthcare financing systems are highly different in the Member States of the Union, it is far from simple to create a harmonised reimbursement system for medical costs. In this respect, the obligation to apply the principle of non-discrimination between domestic and foreign patients is a good first step, but the issue in question calls for further elaboration.[939]

If there is no price list for domestic patients, then the only requirement is that the calculation of the fee must be based on objective and non-discriminatory criteria.[940]

Another concern is whether the *same-tariff rule* can be *enforced in practice.* In the case of contracted providers, putting a monitoring system into operation should be possible. However, it is still doubtful 'whether healthcare providers will be willing to charge lower prices (negotiated with home health insurance providers) for non-referred cross-border patients'.[941] Monitoring the pricing policy of private, non-contracted providers seems to be even more challenging.

If each provider could be required to publish a list of prices of the treatments it provides, that would clarify this question and would allow patients to calculate the fee they can expect. However, setting up such a list might prove to be difficult in certain healthcare schemes.[942] Nevertheless, even if there is not an exhaustive list of medical fees, 'Member States shall have a transparent mechanism for calculation of costs of cross-border healthcare that are to be reimbursed to the insured person by the Member State of affiliation'.[943] Furthermore, the cost

939 Interestingly enough, the Guidance note of the Commission (AC 246/12, above n. 264) does not even touch upon this subject.

940 Article 4(4) PMD.

941 STRBAN, above n. 126, p. 399.

942 On the one hand, also under the Regulation's regime, healthcare providers – irrespective of operating within a reimbursement, a benefit in kind or a national health service type of system – have introduced claims indicating the price of the treatments provided for cross-border patients. So – in theory – it is not impossible to set up such kind of price lists. On the other hand, the reimbursement mechanism within the coordination system is different from the one in the Directive and is not always based on the actual expenditures. On this matter, see section 1. above in this chapter. See also PENNINGS, above n. 8, pp. 443–444.

943 Article 7(6) PMD.

calculation mechanism 'shall be based on objective, non-discriminatory criteria known in advance and applied at the relevant administrative level'.[944]

2.3. ELIGIBILITY CRITERIA AND ADMINISTRATIVE FORMALITIES

Whereas the same-tariff rule is related to non-discrimination between foreign and domestic patients, the issue of *equality of eligibility criteria and administrative formalities* again concerns the other dimension of equal treatment, namely between patients affiliated to the same Member States using their cross-border healthcare rights and the ones who are not using them. The Directive authorises the Member States to make the reimbursement of medical costs subject to 'the same conditions, criteria of eligibility and regulatory and administrative formalities as they would impose if the healthcare were provided in their territory'.[945] The fulfilment of eligibility criteria and certain administrative formalities, such as a gatekeeping scheme, functions in many countries. What the Directive says is that in order to get reimbursement border-crossing patients might be required to go through all the same steps when obtaining healthcare abroad as they would when receiving the healthcare in the Member State concerned. For instance, if there is a referral system in place in the Member State of affiliation, patients need to be able to present a referral. Otherwise reimbursement can be legitimately denied on the grounds of non-fulfilment of the administrative formalities. These conditions and formalities must nevertheless be non-discriminatory and must not constitute an obstacle to free movement.[946]

In practice, it seems that not all the Member States transposed the Directive accordingly and in some Member States interesting conditions were introduced that the reimbursement is dependent on. Palm mentions the examples of the UK that requires a document reasoning the medical necessity of a particular treatment abroad; Bulgaria, where patients need to present a sworn translation of the foreign invoices;[947] and Greece that obliges patients to certify all documents by the local consular official.[948]

Although as a main rule, under the Directive's regime, patients are required to pay for the medical treatments upfront, the Directive nevertheless offers the possibility for the Member States to 'choose to apply the mechanisms of financial

---

944 Ibid. It is up to the Member State of affiliation to determine whether reimbursement is provided at a national, regional or national level. Article 7(3) PMD.

945 Article 7(7) PMD.

946 Ibid. See Strban, above n. 126, p. 400.

947 Not only Bulgaria imposes this requirement, the Report says that at least four Member States requires this. COM (2015) 421, above n. 680, p. 5. Poland does this too. Kowalska-Bobko et al, above n. 809, p. 1238.

948 Palm, above n. 714, p. 21.

compensation between the competent institutions as provided for by Regulation (EC) No 883/2004'.[949] If a Member State decides not to use the Regulations' reimbursement mechanisms, it is then required to 'ensure that patients receive reimbursement without undue delay'.[950] In my opinion, this provision is very unclear and cannot safeguard *patients' right to a timely reimbursement*. It would be all the more desirable to fix a maximum – appropriately short and enforceable – deadline for reimbursement to avoid legal uncertainty and diverse national implementation. At the same time, for the sake of clarity and a speedy settling of claims, a deadline should be set also for patients for introducing the claim to the Member State of affiliation.

The conclusion can be drawn that the Directive followed the path of the case law of the Court and introduced a reimbursement system which enables border-crossing patients to claim reimbursement – in principle – up to the level of domestic tariffs in the Member State of affiliation, while they pay the same scale of medical fees as the patients affiliated to the Member State of treatment. Under the Directive's regime, the patient advances the medical costs.

This concisely summarised financing mechanism shows some gradual differences in comparison with the Coordination Regulation. Therefore, the next section is dedicated to a brief critical analysis of their discrepancies from the patients' point of view.

3. EUROPEAN REIMBURSEMENT REGIMES AS AN OBSTACLE TO CROSS-BORDER PATIENT MOBILITY

As already discussed, the Coordination Regulations and the Patient Mobility Directive substantially differ from each other.[951] One of the most obvious differences is the financing of cross-border medical treatments (these differences are outlined in Table 14 below). After examination of both instruments' reimbursement mechanisms,[952] it can be concluded that the most relevant discrepancies between the two routes of patient mobility concern the level of reimbursement and the mechanism of reimbursement.

3.1. LEVEL OF REIMBURSEMENT

The level of reimbursement is basically dependent on which tariffs are applied when calculating the reimbursement. According to the coordination rules – on

949 Article 9(5) PMD.
950 Ibid.
951 See section 4. in Chapter 2. Legal complexity.
952 See sections 1. and 2. above in this chapter.

the grounds of the full integration principle, namely that foreign patients must be treated as if they were insured in the Member State of treatment – the rules of the Member State of treatment apply, including the rules on the calculation of medical fees. Hence, in principle the healthcare costs incurred abroad are fully covered.

However, the Directive's financing mechanism is based on the idea that the reimbursement of cross-border healthcare costs may not affect the financial balance of the Member State of affiliation. Patients can thus claim reimbursement up to the level of domestic tariffs in that country. If the actual costs exceed this amount, the Member States cannot be obliged to bear the difference, which therefore remains at the expense of the patient.

3.2. MECHANISM OF REIMBURSEMENT

Concerning the mechanism of reimbursement, whereas the Regulations primarily require the institutions involved to settle the claim for reimbursement between each other without the patient needing to advance the costs of the treatment, under the Directive, the patient is invited by the healthcare provider to pay the invoice upfront, after which he/she can claim posterior reimbursement from the Member State of affiliation.

From the patients' point of view, both characteristics are more beneficial under the Regulations, and the less favourable financial scheme of the Directive has the potential to prevent patients from using their rights conferred on them by the Directive.

The non-patient-friendly features of the financing system, such as a possible financial burden due to a cost difference and a requirement of advancing medical costs, were already accompanied by concerns before the adoption of the Patient Mobility Directive. Van der Mei raised the question shortly after the *Kohll* and *Decker* judgments and it is still valid today:

> The Court has accepted that insurance organs may reimburse the costs of 'foreign' medical products or services in accordance with their own reimbursement rates. The difference between the price in other Member States and the national reimbursement rates is to be paid by the patient himself. Especially in case of rather expensive products or types of treatment, the financial burden on the patient could be considerable. The danger exists that 'better off' patients will benefit more from Decker and Kohll than the patients with relatively low incomes. Public health insurance schemes are aimed at guaranteeing all residents regardless of their financial status equality of access to medical care. In the State of residence this equality is largely guaranteed, but should not the same apply to the access to medical care in other Member States?[953]

[953] van der Mei, above n. 270, p. 297.

Table 14. Differences in financing of cross-border medical treatments

<table>
<tr><th colspan="3"></th><th>Under the Regulations' regime</th><th>Under the Directive's regime</th></tr>
<tr><td colspan="3">Necessary care</td><td>Reimbursement in accordance with the *tariffs applied by the MS of treatment* (except non-reimbursable local co-payments the nationals of the MS of treatment are also obliged to pay).
Main principle: *reimbursement between institutions*: the patient *does not need to advance the costs* (except the co-payments which remain at his/her expense) unless the MS of treatment operates a reimbursement system.
If the patient advances the costs, reimbursement can be claimed either from the institution in the MS of stay or from the competent institution.</td><td rowspan="2">Reimbursement in accordance with the *tariffs applied by the MS of affiliation*.
If there is a difference between the actual costs (the tariffs of the MS of treatment – the same scale of fees must be applied as to domestic patients) and the reimbursed costs (the tariffs of the MS of affiliation), those costs *remain at the expense of the patient*, unless the MS of affiliation opts to refund the whole amount.
Main principle: *the patient advances the costs.*
Ancillary costs might be reimbursed if the MS of affiliation opts for that, but there is no obligation.</td></tr>
<tr><td rowspan="3">Planned care</td><td rowspan="2">Treatment subject to PA</td><td>PA granted</td><td>In principle, reimbursement in accordance with the *tariffs applied by the MS of treatment*, but *additional reimbursement* can be claimed if the cost coverage is higher in the competent MS.
If *ancillary costs* are reimbursed when arisen from domestic patient movement, they must be reimbursed in the event of obtained planned treatment abroad as well.</td></tr>
<tr><td>PA not granted</td><td>Medical costs are *not covered* by the Coordination Regulations (unless the refusal of the request for PA is deemed unlawful a posteriori).</td><td>Medical costs are *not covered* by the Patient Mobility Directive.</td></tr>
<tr><td colspan="2">Treatment *not* subject to PA</td><td></td><td>Reimbursement in accordance with the *tariffs applied by the MS of affiliation* (see above).</td></tr>
</table>

Source: The author's own summary.

The risk indeed exists that the Patient Mobility Directive exacerbates pro-rich inequality, because it is 'likely to disproportionately benefit wealthy and well informed patients'.[954] So the following question arises: how can equal access to cross-border healthcare be ensured – independently from the financial capacity of the individual patients?[955]

954 Legido-Quigley et al., above n. 347, p. 366.

955 The Petru judgment – however not interpreting the Directive but the Coordination Regulation – can be used as a way of illustration: Mrs Petru's German hospital treatment did

The European Parliament, which acted as an advocate of patients' rights throughout the negotiations of the proposal for the Directive,[956] also articulated its concerns in relation to the financing mechanism[957] and suggested two possible solutions to ensure direct payment from the patients' funder to the healthcare provider, namely the introduction of a *voucher system* and the establishment of a *central clearing house*.

With the voucher system, the intention was to provide cross-border patients with a tool which they can practically take with them and present to the healthcare provider in the Member State of treatment as a guarantee for reimbursement from the Member State of affiliation. This option very much resembles the system of the Regulations under which patients must present either their EHIC, for necessary care, or an S2 form issued to them, for scheduled care, as a proof of entitlement which can be seen as a 'promissory note' from the competent institution. The voucher system would have imposed a considerable additional administrative burden both on the patients themselves and on the national healthcare administrations. Moreover, the preliminary administrative steps necessary for the usage of vouchers would nullify the very aim of the Directive, which is to offer the possibility to obtain cross-border healthcare without authorisation or any other prior administrative arrangements. The Council rejected the creation of a voucher system. Still, a hint of this proposition remained in the Directive in the form of a voluntary system of prior notification, in return for which 'the patient receives a written confirmation of the amount to be reimbursed on the basis of an estimate'.[958] So this confirmation does not target the healthcare provider as was the idea with the voucher system, but instead gives an indication to the patient as to what he/she can expect financially.

Another proposal was to put in place a system of direct reimbursement 'through a Central Clearing House to manage the cross-border, cross-currency, cross-system (Beveridge/Bismark) complications'.[959] Since the details of this idea were not worked out because of the rejection by the Council, it is unclear how this institution would have been constructed and functioned.

---

cost around 18,000 euros. (See n. 633.). One may raise the question how many patients might be in the position to advance such an amount of money in a country where the minimum wage is about 275 euros (in 2017, the minimum wage in Romania is 1250 Romanian leu).

956 See n. 347 above.

957 'When we say the policy should be about patients with needs, not patients with means, we should make it clear we do not wish to see patients having to travel, clutching cash or credit card to pay upfront for often expensive in-hospital treatment.' European Parliament – Committee on the Environment, Public Health and Food Safety, *Report on the proposal for a directive of the European Parliament and of the Council on the application of patients' rights in cross-border healthcare*, 3 April 2009, A6-0233/2009, p. 76.

958 Article 9(5) PMD.

959 EP – ENVI, above n. 957, p. 76.

It is remarkable that a European institution suggested operating a separate institution with the purpose of managing cross-border healthcare issues. The creation of a central body could indeed facilitate the cooperation between the national contact points and could serve as a central base of knowledge and information on cross-border healthcare.

Since neither of the Parliament's proposals made it through the filter of the Council, the current wording of the Directive does not offer any solid solution to tackle the price difference and the upfront payment in order to provide greater equality and equal access to cross-border healthcare. In particular, the lack of a compensation mechanism adversely affects patients with low incomes affiliated to a healthcare scheme with relatively low tariffs. These patients are basically deprived of their cross-border healthcare rights on an economic ground, because they can neither afford to advance a considerable amount of money, nor bear the cost difference between the tariffs of their own Member State and another Member State with a higher scale of medical fees.[960] In my opinion, this situation can easily result in a rather one-sided European patient mobility phenomenon from the Western countries to the Eastern countries, which – despite the considerably lower prices – do offer good quality healthcare services. Therefore, there is an urgent need to address this problem.

In my view, unifying the Regulations' and the Directive's systems might solve these problems, since under the integrated system the Regulations' inter-institutional reimbursement mechanism should be applied and an additional compensation scheme could be put in place.

4. CONCLUSION

Financing cross-border healthcare is likely to be troublesome for patients. Out of the two simultaneously functioning reimbursement mechanisms, the one included in the Coordination Regulations has evident advantages compared to the one in the Patient Mobility Directive. The Directive's financing system fails to tackle both the *problem of financial affordability* since it evokes the risk of expenses remaining on the patients' side and the requirement of advancing medical costs, and the *problem of accessibility of reimbursement schemes* since reimbursement is often subject to the fulfilment of various legal conditions, the scope and level of reimbursement can be strictly limited and the timeliness of the reimbursement is not ensured.

---

960 See also Kowalska-Bobko et al, above n. 809, p. 1238 and S. Olsena, 'Implementation of the Patients' Rights in Cross-border Healthcare Directive in Latvia' *European Journal of Health Law* 2014, vol 21 issue 1, p. 53.

Although the Regulations' system is far from flawless, it is in the interest of the patient to apply an inter-institutional reimbursement system, where he/she is not required to advance the costs of medical treatment abroad; the coordination mechanism's financing process should thus be strengthened in order to ensure equal access to cross-border healthcare. I cannot agree more with Chaytor, who emphasises that '(a)ction to tackle health inequalities is vital, not least because they have significant social and economic costs to both individuals and wider society'.[961]

[961] S. Chaytor, *Future of Healthcare in Europe – Meeting future challenges: Key issues in context*, UCL Policy Briefing, January 2012, p. 2.

CHAPTER 4
INFORMATION OBSTACLES

Being in need of medical care principally implies being in an extremely vulnerable position which often involves 'extraordinary moments of fear, anxiety and doubt'.[962] Accessing healthcare in a state other than the state of residence might significantly increase the number of potential sources of difficulties, which are consequently very likely to add to the feeling of being helpless and exposed in such situations. Rights provided by law are of no use to the addressees of these rights if the rights themselves cannot be effectively used and enforced by the power of law. This is no different for (cross-border) healthcare rights either.

Each patient comes across different boundaries when accessing healthcare, both of a legal and non-legal nature. Busse and his colleagues identified six hurdles of access, namely the population covered by health insurance, the benefits covered, cost-sharing arrangements, geographical barriers, organisational barriers and the utilisation of accessible services,[963] whereas the European Commission mentioned the following barriers: lack of insurance, high costs of care, lack of information about services provided, language and cultural barriers.[964] The obstacles related to information and communication are usually among the first ones cross-border patients faces: *linguistic barriers* and the *lack of reliable information* were explicitly referred to by the Court of Justice of the EU[965] as potentially discouraging factors of cross-border patient movements.

Patients' right to information is a fundamental human right embedded both in international standards and national legislations.[966] In a cross-border setting, this right is possibly even more complicated to enforce, thus problems related to communication and access to information are addressed below.

---

962 J.D. Fowler, *Cultural and Structural Barriers that Affect the Doctor-Patient Relationship: A Bolivian perspective*, http://ir.library.oregonstate.edu/xmlui/bitstream/handle/1957/9896/Fowler.pdf?sequence=1, 2008 (accessed 25.03.2017), p. 1.

963 Busse et al., above n. 122, p. 4.

964 European Commission, *Communication from the Commission to the European Parliament, the Council, the European Economic and Social Committee and the Committee of the Regions. Solidarity in health: Reducing health inequalities in the EU*, COM (2009) 567 final, 20.10.2009, p. 3.

965 C-385/99 *Müller-Fauré and Van Riet*, 95.

966 A.V. Casas and C.R. Parada, *Patients' right to information: a review of the regulatory and ethical framework*, http://bid.ub.edu/21/vall3.htm, 2008 (accessed 07.4.2017).

1. LINGUISTIC BARRIERS

Communication is a key element of healthcare provision,[967] in the course of which it is of essential importance that each party involved expresses him/herself clearly and exactly.[968] If the mutual communication works properly, it 'ultimately leads to an enhanced doctor-patient relationship resulting in satisfaction with the encounter by both parties and thus improved health care outcomes',[969] whereas the lack of or inappropriate information exchange might result in incomplete medical assessment, distrust between the parties and inadequate medical treatment.[970] Interestingly enough, this problem has not been addressed on EU level so far.[971]

1.1. THE LANGUAGE BARRIER

In the currently 28 Member States of the European Union 24 official languages[972] are spoken beside the relatively high number of regional and minority languages.[973] Although the Union is committed to safeguarding multilinguism[974] as a proof and a guarantee of European diversity,[975] this constitutes a serious

967 Both patients and health practitioners claim that there is a need for improved communication between the parties involved. European Commission, *Eurobarometer Qualitative Study: Patient involvement. Aggregate Report*, 2012, p. 13.

968 Mark Twain's famous quote is very appropriate for these situations: 'The difference between the right word and the almost right word is the difference between lightning and the lightning bug.' Quoted by V. Sorlie and R.A. Lopez, 'When Language, Health Literacy, and Miscommunication Collide: Tremors Versus Seizures' *Family Medicine* 2011, vol 43 issue 1, p. 48.

969 Fowler, above n. 962, p. 5. See also M. Simpson, R. Buckman, M. Stewart, P. Maguire, M. Lipkin, D. Novack, J. Till, 'Doctor-patient communication: the Toronto consensus statement' *British Medical Journal* 1991, vol 303, p. 1385.

970 Fowler, above n. 962, pp. 5–6. See also O. Carter-Pokras, M.J.F. O'Neill, V. Cheanvechai, M. Menis, T. Fan and A. Solera, 'Providing Linguistically Appropriate Services to Persons With Limited English Proficiency: A Needs and Resources Investigation' *The American Journal of Managed Care* 2004, vol 10 Special Issue, p. 30.

971 However, the problem was undoubtedly recognised. See COM (2009) 567, above n. 964, p. 3.

972 Regulation No 1 determining the languages to be used by the European Economic Community. OJ 17 of 6 October 1958, Article 1.

973 European Commission, *Eurobarometer: Europeans and their languages*, 2012, p. 2.

974 Although multilingualism can be considered an asset of the Union, language policy is often attacked for its costliness. See, among others, P. Oltermann, 'Something in common: should English be the official language of the EU?' *The Guardian*, 24.04.2013.

975 'It is this diversity that makes the European Union what it is: not a "melting pot" in which differences are rendered down, but a common home in which diversity is celebrated, and where our many mother tongues are a source of wealth and a bridge to greater solidarity and mutual understanding.' European Commission, *Communication from the Commission to the Council, the European Parliament, the European Economic and Social Committee and the*

obstacle in cross-border healthcare situations: if the patient and the healthcare professional do not speak the same language, the risk of misunderstanding and – as a consequence – of misdiagnosis increases significantly, and 'extensive physical examinations and diagnostic tests [are] sometimes required to compensate for the inability to communicate verbally'.[976]

Ideally, this problem could be solved through the improvement of language skills on the part of both patients' and health professionals', so that they have a common language to communicate with. However, in the mirror of the statistical data[977] and the long history of attempts to establish a *lingua franca*,[978] it is not very realistic to expect this scenario to happen in the near future in the European Union.[979] A much more realistic alternative to overcome the language barrier for now is the involvement of an interpreter.

Committee of the Regions. A New Framework Strategy for Multilingualism, COM (2005) 596 final, 22.11.2005, p. 2. See also Article 22 CFREU.

The issue is similarly problematic in the – theoretically monolingual – USA, where a considerable share of the society speaks English as a foreign language and encounters problems when accessing healthcare. The extensive US literature on this topic uses a specific expression for them: LEP aka persons with limited English proficiency. See, among others, Carter-Pokras et al., above n. 970, p. 29; G. Flores, 'The Impact of Medical Interpreter Services on the Quality of Health Care: A Systematic Review' *Medical Care Research and Review* 2005, vol 62 no 3, p. 255 and G. Flores, 'Language Barriers to Health Care in the United States' *The New England Journal of Medicine* 2006, vol 355 no 3, p. 229.

976 S. Priebe, S. Sandhu, S. Dias, A. Gaddini, T. Greacen, E. Ioannidis, U. Kluge, A. Krasnik, M. Lamkaddem, V. Lorant, R. Puigpinósi Riera, A. Sarvary, J.J.F. Soares, M. Stankunas, C. Straßmayr, K. Wahlbeck, M. Welbel, M. Bogic, 'Good practice in health care for migrants: views and experiences of care professionals in 16 European countries' *BMC Public Health* 2011, vol 11 issue 187, p. 4.

See also L.C. Hampers and J.E. McNulty, 'Professional Interpreters and Bilingual Physicians in a Pediatric Emergency Department. Effect on Resource Utilization' *Archives of Pediatrics and Adolescent Medicine* 2002, vol 156 no 11, pp. 1108–1113, describing the phenomenon of 'language-barrier premium', which refers to the increase of resource utilisation in case of language discordance between patient and healthcare professional. Hampers and McNulty, p. 1110.

977 'Just over half of Europeans (54%) are able to hold a conversation in at least one additional language, a quarter (25%) are able to speak at least two additional languages and one in ten (10%) are conversant in at least three. Just over two fifths (44%) of Europeans say that they are able to understand at least one foreign language well enough to be able to follow the news on radio or television.' Eurobarometer, above n. 973, pp. 5–6.

978 European Commission, Directorate General for Translation, *Lingua Franca: Chimera or Reality?* 2011.

979 As an article in the Economist aptly highlights, establishing a *lingua franca* would oblige Member States which did not use that language as their official language 'to accept second-class linguistic citizenship', *The Economist*, 17.09.2013, http://www.economist.com/blogs/prospero/2013/09/language-diversity, 2013 (accessed 25.03.2017). Switching to monolingualism in the EU – although this might seem desirable from certain aspects – is thus a political impossibility in today's Europe.

Nevertheless, promoting the learning of foreign languages has been set high on the EU's agenda; it is one of the main objectives of *life-long learning*. See, among others, European Commission, *Communication from the Commission to the Council, the European Parliament,*

Figure 2. Solutions for the language barrier

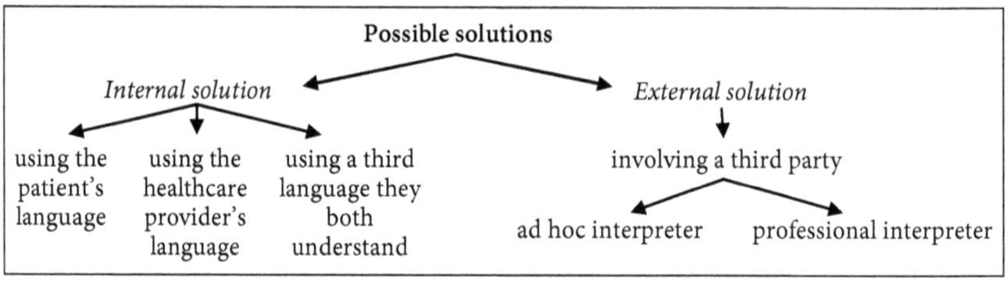

Source: The author's own summary.

Medical interpretation can be provided basically in two different ways:[980] a friend or a family member of the patient or a random person with the required language skills can act as an *ad hoc interpreter;* or a *professional interpreter* can be asked for. In either case, the involvement of a third party raises ethical and legal concerns[981] related to the sensitive nature of the information communicated such as doctor-patient confidentiality, data protection and medical liability.[982] Indirect communication and the presence of a third party make it more difficult to discuss personal intimate issues, which might be highly relevant for the diagnosis. In addition to these disadvantages, ad hoc interpreters tend to translate selectively, to summarise or even to censor, which also leads to loss of information.[983] Moreover, interpretation in general increases process time and – especially when professional interpreters are involved – results in extra costs. However, without the help of a professional interpreter, it might prove difficult or even impossible to take a proper medical history, to discuss the symptoms, to establish a right diagnosis or to explain the treatment and the medical instructions.[984] Therefore, keeping in mind the downsides of the involvement of interpretation, it must be acknowledged that involving a professional medical

the Economic and Social Committee and the Committee of the Regions: Promoting Language Learning and Linguistic Diversity: An Action Plan 2004 – 2006, COM (2003) 449 final, 24.07.2003; Recommendation of the European Parliament and of the Council of 18 December 2006 on key competences for lifelong learning. OJL 394 of 30 December 2006; and European Commission, *Commission Staff Working Document. Language competences for employability, mobility and growth*, SWD (2012) 372 final, 20.11.2012.

980 Carter-Pokras and her colleagues provide a wide variety of interpretation service options pointing out both their positive and negative sides. Carter-Pokras et al., above n. 970, pp. 31–33.

981 Priebe et al., above n. 976, p. 5. Notably, a *lack of interpretation* might also invoke ethical and legal questions, for instance in relation to informed consent. Carter-Pokras et al., above n. 970, p. 31.

982 For instance, the possibility of mistranslation or misinterpretation might shed light on a whole new aspect of medical liability.

983 Priebe et al., above n. 976, p. 5 and Carter-Pokras et al., above n. 970, p. 31.

984 M. Phelan, 'Medical Interpreting and the Law in the European Union' *European Journal of Health Law* 2012, vol 19, pp. 336–337.

interpreter seems to be the best solution to overcome language barriers[985] in the course of cross-border healthcare provision.[986]

1.2. RIGHT TO MEDICAL INTERPRETATION

From a legal point of view, it may be questioned whether European patients hold *a right to medical interpretation*. While no direct reference to medical interpretation can be found in the human rights treaties of the United Nations or the Council of Europe, Phelan argues that the requirement of non-discrimination on language grounds and of equality of treatment implies the provision of interpreters.[987] In the European Union, non-discrimination is a high-rated requirement, but the Treaty provisions on non-discrimination[988] do not enumerate the grounds of language. However, the Treaty stipulates that any discrimination on grounds of nationality is strictly forbidden.[989] At the same time, the Charter of Fundamental Rights of the European Union (CFREU) does specify language as a possible ground of discrimination[990] and within the framework of the right to the integrity of the person it pays special attention to *free and informed consent* as a value which must be particularly respected in the field of healthcare.[991] As Jelfs and Baeten underline, a distinction must be made between *informed consent*, where the patient agrees to a certain treatment while being aware of the risks and possible consequences, and *informed decision*, where the patient has all the relevant information on the different treatment options, procedures and alternatives.[992] In cross-border healthcare situations both informed consent and informed decision-making is essential, and linguistic barriers can easily jeopardise them both. Interestingly,

---

985 See, among others, the findings of W.J. Ferguson and L.M. Candib, 'Culture, Language, and the Doctor-Patient Relationship' *Modern Culture and Physician-Patient Communication* 2002, vol 34 no 5, p. 359.

986 For instance, Luxembourg, that has a large foreign population and has a long-lasting tradition of cross-border healthcare, did adopt a Patient Rights Act which 'specifies that the information by the healthcare providers is validly given in one of three official languages of Luxembourg, which is Luxemburgish, French and German. The healthcare provider may choose another language and the patient may be assisted by a third person that will be in charge of translation.' M. Schwebag, 'Implementation of the Cross-border Care Directive in EU Member States: Luxembourg' *European Journal of Health Law* 2014, vol 21 issue 1, p. 61.

987 Phelan, above n. 984, p. 337.

988 Article 10 TFEU: 'In defining and implementing its policies and activities, the Union shall aim to combat discrimination based on sex, racial or ethnic origin, religion or belief, disability, age or sexual orientation.' See also Article 19(1) TFEU.

989 Article 18 TFEU. See also Article 21(2) CFREU.

990 Article 21(1) CFREU.

991 Article 3(2) CFREU.

992 Jelfs and Baeten, above n. 349, p. 21.

the Proposal for the Patient Mobility Directive (PMD)[993] – referring directly to the Charter – included rules on equity and non-discrimination, where language was mentioned.[994] One may wonder, though, why these rules were not adopted in the final version of the Directive. By adding the above provisions to the right to access to healthcare,[995] Phelan deduces that 'the high level of human health protection could include the provision of translations and of interpreters to people who need such help to access healthcare'.[996]

Despite the fact that the patient's informed consent is likely to be jeopardised by poor communication between the patient and the healthcare professional,[997] I strongly doubt that these legal provisions establish an enforceable obligation for the Member States to provide foreign patients with professional medical interpreters for free. Obviously, the question here not only implies whether patients have access to linguistic services, but also who bears the costs of these services. Currently, in most Member States the costs of interpretation and translation fall on the patients,[998] and these extra costs might constitute another argument against using cross-border healthcare rights. However, since the regulation of language policies belongs to the sole responsibility of the Member States[999] within the Union,[1000] in my opinion, at present the European Union has no solid legal ground to require Member States to guarantee free access to medical interpretation for border-crossing patients. The situation would be slightly different if a specific reference to the *right to interpretation or to equal treatment on language grounds* had been incorporated into the Patient Mobility Directive.[1001] In that case, the Member States would still have had the liberty

---

993 COM (2008) 414, above n. 346.

994 COM (2008) 414, above n. 346, p. 12 and Recital 13 of the Preamble of the Proposal for the PMD.

995 Article 35 CFREU.

996 Phelan, above n. 984, p. 337.

997 Carter-Pokras et al., above n. 970, pp. 31.

998 Jelfs and Baeten, above n. 349, pp. 15–16. See the Finnish practice in M. Kattelus, above n. 923, p. 25.

999 'In principle, EU Member States retain the full capacity to initiate and develop language policies that are suited to their own particular political and cultural context.' J. Bernier, *EU Economic Integration and National Language Policies: An Overlooked Tension*, http://www.sciencessociales.uottawa.ca/crfpp/pdf/debat/Bernier.pdf, 2005 (accessed 20.08.2013), p. 1.

1000 Bernier notes that 'this capacity is significantly circumscribed by internal market rules requiring the unhampered circulation of persons, goods and services'. Bernier, above n. 999, pp. 1–2.

1001 Interestingly enough, in the Preamble of the Directive it is expressly indicated that Member States are required to provide information to patients through their national contact points (Article 6 PMD) 'in any of the official languages of the Member State in which the contact points are situated'. Additionally, 'information may be provided in any other language' (Recital 48, Article 4(5) PMD). Consequently, Member States can voluntarily choose to deliver information in the language which the patient is most familiar with. A study suggests that '(i)n order to make the information on cross-border healthcare accessible

to choose through what kind of measures they wished to provide access to medical interpretation, but they would have been obliged to ensure access to these services. The right to interpretation and translation is not unknown in Union law, Directive 2010/64/EU introduced this right in criminal proceedings for persons who do not speak or understand the language of the criminal proceedings concerned.[1002] In fact, the Directive's provision which establishes the obligation of the Member State of treatment to 'provide relevant information to help patients to make an informed choice'[1003] might be of interest in this respect.

It is not very likely that the obligation *to provide relevant information* is fulfilled without the interpretation or translation of this information: the expressed aim of this rule is to enable patients to make an informed choice. Consequently, the unilateral provision of the information on the healthcare provider's side without an ambition to induce understanding on the patient's side – in my opinion – fails to fulfil the obligation imposed by the Directive.[1004] Nevertheless, Union legislation does not express informed choice as a right for the patient, but as a duty of the Member States, thus it would be interesting to see how the Court interprets this provision.[1005] The question is how the Union can relax the tension between its expressed commitment to linguistic diversity[1006]

---

for both own citizens and visitors from other Member States we recommend to use other relevant (frequently used by groups of citizens or visitors) languages next to the native one'. PRICEWATERHOUSE COOPERS INTERNATIONAL LIMITED, Recommendation Report – A best practice based approach to National Contact Point websites: feasibility study, http://ec.europa.eu/health/cross_border_care/docs/pwc_national_contact_points_website_en.pdf, 2012 (accessed 25.03.2017), p. 27.

It would have been only one step further to integrate in the Directive that Member States are required to give patients information through their national contact points in any of the official languages of the EU according to the patient's request. However, this would not have offered a full solution, since the preamble of the Directive is not legally binding and does not need to be transposed by the Member States.

1002 Directive 2010/64/EU of the European Parliament and of the Council of 20 October 2010 on the right to interpretation and translation in criminal proceedings. OJ L 280 of 26 October 2010.

1003 Article 4(2)(b) PMD. See also Recitals 19–20 of the Preamble of the PMD.

1004 In relation to the requirement set out by Article 6(3) of the Directive, according to which the information shall be easily accessible, NYS rightfully raises the question 'whether information in a language that one cannot understand is not by definition difficult or even impossible to access'. He suggests solving the problem by obliging the Member States to provide information (also) in English. H. NYS, 'The Transposition of the Directive on Patients' Rights in Cross-Border Healthcare in National Law by the Member States: Still a Lot of Effort to Be Made and Questions to Be Answered' *European Journal of Health Law* 2014, vol 21 Special Issue, p. 10.

1005 TAYLOR prognosticates that this right would be 'difficult to enforce given the vagueness of the obligation'. S. TAYLOR, 'Cross-border Patients and Informed Choices on Treatment in English and French Law and the Patients' Rights Directive' *European Journal of Health Law* 2012, vol 19, p. 482.

1006 See n. 975 above.

and its commitment to secure internal market freedoms,[1007] more specifically, the free movement of patients.

1.3. OVERCOMING THE LANGUAGE BARRIER

In my view, two possible solutions could help border-crossing patients to cope with linguistic difficulties in the long run: either establishing an obligation for the Member States to ensure access to medical translation and interpretation services for patients who need them; or establishing a specific organisation within the institutional structure of the European Union, which itself provides professional medical translation and interpretation services for patients lacking sufficient language skills.

Imposing such a duty on the Member States requires a legitimate legal basis the Union can act upon if the Member States fail to fulfil their obligations. As said above, it would have been more than appropriate to have inserted rules on the right to interpretation for patients into the Directive, which is entitled *Directive on the application of patients' rights in cross-border healthcare*. However, adopting a separate legal tool as happened regarding the right to interpretation and translation in criminal proceedings,[1008] would also be a satisfactory way of solving the problem.[1009] The medical interpretation could be carried out by trained staff[1010] at the newly founded national contact points,[1011] where knowledge base on national and cross-border healthcare is given, and which are dedicated to facilitating the exchange of healthcare information in cross-border situations.[1012]

If such an initiative came up, the Member States – without any doubt – would complain about the costliness of providing interpretation. It cannot be denied that professional interpretation services are far from cost neutral,[1013] but 'in any budget discussion, it should be recognized that there are costs associated with not providing language interpretation',[1014] which are mainly related to

1007 Bernier, above n. 999, p. 7.
1008 Directive 2010/64/EU.
1009 Phelan, above n. 984, p. 353.
1010 Flores and his colleagues emphasise the importance of specialised training for medical interpreters: 'medical interpreter training should include a detailed review of medical terms, with attention to linguistic issues such as variation among cultural subsets of a single linguistic group'. G. Flores, M.B. Laws, S.J. Mayo, B. Zuckerman, M. Abreu, L. Medina and E.J. Hardt, 'Errors in Medical Interpretation and Their Potential Clinical Consequences in Pediatric Encounters' *Pediatrics* 2003, vol 111 no 1, p. 11.
1011 Article 6 PMD.
1012 Article 6(2) PMD.
1013 Phelan, above n. 984, p. 353.
1014 Carter-Pokras et al., above n. 970, p. 35.

increased resource utilisation,[1015] a higher risk of medical malpractice,[1016] and decreased patient compliance.

Another alternative to overcome the language barrier would be to set up a special organisation within the institutional framework of the Union: a European medical interpretation agency, which could function as a call centre and provide EU-wide professional medical interpretation services for patients who need them. It could have decentralised national administrators (for example at the national contact points) and a central unit, which would be able to offer prompt services by means of ICT devices. The method of interpretation is apparently also crucial: research results confirmed that the highest patient satisfaction can be reached by *remote simultaneous medical interpretation.*[1017] Although distance provision of services and the involvement of ICT devices also raise concerns,[1018] the opportunity to overcome linguistic barriers and provide cross-border patients with greater certainty in this respect is worth the investment. Either way, it is highly desirable that the European Union makes efforts to improve the access to professional medical interpretation and translation services.[1019]

1015 Hampers and McNulty, above n. 976.
Another US research proved that the length of hospital stays may also be affected by language barriers. It found that 'the length of a hospital stay for LEP patients was significantly longer when professional interpreters were not used at admission or both admission/discharge'. M. Lindholm, J.L. Hargraves, W.J. Ferguson and G. Reed, 'Professional language interpretation and inpatient length of stay and readmission rates' *Journal of General Internal Medicine* 2012, vol 27 issue 10, pp. 1297–1298.

1016 On this issue see K. Quan and J. Lynch, *The High Costs of Language Barriers in Medical Malpractice*, http://www.healthlaw.org/images/stories/High_Costs_of_Language_Barriers_in_Malpractice.pdf, 2010 (accessed 20.08.2013).

1017 See, among others, Flores et al., above n. 1010, p. 10 and F. Gany, J. Leng, E. Shapiro, D. Abramson, I. Motola, D.C. Shield and J. Changrani, 'Patient Satisfaction with Different Interpreting Methods: A Randomized Controlled Trial' *Journal of General Internal Medicine* 2007, vol 22 suppl 2, p. 317.

1018 Beside the concerns originating from the involvement of a third party (see n. 981), both the non-presence of the interpreter and the usage of information and communication technology carry certain risks. Remote (online or telephone) interpretation deprives the interpreter of the non-verbal cues of the communication. Therefore, when training professional interpreters, special attention should to be paid to the development of their ability to decode non-verbal cues from the parties' tone of voice. Carter-Pokras et al., above n. 970, p. 32.

1019 The access to professional medical interpretation and translation services is of high importance not only in the course of the communication between the healthcare provider and the patient, but also between two (or more) healthcare professionals in different Member States, involved in the cross-border healthcare situation. Linguistic problems can easily manifest themselves for instance if a consultation is needed between the patient's former and current doctor and they do not share a common language. These difficulties also affect the provision of cross-border healthcare and the patient him/herself.

2. LACK OF RELIABLE INFORMATION ON CROSS-BORDER PATIENT MOBILITY

How can European citizens be expected to use their cross-border healthcare rights if they are not even aware of the existence of these rights and of the functioning of these mechanisms? The Patient Mobility Directive clearly articulates the patients' need for information on cross-border healthcare.[1020] It acknowledges that 'appropriate information on all essential aspects of cross-border healthcare is necessary in order to enable patients to exercise their rights on cross-border healthcare in practice'.[1021] Statistics show, however, that the European citizens' awareness of their cross-border healthcare rights is rather low: an EU-wide survey demonstrated in 2014,[1022] and a cross-border healthcare simulation also confirmed,[1023] that a large share of the European population has no or very little information about the opportunity to receive medical treatment in another EU country and to be reimbursed for that treatment by their national health authority or healthcare insurer.[1024] So who should spread the knowledge and supply patients with reliable information on cross-border healthcare?

2.1. INFORMATION DUTIES UNDER THE REGULATIONS

In the framework of the principle of *good administration*, the current set of Coordination Regulations provides rules on the Member States' information duties. According to these rules, the healthcare authorities[1025] are required 'to respond to all queries within a reasonable period of time and to provide

1020 See Recital 19 of the Preamble of the PMD, which stipulates that 'when a patient receives cross-border healthcare, it is essential for the patient to know in advance which rules will be applicable'. A study found that 'cross-border patients want to be informed on multiple health-related aspects of care', such as the risk of treatment and infection rates, and financial issues. M. Tinelli, Z. Nikoloski and D. Panteli, 'What information do patients want when choosing a hospital at home or abroad? A case study from Germany' *Eurohealth* 2013, vol 19 no 4.

1021 Recital 48 of the Preamble of the PMD.

1022 See n. 14 above.

1023 Jelfs and Baeten, above n. 349, p. 20.

1024 Patient organisations complain that 'patients are faced with a labyrinth of confusing, sometimes insufficient and sometimes too detailed information'. COM (2015) 421, above n. 680, p. 8.

1025 According to Article 1(p) BR, *institution* means, in respect of each Member State, the body or authority responsible for applying all or part of the legislation. In the field of healthcare, these authorities are the healthcare funds, insurers and national healthcare services. Article 1(2)(b) IR uses the expression 'liaison body' for those bodies designated by the competent authority of a Member State for one or more of the branches of social security to respond to requests for information and assistance for the purposes of the application of the Basic Regulation and the Implementing Regulation.

the persons concerned with any information required for exercising the rights conferred on them' by the Coordination Regulations.[1026] Although the declaration of this obligation is very welcome, there are some blurred points in its phrasing: both the method and the content of the information provision raise doubts.

First of all, it is highly questionable what can be considered 'a reasonable period of time'. As a tool of coordination, the Regulations do not intend and make no effort to harmonise the processing times in the Member States, but the lack of definition gives this obligation a sense of uncertainty since the patient has no indication how long it takes to receive the required information.[1027] For the sake of certainty, *a maximum time span could be inserted in the legislation on EU level.* The question can be raised whether a deadline could be inserted into the Regulations stipulating that all queries must be answered within – for example – five working days unless a longer time span is justified by the special nature of the question (e.g. if advice from an expert has to be sought in order to provide an answer).

An additional question, to which there is no reference in the Regulation, is in which language the requested information should be provided by the Member State. In this respect, one may presume that the national policies on language regime must be applied, and national authorities can be expected to communicate in the official languages of their Member State. However, if the patient who is asking for information in the Member State concerned is familiar with none of these languages, which might easily occur if a foreign patient tries to collect information about treatment options in a Member State other than the Member State of residence, this directly leads to a linguistic obstacle,[1028] which – for lack of a satisfying alternative solution so far – potentially results in extra costs for the patient.

The last point of concern relates to the material scope of the provision: according to the Regulation, national healthcare authorities are only obliged to

[1026] Article 76(4) BR. Article 3(1) IR adds that 'Member States shall ensure that the necessary information is made available to the persons concerned in order to inform them of the changes introduced by the basic Regulation and by the implementing Regulation to enable them to assert their rights. They shall also provide for user friendly services.' However, the question what the drafters of the Implementing Regulation mean by 'user friendly services' remains unanswered.

[1027] However, in certain Member States, national legislation exists that concerns delays for dealing with requests (e.g. in Belgium and in Germany). Presentations by Chris SEGAERT and Marc SCHNEIDER at *AIM Cross-border Heathcare Workshop – Implementation of the Directive 2011/24/EU: Are we ready?* on 17 September 2013 in Brussels, http://www.aim-mutual.org/fileadmin/events/2013/Cross-Border_Healthcare_Workshop/2013_09_17_-_AIM_CBH_Workshop_Chris_Segaert.pdf and http://www.aim-mutual.org/fileadmin/events/2013/Cross-Border_Healthcare_Workshop/Praes_AIM_170913_Marc_Schreiner.pdf (accessed 20.09.2013).

[1028] On the issues related to linguistic obstacles, see section 1. above in this chapter.

inform the patients about matters related to rights included in the Coordination Regulations. Strictly interpreted, in a cross-border healthcare situation, the Member States can fulfil this requirement without even mentioning the additional entitlements of patients outlined by the Court of Justice or introduced by the Patient Mobility Directive. To sum up, although the codification of information duties is a commendable improvement of the coordination mechanism, it suffers from several weaknesses. It should therefore be made more exact and patient-friendly in order to ensure quick, reliable and understandable cross-border healthcare information for free.

2.2. INFORMATION DUTIES UNDER THE DIRECTIVE

In contrast to the rather general provisions of the Regulations, the Patient Mobility Directive specifies the Member States' obligations and clearly splits the responsibility of delivering reliable information to the patients between the Member State of treatment and the Member State of affiliation (Table 15).

Table 15. The Member States' responsibilities in relation to information provision under the PMD

Responsible MS	The scope of the information provision	The content of the information provision
MS of affiliation	patients' rights and entitlements in that MS relating to receiving cross-border healthcare	information on their rights and entitlements in that MS relating to receiving cross-border healthcare, in particular as regards (1) the terms and conditions for reimbursement of costs and (2) procedures (2a) for accessing and determining those entitlements and (2b) for appeal and redress [Article 5-(b) PMD]
MS of treatment	standards and guidelines on quality and safety laid down by that MS	*from the national contact point*: relevant information on the standards and guidelines, including (1) provisions on supervision and assessment of healthcare providers, (2) information on which healthcare providers are subject to these standards and guidelines and (3) information on the accessibility of hospitals for persons with disabilities [Article 4 (2)-(a) PMD]
		from healthcare providers: relevant information to help individual patients to make an informed choice, including (1) on treatment options, (2) on the availability, quality and safety of the healthcare they provide in that state, (3) on prices, as well as (4) on their authorisation or registration status, their insurance cover or other means of personal or collective protection with regard to professional liability [Article 4-(2)-(b) PMD]

Source: The author's own summary.

Primarily, the Member State of affiliation must provide information on the patients' rights and entitlements in that state in relation to receiving cross-border healthcare[1029] and the Member State of treatment must inform the patient about the standards and guidelines on quality and safety laid down in that state.[1030]

Compared to the rules of the Regulation, the rules of the Directive are more specific and detailed and guarantee access to a broader scale of information. However, they do not offer a solution to the problem that if a patient wants to collect all relevant information concerning a certain treatment abroad, this involves at least three sources he/she needs to contact in (at least) two different Member States. So even if a patient possesses the necessary language skills to acquire the essential information, the multi-source investigation puts a considerable burden on him/her. The question is how this burden can be reduced so that it would not discourage patients from receiving healthcare abroad.

2.3. INFORMATION FLOWS

Since obtaining cross-border healthcare is a multi-player situation, different information flows can be identified between the parties involved, namely information from the healthcare authorities[1031] for the patients and the healthcare providers; information from the healthcare providers for the patients and the healthcare authorities; and information from the patients for the healthcare providers and the healthcare authorities (Table 16).[1032] The question is: are these actors aware of and capable of fulfilling their obligations concerning information provision?

National healthcare authorities – irrespective of how the healthcare system is organised in the Member State concerned – are the most traditional sources of information when it comes to healthcare rights, entitlements and conditions attached to them. They have the required knowledge concerning both legislative background and daily practice. They are often also involved in one way or another in the legislative procedures. Thus, they are very well-positioned to offer expert advice to patients in cross-border healthcare situations and to inform healthcare providers on their duties in such cases.

It should be noted, though, that these authorities, healthcare funds, health insurers – besides taking into account the patients' interests – have financial concerns too: while patients want to benefit from the most favourable situation possible, the national healthcare authorities have to balance between the

1029 Article 5(b) PMD.

1030 Article 4(1) PMD.

1031 Including ministries, healthcare institutions and National Contact Points.

1032 Strban et al., above n. 5, pp. 86–89.

interest of the patient and of the national healthcare system itself. No wonder that in the healthcare cases of the Court, representatives of the national governments often came up with the argument that patient mobility might endanger the financial sustainability of the national healthcare budget.[1033] Therefore, with a good faith assumption, it can be presumed that national healthcare authorities will fully inform patients about all possible options, but it must be kept in mind that, at the same time, they will guard the financial equilibrium of their healthcare system and might tend to encourage patients to opt for the alternative which is more economical for the state. Moreover, as mentioned above, the Regulations oblige the Member States to inform patients only about their rights under the Regulations, so – in theory – they can comply with this obligation without even mentioning that alternatives do exist also outside the scope of the Regulations. Besides, the personnel of these institutions is usually only familiar with the national system of the Member State they work for, which is a disadvantage in cross-border situations where at least one other Member State – and its national healthcare system – is involved.

The Directive precisely determines the scope of information which has to be communicated to patients and created special bodies responsible for providing information for patients in relation to cross-border healthcare: the National Contact Points (NCPs).[1034] Their very existence is a great achievement and an added value of the Directive. They are neutral sources of reliable, transparent and easily accessible[1035] information on cross-border healthcare issues. Since they were created to carry out this specific task,[1036] it can be fully expected that the persons working at the NCPs can answer most of the patients' relevant questions related to cross-border treatments, and in cases where they cannot, they have the competence to find the answer quickly through their professional network of NCPs in other Member States, healthcare providers, healthcare authorities and

[1033] See n. 298 above.

[1034] Article 6 PMD. 'The Member States should decide on the form and number of their national contact points.' Recital 49 of the Preamble of the PMD. Some scholars criticise that 'the Directive is vague about the way these contact points should actually work'. Nys, above n. 1004, p. 9.

[1035] Article 6(5) PMD. It is worth mentioning that special reference is made to the accessibility by persons with a disability.

[1036] On the operation of the NCPs (and cross-border healthcare under the Directive in general) several studies have been presented recently, which serve as resourceful basis for further development. See especially G. Zucca, A. De Negri, A Berényi, A. Kaszap, K.A. Stroetmann, P. Varnai, *Evaluative study on the cross-border healthcare Directive*, Prepared for EC DG SANTE, Luxembourg 2014; COM (2015) 421 final, above n. 680; and T. Clemens, E. Cox, B. van der Zanden, M. Commers and H. Brand, *Implementation of National Contact Points for cross-border healthcare in EU Member States: a comparative analysis using websites and short interviews*, http://www.epecs.eu/theme/epecs/uploads/kcfinder/files/2016_06_13%20NCP%20Activity%20report.pdf, 2016 (accessed 21.04.2017).

other organisations.[1037] Whether this is the case remains uncertain. Therefore, it is very important that the NCPs work closely together both with the European and national institutions involved and with each other.[1038] However, the form of this cooperation is far from clear yet[1039] – as Clemens and his colleagues phrased it, '[c]ooperation among NCPs themselves is still in its infancy'.[1040] Additionally, it would be desirable if they could provide patients with information in the language the patient is most familiar with.[1041] Whether this is always the case in practice, is doubtful.[1042]

According to data from the Member States, most NCPs received only a few hundred (or fewer) inquiries in 2015. The reason for this might be found in the relatively low awareness of insured persons of their cross-border healthcare rights[1043] or of the existence of NCPs, or simply the reluctance to seek treatment abroad.[1044]

Reportedly, national authorities often receive inquiries not only from patients but also from healthcare providers in relation to cross-border healthcare. Since – as mentioned above – national authorities have the required expertise on these – mostly legal – issues, they should cooperate with the healthcare providers and inform them on all relevant aspects. Targeted seminars, webpages designed for healthcare professionals or a hotline for providers are possible good practices.

Although patients might trust *healthcare providers* the most – as they usually have direct, face-to-face contact with them – and expect the information

---

1037 'National contact points should be established in an efficient and transparent way and they should be able to consult with patient organisations, healthcare insurers and healthcare providers.' Recital 49 of the Preamble of the PMD and Article 6(1) PMD.

1038 Article 6(2) PMD. On this issue, see Clemens et al., above n. 1036, pp. 19–20.

1039 For instance, organising joint training, frequent multilateral consultations or seminars, sharing experience and good practices and building up a common online platform to enable the administrators to promptly contact each other at different NCPs would be efficient ways to cooperate.

1040 Clemens et al., above n. 1036, p. 20.

1041 On this issue, see section 1. above in this chapter. Most of the NCPs provide information to patients in English next to the official language of their Member State. However, there are exemplary attempts by certain Member States which aim to be able to provide information in more than twenty different languages (e.g. the Czech Republic). Presentation by Sarga Polakova at *AIM Cross-border Heathcare Workshop – Implementation of the Directive 2011/24/EU: Are we ready?* on 17 September 2013 in Brussels, http://www.aim-mutual.org/fileadmin/events/2013/Cross-Border_Healthcare_Workshop/AIM-Brussels-Directive_CMU_Mgr._Sarka_Polakova.pdf, (accessed 18.09.2013).

1042 I have recently started a project analysing the replies of NCPs to patients' inquires. The results – yet to be published – show that some NCPs tend to answer in their national language even if the patient's inquiry was in English.

1043 See n. 1021–1022.

1044 J. Olsson, *Member State data on cross-border healthcare following Directive 2011/24/EU*, Prepared for EC DG SANTE, Brussels 2016, pp. 8–9.

primarily from them,[1045] they are often neither trained nor willing to function as a source of non-medical information.[1046] The Directive, however, confers a specific obligation on them as well: they have to provide individual patients with all relevant information to help them make an informed choice, including information on treatment options, on the availability, quality and safety of the healthcare they provide in that state, on prices, as well as on their authorisation or registration status, their insurance cover or other means of personal or collective protection with regard to professional liability.[1047] Taylor asserts the eminent relevance of such information 'since it goes to the heart of patient autonomy'.[1048] One may wonder though whether healthcare providers are prepared to fulfil these obligations.

Training opportunities should be offered for healthcare professionals and for other staff members of healthcare providers to enable them to provide patients with the information required. At the same time, national healthcare authorities – in cooperation with the European Commission – should develop a monitoring system to ensure that all the obliged parties fulfil their information obligations.

Healthcare providers do not only need to provide information for patients, they have to communicate financial information (and other relevant information related to the specific healthcare provision in question) to the national healthcare authorities in order to receive reimbursement for the costs of the treatment provided for a foreign patient under the coordination regime.

Certain information has to be provided by the *patients* as well: they have to provide information on their entitlement for healthcare providers by presenting proof (usually an EHIC, PRC, PD S2, authorisation under the Directive or a medical referral in the absence of an authorisation, where applicable) and to communicate financial information (and other relevant information related to the specific healthcare provision in question) to the national healthcare authorities in order to receive reimbursement for the costs of the treatment received from a foreign provider under the Directive's regime (and also under the coordination regime in the case of reimbursement systems where patients are invited to pay the costs of the treatment on the spot).

Normally, this latter information provision takes the form of an invoice. Patients are required to hand in the original invoices and other relevant medical documentation. Some Member States insist on official translations of

---

1045 European Commission, *Eurobarometer: European Union citizens and sources of information about health*, 2003, p. 5.

1046 Jelfs and Baeten note that the preparedness of healthcare providers to fulfil their obligation concerning information provision under the Directive is questionable. Jelfs and Baeten, above n. 349, p. 21.

1047 Article 4(2)(b) of Directive 2011/24/EU.

1048 Taylor, above n. 1005, p. 468.

these documents which might cause considerable costs for patients and the exact content of the invoices are also not always clear. The Directive obliges the healthcare providers to issue clear invoices[1049] and the Member States to cooperate in order to clarify the content of invoices.[1050] Nevertheless, the difficulties related to unclear invoices and different invoicing methods could be significantly reduced by introducing a *standardised European invoice*, the form of which would be the same in each Member State just like the Portable Documents used under the Regulation regime.

Table 16. Information flows in cross-border patient mobility

From / To	Healthcare authorities	Healthcare providers	Patients
Healthcare authorities	*Cooperation* with other healthcare authorities within the country and in other Member States	*Financial information* related to reimbursement under the Regulation	*Financial information* related to reimbursement under the Directive (or the Regulation)
Healthcare providers	Information on different aspects of cross-border healthcare provision, especially on *their obligations*	Not mentioned by the Regulation or the Directive, but existing: professional organisations at national level and at EU level (e.g. Standing Committee of European Doctors, European Hospital and Healthcare Federation)	Presenting *proof of entitlement*, such as an EHIC, PRC, PD S2, authorisation under the Directive or a medical referral in lack of an authorisation where applicable
Patients	Information on different aspects of cross-border healthcare provision, especially on *their rights and entitlements*	Relevant information to help patients to make an *informed choice*	Not mentioned by the Regulation or the Directive, but existing: patient organisations, NGOs at national and EU level (e.g. European Patients' Forum)

Source: The author's own summary.

As shown above, in the Member States various actors are involved in information spreading practices and a great variety of means of information-sharing is used, both of an online and offline nature. Information is shared in various forms: some methods of information-sharing are more traditional (e.g. leaflets, personal or phone consultation) or more widely used (e.g. websites), whereas others (e.g. smart phone applications) are rather new and progressive, setting an example for other countries to follow.[1051] Since

1049 Article 4(2)(b) of Directive 2011/24/EU.
1050 Article 10(1) of Directive 2011/24/EU.
1051 Strban et al., above n. 5, pp. 89–90.

information from the media and the internet 'is rapidly establishing itself as a central source of health information',[1052] it is worth briefly mentioning some of the implications of the usage of ICT in cross-border healthcare information.

2.4. ONLINE INFORMATION IN CROSS-BORDER PATIENT MOBILITY

In the internet era, people get a vast quantity of information each day. Thus, it is of utmost importance to provide them with clear, easily accessible, understandable, up-to-date and accurate information. Patients receive information about health from various sources, but the question is whether this information can be trusted. This is especially important for online information.

John Naisbitt[1053] is credited with the visionary thought that 'the new source of power is not money in the hands of a few but information in the hands of many'.[1054] As the internet grew to be the biggest search engine of health-related information in the past decades,[1055] it became an emerging consideration to provide patients with correct and up-to-date information on online medical platforms. The World Wide Web offers the possibility for healthcare authorities and healthcare providers to disseminate information on a broad range of topics through their websites, for healthcare professionals to give advice on different forums and keep contact with their patients, and for patients to seek information

1052 P.E. Kummervold and R. Wynn, 'Health Information Accessed on the Internet: The Development in 5 European Countries' *International Journal of Telemedicine and Applications* 2012, vol 2012, p. 1. See also M. McMullan, 'Patients using the Internet to obtain health information: How this affects the patient–health professional relationship' *Patient Education and Counseling* 2006, vol 63 issue 1–2, p. 27. See also S. De Rosis, S. Barsanti, 'Patient satisfaction, e-health and the evolution of the patient–general practitioner relationship: Evidence from an Italian survey' *Health Policy* 2016, vol 120, p. 1279.

1053 American author and public speaker in the area of futures studies.

1054 Quoted by Ball and Lillis. M.J. Ball and J. Lillis, 'E-health: transforming the physician/patient relationship' *International Journal of Medical Informatics* 2001, vol 61, p. 1.

1055 Numerous studies show that 'the use of the internet as a source of medical information has become increasingly popular'. See, among others, B.S. Gerber and A.R. Eiser, 'The Patient-Physician Relationship in the Internet Age: Future Prospects and the Research Agenda' *Journal of Medical Internet Research* 2001, vol 3 no 2; J.A. Diaz, R.A. Griffith, J.J. Ng, S.E. Reinert, P.D. Friedmann and A.W. Moulton, 'Patient's Use of the Internet for Medical Information' *Journal of General Internal Medicine* 2002, vol 17 issue 3, p. 180; S.R. Cotton and S.S. Gupta, 'Characteristics of online and offline health information seekers and factors that discriminate between them' *Social Science & Medicine* 2004, vol 59, pp. 1795–1796; N.J. Gray, J.D. Klein, P.R. Noyce, T.S. Sesselberg and J.A. Cantrill, 'Health information-seeking behaviour in adolescence: the place of the internet' *Social Science & Medicine* 2005, vol 60, p. 1467 and N. Pletneva and A. Vargas, *Requirements for the general public health search*, http://www.hon.ch/Global/pdf/Khresmoi/KHRESMOI_general_public_survey_report.pdf, 2011 (accessed 26.03.2017), pp. 6–7 and pp. 17–18.

and share their knowledge and experience. Whereas the internet has numerous beneficial features[1056] and undoubtedly contributes to empowering patients to take a more active role in their healthcare[1057] and to raising their awareness, it certainly has its drawbacks.[1058] One of the main concerns relates to the credibility of the websites,[1059] the quality of which is often questionable. Online content can be not only wrong, outdated or misleading but even harmful for patients who rely on it.[1060] Therefore, it should be crucial to ensure the accuracy of medical information.

In my opinion, the European Union should develop a verification system for medical website content with an easily recognisable emblem. Thus, patients – whether border-crossing or not – would know at first glance that the quality of the information has been verified and reliable. This measure could be a big leap in building public confidence in eHealth.[1061]

2.5. TACKLING THE INFORMATION OBSTACLE

It is essential that both the content and the form of the information are appropriate and that patients receive comprehensive information all at once. It is reported that in several Member States (e.g. in some regions of Spain) information is not only hard to find but also too general to get all the details a patient intending to receive healthcare abroad might need. NCPs have a unique role and a great potential which should be used more effectively in some

---

1056 Among the advantages, Cotton and Gupta mention that the internet 'affords individuals privacy, immediacy, convenience, anonymity, a wide variety of information, and a variety of perspectives on the same topic'. Cotton and Gupta, above n. 1055, p. 1797. Furthermore, Pletneva and Vargas emphasise that '(o)nline health surfing can be very beneficial for the novice users in terms of feelings of reassurance, confidence and relief'. Pletneva and Vargas, above n. 1055, p. 7.

1057 See, among others, Ball and Lillis, above n. 1054, p. 2 and Gerber and Eiser, above n. 1055.

1058 Privacy and anonymity are often mentioned as key issues, but information overload, contradictory information, the use of overly technical language, the lack of user friendliness, a constant changeability and questionable trustfulness of information can also discourage patients. Cotton and Gupta, above n. 1055, p. 1797.

1059 On trust in online content such as medical websites, see A. Beldad, M. de Jong, M. Steehouder, 'How shall I trust the faceless and the intangible? A literature review on the antecedents of online trust' *Computers in Human Behavior* 2010, vol 26, pp. 857–869.

1060 Pletneva and Vargas, above n. 1055, p. 7.
There is a recent phenomenon called *cyberhondria*, which describes the case of 'unfounded escalation of concerns about common symptomatology, based on the review of search results and literature on the Web'. R.W. White and E. Horvitz, *Cyberchondria: Studies of the Escalation of Medical Concerns in Web Search*, Microsoft Research, http://research.microsoft.com/pubs/76529/TR-2008-178.pdf, 2008 (accessed 23.03.2017), p. 1.

1061 COM (2008) 689, above n. 119, p. 7.

Member States. It should be investigated how the development of the network of the NCPs can be facilitated by the Union, for instance via standardising the form and content of their websites, training their staff on EU level or connecting the national entities by a European one. It may be seen as good practice that certain meetings and workshops involving communication and social security experts from national ministries and institutions and from the European Commission have been taking place with the aim of focusing on how to better coordinate EU communication actions with those of the Member States, by creating synergies, avoiding overlaps and filling gaps.

Besides, some Member States do not provide information in English or the information provided in English is not of the same standard (e.g. Portugal, Latvia).[1062] Although Member States are not obliged to share information in any languages other than their own, in practice, it would be very useful to have this content in the most widely used language in Europe. This would also allow the patient to compare the possibilities and circumstances offered in the different Member States.

Moreover, since the European Commission's EHIC application[1063] became popular and proved to be useful in unplanned cross-border healthcare situations, a similar smartphone application could be developed also for other cross-border healthcare rights related to planned care.

In addition to these bodies' obligations laid down in the European legislation, the European Union should make serious efforts to spread proper information on cross-border patient rights. Since the developments in patient mobility were elaborated by the EU institutions through various EU instruments,[1064] it can be seen as much of an obligation of the European Union itself as of the Member States to make information available and easily accessible in order to raise the awareness among European patients.[1065]

In my opinion, patient organisations should also play a greater role in raising patients' awareness, since their basic role is 'to empower patients by providing support, information and education'.[1066] Although initiatives can be seen on European level,[1067] it is questionable whether these efforts reach the patients themselves.

1062 S. Olsena, above n. 960, p. 49.

1063 See n. 548 above.

1064 On this topic, see section 3.7. in Chapter 1. Setting the scene.

1065 The EU has a wide variety of tools to provide information to citizens: the websites of the EU institutions, specialised websites to increase the general understanding of European issues (e.g. the Your Europe portal), leaflets, online campaigns, videos on video sharing sites etc.

1066 Thorn and Dill, above n. 58, p. 24.

1067 For instance, the European Patients Forum not only participates in the negotiations of the PMD by issuing statements and recommendations, but also disseminates information on the Directive through its website and other activities.

3. CONCLUSION

When empowering patients, information and communication is key. Even if a clear and consistent legal framework were available, without tackling the practical obstacles to patient mobility efficiently, patients would not be able to exercise their cross-border healthcare rights. These obstacles were examined in the above sections.

In this chapter, it was concluded that a solution to the matter of the language barrier is currently lacking since the problem is not addressed on a European level. Consequently, both the burden and the costs in relation to translation and interpretation lie with patients.

Patients' information rights were strengthened by the Patient Mobility Directive, but collecting all the relevant information a border-crossing patient might need is a continuing challenge. Whereas the language barrier demands an original solution on Union level, patients' awareness could be effectively raised by empowering the network of national contact points and using their potential more efficiently.

CHAPTER 5
CONCLUSIONS AND SUGGESTIONS

The free countries of Europe must not only demonstrate concern for the maintenance of peace, security and the good organization of their economy; there is another concern we have no right to ignore – human beings. If there is one area where we must act generously, it is in the area of health. If there is one area that seems to lend itself to unification, it is in the struggle against disease.[1068]

The main concept of the research has been to take a look beyond the words of the legislation, to make the patients the centre of interest and to bring a better understanding of the (potential) problems patients face when obtaining healthcare abroad. In searching for the answer as to whether free movement of patients exists in the European Union, the research led to the conclusion that the desired 'borderless Europe' is yet far away for European patients and despite its benefits, the long-awaited Patient Mobility Directive (PMD) did not bring much change in this regard.

One might wonder why it is so difficult to tackle the problems of cross-border healthcare, when it involves a comparatively limited number of patients[1069] and healthcare expenditure.[1070] In my opinion, the main reason is that the field of healthcare is a *multi-player arena* where many different interests (of patients, healthcare providers, healthcare funds, national governments, Union institutions, etc), different competences (basically of the Member States and various EU Institutions, but also within the Member States where competences are often allocated at different levels, e.g. federal, regional, local) and different ideologies collide. This creates a tense political atmosphere in which patients' well-being, which is supposed to be the starting point and the main aim of any health-related arguments, runs the risk of evaporating in the process. This might – at least partly – explain why, after almost sixty years of healthcare coordination and almost two decades since the ground-breaking judgments of

1068 Citation from the speech of Robert SCHUMAN, one of the Founding Fathers of the European Communities, on 12 December 1952 in Paris. http://www.cvce.eu/obj/expose_de_robert_schuman_a_la_conference_preparatoire_a_la_communaute_europeenne_de_la_sante_paris_12_decembre_1952-fr-1fba65da-1ae8-45a4-beb5-e299ed4b4c6c.html (accessed 29.03.2017).

1069 See n. 8 above.

1070 See n. 9 above.

the Court of Justice of the European Union (CJEU),[1071] European patients are still left with restricted cross-border mobility rights and impediments to free movement both from legal and non-legal points of view.

In the former sections of this book I focused on the individual problems accompanying cross-border patient movements within the European Union and suggested some possible solutions to tackle them. In this last chapter, however, I sketch a more comprehensive, global solution to enforce patients' mobility rights in Europe and offer *de lege ferenda* suggestions.

1. REVAMPING EUROPEAN PATIENT MOBILITY LEGISLATION

It was confirmed that European border-crossing patients – although they have the right to access healthcare facilities in another Member State[1072] – face serious difficulties when (intending to) obtain(ing) healthcare in a Member State other than their Member State of residence. The research led to the conclusion that the current Union legislation on cross-border patient mobility cannot fully cope with all the problems identified in the course of the research.

Concerning the legal obstacles, the analysis has shown that there are numerous weak points in the current European legislation on cross-border patient mobility. The legislative body is complex, the relation between the different legal tools is unclear, the administrative procedures are often lengthy and burdensome, the monitoring and enforcing mechanism is poor and the discretion of the national healthcare authorities restricts cross-border patient movements. In order to serve European patients better, both the legislation and the administration of patient mobility should be considerably simplified, the parallelisms should be ceased and the administration should be improved in a patient-friendly way.[1073]

I found that these defects could be overcome by a consistent, integrated legal system which builds on the legacy of sixty years of healthcare coordination and which is complemented by the innovations of case law and the Patient Mobility Directive. The proposed integrated legal scheme is based on equal cross-border healthcare entitlements for each insured person without a distinction between planned and unplanned care, with as little administrative burden as possible and with access to any legally functioning healthcare provider who meets the universalised European standards.

1071 See n. 272 and 273.

1072 See section 3. in Chapter 1. Setting the scene.

1073 See Chapter 2. Legal complexity.

It is absolutely necessary to create a consistent legal framework which takes the interests of the (border-crossing) patients into due account. As I see it, the complexity of the issues related to cross-border patient mobility excludes the possibility to unite all the relevant rules in one single legal tool and requires a fine-tuned, contradiction-free multi-level legislation instead. An integrated European patient mobility legislation has two basic tasks, namely providing patients with clear provisions on their entitlements and serving European patients better by, among others, ceasing the existing parallelisms.

In my opinion, to design the integrated legislation of free movement of patients, the structure of the free movement legislation[1074] could be used by analogy. In the field of free movement of workers, the basic entitlements are incorporated into a Regulation,[1075] and a Directive has recently been adopted in order to facilitate the exercise of rights conferred on the workers.[1076]

I believe that although the Coordination Regulations were initially not drafted for freely moving patients, they provide a solid basis to integrate the core of cross-border patient mobility rights into. The social security coordination legislation has been functioning for more than half of a century and, although it has its limitations, it is undoubtedly one of the strongest shields of social security rights of people moving within the European Union. Therefore, I think that with some conceptual modifications it could be turned into an effective tool in the hands of border-crossing patients.

Besides redesigning the sickness chapter of the Coordination Regulation, the Patient Mobility Directive should be kept as a complementary element of the legislation. It has great assets in relation to issues which do not fit in the Regulations, such as the network of national contact points (NCPs)[1077] and cross-border cooperation.[1078] These provisions do not overlap with the ones in the Regulations and thus the parallelisms cease in this respect. However, the Directive itself should also be improved.

The research underlined the need for a drastic simplification both in terms of legislation and administration. This revision of the Coordination Regulations should definitely involve the prior authorisation requirement, the distinction between planned and unplanned care and the circle of healthcare providers

[1074] This field certainly has common points with patient mobility and – similar to the coordination of social security systems – has long been regulated by EU law. See n. 155.

[1075] Regulation (EU) No 492/2011 of the European Parliament and of the Council of 5 April 2011 on freedom of movement for workers within the Union.

[1076] Directive 2014/54/EU of the European Parliament and of the Council of 16 April 2014 on measures facilitating the exercise of rights conferred on workers in the context of freedom of movement for workers. OJ L 128 of 30 April 2014.

[1077] Article 6 PMD.

[1078] Chapter IV PMD.

which patients can turn to when using their cross-border healthcare rights. These issues are detailed in the next sections below.

1.1. THE PRIOR AUTHORISATION REQUIREMENT

As to prior authorisation required for planned treatment abroad, the baseline of the patient mobility case law was that the Treaty precludes national rules which have the effect of making the provision of services (and the consumption of services) between Member States more difficult than the provision of services purely within one Member State.[1079] Nevertheless, after refusing a series of possible grounds for justification of restrictions, the Court acknowledged that planning objectives can justify the maintenance of prior authorisation schemes.[1080] Might the Member States' heated objection[1081] be – at least partly – responsible for the softening of the Court's approach?[1082] Whether or not this directly or indirectly influenced the jurisprudence, the fact is that opening up the possibility for the Member States to make reimbursement of medical costs occurred abroad subject to prior authorisation eroded patients' rights to cross-border treatments. Moreover, the Patient Mobility Directive took a step further, and introduced grounds for justification – based on the protection of public health – which were not even verified by the Court.[1083] As a consequence, the cross-border mobility of European patients is more restricted today than it was at the end of 1990s.

1.1.1. Abolition of Prior Authorisation

It is clear that the great majority of European patients prefer to use healthcare facilities which are close to their home and which they are familiar with.[1084] Hence, no indicators suggest that cross-border patient movements can be expected to grow into a mass phenomenon in Europe:[1085] as of now it seems that,

---

1079 See n. 277 above.

1080 See n. 662 and 663.

1081 See n. 791.

1082 The question is especially valid in the light of the aftermath of the Court's decisions in the *Pierik* cases. See n. 283.

1083 See n. 689 and 690.

1084 See n. 10 above.

1085 The generally low willingness of insured persons to move across borders in order to obtain healthcare does not predict a radical change in this respect.
Administrative data based on the number of PDs S2 issued in the recent years supports this prognosis: in 2012 about 30,900, in 2013 about 29,400, in 2014 about 39,200, in 2015 about 34,400 PDs S2 were issued in the 32 countries applying the Coordination Regulations, where (depending on the year) circa 40–60 per cent of the prior authorisations were granted by Luxembourg as the, by far, leading exporter country. See Pacolet and De Wispelaere,

patient mobility will remain limited, although very important in certain areas and in certain cases.[1086] Nevertheless, the Member States' vehemence with which they guard their national healthcare (authorisation) schemes against border-crossing patients hardly correlates with the figures on the current volume of cross-border patient movements.[1087]

It might be the right time to raise the question: is the authorisation mechanism still necessary and proportionate? What would the implications be of the removal of the prior authorisation requirement? One might wonder what the impact of the full liberalisation of cross-border patient mobility might be.

Since factual evidence does not support the Member States' argument that the current volume of patient movements would constitute a major risk to their healthcare systems, the justification that prior authorisation should be maintained 'in meeting the desire to control costs and to prevent as far as possible, any wastage of financial, technical and human resources'[1088] is hardly valid in today's circumstances. It can thus be argued that the prior authorisation requirement should be erased from the Regulations. Nevertheless, upon the occasion of abolition of prior authorisation schemes, a practical counterbalance could be introduced into the protection of national healthcare systems against any possible extreme change in patient mobility trends.[1089] An 'in case of emergency' clause (hereinafter also referred to as ICE clause) could be inserted into the Regulations – similar to the one which has been applied to the free movement of workers in the newly accessed Member States – indicating that when a Member State undergoes or foresees disturbances in its national healthcare system which could seriously threaten the standard of healthcare provision or the national healthcare scheme in the given Member State, that

above n. 732, p. 6 and 9; Pacolet and De Wispelaere, above n. 732, p. 4; and De Wispelaere and Pacolet, above n. 54, p. 12.

Similarly, it was repeatedly confirmed that 'the number of patients that made use of cross-border healthcare under [the] Directive is still rather low,' although 'an increase in patient numbers seeking cross-border care may reveal unforeseen concerns'. Zucca et al., above n. 1036, pp. 12–13.

1086 See n. 11 above.

1087 The Commission's report on the operation of the Directive underlines that '[t]he data returns made by the Member States, in general, do not suggest that extensive systems of prior authorisation are justified,' because 'some Member States with prior authorisation systems have received no requests for authorisation at all (and many others have received very few)' – as a matter of fact, Austria, Bulgaria, Cyprus, Estonia, Greece and Portugal recorded no reimbursement under the Directive, whereas fourteen further Member States made fewer than a hundred reimbursements. COM (2015) 421, above n. 680, p. 4 and 16. See also Palm, above n. 714, p. 22. In Olsson's report, slightly higher but still very low numbers are presented. Olsson, above n. 1044, pp. 11–12.

Although these statements concern the Directive's regime, patient numbers under the Regulations are similarly hardly high enough (see above n. 1084) not to question the existence of prior authorisation systems in general.

1088 See n. 313 above.

1089 After all, it does not serve patients' interest if national healthcare systems get hamstrung.

Member State shall inform the Commission and other Member State thereof and shall supply them with all relevant particulars. On the basis of this information, the Member State may request the Commission to permit certain restrictions in order to restore to normal the situation in the healthcare system concerned.[1090]

Thus, the burden of proof would be shifted: instead of the patient being required to request an authorisation from the competent institution in advance and meet the conditions laid down in the legislation in order to receive an authorisation, the Member State has to provide evidence that patient movements put its system at a considerable risk. If such evidence cannot be given, patients are free to access healthcare in any other Member State.

1.1.2. *Arguments against the Abolition of Prior Authorisation*

There are a number of arguments which the Member States would put forward against the idea of removing prior authorisation. I presume that beside the argument that such a measure jeopardises their healthcare planning, Member States would play the 'combating fraud' card and would argue that the maintenance of prior authorisation also serves the purpose of safeguarding quality in the national healthcare schemes. I question whether any of these causes could justify this restriction of free movement of patients for the following reasons.

I have already dealt with the justification based on planning objectives in the former section, where I stated that it is doubtful that the current features of patient movements would significantly influence national healthcare planning objectives. If this were the case, and the individual Member State provides hard evidence, necessary and proportionate restrictions might indeed be permitted by the Commission on the grounds of the aforementioned ICE clause. However, this restriction might not necessarily be the re-invention of prior authorisation.

It is unquestionable that another argument which should be included in any discussion about liberalising healthcare provision is how fraud and abuse can be prevented and combated. Although this is a very complex topic,[1091] it must nevertheless be underlined that more freedom on the one hand requires more control on the other. Without going into detail, I would like to point out that – in my view – controlling mechanisms should be developed at least on three levels,

---

[1090] See by analogy for instance the Act concerning the conditions of accession of the Czech Republic, the Republic of Estonia, the Republic of Cyprus, the Republic of Latvia, the Republic of Lithuania, the Republic of Hungary, the Republic of Malta, the Republic of Poland, the Republic of Slovenia and the Slovak Republic and the adjustments to the Treaties on which the European Union is founded – Annexes to the Act of Accession – 1. Freedom of movement for persons, Article 7.

[1091] On the topic see, among others, A. Rashidian, H. Joudaki and T. Vian, 'No Evidence of the Effect of the Interventions to Combat Health Care Fraud and Abuse: A Systematic Review of Literature' *PLoS One* 2012, vol 7 issue 8 and M. Del Sol, 'Taking Measures Against European Healthcare Fraud' in Hennion and Kaufmann, above n. 8.

namely concerning fraudulent and abusive behaviours of patients, providers and healthcare funds.

To prevent patients who lack entitlement from exercising cross-border healthcare rights, it should be made possible that healthcare providers anywhere in Europe are able to check patients' entitlements. A European database available to each registered and accredited, legally functioning healthcare provider could tackle this problem.[1092] However, considering the difficulties of the EESSI project,[1093] it is highly questionable whether such a database could be put in place in the near future.

An improved version of the European Health Insurance Card[1094] should continue to serve as a universal European document incorporating entitlement to cross-border healthcare. Fraudulent usage of the EHIC (e.g. forged or fake cards or usage by someone other than the person the card was issued for) must be reported and investigated in each case.

Providers must be closely monitored not only in terms of quality, but also their pricing practice and their administrative mechanisms should be checked by independent institutions. It must be confirmed that providers respect the principle of equal treatment[1095] and comply with the European rules of (cross-border) healthcare provision.

Last but not least, healthcare funds should also be subject to monitoring, especially in relation to requests for re-imbursement from the European Healthcare Fund.[1096] It is of utmost importance that the sources of the fund are used rightfully and for the purpose they are intended for.

Although there is no dispute that cross-border fraud must be prevented and tackled, the methods might be different. I cannot share the opinion that prior authorisation is an appropriate tool for that purpose.[1097] I agree with Del Sol on the idea that the key to effectively fight fraud and abuse in the field of healthcare

---

1092 Similar databases on nation level, where providers can check – or are even obliged to check – the entitlement of patients, exist in most Member States. The Hungarian system is outlined in n. 525.

1093 See n. 253 above.

1094 See section 2.3. in Chapter 2. Legal complexity.

1095 See n. 383 above.

1096 See section 2. below in this chapter.

1097 The Court of Justice is reluctant to easily accept the argument of the fight against or the prevention of fraud and abuse of rights as proper justifications for impediments on free movement in relation to non-corporate entities.
See, among others, the Court cases C-200/02 *Kunqian Catherine Zhu and Man Lavette Chen v Secretary of State for the Home Department* [ECLI:EU:C:2004:639], where the Court refused the UK's argument that the appellants in the main proceedings were not entitled to rely on the Community provisions in question, because Mrs Chen's move to Northern Ireland with the aim of having her child acquire the nationality of another Member State constitutes an attempt to improperly exploit the provisions of Community law (34.); and C-577/10 *European Commission v Kingdom of Belgium* [ECLI:EU:C:2012:814], where the Court expressly declared in relation to a prior declaration requirement for foreign posted

is in an efficient inter-institutional cooperation.[1098] I think that a central coordinating institution – as suggested below[1099] – would hugely contribute to the common work of both European and national institutions in this respect.

Member States argue that prior authorisation systems not only enable them to control costs and avoid wastage of resources but also to safeguard the quality of healthcare services,[1100] thus to protect both public health and the health of individual patients.[1101] As described above, these arguments came up at an early phase in the healthcare case law,[1102] and although the Court declined them, they survived and became legal grounds of justification of prior authorisation in the Patient Mobility Directive.[1103] The questions which must be raised here are whether the authorisation system is the right measure to maintain quality, and how the removal of the prior authorisation requirement could be compensated in this respect.

I share the opinion of the Court that the concern related to the quality of services on a more liberal healthcare market cannot justify the restriction of patients' movements. Instead, any entities providing healthcare services on the territory of the Union should be closely monitored. European institutions[1104] and responsible national authorities should effectively cooperate to ensure that in all Member States patients receive good quality healthcare services. To this

employed and self-employed workers that a general presumption of fraud was not sufficient to justify a measure which compromises the objectives of the TFEU (53.).
Furthermore, see on this topic R. de la Feria and S. Vogenauer, *Prohibition of Abuse of Law. A New General Principle of EU Law?* Hart Publishing, Oxford 2011.

1098 Del Sol, above n. 1091, pp. 346–349.

1099 See section 3. below in this chapter.

1100 The issues related to the quality of healthcare services and patient safety are highly relevant in a cross-border context as well, but considering their complexity, they are beyond the scope of this research. See n. 4 above. See also H. Legido-Quigley, M. McKee, E. Nolte and I.A. Glinos, *Assuring the quality of health care in the European Union*, European Observatory on Health Systems and Policies, Brussels 2008, especially chapter III entitled *Patients, quality of care and cross-border care in the European Union.*

1101 To the argument of protecting public health via the supply of goods and the provision of services by persons authorised by law to pursue the profession, the CJEU answered that 'since the conditions for taking up and pursuing regulated professions have been harmonised on Community level, the provision of a treatment by a healthcare provider established in another Member State provides guarantees equivalent to those provided by a healthcare practitioner established in the national territory'. C-215/87 *Schumacher*, 20; C-62/90 *Commission v Germany*, 18; C-120/95 *Decker*, 41–45; C-158/96 *Kohll*, 44–49; C-145/03 *Keller*, 50, 52; C-444/05 *Stamatelaki*, 37. See n. 299.

1102 The argument first appeared before the Court at the end of the 1980s. See n. 1100.

1103 See section 3.2.2. in Chapter 2. Legal complexity, especially n. 689 and 690.

1104 There are a number of Union institutions with a wide range of tasks related to healthcare among which they also have responsibilities in human health and safety protection. The most notable of these agencies are the European Medicines Agency, the European Monitoring Centre for Drugs and Drug Addiction, the European Centre for Disease Prevention and Control and the European Chemicals Agency. On this topic, see G. Permanand and E. Vos, 'EU regulatory agencies and health protection' in Mossialos et al., above n. 118.

end, quality standards should be harmonised[1105] and a European registration and accreditation scheme for healthcare providers should be developed which would ensure that persons and institutions providing healthcare services in the Union meet the universal minimum standards set up on EU level. Furthermore, frequently checks to confirm that these standards are maintained in the daily functioning of the healthcare provider would be necessary. I would find it laudable if a separate supranational institution, a European Monitoring Centre for Healthcare Provision, were established to carry out this task.

Of course, less radical solutions than the abolition of the prior authorisation schemes also exist which are a compromise between national interests and patients' rights, such as a *prior notification system* described above.[1106] However, none of these solutions would be as beneficial for patients as liberating them from the requirement of prior authorisation.

Either way, the Member States would possibly object strongly to any measures that loosened their control over patient movements. Therefore, any alteration requires careful consideration of the interests of each party involved in order to reach a substantive solution.

1.2. THE DISTINCTION BETWEEN PLANNED AND UNPLANNED CARE

The distinction between planned and unplanned care has occupied a place on the list of difficulties of healthcare coordination. From a conceptual point of

1105 Harmonising measures concerning special fields of healthcare already exist, such as (1) Council Directive 90/385/EEC of 20 June 1990 on the approximation of the laws of the Member States relating to active implantable medical devices; (2) Council Directive 93/42/EEC of 14 June 1993 concerning medical devices; (3) Directive 98/79/EC of the European Parliament and of the Council of 27 October 1998 on in vitro diagnostic medical devices; (4) Directive 2001/20/EC of the European Parliament and of the Council of 4 April 2001 on the approximation of the laws, regulations and administrative provisions of the Member States relating to the implementation of good clinical practice in the conduct of clinical trials on medicinal products for human use; (5) Directive 2001/83/EC of the European Parliament and of the Council of 6 November 2001 on the Community code relating to medicinal products for human use; (6) Directive 2002/98/EC of the European Parliament and of the Council of 27 January 2003 setting standards of quality and safety for the collection, testing, processing, storage and distribution of human blood and blood components; (7) Directive 2004/23/EC of the European Parliament and of the Council of 31 March 2004 on setting standards of quality and safety for the donation, procurement, testing, processing, preservation, storage and distribution of human tissues and cells; (8) Regulation (EC) No 726/2004 of the European Parliament and of the Council of 31 March 2004 laying down Community procedures for the authorisation and supervision of medicinal products for human and veterinary use and establishing a European Medicines Agency; (9) Directive 2005/36/EC of the European Parliament and of the Council of 7 September 2005 on the recognition of professional qualifications; and (10) Directive 2010/53/EU of the European Parliament and of the Council of 7 July 2010 on standards of quality and safety of human organs intended for transplantation.

1106 See section 3.3. in Chapter 2. Legal complexity.

view, the difference lies in the (prior) intention of the person concerned, namely whether or not he/she willingly travelled abroad in search of medical treatment. However, a genuine problem is how the *intention of the person* – when not obvious from the circumstances – can be determined.[1107]

From an administrative point of view, the different nature of the health risks explains the different administrative procedures. Whereas necessary care, which may occasionally occur during a temporary stay abroad, can be obtained simply by presenting a valid European Health Insurance Card to the healthcare provider,[1108] in case of planned care, where the aim of the travel is to receive healthcare in another Member State, a prior authorisation from the competent institution must be requested.[1109] However, in a system in which no prior authorisation is required, as proposed above, the legal distinction between occasional and planned care becomes outdated.

The removal of the distinction is in line with the Patient Mobility Directive, although in the Directive the lack of a distinction accompanied by the maintenance of the possibility to require prior authorisation resulted in an inconsistent situation.[1110] Nevertheless, with this change, instead of investigating the person's intention, which is problematic, only the patient's entitlement would be examined.

However, this leads us to the next problem, namely how to define the benefit package patients are entitled to. Moreover on this point, two reverse approaches collide: either the entitlement to benefits provided for by the Member State of treatment or the entitlement to benefits provided for by the competent Member State is granted. Whereas in case of necessary treatment or when the person concerned lives outside of the competent state the *full integration principle* is applied based on equal treatment, so patients are treated as if they were insured in that country and as a consequence have access to the benefits included in that benefit basket;[1111] when obtaining planned care, patients – as a principle – should rely on the benefits determined by the competent Member State.[1112] Hence, the question becomes: if the distinction between planned and unplanned care disappears, which benefit coverage concept should be put in place?

The Directive opted for allowing the competent Member State to define which benefits patients can obtain.[1113] Although the Court has made efforts to limit the discretion of the Member States when determining the benefit

1107 See section 2.1.1. in Chapter 2. Legal complexity.
1108 On the issues related to the EHIC, see section 2.3. in Chapter 2. Legal complexity.
1109 On the issues related to prior authorisation, see section 3.3. in Chapter 2. Legal complexity.
1110 See section 2.2. in Chapter 2. Legal complexity.
1111 See n. 377 and 383.
1112 See section 3.1.2. in Chapter 2. Legal complexity.
1113 Article 7(1) PMD.

coverage,[1114] this choice still belongs to the core of the national autonomy in organising healthcare schemes.[1115] The question arises, though, what must be done when there is no possibility – e.g. due to urgency – to check whether the proposed treatment, which is provided for in the Member State of treatment, is covered by the competent Member State.

In my view, the ideal solution to this dilemma is the progressive *harmonisation of the national benefit packages*,[1116] with the aim to create *standardised European benefit coverage*.[1117] It would guarantee the exact *same entitlements to each insured person* throughout Europe, who could then freely decide in which Member State he/she exercises his/her right to these benefits. However, this development would necessitate tremendous investments in many Member States. The likelihood that this achievement could be reached, which would raise European healthcare policy to a whole new level, is thus rather low under the current political and economic circumstances.[1118]

1.3. THE CIRCLE OF AVAILABLE PROVIDERS

Another long-lasting teething problem of European social security coordination is that only national statutory systems are coordinated. This limitation of the Regulations might have been appropriate at the end of the 1950s, but in today's social security systems the exclusion of the voluntary and supplementary elements of social security coverage is no longer acceptable. The consequence of this characteristic in the field of healthcare is that under the scope of the Regulations, patients can – in principle – obtain treatments only from providers affiliated to the statutory healthcare system of the Member States.[1119] This not only causes uncertainty and misunderstandings concerning the recognition of which providers belong to the system and which do not,[1120] but more importantly, it considerably limits patients' freedom to choose which provider they wish to turn to.

It is a great merit of the Patient Mobility Directive that it covers both public and private providers, thus offering patients significantly more options. This development should be built into the proposed integrated legislation of

1114 See section 3.1.2. in Chapter 2. Legal complexity.

1115 See n. 577 above.

1116 See n. 600 above.

1117 See n. 601 above.

1118 See section 4. below in this chapter.

1119 Of course, competent Member States are free to decide whether they cover costs occurred at private providers, but they are not obliged to do so. See n. 529.

1120 However, as discussed in section 2.3. in Chapter 2. Legal complexity, this problem can be easily fixed. See n. 531 and 532.

European patient mobility, which requires the Regulations to open up for private providers.[1121]

Since the Member States did accept their inclusion for the Patient Mobility Directive, there is a chance that this could be transformed into the Regulations without major objections. Nevertheless, it must not be forgotten that private providers are now included because – by applying the principle of free movement of services – there was no justification to exclude them. However, in case of the Regulations – which are traditionally based on the free movement of persons – this is a considerable change which not only affects the healthcare domain but also the coordination of social security schemes as a whole, and Member States might be reluctant to go beyond the classic coordination measures and move towards harmonisation.[1122]

I think what needs to be understood is that upgrading European patients' legal status is hardly imaginable without deeper social integration, improved coordination and harmonisation.

2. FINANCING CROSS-BORDER TREATMENT IN THE EUROPEAN UNION

In relation to the financing of medical treatments abroad, the research highlighted that the currently existing reimbursement regimes greatly differ and their interaction is not always clear. It is beyond dispute that the Regulation rules on financing are more favourable for patients, since – in principle – they do not need to advance the medical costs and the full cost of medical intervention abroad is covered except for co-payments. In relation to the latter, the introduction of the *Vanbraekel* supplement results in a controversial situation, which – as demonstrated above – leaves room for reverse discrimination.[1123] The single asset of the Directive in this regard is that it offers reimbursement if the treatment was provided by non-contracted healthcare providers, who are excluded from the scope of the Regulations.[1124]

In the integrated scheme of patient mobility legislation, I suggest applying the Regulations' financial mechanism as a default reimbursement regime based on full cost coverage and inter-institutional settlement of financing. To compensate the Member States' healthcare budgets for the expected extra costs resulting from the liberalisation of cross-border patient movements,[1125] a European Healthcare Fund could be set up.

1121 This issue certainly goes beyond the scope of healthcare coordination, and also concerns other social security branches, such as private pension schemes.
1122 See n. 328 and section 4. below in this chapter.
1123 See n. 383 above.
1124 See section 2. in Chapter 3. Financial affordability.
1125 See section 1.1. above in this chapter.

Possibly the most complicated point of combining the Directive's service-based concept with the Coordination Regulations is the highly different financing mechanisms of the two legal tools.[1126] It is also the source of the Member States' deepest concerns, worrying about the possible effects of cross-border patient movements on the financial equilibrium of their national healthcare schemes.

The problem is that, with the intention to avoid affecting the healthcare spending of the Member States, the Court – and by incorporating its case law, the Directive – created a parallel reimbursement mechanism, which is much less beneficial for patients than the Coordination Regulations, and as a result of which many patients are practically deprived of the opportunity to exercise their cross-border healthcare rights.[1127] The question is how to synchronise these regimes under the scope of an integrated system in favour of patients, but without significantly affecting national healthcare budgets.

In my opinion, once again the starting point of the integrated system must be the financing mechanism of the Regulations, since it ensures higher protection for patients. However, if the applicability of the tariff of the Member State of treatment is maintained while no prior authorisation is in place, unpredictable patient movements might produce high medical invoices and feed the Member States' budgetary fears. This might affect especially those Member States in which tariffs are considerably lower than in others. Thus, this scenario has the potential to deepen the division between western and northern Europe as 'patient exporters', where patients can easily access healthcare systems with lower tariffs, and eastern and southern Europe as 'patient importers', where patients have less chance to head towards countries with higher tariffs. A compensation mechanism is needed to tackle this defect.

As an ambitious solution, I suggest setting up a European Healthcare Fund, which compensates Member States for the difference between their domestic tariffs and the foreign tariffs invoiced to them. Hence, cross-border patient movements would leave national healthcare spending basically intact.

For instance, in a given Member State (MS) A the required treatment costs 3,000 euros, and in MS B the same treatment costs 1,000 euros. The patient wishes to obtain the treatment in MS A, whereas he/she is insured in MS B.

1126 See Table 14 above. As discussed in Chapter 3. Financial affordability, the Regulations operate a *protective financing mechanism*, based – in principle – on the *full reimbursement of costs* and *inter-institutional* financial arrangements. In this system, patients are not required to advance the medical costs occurred abroad – unless the same requirement exists for the insured persons of that state (in the countries operating a reimbursement system, patients do advance the costs and get reimbursed afterwards) – and they only need to pay the co-payment. Contrarily, under the Directive's regime, Member States are obliged to reimburse costs *up to a maximum of the level of the domestic tariff* in the Member State of affiliation, which leaves the price difference at the expense of the patient. Moreover, patients are expected to *pay upfront* and request (often only partial) reimbursement afterwards.

1127 See section 3. in Chapter 3. Financial affordability.

There is a co-payment of 50 euros. Currently, the patient has multiple options which result in different financial outcomes on his/her side. He/she uses his/her own means to finance the treatment, the financial burden left on the patient thus being 3,000 euros. He/she requests an authorisation under the Regulation. If the request is declined, he/she can still either use the Directive's mechanism or finance the treatment him/herself. However, if the request is accepted and the authorisation is issued, the financial burden left on the patient is only 50 euros. If the treatment is not subject to authorisation under the Directive, he/she can receive the treatment and pay 3,000 euros upfront, but get back 1,000 euros as a reimbursement, the financial burden left on the patient thus being 2,000 euros. If the treatment is subject to authorisation and the authorisation is provided, the same rules apply, whereas if the request for authorisation is refused, he/she has to bear all the costs.

Under the proposed integrated system, the patient has the right to receive the treatment abroad without prior authorisation. The healthcare provider in MS A has to send the invoice directly to the healthcare fund in MS B to which the patient is affiliated. The financing of the treatment comes from three sources: the patient is invited to pay the co-payment of 50 euros; MS B is obliged to finance up to its domestic tariff, in this case 1,000 euros; the remaining 1,950 euros is financed from the proposed European healthcare fund.

This European healthcare budget would ensure that patients of worse off Member States have the same opportunities in terms of cross-border healthcare as those with better financial conditions. It would thus be a manifestation of European supranational social solidarity.[1128] However, an unavoidable question is where the revenues of this solidaristic fund should come from. In this respect multiple options can be suggested; three of which are outlined below.

A possible alternative, which implies higher Union involvement, is that transfers are made from other European funds, such as the European Social Fund, for this special purpose. The advantage of this option is that it is based on a long-existing European fund. Transfers could thus be made quite promptly. Still, a huge disadvantage is that it takes money away from other (similarly important) social purposes.

Another solution – by analogy to what was proposed by Commissioner Andor in relation to the supranational unemployment scheme[1129] – is that

[1128] The idea of creating a common European fund for specific social purposes received a new stimulus in recent years. In Berlin on 13 June 2014, Commissioner László Andor outlined a scheme where the eurozone states would share the costs of a European short-term unemployment insurance. http://europa.eu/rapid/press-release_SPEECH-14-455_en.htm (accessed 31.03.2017). On a European unemployment insurance, see S. Dullien, A *European unemployment insurance as a stabilization device – Selected issues*, Paper prepared for DG EMPL, http://ec.europa.eu/social/BlobServlet?docId=10437&langId=en, 2012 (accessed 31.03.2017).

[1129] See n. 1128 above.

the Fund functions as a *supranational healthcare insurance scheme*; hence, all Member States pay a part of their revenues in the Fund. To this end, a universal contribution could be introduced to each insured person in Europe.

I find this option fair and promising, because it embraces solidarity and unity, values which I think are supposed to be the leading lights of an enhanced social Union. However, it puts the financial burden directly on the citizens. Nevertheless, I think this burden – since shared by all insured persons in all the Member States – is far less per capita than the burden a patient might face in a cross-border situation without an appropriate financing mechanism. Therefore, I am convinced that this issue is worth further research.

Whereas countries with lower tariffs would need to rely on the Fund to be able to pay medical invoices from other Member States, Member States with higher tariffs would save money if their insured persons received healthcare in a country with lower costs. Another element of cross-national solidarity would be, if a part of these savings were paid into the European healthcare fund. This is all the more reasonable, since otherwise Member States might be motivated to 'outsource' their patients to countries with good quality care but much cheaper treatments to save money.[1130] The aim of the patient mobility legislation is certainly not to push patients – against their will – to receive healthcare services far from where they live, but to guarantee that in case they need or prefer to undergo a medical treatment in another Member State, they have both the right and the real possibility to do so on an equal basis without facing significant hurdles. Therefore, this option also seems to deserve more attention in the future.

Nevertheless, with a well-functioning compensation mechanism in place the financing of cross-border patient movements would not significantly affect the financial balance of the national social security budgets. Hence, Member States cannot use this argument to restrict the free movement of patients.[1131]

Speaking of financial compensation mechanisms, I think the equality component is also essential in this respect. One of the most serious criticisms of the Patient Mobility Directive[1132] and the current patient mobility legislation in general[1133] is that it disproportionately benefits the highly mobile, educated, well-informed patients with higher incomes as opposed to patients who have neither reliable information nor appropriate financial means to exercise their cross-border healthcare rights under the given framework.[1134] Consequently,

---

1130 It cannot be the aim of strengthening patients' cross-border healthcare rights to encourage Member States to send their patients abroad instead of creating ideal circumstances for them to obtain healthcare at home if they prefer to do so. See in relation to long-term care CONNOLLY, above n. 75.

1131 See n. 217 and 298.

1132 See n. 953 above.

1133 See n. 952 above.

1134 The issue of the *non-take-up of benefits* deserves more attention both on a political level and in academic literature, especially nowadays, when its counterpart, the misuse of benefits,

the Directive has the potential to reinforce the already existing healthcare inequalities. However, it can be argued that cross-border healthcare rights form an integral part of European social citizenship,[1135] according to which citizens are granted the same entitlements and equal opportunities have to be ensured for them to enjoy these entitlements.[1136] The suggestions made in this chapter serve this purpose.

3. TACKLING OBSTACLES OF A NON-LEGAL NATURE: CREATING A SOLID INSTITUTIONAL BACKGROUND

Concerning the practical obstacles, the research underlined that the issue of language barriers is not addressed on European level and the information rights of patients are not satisfactorily settled.[1137]

In my opinion, both problems could be tackled efficiently by creating a more empowered network of national contact points functioning as a knowledge and information centre for each party involved in cross-border healthcare provision, and having the means and infrastructure to provide remote interpretation and translation services for patients, coordinated by a central unit on supranational level.

The findings of the research point to the need to create a solid institutional background in order to ensure the smooth functioning of European cross-border healthcare legislation in practice. As discussed above,[1138] the

---

is widely discussed (see also section 4. below in this chapter). On this topic, see W. van Oorschot, 'Non-take-up of Social Security Benefits in Europe' *Journal of European Social Policy* 1991, vol 1 issue 1.

The phenomenon is also known as the *Matthew-effect*, first described by Robert K. Merton in 1968. R.K. Merton, 'Matthew-effect in Science. The reward and communication systems of science are considered' *Science* 1968, vol 159. In relation to healthcare, Joseph defined it as 'the paradox that populations with a poor standard of health seem to achieve only meagre improvements over time, whereas those with a good standard of health seem to show continual, substantial improvement'. K.S. Joseph, 'The Matthew effect in health development' *British Medical Journal* 1989, vol 298, p. 1497.

See also F. Tacconi, 'Freedom of Health and Medical Care Services within the European Union. Recent Jurisprudence of the European Court of Justice, with Particular Reference to Case C-372/04 *Yvonne Watts*, 16 May 2006' *Zeitschrift für ausländisches öffentliches Recht und Völkerrecht* 2008, vol 68, pp. 206–207.

1135 'If there is to be an EU social citizenship, it will have to erode rather than enshrine the differences in the capacity and willingness of Member States to provide social citizenship rights.' S.L. Greer and T. Sokol, 'Rules for Rights: European Law, Health Care and Social Citizenship' *European Law Journal* 2014, vol 20 no 1, p. 86.

1136 However, it is subject to discussion as to what extent an individual need can be prioritised as opposed to the needs of other patients. See Greer and Sokol, above n. 1135, p. 79 on absolute needs vs relative needs of patients.

1137 See Chapter 4. Information obstacles.

1138 See section 2.6. in Chapter 4. Information obstacles.

Patient Mobility Directive did take the first, important step towards the establishment of an institutional background for cross-border patient mobility by imposing the obligation on the Member States to 'designate one or more national contact points for cross-border healthcare'.[1139] However, I find the provisions on the network of national contact points rather vague and I hold the firm opinion that for now, the Union is far from using the full potential of such a network.

According to my ideas, a network of national contact points coordinated by a supranational central unit, a European Coordination Centre of Cross-Border Healthcare, could be the right advocate for European (border-crossing) patients. This system could ensure that patients engaged in cross-border healthcare provision can exercise their rights simply by turning to a single institution on national level.

In order to guarantee that these institutions work both in the best interests of patients and towards the enforcement of Union legislation without external influence, it is desirable that they function independently, separate from national healthcare funds and ministries.[1140] There are a number of tasks in relation to cross-border patient mobility which could be delegated to these institutions. I enumerate the most essential ones below.

The national contact points serve as a knowledge base and information centre for cross-border healthcare. They should both provide information on request and carry out information campaigns aimed at patients and providers. If the request for information concerns another Member State, they should contact the national contact point in that state as soon as possible.[1141] They could easily do so by means of a common online platform.[1142]

1139 Article 6 PMD.

1140 One might wonder though, how impartiality can be safeguarded at institutions such as those in question when functioning on a national level. Nevertheless, the Coordination Centre must monitor closely to ensure that the NCPs fulfil their tasks as required by European law.

1141 Article 6(2) PMD. In this sense, I think they could function similarly to the SOLVIT network, but specialised in cross-border healthcare issues. Yet, differences are that whereas SOLVIT is a service provided by the national administration of each Member State, NCPs must be independent institutions functioning on a national level; whereas SOLVIT mostly deals with cases when public authorities breach Union law, NCPs must have a broader competence and deal with any issues related to cross-border healthcare; and also whereas SOLVIT is mainly approached online, NCPs should offer various means by which they can be contacted by patients.
However, the rules on the establishment and functioning of the SOLVIT network can provide some ideas. See European Commission, *Communication from the Commission to the Council, the European Parliament, the Economic and Social Committee and the Committee of the Regions – Effective Problem Solving in the Internal Market ('SOLVIT')*, COM (2001) 0702 final, 27.11.2001; European Commission, *Commission Recommendation of 7 December 2001 on principles for using 'SOLVIT' – the Internal Market Problem Solving Network*, C (2001) 3901, OJ L 331 of 15 December 2001 and European Commission, *Commission Recommendation of 17 September 2013 on the principles governing SOLVIT*, C (2013) 5869 final, 17.09.2013.

1142 See n.1039 above.

The national contact points should provide interpretation and translation services for patients in order to bridge potential language barriers. Modern information and communication technologies can significantly simplify this exercise.[1143]

The national contact points should establish a 'one-stop shop system'[1144] for patients by connecting each party involved in cross-border healthcare, and cooperate and frequently consult with patient organisations, healthcare providers and healthcare insurers.[1145]

As to the central unit on EU level, its main mission is to enhance cooperation between national contact points, monitor their functioning and deal with the tasks which go beyond borders, such as training and researching on European cross-border healthcare, organising multilateral seminars and consultations where experts can share their experience, working on methods to develop cross-border mechanisms and operating the European Healthcare Fund.[1146]

One could argue that creating this system would add to European bureaucracy and necessitate further investment. Without doubt, investment would be needed. However, taking into account that a network of national contact points is already operational, this reform would not start from but would improve an existing structure in favour of patients. I believe that a measure which could directly lead to increased awareness and comfort for patients makes this investment reasonable and proportionate.

4. THE LEGAL, POLITICAL AND ECONOMIC FEASIBILITY OF THE *DE LEGE FERENDA* SUGGESTIONS

The EU is beset with difficulties at the moment and is facing tension from different sources. If the 'unprecedented displacement crisis'[1147] were not enough

1143 See section 1.3. in Chapter 4. Information obstacles.

1144 The point of a 'one-stop shop for cross-border problems' is very well summarised by the Commission: 'Different mechanisms to assist citizens [...] must also be better co-ordinated. The world looks different through the eyes of a citizen [...] than through the eyes of the public sector. When citizens have a problem in the Internal Market, whether it relates to a bad experience when buying goods across borders or when trying to exercise their civil liberties, they do not wish to wander around looking for a helping hand. They want one door to knock on: A one-stop access to clear information about their rights, advice and a remedy.' COM (2001) 0702, above n. 1141.

1145 Article 6(1) PMD.

1146 See section 2. above in this chapter.

1147 http://ec.europa.eu/echo/refugee-crisis_en, (accessed 01.04.2017).

of a challenge, it also has to deal with Brexit, the shining evidence of recent years' growing Euroscepticism.[1148] Ironically, Article 50 of the Treaty on European Union (TEU) was triggered by the British Prime Minister[1149] just two days after the sixtieth anniversary of the signing of the Treaty of Rome,[1150] where this whole story started. What is Europe going to do now?

We live in a Europe which worships diversity, but where diversity ties our hands. As the Union has grown and pushed its own boundaries not only geographically but also in terms of the fields of life it influences, in the motto 'United in diversity', emphasis shifted to the last word. Whereas in the beginning six – more or less – similar states united under the twelve stars of Europe,[1151] today twenty-eight countries[1152] compete to gain footing, diverse in their national identities, language, culture, political and social environment and economic capacity. In my opinion, the Union has reached the point where a decision must be made: it either rises above the national differences and finds a way to create an enhanced European integration along the line of our common values; or the dream of the United States of Europe[1153] falls apart for good.

Within the area of healthcare the question arises whether European values, such as universality, access to good quality care, equity, solidarity[1154] and the right to healthcare[1155] overcome national diversity and lead to 'Europe for patients'; or whether national fears and interests remain predominant over patients' social rights in a divided healthcare market.[1156]

1148 On this issue, see, among others, J.I. Torreblanca and M. Leonard, *The continent-wide rise of Euroscepticism*, http://eutruth.info/euroscepticism.pdf, 2013 (accessed 01.04.2017) and M. Condruz-Bacescu, *Euroscepticism Across Europe: Drivers and Challenges*, European Journal of Interdisciplinary Studies 2014, vol 6 issue 2.

1149 http://europa.eu/rapid/press-release_MEMO-17-648_en.htm, (accessed 01.04.2017).

1150 https://europa.eu/european-union/eu60_en, (accessed 01.04.2017).

1151 On the relation between European symbols and European identity, see M. Bruter, 'Winning hearts and minds for Europe. The Impact of News and Symbols on Civic and Cultural European Identity' *Comparative Political Studies* 2003, vol 36 no 10.

1152 Thirty-two, if we also count the EEA countries and Switzerland. See n. 266.

1153 'It is to re-create the European Family, or as much of it as we can, and to provide it with a structure under which it can dwell in peace, in safety and in freedom. We must build a kind of United States of Europe. In this way only will hundreds of millions of toilers be able to regain the simple joys and hopes which make life worth living. The process is simple. All that is needed is the resolve of hundreds of millions of men and women to do right instead of wrong and to gain as their reward blessing instead of cursing.' Citation from Winston Churchill's speech to the academic youth in Zürich on 19 September 1946. http://archive.today/hSYZV (accessed 01.04.2017).

1154 See n. 202 above.

1155 See section 3.2. and 3.3. in Chapter 1. Setting the scene.

1156 Healthcare market integration goes further than only benefiting border-crossing patients. By providing patients with the possibility to 'opt-out' of their national healthcare system, the Union puts pressure on the Member States to constantly develop their own systems in order to keep their own and possibly attract foreign patients.

The recent political and economic developments did not serve the idea of free movement in Europe. Although the financial crisis impacted each national economy, it did not affect the different Member States to the same extent. Nevertheless, the increased level of unemployment, the recession and other negative impacts of economic stress fed anti-migration and Euro-sceptical voices[1157] with new arguments, and made some Member States question the very fundamentals of the Union, such as free movement. 'Welfare tourism'[1158] has become an even more fashionable anti-EU slogan ever since.[1159] Without going into great detail, it must be made clear that benefiting from legal opportunities

1157 See for instance F. Markovic, *Restrictions to Freedom of Movement for Labour: the Culture of Something for Nothing*, http://www.europeanpublicaffairs.eu/restrictions-to-freedom-of-movement-for-labour-the-culture-of-something-for-nothing/, 2014 (accessed 01.04.2017).

1158 Various terms are widely used. In the Union, the expressions welfare, social or benefit tourism are most often used with a negative connotation to describe the phenomenon of non-active migrants accessing welfare or social benefits. Several terms connecting healthcare and tourism were dealt with in section 2.3. in Chapter 1. Setting the scene.

1159 The free movement debate reached its zenith in 2013 – ironically, in the year dedicated to European citizenship – and today continues to raise major concerns EU-wide. In April 2013, four ministers of influential Member States addressed a joint letter to the Irish Presidency and 'launched a strong attack regarding the freedom of movement of EU citizens'. Y. Pascouau, *Strong attack against the freedom of movement of EU citizens: turning back the clock*, http://www.epc.eu/pub_details.php?pub_id=3491, 2013 (accessed 01.04.2017).

The ministers claimed that migrant EU citizens from other Member States (whom they referred to as 'immigrants', an expression which is associated to citizens of third countries) 'avail themselves of the opportunities that freedom of movement provides, without, however, fulfilling the requirements for exercising this right'. http://docs.dpaq.de/3604-130415_letter_to_presidency_final_1_2.pdf (accessed 01.04.2017). Soon after the 'letter incident,' then British Prime Minister David Cameron announced that the UK was willing to impose restrictions on the free movement of citizens of newly accessed Member States and called upon other Member States to do the same. Among others, he proposed 'to require a new country to reach a certain income or economic output per head before full free movement was allowed. Individual member states could be freed to impose a cap if their inflow from the EU reached a certain number in a single year.' D. Cameron, 'Free movement within Europe needs to be less free' *Financial Times*, 26 November 2013. As a response, the Foreign Ministers of the Visegrad countries (all of them among the 'new' Member States which joined the Union in 2004) issued a joint statement pointing to data which show how beneficial the immigration of workers from Central and Eastern European countries was to the UK's economy. http://register.consilium.europa.eu/doc/srv?l=EN&f=ST%2017395%202013%20INIT (accessed 01.04.2017).

It is worth mentioning that in Switzerland (although not an EU Member State as it is a member of the European Free Trade Association, citizens of Switzerland enjoy the same rights as the EEA nationals) on 9 February 2014 a referendum resulted in favour of re-introducing restrictions on the free movement of workers between the European Union and Switzerland. In the heated political debate, the European Commission was forced into the position to defend the basic freedoms. In response to the offense, not only did both the then Commissioner László Andor (DG EMPL) and the then Commissioner Viviane Reding (DG JUSTICE) repeatedly commit themselves to the free movement principle as a non-negotiable basic value of the single market, but the Commission also provided factual evidence that the main driver of intra-EU migration is employment and that migrants from other Member States are not more intensive users of welfare than nationals. ICF GHK and

and exercising rights in good faith,[1160] conferred on citizens by the Union legislation, is neither abuse, nor fraud.

When placing the question whether the Union is ready to develop a barrier-free European area for patients in the afore-mentioned political context, it is obvious that the circumstances are far from ideal. The huge differences among the Member States do not leave the European legislation intact: reaching compromises in a tense political atmosphere is getting more and more difficult. Therefore, European legislation currently tends to transform from inflexible, directly applicable legal tools into legal solutions which ensure more flexibility for the Member States in order to apply the rules to their own individual situations. However, providing Member States with more freedom might result in less certainty for the citizens and greater inequalities among them.[1161] At the same time, more freedom for the citizens triggers the Member States' fears of losing (cost) control. It is an invaluable task to find a fine balance between these two.

Having said this, it is reasonable to look into the legal, economic and political feasibility of the suggestions made in this book in more detail. These aspects are not separable from each other. On the contrary, in the European Union the various angles of feasibility create a complex network of requirements, interests and compromises which only a small portion of suggestions can work through. Nevertheless, these aspects are able to articulate what the potential threats are to the – so far purely theoretic – ideas drafted above.

Milieu, *A fact finding analysis on the impact on the Member States' social security systems of the entitlements of non-active intra-EU migrants to special non-contributory cash benefits and healthcare granted on the basis of residence*, Prepared for DG Employment, Social Affairs and Inclusion, http://ec.europa.eu/social/main.jsp?langId=en&catId=89&newsId=1980&furtherNews=yes, 2013 (accessed 01.04.2017), p. 203.

See also another analysis on the topic prepared by the European Parliamentary Research Service: E.-M. Poptcheva, *Freedom of movement and residence of EU citizens*, http://www.europarl.europa.eu/RegData/bibliotheque/briefing/2014/140808/LDM_BRI(2014)140808_REV1_EN.pdf, 2014 (accessed 01.04.2017).

1160 Spaventa points out by referring to the Joined Cases C-151/04 and C-152/04 *Criminal proceedings against Claude Nadin, Nadin-Lux SA* (C-151/04) and *Jean-Pascal Durré* (C-152/04) [ECLI:EU:C:2005:775] that 'the Court refers to the possibility for a Member State to "prevent certain of its nationals from attempting, under cover of the rights created by the [EC] Treaty, improperly to circumvent their national legislation or to prevent individuals from improperly or fraudulently taking advantage of provisions of Community law"'. E. Spaveta, 'Comments on Abuse of Law and the Free Movement of Workers' in de la Feria and Vogenauer, above n. 1097, p. 316.

1161 I agree with Markovic who warns that '(m)ore flexibility would only lead to reinforcement of the existing category of second class member states and EU citizens'. Markovic, above n. 1156. In another vitriolic and remarkable piece of writing he also draws attention to the inequality of citizens in reality despite a supposed legal equality. F. Markovic, *In Europe, We're All Equal (Unless We're Not)*, http://www.europeanpublicaffairs.eu/in-europe-were-all-equal-unless-were-not/, 2013 (accessed 01.04.2017).

4.1. LEGAL FEASIBILITY

The legal feasibility of a suggestion is more or less determined by two issues: whether the legislative body has competence to legislate the question at stake and whether it is possible to integrate the new legislation into the existing legal tools or whether a new tool has to be created.

In accordance with the principle of subsidiarity

> in areas which do not fall within its exclusive competence, the Union shall act only if and in so far as the objectives of the proposed action cannot be sufficiently achieved by the Member States, [...] but can rather, by reason of the scale or effects of the proposed action, be better achieved at Union level.[1162]

It was shown by the European Commission that legislating cross-border healthcare issues on EU level is necessary[1163] and – by adopting the Patient Mobility Directive – the Member States seemed to accept that. However, the Union is entitled to act only within the limits of the competence conferred on it in the Treaty.[1164]

It was thoroughly discussed that patient mobility is a complex legal issue which relates to several European domains such as public health,[1165] free movement of workers[1166] and free movement of services.[1167] Thus, legislative tools in this field are rooted in different legal bases. Whereas Article 48 of the Treaty on the Functioning of the European Union (TFEU) gives power to the Union to introduce only *coordinating* measures in the field of social security as are necessary to provide freedom of movement for workers, Article 114(1) permits it to adopt *harmonising* measures, since healthcare services are considered internal market services within the meaning of the Treaty. However, as pointed out earlier, most Member States have been far from impressed by this expansion of Union competence in healthcare,[1168] which is considered as a cornerstone of national social security systems, thus belonging to the competence that remains with the Member States. No wonder that each new proposal related to European healthcare legislation faces Member States' suspicion and must be carefully tested against going beyond current EU competence.

1162 Article 5(3) TEU. See n. 202.

1163 European Commission, *Commission Staff Working Document. Accompanying document to the Proposal for a Directive of the European Parliament and of the Council on the application of patients' rights in cross-border healthcare. Impact Assessment*, SEC (2008) 2163, 02.07.2008, p. 16.

1164 See n. 197 above.

1165 See section 3.5. in Chapter 1. Setting the scene.

1166 See section 3.6. in Chapter 1. Setting the scene.

1167 See section 3.7. in Chapter 1. Setting the scene.

1168 See n. 791 above.

A major setback of an integrated European patient mobility legislation as detailed above[1169] is that it intends to build on the legacy of social security coordination while aiming to harmonise healthcare schemes to a certain extent. This means that some of the suggestions drafted above are legally feasible and could be inserted into today's legislation on cross-border patient movements, whereas others lack an appropriate legal base. Without repeating what was said about the issue of legal competence, it can be stated that measures such as a maximum timeframe defining undue delay, unified administrative deadlines or a standardised healthcare package, which would largely affect how national healthcare systems are organised, cannot be carried out under the current Treaty provisions on Union competence in healthcare. In order to enable the Union to adopt legal tools in relation to these questions, the division of healthcare competence between Member States and the Union institutions should be changed. From a legal point of view, this can be done with the agreement of all the EU countries. The question whether this could be done in practice leads to the issue of the political feasibility, which is dealt with in the next section.

In my view, clear and consistent European patient mobility legislation does not necessitate the creation of new legal tools but a considerable revision of what we have today. The Treaty, the Coordination Regulations and the Patient Mobility Directive all form an integral part of the body of the legislation. As to the Treaty, modification is only possible if political willingness supports the idea of a shift of competence in healthcare. However, the Regulations and the Directive could be altered by the EU institutions and numerous suggestions could be realised under their scope.[1170] The most important point to keep in mind is that the Regulations and the Directive should complement each other without overlapping or conflicting rules.

4.2. POLITICAL FEASIBILITY

The European Union is an entity which seeks to reconcile concurring political interests: concurring interests of the individual Member States and concurring interests of the Member States and the Union. This not only affects strategic political decision-making but law-making as well. The Treaties are the framework which set the balance: they are the result of a compromise between the Member States and lay down the boundaries of the Union's actions.

The supranational nature of the Union implies that legislative powers are delegated to the institutions of the EU which 'are able to take advantage of their discretion to pursue their own policy preferences – for example, by seeking

[1169] See section 1. above in this chapter.
[1170] See section 5. below in this chapter.

to advance the process of European integration beyond the lowest-common-denominator preferences of the EU member governments'.[1171] Thus, although the playbook of this 'power game' was composed at a certain point in time, European integration can be considered as a work-in-progress, the rules of which are subject to potential changes.

The field of cross-border patient mobility is a prominent example of this 'race for competence'. Whereas healthcare was and still is a severely protected area of national sovereignty, the EU has gained footing step by step and was awarded certain competences in certain domains related to patient mobility, which recently peaked when healthcare services became included in the internal market, thus enabling the EU to adopt harmonising measures concerning the cross-border provision (and consumption) of such services.[1172] As detailed above, this process was dominated by the Court with the strong support of the Commission and the Parliament,[1173] while the Member States were quite hostile and qualified this activism as unwanted and unwarranted.[1174]

Most of the suggestions made in this book have a federalising tendency which requires further integration and extended harmonisation. The question is whether this is politically plausible: are the Member States ready and willing to transfer more of their sovereignty to the Union in this field? After the experience of the adoption of the new pair of Coordination Regulations and the Patient Mobility Directive,[1175] this scenario seems rather unlikely. It does not mean though that this cannot change. Nevertheless, a solid reform of the legislation cannot be carried out without political will.

Each national government has its own agenda and its own preferences. Since healthcare is a major priority for the citizens, it is certainly high on governments' agendas. As Walus points out aptly, '[t]he social and financial implications of healthcare result in the organisation of healthcare becoming a highly sensitive political issue.'[1176] Before turning to the financial implications, there are some important matters with regard to social implications which must be addressed here since they are and will likely remain the focal point of political debates both on national and European level. These issues are related to solidarity, equality and freedom of choice.

Solidarity has been a foundational element of European welfare societies. In social security schemes, the unity of the interests manifests itself as a risk-sharing mechanism: carrying the risks of individual social crises together,

---

1171 M.A. Pollack, *The Engines of European Integration. Delegation, Agency and Agenda Setting in the EU*, Oxford University Press, New York 2003, p. 7.

1172 See section 3.7. in Chapter 1. Setting the scene.

1173 See n. 347 above.

1174 See n. 792 above.

1175 See section 3.7. in Chapter 1. Setting the scene and especially n. 327 and 328.

1176 Walus, above n. 168, p. 53.

so that in case such events occur, each participant is protected. Since solidarity is a common value shared by the Member States, the Union also puts great emphasis on it.[1177]

Solidarity means that we all take on the burden (or part of it) so that we can all benefit from the social coverage when in need. As such, it 'is closely linked to the financial arrangement of our national health systems and the need to ensure accessibility to all'.[1178] One might say though that people who receive treatment in another state break the circle of national solidarity by taking out money from the national healthcare budget brought together by all, since the national healthcare budget can be seen as the result of a common (financial) effort of all citizens or tax payers of the given country. As elaborated above,[1179] this is the argument most often raised by the Member States, namely that cross-border patient movements threaten the financial equilibrium of their healthcare systems.[1180] This danger affects the system as a whole, thus also those patients who stayed in their home country. This concern is valid and deserves due attention.

First, it must be noted that although in certain cases healthcare services abroad indeed mean extra costs for the Member States,[1181] no hard evidence suggests that the current scale of European patient mobility has the potential to endanger national healthcare budgets and/or healthcare planning.[1182] Of course, a reform liberalising patient mobility might change this, but it is argued that this matter should be tackled by reforming the financing of cross-border healthcare[1183] instead of restricting the free movement of patients.

Secondly, sometimes treatments can actually be cheaper abroad, in which case mobile patients do not take money away, but on the contrary, save money for their national healthcare system and contribute to the utilisation of healthcare services.

Thirdly, although from the national healthcare systems' point of view cross-border healthcare is usually looked at as a challenge, it is an opportunity at the same time. Patient mobility concerns not only outgoing but also incoming patients. The latter offers Member States the opportunity to develop their schemes so as to make them more attractive for incoming patients, which provides income for the national healthcare budget. However, it is very important to ensure that such profiting from an integrated European healthcare market does not impair the accessibility of healthcare services for the domestic patients. Incoming patients should not be prioritised over domestic patients but treated equally.

1177 For instance, see title IV of CFREU. See also Council Conclusions, above n. 22.
1178 Council Conclusions, above n. 22.
1179 See Chapter 3. Financial affordability and section 2. above in this chapter.
1180 See n. 863 above.
1181 This occurs when the patient receives treatment under the scope of the Regulation and it is more expensive in the Member State of treatment than it is in the Member State of affiliation.
1182 See n. 9 above.
1183 See sections 1. and 2. above in this chapter.

Fourthly, many of the suggestions made in this book involve the development of national healthcare systems, which benefits each person, both patients who are treated at home and those treated abroad.

Concerning cross-border patient movements, there are two dimensions of equality, which are important to the same extent: equal treatment between nationals of the Member State (domestic patients) and non-nationals of the Member State (incoming patients); and equal treatment between mobile patients (outgoing patients) and 'sedentary' patients (who are treated in their home country).

Whereas the EU legislation on patient mobility ensures equality in the first situation,[1184] the solution to the second is mainly left to the Member States. The EU itself acknowledges that health inequalities and problems related to equal access is a concern of the Member States,[1185] but has no competence to influence the legal status of insured persons under national social legislation. Moreover, certain features of EU legislation add to these inequalities.[1186]

I find it essential to close these gaps by empowering patients, educating them about their entitlements and the possible ways of enforcement of their rights, and tackling inequalities within the EU legislation.

Lastly, the issue of patients' freedom of choice must be briefly addressed. As has been mentioned, the opportunity to obtain healthcare abroad also comes with the risk that Member States may decide not to maintain and/or develop (certain branches of) their healthcare schemes but to send their citizens to another country instead where the treatment needed is provided for a lower price and/or more quickly and/or with better quality.[1187] Whereas this outsourcing technique might be acceptable in some cases,[1188] from the patients' point of view, entitlements in association with treatment abroad conferred on them by the Union legislation should remain an opportunity, not an obligation. The Union legislation on patient mobility does not serve the purpose in any way to force patients to receive healthcare outside their catchment area, but offers the legal possibility to do so.

4.3. ECONOMIC FEASIBILITY

When a new idea appears, in the end, it always comes down to the question: who is going to pay for this? Although much has been said about the financial

1184 See n. 383 above.

1185 'Equity relates to equal access according to need, regardless of ethnicity, gender, age, social status or ability to pay. EU health systems also aim to reduce the gap in health inequalities, which is a concern of EU Member States.' Council Conclusions, above n. 22.

1186 On concerns related to financial inequalities see n. 952–954.

1187 See section 2. above in this chapter.

1188 See n. 102 and 104.

aspect of cross-border patient mobility,[1189] it also seems reasonable to observe the *de lege ferenda* suggestions from this perspective.

The suggestions – although different in nature – have in common that they necessitate financial investment, in particular with regard to setting up new institutions and developing national healthcare schemes in one way or another. I see basically three options where the money required for the changes could come from: the patients themselves; the Union or the Member States.

It can be argued that if patients wish to use their entitlements, they have to pay. However, the example of the Patient Mobility Directive's financial regime showed that putting the financial burden associated with cross-border treatments directly on patients results in magnifying healthcare inequalities and – despite of the equal legal status – in effect restricts the free movement of patients who cannot deal with such additional costs.[1190] This is the main reason why I think the costs of the reforms should not be put on patients. Although it may be possible to share these costs among all insured persons on the grounds of solidarity,[1191] one can rightfully raise the question why patients who do not make use of cross-border healthcare and who are participate in financing their national healthcare systems should be obliged to contribute to the development of such a European feature. So charging patients – though it might be feasible – is not desirable.

The European Union should certainly play a part in financing such changes which aim to upgrade citizens' status and improve free movement within the internal market. Its role is especially important in building the institutional background on EU level. Resources should be ensured for the establishment of a European Coordination Centre of Cross-Border Healthcare, a European Medical Interpretation Agency, a European Monitoring Centre for Healthcare Provision and a European Healthcare Fund.[1192] Taking into account the extensive EU administration, I think that budgetary sources could be found for these specialised purposes if the legislative bodies so decide.

In my view, the Achilles' heel of the economic feasibility is the national side of the issue. In a post-crisis era, when numerous Member States needed to cut back social security budgets, it might not seem realistic to expect Member States to be keen on making investments in order to enable patients to receive healthcare abroad. In particular, suggestions which have a harmonising tendency such as reducing administrative deadlines and setting a deadline for undue delay might require a considerable amount of money. It is highly questionable whether the national governments would be able and willing to transfer money to these areas today. By establishing a European Healthcare Fund, the Member States

1189 See Chapter 3. Financial affordability and section 2. above in this chapter.
1190 See sections 2. and 3. in Chapter 3. Financial affordability.
1191 See section 2. above in this chapter.
1192 See sections 2. and 3. above in this chapter.

could be provided with financial support for these purposes. However, without any external financial sources the economic feasibility of some of the suggestions is, unfortunately, rather low for the moment.

Although, as I see it, it is doubtful that a radical positive change in European cross-border healthcare policy is just around the corner, there are alternatives, as I have shown, to the current politically burdened, incomplete freedom for patients. My suggestions – although perhaps over-ambitious in current political and economic circumstances – aim at such a positive shift towards a (more) Social Europe.[1193]

Since such changes cannot be expected to happen overnight, the next section provides for a detailed step-by-step approach which offers various policy options with various sets of suggestions.

5. POLICY OPTIONS

European legislation and policy making need to seek compromises. It is a very delicate task to reach agreements when there are so many different interests and discrepancies, aspects and circumstances to take into account. Solutions which might seem ideal from certain perspectives might not be feasible or even acceptable from others.

Therefore, in the light of the feasibility test carried out above, I herewith draft a number of policy options which are different in their aims and expected effects. I start with the one which requires the least modifications to the current legislation, and thus holds the highest level of feasibility, but, as a result, cannot tackle many of the issues this research has revealed. After going through a few intermediary options, I end the list with the most radical one, which, with the state of affairs today, is the least feasible, but to my mind, has the biggest potential to create a (greater) freedom of movement for patients in Europe. (Figure 3)

Figure 3. Policy options

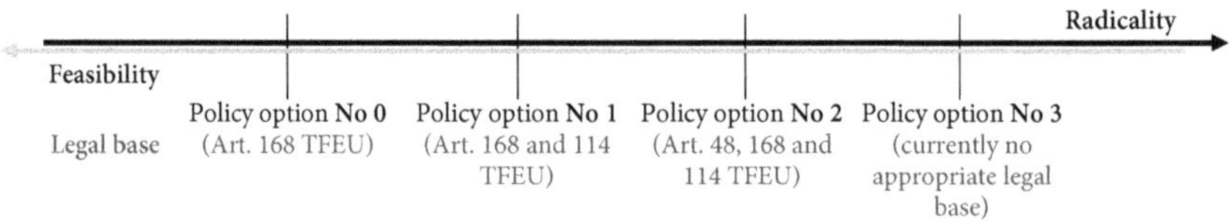

Source: The author's own summary.

1193 It is promising that the Commissioner responsible for healthcare issues, Vytenis Andriukaitis, envisaged 'a single market for health services' and said that 'moving around Europe is taken for granted, so systems should be in place that can take care of everyone wherever they are'. P. O'Donnell, *Andriukaitis calls for an EU health system to take care of everyone, wherever they are*, http://www.europeanvoice.com/article/andriukaitis-calls-for-an-eu-health-system-to-take-care-of-everyone-wherever-they-are/, 2014 (accessed 01.04.2017).

5.1. POLICY OPTION NO 0: SOFT MEASURES

I consider the first alternative the baseline. In the framework of this policy option the body of the legislation remains mostly intact: no measures which would be likely to induce heated political discussions are included. Within the limits of the current competences of the Union, *soft law incentives* could give further stimuli to strengthening inter-institutional cooperation in the field of cross-border healthcare and to the improved enforcement of patients' rights. Article 168 TFEU is a proper legal base for this. It provides that the Union must encourage cooperation between Member States in the field of healthcare in an effort to ensure a high level of human health protection.[1194]

The *open method of coordination* (OMC) in the field of healthcare might be a useful tool. However, its nature and practical outcome is widely debated.[1195] Nevertheless, it is argued that the OMC has gained a growing importance, because 'it commits Member States to work together in reaching joint goals without seeking to homogenize their inherited policy regimes and institutional arrangements'.[1196] Without going into detail, it must be noted that I doubt whether the OMC is capable of efficiently contributing to the development of the right to free movement for patients via its mutual learning technique. Nevertheless, it must be acknowledged that in fields such as healthcare, sitting in the very heart of national sovereignty, this might be the easiest tool to move things forward.

The Union institutions (especially the Commission and the Court) have a huge responsibility in enhancing and effectively controlling the *just and universal application* of the existing legal tools. The Commission should continue and even widen its *information-spreading activities*[1197] in order to make sure that all parties involved are aware of their rights and obligations (patients, providers as well as healthcare institutions) in cross-border healthcare situations. The Administrative Commission remains to serve as a forum for Member State representatives to discuss and solve problems of application

1194 Article 168(1)–(2) TFEU. See also Recital 1 of the Preamble of the Patient Mobility Directive.

1195 The details of this fascinating discussion go beyond the scope of this research, but more information can be found on the scholarly opinions in E. Barcevicius, T. Weishaupt and J. Zeitlin, *Assessing the Open Method of Coordination. Institutional Design and National Influence of EU Social Policy Coordination*, Palgrave Macmillan, Basingstoke 2014. Especially J. Zeitlin, E. Barcevicius, and J.T. Weishaupt, 'Institutional Design and National Influence of EU Social Policy Coordination: Advancing a Contradictory Debate' in Barcevicius et al., pp. 1–15. See also M. Flear, 'The Open Method of Coordination on health care after the Lisbon Strategy II: Towards a neoliberal framing?' in S. Kröger (ed.), *What we have learnt: Advances, pitfalls and remaining questions in OMC research*, European Integration Online Papers 2009, Special Issue 1, vol. 13 no 12.

1196 Zeitlin et al., above n. 1195, p. 4.

1197 See section 2. in Chapter 4. Information obstacles and especially n. 1065.

and interpretation that occur concerning the coordination of, among others, sickness benefits.[1198]

As said, this policy option aims to basically retain the status quo. There are some politically neutral steps, which in the long run might somewhat improve patients' rights, but, in my opinion, their short-term impacts are highly limited.

5.2. POLICY OPTION NO 1: NO RADICAL CHANGES IN LEGISLATION

One step further already involves the change of hard law, but no radical modifications to the legislation take place yet. The alteration of secondary legislation is usually somewhat problematic – especially when it comes to healthcare – but this second policy option requires relatively minor changes, such as clarifying measures and the establishment of coordinating institutions on EU level.

Among the issues waiting for clarification, the debate on the *material scope of the Patient Mobility Directive* should be resolved right in the Directive itself, because for now the different interpretations result in legal uncertainty.[1199] In this respect, I stand by the opinion that the Directive should be applied to both planned and unplanned care.

As to establishing coordinating institutions, I refer to the *European Coordination Centre of Cross-Border Healthcare*, which I made a plea for above,[1200] and which could also include a *European Medical Interpretation Agency*, as an alternative to or coordinating the interpretation and translation services provided by the national contact points.[1201] These additions to the existing network of national contact points have the potential to considerably strengthen patients' information rights and to tackle the language barrier. This exercise could be carried out by way of modifying the Patient Mobility Directive and inserting separate articles on both institutions. In these provisions, it must be stated exactly what the responsibilities of these institutions are and how they function. In order to avoid overlapping competences and malfunctioning, there must be a clear distribution of tasks between the national contact points and the central unit.[1202]

These changes could be carried out within the current limits of EU competence – with Article 168 and 114 TFEU as legal bases, as they served as legal bases for the Directive. Although both financial implications and fear of

1198 Article 72 BR.

1199 See section 2.2. in Chapter 2. Legal complexity.

1200 See section 3. above in this chapter.

1201 See sections 1.3. in Chapter 4. Information obstacles and 3. above in this chapter.

1202 See section 3. above in this chapter.

red tape might result in objections from the Member States, I think agreement could still be reached on these questions.

In my view, these measures definitely go further than the ones in the previous section, but not far enough to offer solutions for each problem which border-crossing patients might encounter.

5.3. POLICY OPTION NO 2: ESSENTIAL CHANGES IN SECONDARY LAW

In my opinion, with this policy option, we cross the line of today's feasibility. When one starts to think out of the box, and redraw the characteristics of legislation which has been in force without much change for decades, one must expect, at least, resistance. I think most of the *de lege ferenda* suggestions made in this chapter fit into this category. Although they are legally feasible – based on Article 48, 114 and 168 TFEU – their political and economic feasibility is rather uncertain.[1203]

Creating an integrated legal system by erasing the parallelisms, removing the prior authorisation requirement, abolishing the distinction between planned and unplanned care, extending the coordination regime to private providers and rethinking the financing of cross-border treatments[1204] are all elements of a *comprehensive reform of patient mobility legislation.* Although none of these suggestions necessitate further harmonisation, but rather build on a renewed framework of coordination, they would break time-worn traditions and require a high level of openness and flexibility from the Member States.

It has been proved in the past that Member States do not easily reach a common standpoint on social security coordination issues.[1205] Even though unanimity is no longer required in the Council,[1206] a gradual change of the Regulations will not happen without long and thorny negotiations. Even more so since, for example, the extension of the scope of coordination to private providers not only concerns the healthcare branch, but also addresses the question whether a modern coordination system can fulfil its role without including the elements of private social security schemes. It goes much further than cross-border healthcare.[1207] Moreover, both prior authorisation and

1203 See section 4. above in this chapter.

1204 See section 1. and 2. above in this chapter.

1205 The adoption of the third generation of Coordination Regulations illustrated the difficulties aptly. See section 3.7. in Chapter 1. Setting the scene.

1206 See n. 234 above.

1207 There are trends which aim to eliminate the flaws of the coordination system. In case of supplementary pension schemes – which do fall outside of the scope of the Regulations – directives were adopted to safeguard the social rights of migrant workers. http://ec.europa.eu/social/main.jsp?catId=468&langId=en (accessed 02.04.2017).

financing touch upon the issue of (cost) control, which is an extremely critical question for all the Member States.

Under this policy option essential changes would redesign both the Regulations and the Directive. The Regulations would exclusively legislate the way insured persons can obtain healthcare services outside of the Member State of affiliation on behalf of the competent institution; whereas the Directive would contain all those rules which are closely connected to cross-border healthcare provision but fall outside the scope of the Regulations, such as the rules on the information rights of patients, institutional background and inter-institutional cooperation.

In my opinion, this relatively radical reform would improve European healthcare legislation in a patient-friendly manner and enable more patients to exercise their cross-border healthcare rights.

5.4. POLICY OPTION NO 3: REFORMING THE WHOLE LEGAL LANDSCAPE

This last policy option is purely an alternative for the future, since for the present it lacks vital components of feasibility: any measures which involve harmonisation of the national healthcare systems invades the autonomy of the Member States and goes against the current wording of the Treaty.[1208] In order to launch any Union action aiming to harmonise any element of national healthcare systems, competence has to be conferred on the Union institutions beforehand. This would erode national sovereignty further, which makes this unlikely to happen any time soon.[1209] Nevertheless, giving the Union the legislative power to harmonise national healthcare schemes would raise European healthcare policy to new heights and open the door to a more integrated European healthcare market with more equal opportunities for each European patient.

As pointed out above, standardising national benefit packages, creating maximum waiting times in relation to undue delay and introducing universal, European deadlines in healthcare administration[1210] go beyond Union competence, since they affect how healthcare services are defined, organised, delivered and financed in the individual Member States.

Since harmonising attempts have not been supported in the past,[1211] these changes seem implausible. Whether social Europe can ever go as far as to

---

1208 Article 168(7) TFEU.

1209 See section 4. above in this chapter.

1210 See section 3. in Chapter 2. Legal complexity.

1211 See n. 328 above.

harmonise social security systems is a question to be answered in the coming decades.

6. CLOSING THOUGHTS

To sum up, the ideal system I find desirable to create in the long run in the European Union in order to serve European (border-crossing) patients best is based on *equality* and is legislated in an *integrated, consistent system of legal tools*. The core entitlements are codified in the Coordination Regulations, which provide access to healthcare in another Member State without prior administrative obstacles, without the limitation of available providers and with a *solidaritarian financing mechanism*, which ensures the opportunity to obtain medical treatment abroad to each insured person who wishes or needs to do so. The additional rules on enhanced cooperation, patients' information rights and institutional background are incorporated in the second pillar of the legislation, namely the Patient Mobility Directive.

The closing thought of Strban et al. fits here nicely.

> [A]ll legal rules pertaining to cross-border healthcare and their interpretation should be to the benefit of mobile and national patients. Access to (cross-border) healthcare has to encompass not only geographical access, but also timely access (which is sometimes lacking in the home country), financial access (which may pose problems if costs of healthcare have to be advanced by the patient, who might not be fully reimbursed), informational access (which is seriously lacking in cross-border healthcare) and procedural access (regarding the steps needed to be taken in order to receive healthcare in another Member State). Next to these forms, access has to be equitable, meaning that all mobile patients should have equal access to cross-border healthcare of the highest quality. At the same time, based on EU citizenship, the same should apply to patients who are (for one reason or other) not moving within the EU.[1212]

To my mind, the mission of science is to visualise future solutions in response to present-day problems. Thus, although I am fully aware that today the suggestions I have made exist only on paper, I considered it to fall under the scope of the mission of this book to offer solutions for the problems I found. After placing these solutions in the context of real-life circumstances, it seems that they might never see the light of day. However, this cannot be a reason not to formulate them in the hope that Europe might actually get there one day.

It must be kept in mind that the most core human value is at stake here: human life and the quality thereof. Healthcare is fundamental to the wellbeing

---

1212 Strban et al, above n. 5, p. 95.

of mankind. The right to access to healthcare is not only a fundamental human right but one of the most basic needs of each person. Thus, individual needs and differences cannot be disregarded. On the contrary, in my understanding, in an ideal healthcare system, it is the need of the patients which gradually defines the healthcare provision.

The controversial issues of cross-border healthcare are just a few of the many examples of the dilemma that are rooted in the Member States' fear of relinquishing more areas of national sovereignty as opposed to the Union's steady intention to develop the internal market and deepen integration. It seems clear that without further harmonisation, the questions surrounding cross-border healthcare entitlements will remain unsolved for a long time. I firmly believe that the European institutions and the Member States must join forces and work towards a more integrated, solidarity-based, socially sensitive European Union, providing equal rights and opportunities for all.

BIBLIOGRAPHY

S. Allin, K. Davaki and E. Mossialos, 'Paying for 'free' health care: the conundrum of informal payments in post-communist Europe' *Global Corruption Report* 2005

N. Azzopardi Muscat, K. Grech, J.M. Cachia and D. Xuereb, 'Sharing capacities – Malta and the United Kingdom' in M. Rosenmöller, M. McKee and R. Baeten (eds.), *Patient Mobility in the European Union – Learning from experience*, European Observatory on Health Systems and Policies, Europe for Patients Project, Brussels 2006

R. Baeten, *The proposal for a Directive on Services in the Internal Market applied to Healthcare Services*, http://www.ose.be/files/publication/rbaeten/baeten_2004_Paper HearingEP111104.pdf, 2004

——, 'Health and social services in the internal market' in C. Degryse and P. Pochet (eds.), *Social Developments in the European Union 2006*, European Observatory on Health Systems and Policies, Brussels 2007

R. Baeten and W. Palm, 'The Compatibility of Health Care Capacity Planning Policies with EU Internal Market Rules' in J.W. van de Gronden, E. Szyszczak, U. Neergaard and M. Krajewski (eds.), *Health Care and EU Law*, T. M. C. Asser Press, The Hague 2011

R. Baeten and L. San Miguel, 'Cross-border recognition of medicines prescriptions: Results from a mystery shopping experiment' *Eurohealth* 2013, vol 19 no 4

M.J. Ball and J. Lillis, 'E-health: transforming the physician/patient relationship' *International Journal of Medical Informatics* 2001, vol 61

E. Barcevicius, T. Weishaupt and J. Zeitlin, *Assessing the Open Method of Coordination. Institutional Design and National Influence of EU Social Policy Coordination*, Palgrave Macmillan, Basingstoke 2014

P. Barlow, 'Health care is not a human right' *British Medical Journal* 1999, vol 319

C. Barnard, *The substantive law of the EU: the four freedoms*, Oxford University Press, Oxford, New York 2010

T.L. Beauchamp and R.R. Faden, 'The Right to Health and the Right to Health Care' *The Journal of Medicine and Philosophy* 1979, vol 4 no 2

A. Beldad, M. de Jong and M. Steehouder, 'How shall I trust the faceless and the intangible? A literature review on the antecedents of online trust' *Computers in Human Behavior* 2010, vol 26

G. Berki, 'A betegmobilitás közösségi jogi keretei az Európai Unióban a szociális biztonsági koordináció nézőpontjából' (The legal framework of patient mobility within the European Union from the social security coordination's point of view) in G. Berki (ed.), *Opuscula Szegediensia 4*, Pólay Elemér Alapítvány, Szeged 2011

—— (ed.), *Opuscula Szegediensia 4*, Pólay Elemér Alapítvány, Szeged 2011

——, 'Az Európai Bíróság újabb ítélete az egészségügyi szolgáltatás tervezett külföldi igénybevételének tárgyában. A tagállami ellátási csomag tartalmának kérdése' (Another CJEU ruling on scheduled treatment abroad: the question of the content of benefit baskets) *Jogesetek Magyarázata* (*Case Law Review*) 2012, vol 3 issue 2

——, 'Az Európai Bíróság ítélete egy "egészségügyi menekült" ügyében: A tartózkodás és a lakóhely fogalmi dilemmája egészségügyi szolgáltatás külföldi igénybevétele esetén' (The CJEU's decision in the case of a 'healthcare refugee': the dilemmas of the place of stay and the place of residence in relation to obtaining healthcare abroad) *Jogesetek Magyarázata* (*Case Law Review*) 2015, vol 6 issue 4

J. Bernier, *EU Economic Integration and National Language Policies: An Overlooked Tension*, http://www.sciencessociales.uottawa.ca/crfpp/pdf/debat/Bernier.pdf, 2005

L. Bertinato, R. Busse, N. Fahy, H. Legido-Quigley, M. McKee, W. Palm, I. Passarani and F. Ronfini, *Cross-Border Health Care in Europe*, European Observatory on Health Systems and Policies, Brussels 2005

K.-J. Bieback, 'Rechtlinie 2011/24/EU – Patientenrechtlinie' in M. Fuchs (ed.), *Europäisches Sozialrecht*, Nomos, Baden-Baden 2013

K.-D. Borchardt, *The ABC of European Union Law*, Publications Office of the European Union, Luxembourg 2010

T.A. Börzel and R.A. Cichowski (eds.), *The State of the European Union Law, Politics and Society*, Oxford University Press, New York 2003

A. Bosco, 'Are national social protection systems under threat? Observations on the recent case law of the Court of Justice' *European Issues* 2000, no 7

M. Brazier, 'Regulating the reproduction business?' *Medical Law Journal* 1999, vol 7

E. Brooks, 'Crossing borders: A critical review of the role of the European Court of Justice in EU health policy' *Health Policy* 2012, vol 105 issue 1

M. Bruter, 'Winning hearts and minds for Europe. The Impact of News and Symbols on Civic and Cultural European Identity' *Comparative Political Studies* 2003, vol 36 no 10

D. Budiani-Saberi and F.L. Delmonico, 'Organ Trafficking and Transplant Tourism: A Commentary on the Global Realities' *American Journal of Transplantation* 2008, vol 8

P. Burge, N. Devlin, J. Appleby, C. Rohr and J. Grant, 'Do patients always prefer quicker treatment? : a discrete choice analysis of patients' stated preferences in the London Patient Choice Project' *Applied Health Economics and Health Policy* 2004, vol 3 issue 4

R. Busse, M. Wörz, T. Foubister, E. Mossialos and P. Berman, *Mapping Health Services Access: National and Cross-Border Issues – Final Report*, HealthACCESS Project, 2006

R. Busse, E. Van Ginneken, J. Schreyögg and M. Velasco Garrido, 'Benefit baskets and tariffs' in M. Wismar, W. Palm, J. Figueras, K. Ernst and E. van Ginneken (eds.), *Cross-border Health Care in the European Union – Mapping and analysing practices and policies*, European Observatory on Health Systems and Policies, Brussels 2011

P. Cablar, 'Cross-border medical care in the European Union – bringing down a first wall' *European Law Review* 1999, vol 24 issue 4

M. Calnan, W. Palm, F. Sohy and D.N.A. Quaghebeur, 'Cross-border use of health care – A survey of frontier workers' knowledge, attitudes and use' *European Journal of Public Health* 1997, vol 7 suppl 3

D. Cameron, 'Free movement within Europe needs to be less free' *Financial Times*, 26.11.2013

C.T. Carlstrom, 'The Government's Role in the Health Care Industry: Past, Present, and Future' *Economic Commentary*, 1 June 1994

P.M. Carrera and J.F.P. Bridges, 'Globalization and healthcare: understanding health and medical tourism' *Expert Review of Pharmacoeconomics & Outcomes Research* 2006, vol 6 no 4

O. Carter-Pokras, M.J.F. O'Neill, V. Cheanvechai, M. Menis, T. Fan and A. Solera, 'Providing Linguistically Appropriate Services to Persons With Limited English Proficiency: A Needs and Resources Investigation' *The American Journal of Managed Care* 2004, vol 10, Special Issue

A.V. Casas and C.R. Parada, *Patients' right to information: a review of the regulatory and ethical framework*, http://bid.ub.edu/21/vall3.htm, 2008

S. Chaytor, *Future of Healthcare in Europe – Meeting future challenges: Key issues in context*, UCL Policy Briefing, January 2012

A. Clarke and R. Rosen, 'Length of stay – How short should hospital care be?' *European Journal of Public Health* 2001, vol 11 issue 2

T. Clemens, E. Cox, B. van der Zanden, M. Commers and H. Brand, *Implementation of National Contact Points for cross-border healthcare in EU Member States: a comparative analysis using websites and short interviews*, http://www.epecs.eu/theme/epecs/uploads/kcfinder/files/2016_06_13%20NCP%20Activity%20report.pdf, 2016

M. Condruz-Bacescu, 'Euroscepticism Across Europe: Drivers and Challenges' *European Journal of Interdisciplinary Studies* 2014, vol 6 issue 2

J. Connell, 'Medical tourism: Sea, sun, sand … and surgery?' *Tourism Management* 2006, vol 27

——, 'Contemporary medical tourism: Conceptualisation, culture and commodification' *Tourism Management* 2013, vol 34

K. Connolly, 'Germany "exporting" old and sick to foreign care homes' *The Guardian*, 26.12.2012

R. Cornelissen, 'The Principle of territoriality and the Community regulations on social security (Regulations 1408/71 and 574/72)' *Common Market Law Review* 1996, vol 33

——, '50 years of social security coordination' *European Journal of Social Security* 2009, vol 11 issue 1–2

——, 'Achievements of 50 years of European Social Security Coordination' in Y. Jorens (ed.), *50 years of Social Security Coordination: Past – Present – Future*, Publications Office of the European Union, Luxembourg 2010

S.R. Cotton and S.S. Gupta, 'Characteristics of online and offline health information seekers and factors that discriminate between them' *Social Science & Medicine* 2004, vol 59

M. Coucheir, *EHIC Report 2013*, trESS Network, Ghent 2013

M. Coucheir and Y. Jorens, *The European Legal Framework in Relation to Patient Mobility*, Europe for Patients Project 2005

M. Coucheir and M. Sakslin (eds.), S. Giubboni, D. Martinsen and H. Verschueren, *The relationship and interaction between the coordination Regulations and Directive 2004/38/EC*, trESS Network, Ghent 2008

M. Cousins, *Habitual residence: fact or (legal fiction)? Case C-255/13, I v. Health Service Executive*, https://works.bepress.com/mel_cousins/82/, 2014

V.A. Crooks, P. Kingsbury, J. Snyder and R. Johnston, 'What is known about the patient's experience of medical tourism? A scoping review' *BMC Health Services Research* 2010, vol 10

A.J. Culyer, *The Dictionary of Health Economics*, Edward Elgar Publishing, Cheltenham, UK, Northampton, MA, USA 2005

N.M. Daysal, M. Trandafir and R. van Ewijk, 'Saving lives at birth: The impact of home births on infant outcomes' *Discussion Paper Series* 2012, Forschungsinstitut zur Zukunft der Arbeit, No. 6879

C.G. De Cortazar, 'Kohll and Decker, or That is Somebody Else's Problem. The Challenge Facing Spain' *European Journal of Health Law* 1999, vol 6

A. de Jonge, B.Y. van der Goes, A.C.J. Ravelli, M.P. Amelink-Verburg, B.W.J. Mol, J.G. Nijhuis, J. Bennebroek Gravenhorst and S.E. Buitendijk, 'Perinatal mortality and morbidity in a nationwide cohort of 529 688 low-risk planned home and hospital births' *An International Journal of Obstetrics & Gynaecology* 2009, vol 116 issue 9

R. de la Feria and S. Vogenauer, *Prohibition of Abuse of Law. A New General Principle of EU Law?*, Hart Publishing, Oxford 2011

S. de la Rosa, 'The Directive on Cross-Border Healthcare or the art of codifying complex case law' *Common Market Law Review* 2012, vol 49

C.M. de Pancorbo and L. Moral, 'Improving Waiting List Information Systems' in HOPE, Waiting lists and waiting times in health care – Managing demand and supply', http://www.hope.be/05eventsandpublications/docpublications/60_waiting/60_waitinglists_2001.pdf, 2001

S. De Rosis and S. Barsanti, 'Patient satisfaction, e-health and the evolution of the patient–general practitioner relationship: Evidence from an Italian survey' *Health Policy* 2016, vol 120

F. De Wispelaere and J. Pacolet, *Coordination of social security systems at a glance: 2016 Statistical Report*, Network Statistics FMSSFE, Leuven 2016

——, *Planned cross-border healthcare*, Network Statistics FMSSFE, Leuven 2016

E. Declercq, R. DeVries, K. Viisainen, H.B. Salvesen and S. Wrede, 'Where to give birth? Politics and the Place of Birth' in R. DeVries, S. Wrede, E. van Teijlingen and C. Benoit (eds.), *Birth by Design: Pregnancy, Maternity Care, and Midwifery in North America and Europe*, Routledge, New York, London 2002

C. Degryse and P. Pochet (eds.), *Social Developments in the European Union 2006*, European Observatory on Health Systems and Policies, Brussels 2007

M. Del Sol, 'Taking Measures Against European Healthcare Fraud' in S. Hennion and O. Kaufmann (eds.), *Unionsbürgerschaft und Patientenfreizügigkeit*, Springer, Berlin, Heidelberg 2014

A. den Exter, 'Patient Mobility in European Union: Health Spas in Ischia, Italy' *Croatian Medical Journal* 2005, vol 46 issue 2

R. DeVries, S. Wrede, E. van Teijlingen and C. Benoit (eds.), *Birth by Design: Pregnancy, Maternity Care, and Midwifery in North America and Europe*, Routledge, New York, London 2002

J.A. Diaz, R.A. Griffith, J.J. Ng, S.E. Reinert, P.D. Friedmann and A.W. Moulton, 'Patient's Use of the Internet for Medical Information' *Journal of General Internal Medicine* 2002, vol 17 issue 3

S. Douglas-Scott, *Constitutional Law of the European Union*, Dorset Press, Dorchester 2002

S. Dullien, *A European unemployment insurance as a stabilization device – Selected issues*, Paper prepared for DG EMPL, http://ec.europa.eu/social/BlobServlet?docId=10437&langId=en, 2012

M. Eliantonio and C. Backes, 'Taking constitutionalization one step too far? The need for revision of the Rheinmühlen case law in the light of the AG opinion and the ECJ's ruling in Elchinov' *Maastricht Faculty of Law Working Paper* 2010/9

European Patients Forum, EU *Directive 2011/24/EU on the application of patients' rights in cross-border healthcare: Legislation Guidance for Patient Organisations*, http://www.eu-patient.eu/Documents/Policy/Cross-borderHealthcare/2013%2011%2018_CBHC_guidance-final.pdf, 2013

G. Esping-Andersen, *The Three Worlds of Welfare Capitalism*, Polity Press, Cambridge 1990

Eurostat, *European social statistics*, 2013 edition, Publications Office of the European Union, Luxembourg 2013

E. Felten, 'Patientmobilität im Spiegel des primären und sekundären Gemeinschaftsrecht' (Patient mobility in the mirror of the primary and secondary Community law) *Das Recht der Arbeit* 2008, issue 1

W.J. Ferguson and L.M. Candib, 'Culture, Language, and the Doctor-Patient Relationship' *Modern Culture and Physician-Patient Communication* 2002, vol 34 no 5

M. Ferrera, 'Reconstructing the welfare state in Southern Europe' in S. Kuhnle (ed.), *Survival of the European Welfare State*, Routledge, London 2000

K. Ficsór, 'Az egészségügyi ellátórendszer finanszírozási modelljei – nemzetközi kitekintés' (Financial models of healthcare systems) in G. Berki (ed.), *Opuscula Szegediensia 4*, Pólay Elemér Alapítvány, Szeged 2011

M. Flear, 'Case C-385/99 V.G. Müller-Fauré v. Onderlinge Waarborgmaatschappij O.Z. Zorgverzekeringen U.A. and E.E.M. van Riet v. Onderlinge Waarborgmaatschappij Z.A.O. Zorgverzekeringen, Judgement of the Court of 13 May 2003' *Common Market Law Review* 2004, vol 41 issue 1

——, 'The Open Method of Coordination on health care after the Lisbon Strategy II: Towards a neoliberal framing?' in S. Kröger (ed.), *What we have learnt: Advances, pitfalls and remaining questions in OMC research*, European Integration Online Papers 2009, Special Issue 1, vol. 13 no 12

G. Flores, 'The Impact of Medical Interpreter Services on the Quality of Health Care: A Systematic Review' *Medical Care Research and Review* 2005, vol 62 no 3

——, 'Language Barriers to Health Care in the United States' *The New England Journal of Medicine* 2006, vol 355 no 3

G. Flores, M.B. Laws, S.J. Mayo, B. Zuckerman, M. Abreu, L. Medina and E.J. Hardt, 'Errors in Medical Interpretation and Their Potential Clinical Consequences in Pediatric Encounters' *Pediatrics* 2003, vol 111 no 1

K. Footman, C. Knai, R. Baeten, K. Glonti and M. McKee, *Cross-border health care in Europe*, http://www.euro.who.int/__data/assets/pdf_file/0009/263538/Cross-border-health-care-in-Europe-Eng.pdf, 2014

J.D. Fowler, *Cultural and Structural Barriers that Affect the Doctor-Patient Relationship: A Bolivian perspective*, http://ir.library.oregonstate.edu/xmlui/bitstream/handle/1957/9896/Fowler.pdf?sequence=1, 2008

G. France, 'Cross-border flows of Italian patients within the European Union – An international trade approach' *European Journal of Public Health* 1997, vol 7 suppl 3

E. Fries-Tersch and V. Mabilia, *2015 Annual Report on Labour Mobility*, Network Statistics FMSSFE, Brussels 2015

M. Frischhut, 'Legal and Ethical Issues of Cross-Border Reproductive Care from an EU Perspective' in M.K. Smith and L. Puczkó (eds.), *The Routledge Handbook of Health Tourism*, Taylor & Francis, London, New York 2017

M. Fuchs (ed.), *Europäisches Sozialrecht*, Nomos, Baden-Baden 2013

F. Gany, J. Leng, E. Shapiro, D. Abramson, I. Motola, D.C. Shield and J. Changrani, 'Patient Satisfaction with Different Interpreting Methods: A Randomized Controlled Trial' *Journal of General Internal Medicine* 2007, vol 22 suppl 2

B.S. Gerber and A.R. Eiser, 'The Patient-Physician Relationship in the Internet Age: Future Prospects and the Research Agenda' *Journal of Medical Internet Research* 2001, vol 3 no 2

I.A. Glinos and R. Baeten, *A Literature Review of Cross-Border Patient Mobility in the European Union*, European Observatory on Health Systems and Policies, Europe for Patients Project, Brussels 2006

I.A. Glinos, R. Baeten and N. Boffin, 'Cross-border contracted care in Belgian hospitals' in M. Rosenmöller, M. McKee and R. Baeten (eds.), *Patient Mobility in the European Union – Learning from experience*, European Observatory on Health Systems and Policies, Europe for Patients Project, Brussels 2006

I.A. Glinos, R. Baeten, M. Helble and H. Maarse, 'A typology of cross-border patient mobility' *Health and Place* 2010, vol 16 issue 6

I.A. Glinos and M. Wismar, *Hospitals and Borders – Seven case studies on cross-border collaboration and health system interactions*, European Observatory on Health Systems and Policies, Brussels 2013

O. Golynker, 'Patient Mobility and healthcare in the EU' in F. Pennings and G. Vonk (eds.), *Research Handbook on European Social Security Law*, Edward Elgar Publishing, Cheltenham 2015

Grail Research, *The Rise of Medical Tourism*, http://www.grailresearch.com/pdf/ContenPodsPdf/Rise_of_Medical_Tourism_Summary.pdf, 2009

N.J. Gray, J.D. Klein, P.R. Noyce, T.S. Sesselberg and J.A. Cantrill, 'Health information-seeking behaviour in adolescence: the place of the internet' *Social Science & Medicine* 2005, vol 60

S.L. Greer, *The politics of European Union health policies*, Open University Press, Berkshire 2009

S.L. Greer and T. Sokol, 'Rules for Rights: European Law, Health Care and Social Citizenship' *European Law Journal* 2014, vol 20 no 1

J. Hajdú, *Az Európai Unió szociális joga, különös tekintettel a szociális biztonsági koordinációra* (Social law in the European Union, with special regard to the social security coordination), JATE Press, Szeged 2008

——, 'Cross border health care under the 1408/71 EC Regulation' *Studia Juridica Caroliensia*, vol 3, Károli Gáspár Református Egyetem Állam- és Jogtudományi Kar, Budapest 2008

L.C. Hampers and J.E. McNulty, 'Professional Interpreters and Bilingual Physicians in a Pediatric Emergency Department. Effect on Resource Utilization' *Archives of Pediatrics and Adolescent Medicine* 2002, vol 156 no 11

C. Harvey and R.P. Barnidge, *The right to leave one's own country under international law*, http://www.qub.ac.uk/schools/SchoolofLaw/Research/HumanRightsCentre/Publications/ResearchReports/researchfilestore/Filetoupload,56100,en.pdf, 2005

V. Hatzopoulos and T.U. Do, 'The case law of the ECJ concerning the free provision of services: 2000–2005' *Common Market Law Review* 2006, vol 43

V. Hatzopoulos and T. Hervey, 'Coming into line: the EU's Court softens on cross-border health care' *Health Economics, Policy and Law* 2013, vol 8 issue 1

O. Hawkins, *Migration Statistics*, Briefing Paper, Number SN06077, House of Commons Library, London 2017

K-G. Hem, B. Kalseth and A. Wilson, *Patient mobility in the Nordic Countries. Volume and obstacles*, http://www.nordicinnovation.org/Global/_Publications/Reports/2011/2011_patientMobility_report.pdf, 2011

W. Henn, 'Genetic screening with the DNA chip: a new Pandora's box?' *Journal of Medical Ethics* 1999, vol 25

S. Hennion and O. Kaufmann (eds.), *Unionsbürgerschaft und Patientenfreizügigkeit*, Springer, Berlin, Heidelberg 2014

T. Hervey and B. Vanhercke, 'Health care and the EU: the law and policy patchwork' in E. Mossialos, G. Permanand, R. Baeten and T.K. Hervey (eds.), *Health Systems Governance in Europe – The Role of European Union Law and Policy*, Cambridge University Press, New York 2010

M. Huber, 'Health Care Financing in European Union Member States. An Initial Perspective Based on Recent OECD Work on Overall Social Trends' in R. Leidl (ed.), *Health Care and its Financing in the Single European Market*, IOS Press, Amsterdam 1998

T. Hunter, 'Holidaymakers warned as Spain blocks EHIC usage' *The Telegraph*, 31.03.2013

ICF GHK and Milieu, *A fact finding analysis on the impact on the Member States' social security systems of the entitlements of non-active intra-EU migrants to special non-contributory cash benefits and healthcare granted on the basis of residence*, Prepared for DG Employment, Social Affairs and Inclusion, http://ec.europa.eu/social/main.jsp?langId=en&catId=89&newsId=1980&furtherNews=yes, 2013

International Organisation for Migration, *Glossary on migration*, http://publications.iom.int/bookstore/free/Glossary%202nd%20ed%20web.pdf, 2011

D. Jacobson, *Rights across borders: Immigration and the decline of citizenship*, Johns Hopkins University Press, Baltimore 1996

E. Jelfs and R. Baeten, *Simulation on the EU Cross-Border Care Directive. Final Report*, http://www.uems.net/uploads/media/CrossBorderHealthcareSimulation_FinalRep_09052012.pdf, 2011

R. Jennissen, *Macro-economic determinants of international migration in Europe*, Dutch University Press, Amsterdam 2004

C. Jinks, B.N. Ong and C. Paton, 'Mobile medics? The mobility of doctors in the European Economic Area' *Health Policy* 2000, vol 54 issue 1

Y. Jorens, *European Integration and Health Care Systems: a Challenge for Social Policy EC Regulations 1408/71 between Status Quo and Upgrading*, http://www.ose.be/health/papers/jorenpaper2.pdf, 2001

——, 'The Right to Health Care across Borders' in M. McKee, E. Mossialos and R. Baeten (eds.), *The Impact of EU Law on Health Care Systems*, P.I.E.-Peter Lang, Brussels 2002

—— (ed.), *50 years of Social Security Coordination: Past – Present – Future*, Publications Office of the European Union, Luxembourg 2010

Y. Jorens and J. De Coninck, *Reply to an ad hoc request for comparative analysis of national legislations. Administrative procedures for cross-border healthcare*, FreSsco Network, Ghent 2015

Y. Jorens and J.-P. Lhernould, *European Report 2013.* trESS Network, Ghent 2013

Y. Jorens and B. Schulte (eds.), *Coordination of social security schemes in connection with the accession of Central and Eastern European States – 'The Riga Conference'*, la Charte, Brussels 1999

Y. Jorens and F. Van Overmeiren, 'General principles of coordination in Regulation 883/2004' *European Journal of Social Security* 2009, vol 11 nos 1–2

Y. Jorens, M. Coucheir and F. Van Overmeiren, 'Access to health care in an internal market: impact for statutory and complementary systems' *Bulletin luxembourgeois des questions sociales* 2005, vol 18

Y. Jorens, B. de Schuyter and C. Salamon, *Towards a rationalisation of the EC Co-ordination Regulations concerning Social Security?*, Academia Press, Ghent 2007

Y. Jorens, J.-P. Lhernould and S. Roberts, *Handbook on European Social Security Law*, http://www.sgk-kap.org/en/database/db/B2_C8_717.pdf, 2011

K.S. Joseph, 'The Matthew effect in health development' *British Medical Journal* 1989, vol 298

S.S. Juss, 'Free Movement and the World Order' *International Journal of Refugee Law* 2004, vol 16 issue 3

K. Jutten and P. Janssens (eds.), *Patients without borders: Cross-border patient flows in the BENELUX*, General Secretariat of the Benelux Union, 2016

A. Kaczorowska, 'A Review of the Creation by the European Court of Justice of the Right to Effective and Speedy Medical Treatment and its Outcomes' *European Law Journal* 2006, vol 12 no 3

P. Kanavos, M. McKee and T. Richards, 'Cross border health care in Europe. European court rulings have made governments worried' *British Medical Journal* 1999, vol 319 issue 7192

B. Kangas, 'Traveling for Medical Care in a Global World' *Medical Anthropology: Cross-Cultural Studies in Health and Illness*, Special Issue: Medical Travel 2010, vol 29 issue 4

C. Karner, 'Nemzetközi egészségügyi finanszírozási modellek és az állam szerepvállalása' (International models of healthcare financing and the role of the state) *Egészségügyi Gazdasági Szemle (Journal of Health Economics)* 2008, vol 46 issue 2

M. Kattelus, 'Implementation of the Directive on the Application on Patient's Rights in Cross-border Healthcare (2011/24/EU) in Finland' *European Journal of Health Law* 2014, vol 21, issue 1

K. Kesteloot, S. Pocceschi and E. van der Schueren, 'The reimbursement of the expenses for medical treatment received by "transnational" patients in EU-countries' *Health Policy* 1995, vol 33 issue 1

Gy. Kincses, I. Borbás, P. Mihalicza, E. Varga and E. Udvardy, 'A gyógyturizmus tendenciái a világban' (Tendencies of health tourism around the world), *Egészségügyi Gazdasági Szemle (Journal of Health Economics)* 2009, issue 5

I. Kowalska-Bobko, A. Mokrzycka, A. Sagan, W.C. Włodarczyk and M. Zabdyr-Jamróz, 'Implementation of the Cross-Border Healthcare Directive in Poland: How Not to Encourage Patients to Seek Care Abroad?' *Health Policy* 2016, vol 120 issue 11

S. KUHNLE, *Survival of the European Welfare State*, http://www.sv.uio.no/arena/english/research/publications/arena-working-papers/1994-2000/1999/wp99_19.htm, 1999

—— (ed.), *Survival of the European Welfare State*, Routledge, London 2000

P.E. KUMMERVOLD and R. WYNN, 'Health Information Accessed on the Internet: The Development in 5 European Countries' *International Journal of Telemedicine and Applications* 2012, vol 2012

S. KUMPUNEN and L. TRIGG, 'Intra-European retirement migrants' access to state-funded long-term care and health entitlements' *Eurohealth* 2013, vol 19 no 4

J.M. LAST, *A Dictionary of Public Health*, Oxford University Press, Oxford 2007

H. LEGIDO-QUIGLEY, M. MCKEE, E. NOLTE and I.A. GLINOS, *Assuring the quality of health care in the European Union*, European Observatory on Health Systems and Policies, Brussels 2008

H. LEGIDO-QUIGLEY, I.A. GLINOS, K. WALSHE, B. VAN BEEK, C. CUCIC and M. MCKEE, 'Quality and safety' in M. WISMAR, W. PALM, J. FIGUERAS, K. ERNST and E. VAN GINNEKEN (eds.), *Cross-border Health Care in the European Union – Mapping and analysing practices and policies*, European Observatory on Health Systems and Policies, Brussels 2011

H. LEGIDO-QUIGLEY, I. PASSARANI, C. KNAI, R. BUSSE, W. PALM and M. WISMAR, 'Cross-border healthcare in Europe: clarifying patients' rights' *British Medical Journal* 2011, vol 342

R. LEIDL (ed.), *Health Care and its Financing in the Single European Market*, IOS Press, Amsterdam 1998

M. LEWIS, 'Informal health payments in central and eastern Europe and the former Soviet Union: issues, trends and policy implications' in E. MOSSIALOS, A. DIXON, J. FIGUERAS and J. KUTZIN (eds.), *Funding health care: options for Europe*, Open University Press, Buckingham, Philadelphia 2002

J.-P. LHERNOULD, 'Access to Healthcare by Cross-Border *Patients*' in S. HENNION and O. KAUFMANN (eds.), *Unionsbürgerschaft und Patientenfreizügigkeit*, Springer, Berlin, Heidelberg 2014

J.-P. LHERNOULD, B. SCHULTE (eds.), J.-C. FILLON, J. HAJDÚ and H. VERSCHUEREN, *Healthcare provided during a temporary stay in another Member State to persons who do not fulfil conditions for statutory health insurance coverage*, trESS Network, Ghent 2010

M. LINDHOLM, J.L. HARGRAVES, W.J. FERGUSON and G. REED, 'Professional language interpretation and inpatient length of stay and readmission rates' *Journal of General Internal Medicine* 2012, vol 27 issue 10

K. LIPSTEIN, *The Law of the European Economic Community*, Butterworths, London 1974

N. LOWE and G. DOUGLAS (eds.), *Families Across Frontiers*, Kluwer Academic Publisher, The Hague 1996

N. LUNT and P. CARRERA, 'Medical tourism: Assessing the evidence on treatment abroad' *Mauritas* 2010, vol 66

T. MAINIL, *Transnational health care and medical tourism: Understanding 21st-century patient mobility – Towards a rationale of transnational health region development*, NRIT Media, Nieuwegein 2012

B. MARCHAL and G. KEGELS, 'Health workforce imbalances in times of globalization: brain drain or professional mobility?' *The International Journal of Health Planning and Management* 2003, vol 18 issue S1

F. Marhold (ed.), *Das neue Sozialrecht der EU* (The new social law of the EU), Linde Verlag, Wien 2005

——, 'Modernisation of European coordination of sickness benefits' *European Journal of Social Security* 2009, vol 11 issue 1–2

F. Markovic, *In Europe, We're All Equal (Unless We're Not)*, http://www.europeanpublicaffairs.eu/in-europe-were-all-equal-unless-were-not/, 2013

——, *Restrictions to Freedom of Movement for Labour: the Culture of Something for Nothing*, http://www.europeanpublicaffairs.eu/restrictions-to-freedom-of-movement-for-labour-the-culture-of-something-for-nothing/, 2014

D.S. Massey, J. Arango, G. Hugo, A. Kouaouci, A. Pellegrino and J.E. Taylor, 'Theories of International Migration: A Review and Appraisal' *Population and Development Review* 1993, vol 19 no 3

A. Maynard and A. Dixon, 'Private health insurance and medical savings accounts: theory and experience' in E. Mossialos, A. Dixon, J. Figueras and J. Kutzin (eds.), *Funding health care: options for Europe*, Open University Press, Buckingham, Philadelphia 2002

M. McKee and E. Mossialos, 'Health policy and European law: Closing the gaps' *Public Health* 2006, vol 120 issue 11

M. McKee, E. Mossialos and R. Baeten (eds.), *The Impact of EU Law on Health Care Systems*, P.I.E.-Peter Lang, Brussels 2002

M. McKee, R. Busse, R. Baeten and I. Glinos, 'Cross-border healthcare collaboration in the European Union: Placing the patient at the centre' *Eurohealth* 2013, vol 19 no 4

A. McKelvey, A.L. David, F. Shefield and E.R. Jauniauxc, 'The impact of cross-border reproductive care or "fertility tourism" on NHS maternity services' *BJOG: An International Journal of Obstetrics & Gynaecology* 2009, vol 116 issue 11

H. McKenna, 'Five big issues for health and social care after the Brexit vote', https://www.kingsfund.org.uk/publications/articles/brexit-and-nhs, 2016

M. McMullan, 'Patients using the Internet to obtain health information: How this affects the patient–health professional relationship' *Patient Education and Counseling* 2006, vol 63 issue 1–2

R.K. Merton, 'Matthew-effect in Science. The reward and communication systems of science are considered' *Science* 1968, vol 159

H. Meyer, 'Spain's Ehic refusal prompts legal action from European Commission' *The Guardian*, 30.05.2013

E. A. Miller, *Telemedicine and the Provider-Patient Relationship: What We Know So Far*, Report Prepared for the Nuffield Council's Working Party on Medical Profiling and Online Medicine: The Ethics of 'Personalised' Medicine in a Consumer Age, 2010

D.S. Miller and C. Gonzalez, 'When Death is the Destination: The Business of Death Tourism – Despite Legal and Social Implications' *International Journal of Culture, Tourism and Hospitality Research* 2013, vol 7 issue 3

E. Mossialos and S.M.S. Thomson, 'Voluntary health insurance in the European Union' in E. Mossialos, A. Dixon, J. Figueras and J. Kutzin (eds.), *Funding health care: options for Europe*, Open University Press, Buckingham, Philadelphia 2002

E. Mossialos, A. Dixon, J. Figueras and J. Kutzin (eds.), *Funding health care: options for Europe*, Open University Press, Buckingham, Philadelphia 2002

E. Mossialos, G. Permanand, R. Baeten and T.K. Hervey (eds.), *Health Systems Governance in Europe – The Role of European Union Law and Policy*, Cambridge University Press, New York 2010

C. Murphy, 'An Effective Right to Cross-Border Healthcare? On Patients, Primacy and Procedural Autonomy: Comment on Elchinov' *European Law Review* 2011, No 4

U. Neergaard, E. Szyszczak, J.W. van de Gronden and M. Krajewski, *Social Services of General Interest in the EU*, T.M.C. Asser Press, The Hague 2013

Gy. Németh, '*Az egészségbiztosítási rendszerekről – nemzetközi összehasonlításban I.*' (Healthcare schemes – in international context*) Egészségügyi Gazdasági Szemle (Journal of Health Economics)* 2007, vol 45 issue 5–6

P. Neroth, 'Can health survive the single market?' *The Lancet* 2005, vol 365 issue 9458

C. Newdick, 'The European Court of Justice, transnational health care and social citizenship – Accidental death of a concept?' *Wisconsin International Law Journal* 2009, vol 26 issue 3

L. Nielsen, 'Procreative Tourism, Genetic Testing and The Law' in N. Lowe and G. Douglas (eds.), *Families Across Frontiers*, Kluwer Academic Publisher, The Hague 1996

H. Nys, 'The Transposition of the Directive on Patients' Rights in Cross-Border Healthcare in National Law by the Member States: Still a Lot of Effort to Be Made and Questions to Be Answered' *European Journal of Health Law* 2014, vol 21, Special Issue

A.J. Obermaier, *Fine-tuning the Jurisprudence: The ECJ's Judicial Activism and Self-restraint*, Institute for European Integration Research, Working Paper No. 02/2008

L. O'Carroll, 'Hundreds of thousands of retired Britons in EU "may be forced to return"' *The Guardian*, 18.01.2017

P. O'Donnell, *Andriukaitis calls for an EU health system to take care of everyone, wherever they are*, http://www.europeanvoice.com/article/andriukaitis-calls-for-an-eu-health-system-to-take-care-of-everyone-wherever-they-are/, 2014

OECD, Eurostat and WHO, *A Proposal for the Main Categories of the Classification of Financing Schemes*, http://www.oecd.org/dataoecd/17/32/41016651.pdf

S. Olsena, 'Implementation of the Patients' Rights in Cross-border Healthcare Directive in Latvia' *European Journal of Health Law* 2014, vol 21 issue 1

J. Olsson, *Member State data on cross-border healthcare following Directive 2011/24/EU*, Prepared for EC DG SANTE, Brussels 2016

P. Oltermann, 'Something in common: should English be the official language of the EU?' *The Guardian*, 24.04.2013

A. Osterle, P. Balazs and J.J. Delgado, 'Travelling for teeth: characteristics and perspectives of dental care tourism in Hungary' *British Dental Journal* 2009, vol 206 no 8

J. Pacolet, F. De Wispelaere and A. De Coninck, *The social security rights of frontier workers – A survey on their knowledge, use and satisfaction, focusing on sickness benefits*, SSCALA Project, Leuven 2012

J. Pacolet and F. De Wispelaere, *The European Health Insurance Card*, Network Statistics FMSSFE, Leuven 2014

——, *Planned cross-border healthcare*, Network Statistics FMSSFE, Leuven 2014

——, *Planned cross-border healthcare*, Network Statistics FMSSFE, Leuven 2015

——, *The entitlement to and use of sickness benefits by persons residing in a Member State other than the competent Member State*, FMSSFE, Leuven 2016

——, *The European Health Insurance Card*, Network Statistics FMSSFE, Leuven 2016

W. Palm, 'The cross-border care Directive: implementation *status*' *Eurohealth* 2016, vol 22 no 1

W. Palm and I.A. Glinos, 'Enabling patient mobility in the EU: between free movement and coordination' in E. Mossialos, G. Permanand, R. Baeten and T.K. Hervey (eds.), *Health Systems Governance in Europe – The Role of European Union Law and Policy*, Cambridge University Press, New York 2010

W. Palm, J. Nickless, H. Lewalle and A. Coheur, *Implications of recent jurisprudence on the co-ordination of health care protection systems*, Association Internationale de la Mutualite, Brussels 2000

W. Palm, M. Wismar, E. van Ginneken, R. Busse, K. Ernst and J. Figueras, 'Towards a renewed Community framework for safe, high-quality and efficient cross-border health care within the European Union' in M. Wismar, W. Palm, J. Figueras, K. Ernst and E. van Ginneken (eds.), *Cross-border Health Care in the European Union – Mapping and analysing practices and policies*, European Observatory on Health Systems and Policies, Brussels 2011

Y. Pascouau, *Strong attack against the freedom of movement of EU citizens: turning back the clock*, http://www.epc.eu/pub_details.php?pub_id=3491, 2013

V. Paskalia, *Free movement, social security and gender*, Hart Publishing, Oxford, Portland 2007

——, 'Cross-border Healthcare in the EU: And What if Something Goes Wrong?' *European Journal of Health Law* 2016, http://booksandjournals.brillonline.com/content/journals/10.1163/15718093-12341435

M. Peeters, 'Free Movement of Patients: Directive 2011/24 on the Application of Patients' Rights in Cross-Border Healthcare' *European Journal of Health Law* 2012, vol 19

M. Peeters, M. McKee and S. Merkur, 'EU law and health professionals' in E. Mossialos, G. Permanand, R. Baeten and T.K. Hervey (eds.), *Health Systems Governance in Europe – The Role of European Union Law and Policy*, Cambridge University Press, New York 2010

F. Pennings, 'The European Commission Proposal to Simplify Regulation 1408/71' *European Journal of Social Security* 2001, vol 3 issue 1

——, 'Overview of Recent Cases Before the European Court of Human Rights and the European Court of Justice' *European Journal of Social Security* 2001, vol 3 issue 3

——, 'Introduction: Regulation 883/2004 – the third coordination regulation in a row' *European Journal of Social Security* 2009, vol 11 issue 1–2

——, 'Conclusion: Simplification, Modernisation and Regulation 883/2004' *European Journal of Social Security* 2009, vol 11 issue 1–2

——, *European Social Security Law*, Intersentia, Antwerp 2010

——, 'The Cross-border Health Care Directive: More Free Movement for Citizens and More Coherent EU Law?' *European Journal of Social Security* 2011, vol 13 issue 4

G. Pennings, 'Reproductive tourism as moral pluralism in motion' *Journal of Medical Ethics* 2002, vol 28

——, 'Legal harmonization and reproductive tourism in Europe' *Human Reproduction* 2004, vol 19 no 12

F. Pennings and G. Vonk (eds.), *Research Handbook on European Social Security Law*, Edward Elgar Publishing, Cheltenham 2015

C. Perdue and S. Noble, 'Foreign travel for advanced cancer patients: a guide for healthcare professionals' *Postgraduate Medical Journal* 2007, vol 83 issue 981

G. Permanand and E. Vos, 'EU regulatory agencies and health protection' in E. Mossialos, G. Permanand, R. Baeten and T.K. Hervey (eds.), *Health Systems Governance in Europe – The Role of European Union Law and Policy*, Cambridge University Press, New York 2010

M. Phelan, 'Medical Interpreting and the Law in the European Union' *European Journal of Health Law* 2012, vol 19

N. Pletneva and A. Vargas, *Requirements for the general public health search*, http://www.hon.ch/Global/pdf/Khresmoi/KHRESMOI_general_public_survey_report.pdf, 2011

M.A. Pollack, *The Engines of European Integration. Delegation, Agency and Agenda Setting in the EU*, Oxford University Press, New York 2003

E.-M. Poptcheva, *Freedom of movement and residence of EU citizens*, http://www.europarl.europa.eu/RegData/bibliotheque/briefing/2014/140808/LDM_BRI(2014)140808_REV1_EN.pdf, 2014

G. Price, 'Polish women increasingly head abroad for abortions' *Warsaw Business Journal*, 27 August 2010

S. Priebe, S. Sandhu, S. Dias, A. Gaddini, T. Greacen, E. Ioannidis, U. Kluge, A. Krasnik, M. Lamkaddem, V. Lorant, R. Puigpinósi Riera, A. Sarvary, J.J.F. Soares, M. Stankunas, C. Straßmayr, K. Wahlbeck, M. Welbel and M. Bogic, 'Good practice in health care for migrants: views and experiences of care professionals in 16 European countries' *BMC Public Health* 2011, vol 11 issue 187

Pricewaterhouse Coopers International Limited, *Recommendation Report – A best practice based approach to National Contact Point websites: feasibility study*, http://ec.europa.eu/health/cross_border_care/docs/pwc_national_contact_points_website_en.pdf, 2012

K. Quan and J. Lynch, *The High Costs of Language Barriers in Medical Malpractice*, http://www.healthlaw.org/images/stories/High_Costs_of_Language_Barriers_in_Malpractice.pdf, 2010

E. Randall, *The European Union and health policy*, Palgrave, New York 2001

K.M. Raptopoulou, 'The Directive on cross-border health care: signalling the coordination or the harmonisation of public health systems?' *European Journal of Social Law* 2012, vol 2 issue 3

A. Rashidian, H. Joudaki and T. Vian, 'No Evidence of the Effect of the Interventions to Combat Health Care Fraud and Abuse: A Systematic Review of Literature' *PLoS One* 2012, vol 7 issue 8

N. Rennuy, 'Assimilation, territoriality and reverse discrimination: a shift in European social security law' *European Journal of Social Law* 2011, vol 1 no 4

C.M. Rieder, 'Cross-border Movement of Patients in the EU: A Re-Appraisal' *European Journal of Health Law* 2016, http://booksandjournals.brillonline.com/content/journals/10.1163/15718093-12341419

S. Roberts, 'A short history of social security coordination' in Y. Jorens (ed.), *50 years of Social Security Coordination: Past – Present – Future*, Publications Office of the European Union, Luxembourg 2010

S. Roberts and B. Schulte (eds.), C.G. de Cortazar, T. Medaiskis and H. Verschueren, *Healthcare for Pensioners*, trESS Network, Ghent 2009

R. Robinson, 'User charges for healthcare' in E. Mossialos, A. Dixon, J. Figueras and J. Kutzin (eds.), *Funding health care: options for Europe*, Open University Press, Buckingham, Philadelphia 2002

C.C. Ros, P.P. Groenewegen and D.M.J. Delnoij, 'All rights reserved, or can we just copy? Cost sharing arrangements and characteristics of health care systems' *Health Policy* 2000, vol 52 no 1

M. Rosenmöller, M. McKee and R. Baeten (eds.), *Patient Mobility in the European Union – Learning from experience*, European Observatory on Health Systems and Policies, Europe for Patients Project, Brussels 2006

M. Rosenmöller, M. McKee, R. Baeten and I.A. Glinos, 'Patient mobility: the context and issues' in M. Rosenmöller, M. McKee and R. Baeten (eds.), *Patient Mobility in the European Union – Learning from experience*, European Observatory on Health Systems and Policies, Europe for Patients Project, Brussels 2006

V. Runnels and P.M. Carrera, 'Why do patients engage in medical tourism?' *Mauritas* 2012, vol 73, p. 303.

K.A. Ryan, A.N. Sanders, D.D. Wang and A.D. Levine, 'Tracking the rise of stem cell tourism' *Regenerative Medicine* 2010, vol 5 issue 1

E. Rynning, 'The Ageing Populations of Europe – Implications for Health Systems and Patients' Rights' *European Journal of Health Law* 2008, vol 15

M. Sakslin, 'Social Security Co-ordination – Adapting to Change' *European Journal of Social Security* 2000, vol 2 issue 2

J. Sári, *Alapjogok (Fundamental rights)*, Osiris Kiadó, Budapest 2005

A. Schopenhauer, *Wisdom of Life*, Cosimo Classics, New York 2007

——, *Aphorismen zur Lebensweisheit (Separatausgabe aus 'Parerga und Paralipomena')*, F. A. Brockhaus, Leipzig 1886

M. Schwebag, 'Implementation of the Cross-border Care Directive in EU Member States: Luxembourg' *European Journal of Health Law* 2014, vol 21 issue 1

L. Senden, *Soft Law in European Community Law*, Hart Publishing, Oxford 2004

S. Shmanske, 'Information Asymmetries in Health Services. The Market Can Cope' *The Independent Review* 1996, vol 1 no 2

M. Simpson, R. Buckman, M. Stewart, P. Maguire, M. Lipkin, D. Novack and J. Till, 'Doctor-patient communication: the Toronto consensus statement' *British Medical Journal* 1991, vol 303

M.K. Smith and L. Puczkó (eds.), *The Routledge Handbook of Health Tourism*, Taylor & Francis, London, New York 2017

T. Sokol, 'Rindal and Elchinov: A(n) (Impending) Revolution in EU Law on Patient Mobility' *Croatian Yearbook of European Law and Policy* 2010, vol 6 no 6

P.P. Song, 'Biotech pilgrims and the transnational quest for stem cell cures' *Medical Anthropology* 2010, vol 29 issue 4

V. Sorlie and R.A. Lopez, 'When Language, Health Literacy, and Miscommunication Collide: Tremors Versus Seizures' *Family Medicine* 2011, vol 43 issue 1

E. Spaveta, 'Comments on Abuse of Law and the Free Movement of Workers' in R. de la Feria and S. Vogenauer (eds.), *Prohibition of Abuse of Law. A New General Principle of EU Law?*, Hart Publishing, Oxford 2011

B. Spiegel, 'Die neue europäische Sozialrechtskoordinierung. Wie neu ist die Verordnung 883/2004? Allgemeine Überlegungen' (The new European social security coordination.

How new is the Regulation 883/2004? General considerations) in F. MARHOLD (ed.), *Das neue Sozialrecht der EU* (The new social law of the EU), Linde Verlag, Wien 2005

STANDING COMMITTEE OF EUROPEAN DOCTORS, *Free movement of patients: When is a treatment sufficiently tried and tested – How to decide?*, http://cpme.dyndns.org:591/adopted/CPME_AD_Brd_290303_9_EN_fr.pdf, 2003

A.M. E.W. STERLING, 'European Union and Abortion Tourism: Liberalizing Ireland's Abortion Law' *Boston College International and Comparative Law Review* 1997, vol 20 issue 2

E. STEYGER, 'National Health Care Systems Under Fire (but not too heavily)' *Legal Issues of Economic Integration* 2002, vol 29 issue 1

N. STIEMER, 'Sickness Insurance – Viewpoint of the EU-Member States' in Y. JORENS and B. SCHULTE (eds.), *Coordination of social security schemes in connection with the accession of Central and Eastern European States – 'The Riga Conference'*, la Charte, Brussels 1999

A. STONE SWEET, 'European Integration and the Legal System' in T.A. BÖRZEL and R.A. CICHOWSKI (eds.), *The State of the European Union. Law, Politics and Society*, Oxford University Press, New York 2003

G. STRBAN, 'Patient mobility in the European Union: between social security coordination and free movement of services' *ERA Forum* 2013, vol 14 number 3

G. STRBAN (ed.), G. BERKI, D. CARRASCOSA and F. VAN OVERMEIREN, *Access to healthcare in cross-border situations*, FreSsco Network, Ghent 2017

J. SYLVEST, C. ADAMSEN, A. BEALE and S. PAGE, *The Impact of the European Court of Justice Case Law on National Systems for Cross-Border Health Service Provision*, IPOL/A/IMCO/NT/2006-24, Brussels 2007

P. SYRPIS (ed.), *The Judiciary, the Legislature and the EU Internal Market*, Cambridge University Press, New York 2012

E. SZYSZCZAK, J. DAVIES, M. ANDENÆS and T. BEKKEDAL (eds.), *Developments in Services of General Interest*, T.M.C. Asser Press, The Hague 2011

F. TACCONI, 'Freedom of Health and Medical Care Services within the European Union. Recent Jurisprudence of the European Court of Justice, with Particular Reference to Case C-372/04 Yvonne Watts, 16 May 2006' *Zeitschrift für ausländisches öffentliches Recht und Völkerrecht* 2008, vol 68

S. TAYLOR, 'Cross-border Patients and Informed Choices on Treatment in English and French Law and the Patients' Rights Directive' *European Journal of Health Law* 2012, vol 19

S. THOMSON, T. FOUBISTER and E. MOSSIALOS, *Financing health care in the European Union: Challenges and policy responses*, World Health Organization, Copenhagen 2009

P. THORN and S. DILL, 'The role of patients' organizations in cross-border reproductive care' *Fertility and Sterility* 2010, vol 94 no 1

M. TINELLI, Z. NIKOLOSKI and D. PANTELI, 'What information do patients want when choosing a hospital at home or abroad? A case study from Germany' *Eurohealth* 2013, vol 19 no 4

B.C.A. TOEBES, *The Right to Health as a Human Right in International Law*, Intersentia, Antwerp, Groningen, Oxford 1999

Zs. TOLNAI, B. BILLIK and P. FUCHS, 'Magyarország és a fogászati turizmus (Hungary and the dental tourism)' *Egészségügyi Gazdasági Szemle (Journal of Health Economics)* 2009, issue 4

J.I. Torreblanca and M. Leonard, *The continent-wide rise of Euroscepticism*, http://eutruth.info/euroscepticism.pdf, 2013

L. Trócsányi (ed.), *A mi alkotmányunk* (Our constitution), Complex Kiadó Kft., Budapest 2006

L. Turner, 'Cross-border dental care: 'dental tourism' and patient mobility' *British Dental Journal* 2008, vol 204 no 10

J.W. van de Gronden, 'Social Services of General Interest and EU Law' in E. Szyszczak, J. Davies, M. Andenæs and T. Bekkedal (eds.), *Developments in Services of General Interest*, T.M.C. Asser Press, The Hague 2011

J.W. van de Gronden, E. Szyszczak, U. Neergaard and M. Krajewski (eds.), *Health Care and EU Law*, T. M. C. Asser Press, The Hague 2011

A.-M. van den Bossche and P. Ploscar, 'Rights of Dental Patients in the EU – A Legal Assessment' *Journal of Forensic Odonto-Stomatology* 2012, vol 30 suppl 1

D. van den Steen, 'Cross-border health care: Common rules on medical prescriptions when travelling to another EU country' *Eurohealth* 2013, vol 19 no 4

A.P. van der Mei, 'Cross-Border Access to Medical Care within the European Union – Some Reflections on the Judgments in Decker and Kohll' *Maastricht Journal of European and Comparative Law* 1998, vol 5

——, 'Cross-Border Access to Health Care within the European Union: Some Reflections on Geraets-Smits and Peerbooms and Vanbraekel' *Maastricht Journal of European and Comparative Law* 2002, vol 9 issue 2

——, *Free Movement of Persons Within the European Community – Cross-Border Access to Public Benefits*. Hart Publishing, Oxford 2003

——, 'Case C-512/08, Commission v. France, Judgement of the European Court of Justice (Grand Chamber) of 5 October 2010 and Case C-173/09, Georgi Ivanov Elchinov v. Natsionalna zdravnoosiguritelna kasa, Judgement of the Court of Justice (Grand Chamber) of 5 October 2010' *Common Market Law Review* 2011, vol 48 issue 4

W. van Oorschot, 'Non-take-up of Social Security Benefits in Europe' *Journal of European Social Policy* 1991, vol 1 issue 1

H. Verschueren, 'Financing Social Security and Regulation (EEC) 1408/71' *European Journal of Social Security* 2001, vol 3 issue 1

——, 'The EU social security co-ordination system: A close interplay between the EU legislature and judiciary' in P. Syrpis (ed.), *The Judiciary, the Legislature and the EU Internal Market*, Cambridge University Press, New York 2012

M. Versteegh, K. Weistra, W. Oortwijn, S. de Groot, K. Redekop, F. Rutten and P. Davis, *Literature-based approach to defining the concept of healthcare which requires 'highly specialised and costintensive medical infrastructure or medical equipment'*, Prepared for EC DG SANTE, Luxembourg 2014

W. Vogelaar, 'The Approximation of the Laws of Member States under the Treaty of Rome' *Common Market Law Review* 1975, vol 12 issue 2

C. Wagner and F. Verheyen, 'Aspects of Planned EU Cross-border Care' in S. Hennion and O. Kaufmann (eds.), *Unionsbürgerschaft und Patientenfreizügigkeit*, Springer, Berlin, Heidelberg 2014

A. Walus, 'National healthcare planning and the internal market: A conceptual view on the impact of EU law on Member States' regulatory autonomy in the field of healthcare' *European Journal of Social Security* 2015, vol 17 no 1

T. Ward and E. Ozdemir, *Disparities in access to essential services*. Research note 2012/8, Prepared for the use of the European Commission DG EMPL

A.M. Warnes and A. Williams, 'Older Migrants in Europe: A New Focus for Migration Studies' *Journal of Ethnic and Migration Studies* 2007, vol 32 issue 8

P. Watson, *Social Security Law of the European Communities*, Mansell Publishing, London 1980

R.C.A. White, *Workers, Establishment and Services in the European Union*, Oxford University Press, Oxford, New York 2004

R.W. White and E. Horvitz, *Cyberchondria: Studies of the Escalation of Medical Concerns in Web Search*, Microsoft Research, http://research.microsoft.com/pubs/76529/TR-2008-178.pdf, 2008

A. Whittaker, '*Pleasure and pain: Medical travel in Asia*' Global Public Health 2008, vol 3 issue 3

World Health Organization, '*The Right to Health*' Fact Sheet No. 31, http://www.ohchr.org/Documents/Publications/Factsheet31.pdf, 2008

E. Wicks, *Human Rights and Healthcare*, Hart Publishing, Oxford, Portland 2007

J.N. Wilford, 'Skull Supports Theory of Human Migration' *The New York Times*, 12.01.2007

J. Winkelmann, M.M. Hofmarcher, E. Kovacs and G. Szocska, 'Cross-border dental care between Austria and Hungary' *Eurohealth* 2013, vol 19 no 4

M. Wismar, W. Palm, J. Figueras, K. Ernst and E. van Ginneken (eds.), *Cross-border Health Care in the European Union – Mapping and analysing practices and policies*, European Observatory on Health Systems and Policies, Brussels 2011

M. Wismar, W. Palm, E. van Ginneken, R. Busse, K. Ernst and J. Figueras, 'The Health Service Initiative: supporting the construction of a framework for cross border health care' in M. Wismar, W. Palm, J. Figueras, K. Ernst and E. van Ginneken (eds.), *Cross-border Health Care in the European Union – Mapping and analysing practices and policies*, European Observatory on Health Systems and Policies, Brussels 2011

M. Wismar, I.A. Glinos, C.B. Maier, G. Dussault, W. Palm, J. Bremner and J. Figueras, 'Health professional mobility and health systems: evidence from 17 European countries' *Euro Observer* 2011, vol 13 no 2

J. Zeitlin, E. Barcevicius, and J.T. Weishaupt, 'Institutional Design and National Influence of EU Social Policy Coordination: Advancing a Contradictory Debate' in E. Barcevicius, T. Weishaupt and J. Zeitlin (eds.), *Assessing the Open Method of Coordination. Institutional Design and National Influence of EU Social Policy Coordination*, Palgrave Macmillan, Basingstoke 2014

G. Zucca, A. De Negri, A Berényi, A. Kaszap, K.A. Stroetmann and P. Varnai, *Evaluative study on the cross-border healthcare Directive*, Prepared for EC DG SANTE, Luxembourg 2014

INDEX

www.ingramcontent.com/pod-product-compliance
Ingram Content Group UK Ltd.
Pitfield, Milton Keynes, MK11 3LW, UK
UKHW051921100926
8556IPUK00021B/1302

9 781780 685755